*A Biographical Dictionary
of the Baseball Hall of Fame*

A Biographical Dictionary of the Baseball Hall of Fame

JOHN C. SKIPPER

McFarland & Company, Inc., Publishers
Jefferson, North Carolina, and London

Library of Congress Cataloguing-in-Publication Data

Skipper, John C., 1945–
   A biographical dictionary of the Baseball Hall of Fame /
John C. Skipper.
      p.   cm.
   Includes bibliographical references (p.   ) and index.
   ISBN 0-7864-0603-8 (library binding : 50# alkaline paper) ∞
   1. Baseball players—United States—Biography—Dictionaries.
2. Baseball players—United States—Statistics. 3. National
Baseball Hall of Fame and Museum—History. I. Title.
GV865.A1S516   2000
796.357'092'273—dc21   99-15656
[B]   CIP

British Library Cataloguing-in-Publication data are available

Manufactured in the United States of America

McFarland & Company, Inc., Publishers
  Box 611, Jefferson, North Carolina 28640
    www.mcfarlandpub.com

For Dan and Kay Bjerke
In honor of our friendship

Acknowledgments

In compiling the information for this book, the author rediscovered what he learned long ago — that a project like this is not only an exercise in writing and research but a living, breathing example of a math formula: The whole is equal to the sum of its parts.

This book, in its whole, could not have been accomplished without the parts contributed by a great many people.

The author gratefully acknowledges the assistance of Andrew Alexander, Chuck Hoefer and Richard Johnson in Mason City, Iowa; Bruce Markuson of the Baseball Hall of Fame in Cooperstown, New York; author Rich Marazzi; baseball historian Lloyd Johnson; Mark Alvarez, editor of *National Pastime*; WGN radio and television in Chicago; the Society for American Baseball Research; former ballplayers Hank Sauer, Pete Milne and Johnny Sain; Hall of Famers Yogi Berra, Lou Boudreau, Jim Bunning, Bobby Doerr, Bob Feller, Monte Irvin, Ferguson Jenkins, George Kell, Robin Roberts, Brooks Robinson and Enos Slaughter; and to the Babe Ruth Museum in Baltimore.

As always, a special thanks to a special person: my wife Sandi Skipper.

Table of Contents

Preface

This is a reference book. The reader has the right to expect a clearly defined scope, specific criteria for inclusion, and 100 percent inclusion of everything that meets those criteria.

Those objectives are easily met in this book because of the work of others, primarily the Baseball Writers Association of America and an adjunct group called the Veterans Committee. Each year, they elect members to the Hall of Fame. It is not the purpose of this book to evaluate their work or their judgment. Rather, the purpose is to acknowledge the results by providing biographical information and data on each Hall of Fame member — and leave it to the readers to make their own evaluations.

The statistics of baseball are as precise as the game itself is imprecise. Baseball has been described as "a game of inches" whereby a ball hit or thrown "just a little more this way or that way" would have affected the outcome. Success or failure of a team has often come down to a "this way" or "that way" direction of the ball. If Willie McCovey's line drive with two outs in the ninth inning of the 1962 World Series had been two inches higher, Yankee second baseman Bobby Richardson wouldn't have caught it, two runs would have scored, and the Giants — not the Yankees — would have won the World Series. The "this way, that way" uncertainty of baseball is one of the things that keep the game interesting and is certainly one of the delights of the game for its fans.

In contrast, the fascination of baseball for the researcher is the precision of its record-keeping for well over a century. Henry Chadwick, a native of Great Britain, was a journalist in New York when he became fascinated with the American game of baseball. In 1857, he watched a game in Brooklyn between two local teams — the Excelsiors and the Stars — and wrote an account of it for a weekly paper, the *New York Clipper*. Along with his account, he included a listing of the names and positions of each player as well as several columns that gave a numerical breakdown of what each player had done during the game. He is credited with creating the "box score."

Chadwick's little chart to help readers of a weekly newspaper 140 years ago is the embryo from which all of baseball research has evolved. The box score is precise and concise and tells specifically what players and teams accomplish on a game-to-game basis. Collectively, box scores provide the statistics that preserve the history of the game and are the basis for individual honors such as the Most Valuable Player, Cy Young and Rookie of the Year awards, all of which are recognized as credentials for the Hall of Fame.

Included in this work are the biographies of players, managers, coaches, umpires, executives, sportswriters and broadcasters who have been elected to the Hall of Fame, followed, when applicable, by statistical summaries of their careers — information that was compiled because of the diligence of writers and researchers for more than 100 years, following up on Chadwick's charts.

Statistics, then, are necessarily an important part of this work. More than anything else, they are the documentation — the overriding reasons for the election of players to the Hall of Fame.

The bibliography at the end of this work is acknowledgment of one of the essential tools of research: the careful work of others — contemporaries and those who wrote and recorded accounts of events in another era. Their goal was the same as mine in *A Biographical Dictionary of the Baseball Hall of Fame*—to provide the serious researcher as well as the casual reader with an unbiased, carefully prepared, concise yet all-inclusive factual instrument depicting the lives and statistical accomplishments of everyone in the Hall of Fame. In its adherence to facts, there is no "this way" or "that way."

Introduction

The National Baseball Hall of Fame and Museum is the result of two men trying to figure out what to do with an old baseball. They sought an answer to that at about the same time baseball executives were trying to decide how they could best celebrate the game's 100th birthday.

But the history of the Hall of Fame really begins long before that, when a group of patriotic citizens formed a commission to determine the origin of baseball. In 1905, Albert G. Spalding, a baseball pioneer and entrepreneur whose last name still graces baseball equipment, saw an article by baseball writer Henry Chadwick in which Chadwick, a native of Great Britain, said baseball was a derivation of the English game of rounders. Spalding set out to determine if Chadwick was right.

A blue-ribbon panel of baseball experts and enthusiasts was formed. It included three former National League presidents: U.S. Sen. Morgan Bulkeley of Connecticut, the league's first president in 1876; A.G. Mills of New York, league president from 1882 to 1884; and Nicholas Young of Washington, D.C., league president from 1884 to 1892. Other commission members were U.S. Sen. Arthur Gorman of Maryland, who once owned the Washington ball club; Alfred Reach of Philadelphia and George Wright of Boston, successful businessmen and former players; and James Sullivan of New York, president of the Amateur Athletic Union.

The commission researched the issue and held several meetings over a period of three years. When the public learned of the commission and its purpose, the panel was inundated with unsolicited opinions and ideas.

One of those who wrote was a man named Abner Graves, a mining engineer from Denver. He said he saw an old classmate of his, Abner Doubleday, make changes to a game called "Town Ball" while he played with some children on a playground in their hometown of Cooperstown, New York.

"Town Ball" was a game in which teams of 20 or 30 ran around hitting a round ball with a stick. Doubleday, according to Graves, cut the teams down to a more workable number, put in a pitcher and a catcher and, to create a more concrete objective than just hitting and chasing a ball, added bases.

1

The committee was impressed. When it reported its findings in 1907, it concluded that the first plan for "baseball" was invented by Doubleday in 1839 on that playground in his hometown of Cooperstown. (However, the committee's findings have since been challenged by the fact that Doubleday was a West Point Cadet in 1838, and that no mention of baseball was made in either Doubleday's prolific writings or his *New York Times* obituary.)

In 1932, some people rummaging through a farmhouse attic near Cooperstown came across some belongings of the late Abner Graves. Among these was a tattered baseball. When the discovery was made known, Stephen Clark, a Cooperstown businessman, purchased the ball for $5 with the idea of displaying it, as well as other baseball relics, in a room at a social club in Cooperstown. His idea was an immense success. The old ball drew crowds of interested onlookers.

Clark was inspired to do more. With the help of a business associate, Alexander Cleland, he decided to take the idea a step further — to establish a National Baseball Museum in Cooperstown. The two men got the backing of National League president Ford Frick. Frick enthusiastically approached American League president Will Harridge and Commissioner Kenesaw Mountain Landis and they too supported the idea.

At about the same time that Clark and Cleland were pushing their museum idea, Major League baseball officials were starting to make plans for baseball's centennial celebration in 1939. Frick suggested that a Hall of Fame be established at the museum to honor the best ballplayers — an idea that was heartily accepted.

The Baseball Writers Association of America was called upon to elect the Hall of Fame members. In January 1936, they elected Ty Cobb, Babe Ruth, Honus Wagner, Christy Mathewson and Walter Johnson.

The National Baseball Hall of Fame and Museum was dedicated on June 12, 1939. By that time, 25 players had been elected. Only 11 were still alive, and all 11 attended the ceremonies.

Today, 237 players, managers, coaches, umpires and executives have been inducted into the Hall. There have been many changes over the years. Players from the old Negro leagues, who never had the chance to play Major League baseball, have been inducted. A Veterans Committee each year considers deserving old-timers. Writers and broadcasters also have been given places of honor.

There is an irony about the place that cherishes the facts and figures of the people it honors. Research done long after the blue-ribbon commission issued its report in 1907 calls into question whether Doubleday actually invented baseball. The Hall of Fame itself, in its literature, says contradictory theories are well documented.

Chadwick, who wrote the story about "rounders," and Spalding, who questioned the story, are both in the Hall of Fame, as are Bulkeley, who served on the commission, Frick, who suggested the Hall of Fame, and Landis and Harridge, baseball officials who helped it come to pass. Doubleday is not.

The Hall of Fame
Members

Henry Louis Aaron

Born February 5, 1934, in Mobile, Alabama. 6', 190 lbs., bats right, throws right. Years in minor leagues: 2; Major League debut: April 13, 1954; years in Major Leagues: 23. Elected to Hall of Fame: 1982. Nickname: Hammerin' Henry — bestowed upon him by the news media because of his hitting ability.

Henry (Hank) Aaron's 755 career home runs would surely be enough to earn him a spot in the Hall of Fame — but his accomplishments aside from his home runs also add up to Hall of Fame credentials. In 23 seasons with the Milwaukee Braves, Atlanta Braves and Milwaukee Brewers, he twice led the league in runs scored and tied for the lead once. He also led the league in hits twice, runs batted in four times and batting average twice. He finished with 3,771 career hits and a lifetime batting average of .305. He played in the World Series in 1957 and 1958 and hit .364 in 14 games.

As for home runs, he led the league three times and tied for the lead once. He hit 40 or more home runs eight times, and in four of those years, he hit 44 — his uniform number. In one of the years in which he hit 44, he tied for the league lead with the Giants' Willie McCovey, who also wore uniform number 44. Perhaps the best way to put Aaron's home run record in perspective is this: If a player hits 35 home runs each year for 20 consecutive years, he would still fall 55 homers short of Aaron's all-time record.

An oddity: Aaron finished his career with 2,174 runs scored — exactly the number Babe Ruth had at the end of his career. Aaron holds the all-time record for number of games played, at-bats, total bases, home runs, RBIs and appearances in All-Star games (24). His most famous hit is his 715th home run — the one that put him ahead of Ruth — hit off Dodger lefthander Al Downing on April 8, 1974. But another important hit for him never left the infield. On May 17, 1970, he beat out a hit off Cincinnati Reds righthander Wayne Simpson that gave him 3,000 hits for his career. It marked the first time in baseball history that anyone had 3,000 hits and 500 home runs.

Year	Team	G	AB	R	H	D	T	HR	RBI	AVE.
1954	Mil (N)	122	468	58	131	27	6	13	69	.280
1955	Mil	153	602	105	189	37	9	27	106	.314
1956	Mil	153	609	106	200	34	14	26	92	.328
1957	Mil	151	615	118	198	27	6	44	132	.322
1958	Mil	153	601	109	196	34	4	30	95	.326
1959	Mil	154	629	116	223	47	6	39	123	.355
1960	Mil	153	590	112	172	20	11	40	126	.292
1961	Mil	155	603	115	197	39	10	34	120	.327
1962	Mil	156	592	127	191	28	6	45	128	.323
1963	Mil	161	631	121	201	29	4	44	130	.319
1964	Mil	145	570	103	187	30	3	24	95	.328
1965	Mil	150	570	109	181	40	1	32	89	.318
1966	Atl	158	603	117	168	23	1	44	127	.279
1967	Atl	155	600	113	184	37	3	39	109	.307
1968	Atl	160	606	84	174	33	4	29	86	.287

Year	Team	G	AB	R	H	D	T	HR	RBI	AVE.
1969	Atl	147	547	100	164	30	3	44	97	.300
1970	Atl	150	516	103	154	26	1	38	118	.298
1971	Atl	139	495	95	162	22	3	47	118	.327
1972	Atl	129	449	75	119	10	0	34	77	.265
1973	Atl	120	392	84	118	12	1	40	96	.301
1974	Atl	112	340	47	91	16	0	20	69	.268
1975	Mil (A)	137	465	45	109	16	2	12	60	.234
1976	Mil	85	271	22	62	8	0	10	35	.229
23 years		3298	2364	2174	3771	624	98	755	2297	.305

Transactions: Nov. 2, 1974: Traded from Atlanta Braves to Milwaukee Brewers for Dave May and Roger Alexander.

WORLD SERIES

Year	Team	G	AB	R	H	D	T	HR	RBI	AVE.
1957	Mil.	7	28	5	11	0	1	3	7	.393
1958	Mil.	7	27	3	9	2	0	0	2	.333
2 years		14	55	8	20	2	1	3	9	.364

Bob Addie

Sportswriter. Elected to Hall of Fame: 1981.

Bob Addie covered the Washington Senators for 37 years, writing for the *Washington Times-Herald* and the *Washington Post*. During that time, he literally saw them come and go — the original Senators moved to Minnesota and were replaced by an expansion team in Washington that eventually moved to Texas. It was during Addie's tenure that Washington developed the reputation of being first in war, first in peace and last in the American League.

He was elected to the Hall of Fame in 1981, one year before his death.

Grover Cleveland Alexander

Born February 26, 1887, in Elba, Nebraska; died November 4, 1950, in St. Paul, Nebraska. 6'1", 185 lbs., bats right, throws right. Years in minor leagues: 2; Major League debut: April 15, 1911; years in Major Leagues: 20. Elected to Hall of Fame: 1938. Nickname: Pete — believed to be because of his love of alcohol. During the Prohibition era, when liquor was illegal, one of the slang terms for it was "Sneaky Pete," and Alexander was known to sneak after it on many occasions.

Grover Cleveland Alexander holds several Major League records as a starting pitcher that may never be broken. In a three-year stretch between 1915 and 1917, pitching for the Philadelphia Phillies, he won 94 games: 31, 33 and 30, respectively.

In 1915, he threw four one-hitters and in 1916 tossed 16 shutouts. In his 20-year National League career, hurling for the Phillies, St. Louis Cardinals and Chicago Cubs, he had 90 shutouts — only Walter Johnson had more. His lifetime total of 373 wins ties him with Christy Mathewson as third-best all-time, behind Cy Young and Johnson. He led the league in wins six times, in earned run average five times (each time being under 2.00), in complete games six times, innings pitched six times, strikeouts six times and shutouts five times.

Despite his brilliant career as a starter, one of the great moments of his career occurred on October 10, 1926, when Alexander came on in relief for the St. Louis Cardinals in the seventh game of the World Series against the New York Yankees. He struck out Tony Lazzeri with the bases loaded and then held the Yankees hitless the rest of the way to preserve a 3–2 Cardinal victory, one day after he started and won a 10–2 decision over the Yankees. Alexander gave fans a hint of what was to come in his great career when, in his rookie season in 1911, he beat Cy Young in 12 innings in Young's last start of his Major League career. Young had to settle for a lifetime total of 511 wins — still the all-time record.

In the modern era of Major League baseball, much has been made of the amount of time stars like Ted Williams and Bob Feller lost because of military service — and how that lost time affected their lifetime statistics. It is fair to point out that Alexander joined the Army in 1918 (after pitching in only three games) and was sent to France as an infantry sergeant during World War I. While he only missed the one season, it came the year following his three successive 30-win seasons. His military service surely cost him the opportunity to be alone as third winningest pitcher in baseball history. In addition, Alexander developed epilepsy overseas and was never quite the same after that, probably preventing him from winning 400 games.

Year	Team	W-L	ERA	G	IP	H	BB	SO
1911	Phil (N)	28–13	2.57	48	367	285	129	227
1912	Phil	19–17	2.81	46	310.1	289	105	195
1913	Phil	22–8	2.79	47	306.1	288	75	159
1914	Phil	27–15	2.38	46	355	327	76	214
1915	Phil	31–10	1.22	49	376.1	253	64	241
1916	Phil	33–12	1.55	48	388.2	323	50	167
1917	Phil	30–13	1.86	45	387.2	336	58	201
1918	Chi (N)	2–1	1.73	3	26	19	3	15
1919	Chi	16–11	1.72	30	235	180	38	121
1920	Chi	27–14	1.91	46	363.1	335	69	173
1921	Chi	15–13	3.39	31	252	286	33	77
1922	Chi	16–13	3.63	33	245.2	283	34	48
1923	Chi	22–12	3.19	39	305	308	30	72
1924	Chi	12–5	3.03	21	169.1	183	25	33
1925	Chi	15–11	3.39	32	236	270	29	63
1926	Chi–StL (N)	12–10	3.05	30	200.1	191	30	47
1927	StL	21–10	2.52	37	268	261	38	48
1928	StL	16–9	3.36	34	243.2	262	37	59

Year	Team	W-L	ERA	G	IP	H	BB	SO
1929	StL	9–8	3.89	22	132	149	23	33
1930	Phil (N)	0–3	9.14	9	21.2	40	6	6
20 years		373–208	2.56	696	5189.1	4868	953	2199

Transactions: Dec. 11, 1917: Traded with Bill Killefer to Chicago Cubs for Mike Prendergast, Pickles Dillhoefer and $55,000. June 22, 1926: Placed on waivers by Chicago Cubs and obtained by St. Louis Cardinals. Dec. 11, 1929: Traded with Harry McCurdy to Philadelphia Phillies for Homer Peel and Bob McGraw.

WORLD SERIES

Year	Team	W-L	ERA	G	IP	H	BB	SO
1915	Phil (N)	1–1	1.53	2	17.2	14	4	10
1926	StL (N)	2–0	0.89	3	20.1	12	4	17
1928	StL (N)	0–1	19.80	2	5	10	4	2
3 years		3–2	3.35	7	43	36	12	29

Melvin Allen Israel (Mel Allen)

Broadcaster. Elected to Hall of Fame: 1978.

Melvin Allen Israel, the son of Russian immigrants, grew up in Alabama and might have become a school teacher had it not been for his circumstances at the University of Alabama. He once described himself as the "utility infielder" on the Crimson Tide football team — which meant he was the water boy, equipment manager and public address announcer. Of all the odd jobs, he liked announcing the best, and a career was born. He became "Mel Allen" and worked his way up in broadcasting to become the voice of the New York Yankees, a position he held from 1939 to 1964. He also did the voice-overs on the Movietime newsreels of baseball and was the host of television's "This Week in Baseball" until his death in 1996. He also had a brief stint as broadcaster for the Cleveland Indians in 1968.

Variety, the newspaper of the entertainment industry, rated Allen's voice as one of the 25 most recognizable in the world. Allen the Alabaman never lost the Southern twang that punctuated his speech. On the air, he was enthusiastic and he brought many now-popular phrases into the baseball lexicon, including "going ... going ... gone" on a home run and his trademark "How about that!" Though he was the voice of the Yankees in the days long before coast-to-coast cable broadcasts, Allen was known all over the country because he broadcast 20 World Series and 24 All-Star games in his long career.

In 1978, Allen and Red Barber, who at one time were partners in the broadcast booth, became the first broadcasters inducted into the Hall of Fame.

Walter Emmons Alston

Born December 1, 1911, in Venice, Ohio; died October 1, 1984, in Oxford, Ohio. 6'2", 195 lbs., bats right, throws right. Years in minor leagues: 13 as manager; Major League debut: September 27, 1936; years in Major Leagues: 1 game as player; 23 years as manager. Elected to Hall of Fame: 1983. Nickname: Smokey—which stuck with him from elementary school when he had a pretty good fastball and word got around that he could really "smoke" it.

After the 1953 baseball season, veteran Brooklyn Dodger manager Chuck Dressen asked for a long-term contract. He and his Dodgers had been in the World Series two years in a row, though they lost both times to the New York Yankees. Dodger owner Walter O'Malley didn't believe in long-term contracts. So instead of rehiring Dressen, he dumped him and introduced the world to his new manager: Walter Alston, a bald, soft-spoken man whose Major League experience totaled exactly one game, a game in which he struck out in his only at-bat and made an error in the field as a first baseman.

This unknown newcomer took the helm of the two-time defending National League champions in 1954, the year the Giants won the pennant and then stunned the Cleveland Indians with a four-game sweep of the World Series. But in 1955, Alston's Dodgers won the National League pennant and then beat the Yankees in the World Series — the Dodgers' first World Series championship ever. Brooklyn won the pennant again in 1956. In 1958, the Dodgers moved to Los Angeles, and one year later, Alston led his troops to another World Series championship. Under Alston, the Dodgers won the pennant again in 1963, 1965, 1966 and 1974 and World Series titles in 1963 and 1965. The Dodgers finished in the first division in 18 of Alston's 23 years as manager.

When he announced his retirement on September 27, 1976, it marked the end of a Major League managerial career that resulted in 2,040 victories. Only John McGraw with the Giants and Connie Mack with the Philadelphia A's managed one team longer than Alston managed the Dodgers. Alston did it all without the long-term security that his predecessor sought and that has become a staple of Major League contracts today. Alston signed one-year contracts for 23 consecutive years.

As a Player

Year	Team	G	AB	R	H	D	T	HR	RBI	AVE.
1936	StL (N)	1	1	0	0	0	0	0	0	.000

As a Manager

Year	Team	Record	Standing
1954	Brooklyn	92–62	Second
1955	Brooklyn	98–55	First

Year	Team	Record	Standing
1956	Brooklyn	93–61	First
1957	Brooklyn	84–70	Third
1958	Los Angeles	71–83	Seventh
1959	Los Angeles	88–68	First
1960	Los Angeles	82–72	Fourth
1961	Los Angeles	89–65	Second
1962	Los Angeles	102–63	Second
1963	Los Angeles	99–63	First
1964	Los Angeles	80–82	Sixth
1965	Los Angeles	97–65	First
1966	Los Angeles	95–67	First
1967	Los Angeles	73–89	Eighth
1968	Los Angeles	76–86	Seventh
1969	Los Angeles	85–77	Fourth
1970	Los Angeles	87–74	Second
1971	Los Angeles	89–73	Second
1972	Los Angeles	85–70	Third
1973	Los Angeles	95–66	Second
1974	Los Angeles	102–60	First
1975	Los Angeles	88–74	Second
1976	Los Angeles	90–68	Second
23 years		**2040–1613**	

LEAGUE CHAMPIONSHIP SERIES

1974	Los Angeles	3–1

WORLD SERIES

1955	Brooklyn	4–3
1956	Brooklyn	3–4
1959	Los Angeles	4–2
1963	Los Angeles	4–0
1965	Los Angeles	4–3
1966	Los Angeles	0–4
1974	Los Angeles	1–4
7 years		**20–20**

Adrian Constantine Anson

Born April 17, 1852, in Marshalltown, Iowa; died April 14, 1922, in Chicago, Illinois. 6′, 202 lbs., bats right, throws right. Years in minor leagues: 6; Major League debut: May 6, 1871; years in Major Leagues: 22. Elected to Hall of Fame: 1939. Nickname: Cap — short for captain, the head of the ship. Anson was a player-manager for 20 years of his 22-year career.

Cap Anson was unquestionably baseball's first superstar. He played 22 years for the Chicago White Stockings of the old National League — all before 1900.

He never hit .400 for a season but hit .399 one year and .396 in another. Anson won four batting titles and had a lifetime batting average of .339. In his last Major League season, he hit .302 at the age of 45. Because Anson was a trailblazer in a new sport, he is credited with many firsts. Though he only hit 92 home runs in his long career, he was the first to hit three in one game and to hit five in two consecutive games.

Anson was a formidable figure at the plate. He had a thick handlebar moustache made famous 100 years later by another Hall of Famer, Rollie Fingers. Standing with his heels together and carrying a heavy bat, Anson displayed amazing dexterity and lightning quick reflexes. Despite the stiff, awkward batting stance, he was never hit by a pitch in his long career because of how quickly he could duck or back away from errant pitches.

He was one of the most versatile fielders of all time. Anson was most comfortable at first base where he appeared in 2,058 games and was the first player to accomplish two unassisted double plays at that position in the same game. He also appeared in 118 games at third base, 83 games at shortstop, 49 as an outfielder, 13 games at second base, 3 games as a catcher and three as a pitcher. In 20 years as a manager—19 with Chicago and one with New York—Anson's teams finished first five times, second four times and third twice. His teams won 1,297 games while losing 957, a percentage of .575. Before playing professional baseball, Anson attended the University of Notre Dame where he is credited with forming the school's first baseball team.

Year	Team	G	AB	R	H	D	T	HR	RBI	AVE.
1876	Chi (N)	66	309	63	110	13	7	1	59	.356
1877	Chi	59	255	52	86	19	1	0	32	.337
1878	Chi	60	261	55	89	12	2	0	40	.341
1879	Chi	51	227	40	90	20	1	0	34	.396
1880	Chi	86	356	54	120	24	1	1	74	.337
1881	Chi	84	343	67	137	21	7	1	82	.399
1882	Chi	82	348	69	126	29	8	1	83	.362
1883	Chi	98	413	70	127	36	5	0		.308
1884	Chi	112	475	108	159	30	3	21		.335
1885	Chi	112	464	100	144	35	7	7	114	.310
1886	Chi	125	504	117	187	35	11	20	147	.371
1887	Chi	122	472	107	164	33	13	7	102	.347
1888	Chi	134	515	101	177	20	12	12	84	.344
1889	Chi	134	518	100	177	32	7	7	117	.342
1890	Chi	139	504	95	157	14	5	7	107	.312
1891	Chi	136	540	81	157	24	8	8	120	.291
1892	Chi	146	559	62	152	25	9	1	74	.272
1893	Chi	103	398	70	125	24	2	0	91	.314
1894	Chi	83	347	82	137	28	4	5	99	.395
1895	Chi	122	474	87	159	23	6	2	91	.335
1896	Chi	108	402	72	133	18	2	2	90	.331
1897	Chi	114	424	67	128	17	3	3	75	.302
22 years		2276	9108	1719	3041	532	124	96	1715	.339

Luis Ernesto Aparicio

Born April 29, 1934, in Maracaibo, Venezuela. 5'9", 160 lbs., bats right, throws right. Years in minor leagues: 2; Major League debut: April 17, 1956; Years in Major Leagues: 18. Elected to Hall of Fame: 1984. Nickname: Little Looie — because he was physically small.

In an era dominated by slugging future Hall of Famers such as Mantle, Mays, McCovey, Banks, Killebrew and many others, Luis Aparicio used other skills to become the premier shortstop in the Major Leagues for almost 20 years. He was part of two infield combinations that made their way into the Hall of Fame. In the early part of his career, Aparicio and Nellie Fox were the shortstop–second baseman tandem for the Chicago White Sox. Later, he teamed with Baltimore's great third baseman Brooks Robinson to form the left side of an infield that was almost impossible to hit a ground ball through.

Aparicio's fielding statistics are impressive but they don't begin to demonstrate his range in the field — and there was nobody better in his day. Aparicio consistently took base hits away from hitters and stopped rallies by racing onto the outfield grass to spear ground balls and then throw the runners out at first.

He broke in with the White Sox in 1956 and was the American League's Rookie of the Year. He led the American League in stolen bases nine years in a row — his first nine years in the Majors — and stole more than 50 bases in four different seasons. In 1959, the only season since 1919 that the White Sox have won the American League championship, Aparicio was the leadoff man and stole 56 bases on a team that came to be known as the "Go-Go White Sox." He then played for the Orioles and the Boston Red Sox before retiring after the 1973 season. Aparicio holds the record for most games at shortstop, 2,581; assists, 8,016; chances, 12,564; and double plays, 1,553. Aparicio's father was a great shortstop in Venezuela when Luis was growing up, retiring only when his son came along and replaced him.

Year	Team	G	AB	R	H	D	T	HR	RBI	AVE.
1956	Chi (A)	152	533	69	142	19	6	3	56	.256
1957	Chi	143	575	82	148	22	6	3	41	.257
1958	Chi	145	557	76	148	20	9	2	40	.266
1959	Chi	152	612	98	157	18	5	6	51	.257
1960	Chi	153	600	86	166	20	7	2	61	.277
1961	Chi	156	625	90	170	24	4	6	45	.272
1962	Chi	153	581	72	140	23	5	7	40	.241
1963	Balt	146	601	73	150	18	8	5	45	.250
1964	Balt	146	578	93	154	20	3	10	37	.266
1965	Balt	144	564	67	127	20	10	8	40	.225
1966	Balt	151	659	97	182	25	8	6	41	.276
1967	Balt	134	546	55	127	22	5	4	31	.233
1968	Chi (A)	155	622	55	164	24	4	4	36	.264
1969	Chi	156	599	77	168	24	5	5	51	.280

Year	Team	G	AB	R	H	D	T	HR	RBI	AVE.
1970	Chi	146	552	86	173	29	3	5	43	.313
1971	Bos	125	491	56	114	23	0	4	45	.232
1972	Bos	110	436	47	112	26	3	3	39	.257
1973	Bos	132	499	56	135	17	1	0	49	.271
18 years		**2599**	**10230**	**1335**	**2677**	**394**	**92**	**83**	**791**	**.262**

Transactions: Jan. 14, 1963: Traded with outfielder Al Smith to the Baltimore Orioles for pitcher Hoyt Wilhelm, third baseman Pete Ward, shortstop Ron Hansen and outfielder Dave Nicholson. Nov. 29, 1967: Traded with outfielder Russ Snyder and outfielder John Matias to Chicago White Sox for infielder Don Buford and pitchers Bruce Howard and Roger Nelson. Dec. 1, 1970: Traded to Boston Red Sox for infielder Mike Andrews and infielder Luis Alvarado.

WORLD SERIES

Year	Team	G	AB	R	H	D	T	HR	RBI	AVE.
1959	Chi (A)	6	26	1	8	1	0	0	0	.306
1966	Balt	4	16	0	4	1	0	0	2	.250
2 years		**10**	**42**	**1**	**12**	**2**	**0**	**0**	**2**	**.286**

Lucius Benjamin Appling

Born April 2, 1907, in High Point, North Carolina; died January 3, 1991, in Cumming, Georgia. 5'10", 183 lbs., bats right, throws right. Years in minor leagues: 1; Major League debut: September 10, 1930; Years in Major Leagues: 20. Elected to Hall of Fame: 1964. Nickname: Old Aches and Pains — because of his frequent complaints about injuries, real and imagined.

Luke Appling played 20 years in the Major Leagues, all with the same team — the Chicago White Sox — and had a lifetime batting average of .310. He batted over .300 in 16 of his 20 seasons and won two batting titles. His .388 average in 1936 remains the White Sox record for highest batting average. Like so many other athletes of his day, Appling lost a prime time year to military service. He missed the entire 1944 season for service in World War II, after winning the 1943 batting title with a .328 average.

He returned in 1945 and played in just 18 games but managed to hit .362 in that limited time. He then had four more years where he hit over .300, including 1948 and 1949 when, at the ages of 41 and 42 respectively, he hit .314 and .301. Appling is perhaps best remembered for two things. One was his ability to foul off pitches, often spoiling seven or eight in a row until he either walked or got the pitch he wanted and stroked it for a hit.

The other memorable circumstance occurred long after his playing days were over. In an Old-Timers contest prior to the 1982 All-Star Game at RFK Stadium in Washington, Appling hit a 275-foot home run over a temporary left field fence.

He was 75 years old. The homer is even more amazing in light of the fact that Appling hit only 48 home runs in his entire career of two decades and nearly 9,000 at-bats. The pitcher who gave up the gopher ball was Hall of Famer Warren Spahn.

Year	Team	G	AB	R	H	D	T	HR	RBI	AVE.
1930	Chi (A)	6	26	2	8	2	0	0	2	.308
1931	Chi	96	297	36	69	13	4	1	28	.232
1932	Chi	139	489	66	134	20	10	3	63	.274
1933	Chi	151	612	90	197	36	10	6	85	.322
1934	Chi	118	452	75	137	28	6	2	61	.303
1935	Chi	153	525	94	161	28	6	1	71	.307
1936	Chi	138	526	111	204	31	7	6	128	.388
1937	Chi	154	574	98	182	42	8	4	77	.317
1938	Chi	81	294	41	89	14	0	0	44	.303
1939	Chi	148	516	82	162	16	0	6	56	.314
1940	Chi	150	566	96	197	27	13	0	79	.348
1941	Chi	154	592	93	186	26	8	1	57	.314
1942	Chi	142	543	78	142	26	4	3	53	.262
1943	Chi	155	585	63	192	33	2	3	80	.328
1945	Chi	18	58	12	21	2	2	1	10	.362
1946	Chi	149	582	59	180	27	5	1	55	.309
1947	Chi	139	503	67	154	29	0	8	49	.306
1948	Chi	139	497	63	156	16	2	0	47	.314
1949	Chi	142	492	82	148	21	5	5	58	.301
1950	Chi	50	128	11	30	3	4	0	13	.234
20 years		**2422**	**8857**	**1319**	**2749**	**440**	**102**	**45**	**1116**	**.310**

Donn Richard Ashburn

Born March 19, 1927, in Tilden, Nebraska; died September 9, 1997, in New York, New York. 5'10", 170 lbs., bats left, throws right. Years in minor leagues: 3; Major League debut: April 20, 1948; years in Major Leagues: 15. Elected to Hall of Fame: 1996. Nickname: Putt Putt—attributed to Ted Williams who said the speedy Ashburn had twin engines in his speedy legs; was most often referred to as Richie, a derivation of his middle name.

With the exception of one season, Richie Ashburn had the unfortunate distinction of playing his entire career with teams that finished at or near the bottom of the National League. The exception was the 1950 Philadelphia Phillies who beat out the Brooklyn Dodgers for the pennant on the last day of the season. A key play in that game occurred when center fielder Ashburn threw out Cal Abrams at the plate to preserve a 1–1 tie. The Phillies won it in the tenth inning on a Dick Sisler three-run homer. Philadelphia then lost to the New York Yankees in the World Series. Ashburn broke in in 1948, hit .333 and led the league in stolen bases. He had a 23-game hitting streak that year which, at the time, was the longest hitting streak ever for a rookie.

He played 12 years with the Phillies, two years with the Chicago Cubs and finished his career as a member of the first New York Mets team. He led the league in hits three times and won the batting title twice. He was a leadoff man most of his career and led the league in walks three times. He was the best bunter of his day and often beat out bunts for hits. He finished with a lifetime batting average of .308. But Ashburn's greatest skill was often overshadowed because of flashy competition. He was one of the greatest fielding center fielders of all time, but he played at the same time as Willie Mays of the Giants, Duke Snider of the Dodgers and, in the American League, Mickey Mantle of the Yankees.

While those sluggers were hitting home runs, Ashburn was setting fielding records. He had more than 400 putouts in a season nine times, and in four of those years he exceeded 500. He led the Major Leagues in putouts in nine different seasons. Only Pittsburgh's Max Carey equaled that. When his playing career was over, he returned to the Phillies as a broadcaster for 35 years.

Year	Team	G	AB	R	H	D	T	HR	RBI	AVE.
1948	Phil (N)	117	463	78	154	17	2	4	40	.333
1949	Phil	114	662	84	188	18	11	1	37	.284
1950	Phil	151	594	84	180	25	14	2	41	.303
1951	Phil	154	643	92	221	31	5	4	63	.344
1952	Phil	154	613	93	173	31	6	1	42	.282
1953	Phil	156	622	110	205	25	9	2	57	.330
1954	Phil	153	559	111	175	16	8	1	41	.313
1955	Phil	140	533	91	180	32	9	3	42	.338
1956	Phil	154	628	94	190	26	8	3	50	.303
1957	Phil	156	626	93	186	26	8	0	33	.297
1958	Phil	152	615	98	215	24	13	2	33	.350
1959	Phil	153	564	86	150	16	2	1	20	.266
1960	Chi (N)	151	547	99	159	16	5	0	40	.291
1961	Chi	109	307	49	79	7	4	0	19	.257
1962	NY (N)	135	389	60	119	7	3	7	28	.306
15 years		**2189**	**8365**	**1322**	**2574**	**317**	**109**	**29**	**586**	**.308**

Transactions: Jan. 11, 1960: Traded to Chicago Cubs for pitcher John Buzhardt, infielder Alvin Dark and outfielder Jim Woods. Dec. 8, 1961: Sold to New York Mets as part of expansion draft.

WORLD SERIES

Year	Team	G	AB	R	H	D	T	HR	RBI	AVE.
1950	Phil (N)	4	17	0	3	1	0	0	1	.176

Howard Earl Averill

Born May 21, 1902, in Snohomish, Washington; died August 15, 1983, in Everett, Washington. 5'9", 172 lbs., bats left, throws right. Years in minor leagues: 3; Major League debut: April 16, 1929; Years in Major Leagues: 13.

Elected to Hall of Fame: 1975. Nickname: Rock—apparently because of his sturdy build; often called "the rock of Snohomish." Was best known by his middle name.

Earl Averill played 13 years in the Major Leagues, one of the shortest tenures for a Hall of Famer. He didn't break in until he was 27 years old, after three sensational years in the minor leagues. But he made up for lost time quickly. Averill, playing for the Cleveland Indians, was the first player in the American League to homer in his first Major League at-bat, hitting it off of Detroit's Earl Whitehill on April 16, 1929. Averill and Hoyt Wilhelm are the only two Hall of Famers to have homered in their first Major League at-bats.

Averill had amazing power for a man his size, and he had some amazing games during his career. On September 17, 1930, he hit three home runs in a game against the Washington Senators and just missed a fourth on a drive that had the distance but landed in foul territory. That game was part of a doubleheader in which he also homered in the other game. He finished the day with 4 homers and 11 RBIs. At the time, he held the record for most homers in a doubleheader. In 1931, he drove in seven runs in one game and hit two homers in a game three times. On August 2, 1931, Averill set a Major League record when he walked five times in a game against the Boston Red Sox. In 1933, he hit for the cycle in a game against the Philadelphia A's.

He hit over .300 his first six years, including .332 in his rookie year, 1929. In 1936, he hit .378 and led the American League with 232 hits. He drove in more than 100 runs five times and finished with a lifetime batting average of .318. Averill played in five All-Star games and, despite all the accomplishments of his career, is best remembered by some for an incident in the 1937 All-Star game in Washington. Averill hit a line drive off the foot of National League pitcher Dizzy Dean; the resulting injury affected the rest of the great pitcher's career.

Year	Team	G	AB	R	H	D	T	HR	RBI	AVE.
1929	Cleve	152	602	110	199	43	13	18	97	.332
1930	Cleve	139	534	102	181	33	8	19	119	.339
1931	Cleve	155	627	140	209	36	10	32	143	.333
1932	Cleve	153	631	116	198	37	14	32	124	.314
1933	Cleve	151	599	83	180	39	16	11	92	.301
1934	Cleve	154	598	128	187	48	6	31	113	.313
1935	Cleve	140	563	109	162	34	13	19	79	.288
1936	Cleve	152	614	136	232	39	15	28	126	.378
1937	Cleve	156	609	121	182	33	11	21	92	.299
1938	Cleve	134	482	101	159	27	15	14	93	.330
1939	Cle-Det	111	364	66	96	28	6	11	65	.264
1940	Det	64	118	10	33	4	1	2	20	.280
1941	Bos (N)	8	17	2	2	0	0	0	2	.118
13 years		1669	6358	1224	2020	401	128	238	1165	.318

Transactions: June 14, 1939: Traded to Detroit Tigers for Harry Eisenstat and cash.

WORLD SERIES

| 1940 | Det | 3 | 3 | 0 | 0 | 0 | 0 | 0 | 0 | .000 |

John Franklin Baker

Born March 13, 1886, in Trappe, Maryland; died June 28, 1963, in Trappe, Maryland. 5'11", 173 lbs., bats left, throws right. Years in minor leagues: 2; Major League debut: September 21, 1908; Years in Major Leagues: 13. Elected to Hall of Fame: 1955. Nickname: Home Run — Not because of the number he hit or the distance they went, both common misconceptions, but because he hit homers in consecutive games in the 1911 World Series.

"Home Run" Baker, whose given name was John but went by his middle name, Frank, played 13 years in the Major Leagues and hit a total of 96 home runs, never more than 12 in one year, which was a good output in the "dead ball" era. In the second game of the 1911 World Series, Baker, playing for the Philadelphia A's, hit a home run off of future Hall of Famer Rube Marquard of John McGraw's New York Giants. The homer broke a 1–1 tie and set the stage for a Philadelphia victory. In the next game, Baker connected off another baseball legend, Christy Mathewson, in the ninth inning, costing Mathewson what would have been a 1–0 victory.

From those two games, two nicknames were born: John Baker was forever known as "Home Run" Baker and, for many years, home runs were referred to as "Bakers." Baker was the third baseman in Connie Mack's prized "$100,000 infield" that also featured Jack Barry, Eddie Collins and Stuffy McInnis.

An unusual feature of Baker's career is that he sat out two seasons: 1915 when he refused to play because he didn't get a pay raise, and 1920, when he retired, only to return in 1921 to play two more seasons. His great career with the great A's teams came to an abrupt end when he sat out the 1915 season. Mack sold him to the Yankees for $37,500. Baker had a lifetime batting average of .307 and led the American League in home runs four years in a row. In his 13-year career, his team made it to the World Series six times, and Baker's lifetime World Series batting average is .363. (In 1914, he homered off Marquard again and hit .450 in that World Series.) He led the league in RBIs twice, and it was not an exaggeration to say he swung a heavy bat — it weighed 52 ounces.

Year	Team	G	AB	R	H	D	T	HR	RBI	AVE.
1908	Phil (A)	9	31	5	9	3	0	0	5	.290
1909	Phil	148	541	73	165	27	19	4	73	.305
1910	Phil	146	561	83	159	25	15	2	83	.283
1911	Phil	148	592	96	198	40	14	11	96	.334
1912	Phil	149	577	116	200	40	21	10	116	.347
1913	Phil	149	565	116	190	34	9	12	116	.336
1914	Phil	150	570	84	182	23	10	9	84	.319

Year	Team	G	AB	R	H	D	T	HR	RBI	AVE.
1916	NY (A)	100	360	46	97	23	2	10	46	.269
1917	NY	146	553	57	156	24	2	6	57	.282
1918	NY	126	504	65	154	24	5	6	68	.306
1919	NY	141	567	70	166	22	1	10	83	.293
1921	NY	94	330	46	97	16	2	9	71	.294
1922	NY	69	234	30	65	12	3	7	36	.278
13 years		1575	5985	887	1838	313	103	96	1013	.307

Transactions: Feb. 15, 1916: Sold to New York Yankees for $37,500.

WORLD SERIES

Year	Team	G	AB	R	H	D	T	HR	RBI	AVE.
1910	Phil (A)	5	22	6	9	3	0	0	4	.409
1911	Phil	6	24	7	9	2	0	2	5	.375
1913	Phil	5	20	2	9	0	0	1	7	.450
1914	Phil	4	16	0	4	2	0	0	2	.250
1921	NY (A)	4	8	0	2	0	0	0	0	.250
1922	NY	1	1	0	0	0	0	0	0	.000
6 years		25	91	15	33	7	0	3	18	.363

David James Bancroft

Born April 20, 1891, in Sioux City, Iowa; died October 9, 1972, in Superior, Wisconsin. 5'9", 160 lbs., bats both, throws right. Years in minor leagues: 6; Major League debut: April 14, 1915; Years in Major Leagues: 16. Elected to Hall of Fame: 1971. Nickname: Beauty—Attributed to how well he fielded his shortstop position and also, an expression he used to describe a good fielding play or a good pitch.

Those who saw him play said there was only one thing stopping Dave Bancroft from being the greatest shortstop of his time: Honus Wagner. Bancroft was a master at grabbing every ground ball hit near him and he set the standard for how to cut off a ball thrown from the outfield and relay it to the proper base. Bancroft spent six years in the minor leagues before being called up to the lowly Philadelphia Phillies in 1915. The year before, the Phillies were one of the teams left in the shadows of the "Miracle Braves" who won the 1914 championship. The Phillies finished sixth. In 1915, with Bancroft playing 153 games at shortstop, the Phillies won their first National League pennant. He played five years with the Phillies and then was traded to John McGraw's Giants where he helped them win three consecutive National League championships.

After his playing days were over, Bancroft managed the Boston Braves for four years, then was a coach with the Brooklyn Dodgers, then back with McGraw as a coach and played in 10 games with the Giants in 1930. Then he managed the Minneapolis Millers in the American Association. He rounded out his career with managerial stints with the Battle Creek Belles and the South Bend Blue Sox of the All-American Girls Professional Baseball League. As a Major League player, he hit over .300 six times (and .299 once), finished with a lifetime batting average of .279 and had 2,004 hits. But it is the number of hits he took away from others, by his range defensively, that sets Bancroft apart from most others who played in his time.

Year	Team	G	AB	R	H	D	T	HR	RBI	AVE.
1915	Phil (N)	153	563	85	143	18	2	7	30	.254
1916	Phil	142	477	53	101	10	0	3	33	.212
1917	Phil	127	478	56	116	22	5	4	43	.243
1918	Phil	125	499	69	132	19	4	0	26	.265
1919	Phil	92	335	45	91	13	7	0	25	.272
1920	Phi-NY (N)	150	613	102	183	36	9	0	36	.299
1921	NY	153	606	121	193	26	15	6	67	.318
1922	NY	156	651	117	209	41	5	4	60	.321
1923	NY	107	444	80	135	33	3	1	31	.304
1924	Bos (N)	79	319	49	89	11	1	2	21	.279
1925	Bos	128	479	75	153	29	8	2	49	.319
1926	Bos	127	453	70	141	18	6	1	44	.311
1927	Bos	111	375	44	91	13	4	1	31	.243
1928	Brklyn	149	515	47	127	19	5	0	51	.247
1929	Brklyn	104	358	35	99	11	3	1	44	.277
1930	NY (N)	10	17	0	1	0	0	0	0	.059
16 years		**1913**	**7182**	**1048**	**2004**	**320**	**77**	**32**	**591**	**.279**

Transactions: June 8, 1920: Traded to New York Giants for Art Fletcher, Bill Hubbell and cash. Nov. 12, 1923: Traded to Boston Braves with Casey Stengel and Bill Cunningham for Billy Southworth and Joe Oeschger (and then named manager of the Braves).

WORLD SERIES

Year	Team	G	AB	R	H	D	T	HR	RBI	AVE.
1915	Phil (N)	5	17	2	5	0	0	0	0	.294
1921	NY (N)	8	33	3	5	1	0	0	0	.152
1922	NY	5	19	4	4	0	0	0	0	.211
1923	NY	6	24	1	2	0	0	0	0	.083
4 years		**24**	**93**	**10**	**16**	**1**	**0**	**0**	**0**	**.172**

Ernest Banks

Born January 31, 1931, in Dallas, Texas. 6'1", 180 lbs., bats right, throws right. Years in minor leagues: None; Major League debut: September 17, 1953; Years in Major Leagues: 19. Elected to Hall of Fame: 1977. Nickname: Mr. Cub — because of his loyalty and enthusiasm for the only team he ever played for, and because he was the best player on that team for most of his career.

Ernie Banks was the first black player for the Chicago Cubs. He was a star almost from the first day he took the field. Banks is remembered not only for his home runs — he hit 512 — but for his enthusiastic approach to the game. Rain or shine, Ernie would say, "It's a beautiful day — let's play two!" He was a slick field-ing, durable shortstop for the first eight years of his career but switched to first base in 1961 to ease his ailing knees. At shortstop, Banks had a string of 717 consecutive games played — almost five years straight. He won Gold Glove awards at both short-stop and first base. For several years, he was part of an "All-Star infield" that included Ron Santo at third, Don Kessinger at shortstop and Glenn Beckert at second base.

As a batter, he would grip the bat tightly but move his fingers as he waited for the pitch, then use lightning quick wrists to get around on the ball. In 1955, he hit 44 home runs in his second full season with the Cubs. It was one of five seasons in which Banks hit 40 or more home runs. In 1958 and 1959, he hit 47 and 45 home runs, respectively, and won the Most Valuable Player award both years, helping the Cubs to fifth place finishes both years — their highest standing of the decade. His 47 home runs in 1958 is still the Major League record for a shortstop. He drove in more than 100 runs eight times in his career. His 143 RBIs in 1959 were 91 more than any other Cub player that year, which is also a Major League record. Banks is one of the few players to have spent so many seasons in the Major Leagues (19) without playing in a World Series.

Year	Team	G	AB	R	H	D	T	HR	RBI	AVE.
1953	Chi (N)	10	35	3	11	1	1	2	6	.314
1954	Chi	154	593	70	163	19	7	19	79	.275
1955	Chi	154	596	98	176	29	9	44	117	.295
1956	Chi	139	538	82	160	25	8	28	85	.297
1957	Chi	156	594	113	169	34	6	43	102	.285
1958	Chi	154	617	119	193	23	11	47	129	.313
1959	Chi	155	589	97	179	25	6	45	143	.304
1960	Chi	156	597	94	162	32	7	41	117	.271
1961	Chi	138	511	75	142	22	4	29	80	.278
1962	Chi	154	610	87	164	20	6	37	104	.269
1963	Chi	130	432	41	98	20	1	18	64	.227
1964	Chi	157	591	67	156	29	6	23	95	.264
1965	Chi	163	612	79	162	25	3	28	106	.265
1966	Chi	141	511	52	139	23	7	15	75	.272
1967	Chi	151	573	68	158	26	4	23	95	.276
1968	Chi	150	552	71	136	27	0	32	83	.246
1969	Chi	155	565	60	143	19	2	23	106	.253
1970	Chi	72	222	25	56	6	2	12	44	.252
1971	Chi	39	83	4	16	2	0	3	6	.193
19 years		2528	9421	1305	2583	407	90	512	1636	.274

Walter Lanier Barber

Broadcaster. Elected to Hall of Fame: 1978. Nickname: Red, The Ol' Red-head — for the color of his hair.

Red Barber set many standards as a broadcaster for the Cincinnati Reds, Brooklyn Dodgers, New York Yankees and for many of the great sports events of his generation. A southerner, he brought his own style of language to the ballpark with him as he broadcast the games from "the catbird seat" (as he called his radio booth) and introduced fans to such terms as "rhubarb"—his term for a fight on the field.

He began his broadcasting career in 1934 with Cincinnati, was the announcer for Major League baseball's first televised game between Brooklyn and Cincinnati in August 1939, broadcast Brooklyn Dodger games from 1939 through 1953, then teamed with Mel Allen on New York Yankee broadcasts for ten years. Barber was the announcer for five All-Star games, ten World Series and, in the "off season" broadcast Rose Bowl, Orange Bowl, Sugar Bowl and Army-Navy games.

Barber was known for his command of the language, always grammatical and proper, almost reverent, and he was a reporter, rather than a fan, with a microphone. One of his early habits was to have an egg-timer in the radio booth with him — a reminder to him to tell the score of the game frequently. Barber and Allen, both pioneers in their professions, colleagues for 25 years and partners for 10, were each inducted into the Hall of Fame in 1978, the first broadcasters to receive the honor.

Albert J. Barlick

Born April 2, 1915, in Springfield, Illinois; died December 27, 1995, in Springfield, Illinois. Years in Major Leagues: 27 (as National League umpire). Elected to Hall of Fame: 1989.

Al Barlick became a Major League umpire at the age of 25 and quickly earned the respect of players, managers and his fellow umpires for his decisiveness, his ability to control a game and his booming voice. He umpired in the National League for 27 full seasons, but in three different stints: 1940–43, 1946–55 and 1958 to 1971. Perhaps the best testimony to his greatness is what others said about him: "Without the help of Al Barlick, I would have never made it," said retired National League umpire Dutch Rennert, referring to how Barlick took him under his wing. Doug Harvey, regarded as one of the National League's finest umpires, refers to his colleague as "the great Al Barlick."

Ken Burkhart recalls Barlick's authority and the respect he commanded. "Al Barlick — now there's a guy who could run a ball game," he said. American League umpire Bill Haller, who was on the field for some classic games during his career, says one of his greatest thrills was working the 1970 All-Star Game, because it was the only time in his career that he worked a game with Barlick. "What an umpire. He was very loud and he swore all the time, but he was a great umpire. He was a 'go get 'em' kind of guy. He knew the rules and he could control a ball game," said Haller.

Barlick worked in seven World Series and seven All-Star games. He moved up the minor league ladder quickly on the recommendation of Bill Klem, himself a Hall of Fame umpire, who saw Barlick work and liked what he saw. Ironically, when Barlick started full-time work in the National League, he replaced Klem, who had been on the job for 37 years before he retired.

Edward Grant Barrow

Born May 18, 1868, in Springfield, Illinois; died December 15, 1951, in Port Chester, New York. Years in Major Leagues: 30 (5 as field manager, 25 as general manager). Elected to Hall of Fame: 1953.

Ed Barrow won a World Series championship as manager of the Boston Red Sox and then built a dynasty as general manager of the New York Yankees. Under Barrow, the Yankees won 14 pennants and 10 World Series championships between 1921 and 1945.

Barrow was a shrewd judge of talent, which enabled him to make wise trades and build a formidable farm system. He is perhaps best remembered as the man who converted Babe Ruth from a pitcher to an outfielder to take advantage of the Babe's great hitting prowess. Barrow did that as manager of the Red Sox in 1918. In 1921, he reaped the benefits of his decision when he became general manager of the Yankees, whom Ruth had joined in 1920. Ruth hit 54 home runs in Barrow's first year, on his way to becoming the greatest slugger of his generation.

Barrow was a strict disciplinarian whose success was based on performance rather than personality. He was not well liked but was well respected as he signed players such as Lou Gehrig, Tony Lazzeri, Joe DiMaggio and many other stars that kept the Yankees at the top for a quarter of a century.

Jacob Peter Beckley

Born August 4, 1867, in Hannibal, Missouri; died January 25, 1918, in Kansas City, Missouri. 5'10", 180 lbs., bats left, throws left. Years in minor leagues: 3; Major League debut: 1888; Years in Major Leagues: 20. Elected to Hall of Fame: 1971. Nickname: Old Eagle Eye—for his ability to distinguish balls and strikes as a hitter.

Jake Beckley was one of the greatest hitters in the late 1800s and the start of the 20th century. When he retired in 1907, he had more hits than anyone in baseball history—2,931—just 69 short of the coveted 3,000 mark that would be the benchmark for greatness a century later. Beckley hit over .300 in 13 of his 20 Major League seasons and finished with a lifetime batting average of .308. He had an excellent batting eye and only struck out 270 times in his career, an average of just 14 strikeouts a season. His 244 triples rank him fourth on the all-time list.

Beckley, a first baseman, was not as adept in the field as he was with a bat in his hand; in fact, he was well known for his wild throws. He is credited with creating the "hidden ball trick" on runners—by hiding the ball under one corner of first base. He would wait until an opposing base runner took a step or two off the bag, then would quickly reach down and grab the ball and tag the runner out.

Beckley played his entire career at first base, setting a record for most games at that position, 2,386. In 1906, Beckley played in 22 games, then tried his hand at umpiring, before returning as a player for one more season. His brief stint as an umpire gives him the distinction of being one of two men who both played and umpired in the Major Leagues who were inducted into the Hall of Fame because of their playing skills rather than their umpiring. The other was Ed Walsh.

Year	Team	G	AB	R	H	D	T	HR	RBI	AVE.
1888	Pitt	71	283	35	97	15	3	0	27	.343
1889	Pitt	123	522	91	157	24	10	9	97	.301
1890	Pitt	121	516	109	167	38	22	10	120	.324
1891	Pitt	133	554	94	162	20	20	4	73	.292
1892	Pitt	151	614	102	145	21	19	10	96	.236
1893	Pitt	131	542	106	144	32	19	5	106	.303
1894	Pitt	131	533	121	183	36	17	8	120	.343
1895	Pitt	129	530	104	174	30	20	5	110	.328
1896	Pitt-NY	105	399	81	110	15	9	8	70	.276
1897	NY-Cin	114	433	84	143	19	12	8	87	.330
1898	Cin	118	459	86	135	20	12	4	72	.294
1899	Cin	134	513	87	171	27	16	3	99	.333
1900	Cin	141	558	98	190	26	10	2	94	.341
1901	Cin	140	580	79	178	39	13	3	79	.307
1902	Cin	129	532	82	176	23	7	5	69	.331
1903	Cin	120	459	85	150	29	10	2	81	.327
1904	StL (N)	140	551	72	179	22	9	1	67	.325
1905	StL	134	514	48	147	20	10	1	57	.286
1906	StL	87	320	29	79	16	6	0	44	.247
1907	StL	22	115	6	24	2	0	0	7	.209
20 years		**2386**	**9527**	**1600**	**2931**	**475**	**244**	**88**	**1575**	**.308**

Transaction: February 1904: Sold by Cincinnati to St. Louis

James Bell

Born May 17, 1903, in Starksville, Mississippi; died March 7, 1991, in St. Louis, Missouri. 6', 143 lbs., bats both, throws left. Years in minor leagues (Negro Leagues): 28; Years in Major Leagues: None. Elected to Hall of Fame: 1974. Nickname: Cool Papa—given to him by one of his managers because he played well (cool) in front of large crowds.

Those who saw him play said Cool Papa Bell was the fastest man to ever play baseball. He is said to have been clocked running the bases in 13.1 seconds, and he said he could have made it in 12 if the field hadn't been wet! Bell once scored from first on a sacrifice bunt — taking off from first as the pitcher delivered the ball, rounding second as the third baseman ran in to make the play at first, then rounding third and heading home as the first baseman threw to the plate too late to get the speedy Bell.

His teammate, the great pitcher Satchel Paige, has contributed to the legend of Cool Papa with two descriptions of his speed. Paige said Cool Papa could turn off the lights and be in bed before the room was dark. He also said Bell once hit a ball up the middle and it hit him in the back as he slid into second base. Told these two stories about a year before he died at the age of 88, Bell replied, "Now that second one's an exaggeration."

Bell played for the St. Louis Stars, the Pittsburgh Crawfords, the Homestead Grays and the Kansas City Stars in the Negro Leagues. Though his talent was unquestionable, he was in his prime about a decade before black players were allowed into the Major Leagues. He was 44 years old when Jackie Robinson broke the color barrier in 1947 to become the first black Major League ballplayer.

Though no official records were ever kept, Bell is believed to have hit over .400 in several seasons and had a batting average of over .350 against Major League pitchers in exhibition games. In a game in Cuba in 1931, Bell hit three home runs off of Johnny Allen, later a star pitcher with the Cleveland Indians and New York Yankees. Bell's own personal statistics show he had a lifetime batting average of .339. When he was inducted into the Hall of Fame in 1974, he shared the platform with Mickey Mantle, Whitey Ford and Jocko Conlan.

Johnny Lee Bench

Born December 7, 1947, in Oklahoma City, Oklahoma. 6'1", 197 lbs., bats right, throws right. Years in minor leagues: 4; Major League debut: August 28, 1967; Years in Major Leagues: 17. Elected to Hall of Fame: 1989. Nickname: None.

Johnny Bench was the best catcher of his generation. He was a great clutch hitter who could hit with power and was an outstanding defensive player. Bench became famous for his snap throws to first base, attempting to pick off base runners — from a squatting position behind the plate. He won 10 Gold Glove awards.

Bench played his entire career with the Cincinnati Reds. He was Rookie of the Year in 1968 and was part of the "Big Red Machine" that was a dominant force in the National League in the 1970s. He led the National League in home runs twice and in runs batted in three times. Bench drove in more than 100 runs in six seasons. When he retired in 1983, he held the all-time record for home runs by a catcher — 327 — and had 389 homers altogether. Bench had many famous clutch hits in his career. In the fifth game of the National League championship playoffs in 1972, Pittsburgh was winning 3–2 and was three outs away from going to the World Series when Bench hit a game-tying home run in the bottom of the ninth. The Reds later scored the winning run on a wild pitch.

In 1973, his homer in the bottom of the ninth gave the Reds a 2–1 victory over the Mets in the first game of the National League playoffs. In 1976, Bench's ninth inning home run helped the Reds come from behind in the pennant clincher over the Philadelphia Phillies. In the 1976 World Series, two great catchers — Bench and the New York Yankees' Thurman Munson — were both spectacular. The Reds swept the Yankees as Bench hit .533 and Munson .529 in the four games. In the final game, won by the Reds 7–2, Bench hit two home runs and drove in five runs. He played in a league championship series six times and was in the World Series four times.

Year	Team	G	AB	R	H	D	T	HR	RBI	AVE.
1967	Cin	26	86	7	14	3	1	1	6	.143
1968	Cin	154	564	67	155	40	2	15	82	.275
1969	Cin	148	532	83	156	23	1	26	90	.293
1970	Cin	158	605	97	177	35	4	45	148	.293
1971	Cin	149	562	80	134	19	2	27	80	.238
1972	Cin	147	538	87	145	22	2	40	125	.270
1973	Cin	152	557	83	141	17	3	25	104	.253
1974	Cin	160	621	108	174	38	2	33	129	.280
1975	Cin	142	530	83	150	39	1	28	110	.283
1976	Cin	135	465	62	109	24	1	16	74	.234
1977	Cin	142	494	67	136	34	2	31	109	.275
1978	Cin	120	393	52	102	17	1	23	73	.260
1979	Cin	130	464	73	128	19	0	22	80	.276
1980	Cin	114	360	52	90	12	0	24	68	.250
1981	Cin	52	178	14	55	8	0	8	25	.309
1982	Cin	119	399	44	103	16	0	13	38	.258
1983	Cin	110	310	32	79	15	2	12	54	.255
17 years		**2158**	**7658**	**1091**	**2048**	**381**	**24**	**389**	**1376**	**.267**

LEAGUE CHAMPIONSHIP SERIES

Year	Team	G	AB	R	H	D	T	HR	RBI	AVE.
1970	Cin	3	9	2	2	0	0	1	1	.222
1972	Cin	5	18	3	6	1	1	1	2	.333
1973	Cin	5	19	1	5	2	0	1	1	.263
1975	Cin	3	13	1	1	0	0	0	0	.077
1976	Cin	3	12	3	4	1	0	1	1	.333
1979	Cin	3	12	1	3	0	1	1	1	.250
6 years		**22**	**83**	**11**	**21**	**4**	**2**	**5**	**6**	**.253**

WORLD SERIES

Year	Team	G	AB	R	H	D	T	HR	RBI	AVE.
1970	Cin	5	19	3	4	0	0	1	3	.211
1972	Cin	7	23	4	6	1	0	1	1	.261
1975	Cin	7	29	5	6	2	0	1	4	.207
1976	Cin	4	15	4	8	1	1	2	6	.533
4 years		**23**	**86**	**16**	**24**	**4**	**1**	**5**	**14**	**.279**

Charles Albert Bender

Born May 5, 1884, in Brainerd, Minnesota; died May 22, 1954, in Philadelphia, Pennsylvania. 6'2", 185 lbs., bats right, throws right. Years in minor leagues: None; Major League debut: April 20, 1903; Years in Major Leagues: 15. Elected to Hall of Fame: 1953. Nickname: Chief—a common nickname for men of Indian descent; Bender was half Chippewa Indian.

Chief Bender won 210 games in his 15-year Major League career that began in 1903. He finished with a won-loss percentage of .623. A modern comparison: Bob Feller's won-loss percentage was .621. Bender won over 20 games in two seasons and had the best won-loss percentage in three seasons. He appeared in five World Series for the Philadelphia A's, winning six games and losing four. He had nine complete games in World Series play. In 1910, he threw a no-hitter against the Cleveland Indians, winning 4–0. It was not a perfect game, but the Chief faced 27 batters. He walked one batter, the only base runner of the game, who was thrown out trying to steal.

In 1915, Bender bolted to the Federal League where he was paid more than twice his American League salary. After one season — in which he won only 4 games and lost 16 — he returned to the American League for two more seasons. He then retired for a year, pitched six years in the minor leagues and tried a Major League comeback with the Chicago White Sox in 1925. He pitched one inning, gave up a walk and a home run. He was a workhorse who threw 29 complete games in his rookie year. Throughout his career, he always had the confidence of his manager, Connie Mack. Many years after Bender retired, Mack reflected on all the pitchers he had managed over the years. He said if he had a game he had to win, he'd give the ball to Chief Bender.

Year	Team	W-L	ERA	G	IP	H	BB	SO
1903	Phil (A)	17-15	3.07	36	270	239	65	127
1904	Phil	10-11	2.87	29	203.2	167	59	149
1905	Phil	16-10	2.83	35	229	193	90	142
1906	Phil	15-10	2.53	36	238.1	208	48	159
1907	Phil	16-8	2.05	33	219.1	185	34	112
1908	Phil	8-9	1.75	18	138.2	121	21	85
1909	Phil	18-8	1.66	34	250	196	45	161
1910	Phil	23-5	1.58	30	250	182	47	155
1911	Phil	17-5	2.16	31	216.1	198	58	114
1912	Phil	13-8	2.74	27	171	169	33	90
1913	Phil	21-10	2.21	48	236.2	208	59	135
1914	Phil	17-3	2.26	28	179	159	55	107
1915	Phil	4-16	3.99	26	178.1	198	37	89
1916	Phil	7-7	3.74	27	122.2	137	34	43
1917	Phil	8-2	1.67	20	113	84	26	43
1925	Chi (A)	0-0	18.00	1	1	1	1	0
15 years		**210-127**	**2.44**	**459**	**3017**	**2645**	**712**	**1711**

WORLD SERIES

Year	Team	W-L	ERA	G	IP	H	BB	SO
1905	Phil (A)	1-1	1.06	2	17	9	6	13
1910	Phil	1-1	1.93	2	18.2	12	4	14
1911	Phil	2-1	1.04	3	26	16	8	20
1913	Phil	2-0	4.00	2	18	19	1	9
1914	Phil	0-1	10.13	1	5.1	8	2	3
5 years		**6-4**	**2.44**	**10**	**85**	**64**	**21**	**59**

Lawrence Peter Berra

Born May 12, 1925, in St. Louis, Missouri. 5'8", 191 lbs., bats left, throws right. Years in minor leagues: 2; Major League debut: September 22, 1946; Years in Major Leagues: 19. Elected to Hall of Fame: 1972. Nickname: Yogi — given to him as a child because of his resemblance to a character in a film travelogue whose name was Yogi.

Yogi Berra is probably more famous for his misuse of the English language than for his skills as a ballplayer — but only from people who never saw him play. He was a leading member of one of the greatest teams for nearly two decades. Berra spent most of his career as a catcher for the New York Yankees. He played in 14 World Series — and the Yankees won 10 of them. He ranks first all-time in number of World Series games played, 75; first in times at bat, 259; first in hits, 71; and first in doubles, 10. He ranks second in World Series runs scored, 41; second in RBIs, 39; third in home runs, 12; and third in walks, 32. Berra was the first man to hit a pinch-hit home run in World Series history (1947) and also hit a grand-slam home run (1956). He played 19 years in the Major Leagues and was a notorious bad ball hitter. He once hit a home run off of Don Newcombe of the Brooklyn Dodgers in the World Series and shouted to him that it was a "good pitch" as he rounded the bases.

Berra had a lifetime batting average of .285 with 385 home runs. At the time he retired, he had the most home runs for a catcher. He won the American League's Most Valuable Player award three times, drove in more than 100 runs in four straight seasons and was behind the plate in many memorable no-hitters. He caught Don Larsen's perfect game in the 1956 World Series and was behind the plate in 1951 when Allie Reynolds had one more hitter to get out for a no-hitter — but the batter was Ted Williams. Williams hit a routine pop-up behind the plate, but Berra dropped the ball. Given another chance, Williams once again popped the ball up in Berra's direction, and this time Yogi caught it. In 1964, he managed the Yankees to a pennant but was fired after they lost the World Series to the St. Louis Cardinals. In 1973, he managed the New York Mets to a championship, but they fell to the Oakland A's in the World Series. Berra's off-the-cuff remarks are part of his legend — so much so that it is hard to separate fact from fiction. Two eyewitness accounts will suffice. Mickey Mantle claimed that Berra once arrived at a ballpark in Florida for an exhibition game wearing a sport shirt and shorts. A woman fan noticed him and said, "Mr. Berra, you certainly look cool today." Yogi looked up and said, "You don't look so hot yourself, lady."

Retired umpire John Flaherty said he was working behind the plate one day in Yankee Stadium and, between innings, chatted with Berra behind the plate. "You know, Yogi, I'm not infallible," Flaherty told the catcher. "What does that mean?" Berra asked. "It means I miss one once in a while," said Flaherty. "Heck, you're the most infallible umpire in the league," said Berra.

Year	Team	G	AB	R	H	D	T	HR	RBI	AVE.
1946	NY (A)	7	22	3	8	1	0	2	4	.364
1947	NY	83	293	41	82	15	3	11	54	.280
1948	NY	125	469	70	143	24	10	14	98	.305
1949	NY	116	415	59	115	20	2	20	91	.277
1950	NY	151	597	116	192	30	6	28	124	.322
1951	NY	141	547	92	161	19	4	27	88	.294
1952	NY	142	534	97	146	17	1	30	98	.273
1953	NY	137	503	80	149	23	5	27	108	.296
1954	NY	151	584	88	179	28	6	22	125	.307
1955	NY	147	541	84	147	20	3	27	108	.272
1956	NY	140	521	93	155	29	2	30	105	.298
1957	NY	134	482	74	121	14	2	24	82	.251
1958	NY	122	433	60	115	17	3	22	90	.266
1959	NY	131	472	64	134	25	1	19	69	.284
1960	NY	120	359	46	99	14	1	15	62	.276
1961	NY	119	395	62	107	11	0	22	61	.271
1962	NY	86	232	25	58	8	0	10	35	.224
1963	NY	64	147	20	43	6	0	8	28	.293
1965	NY (N)	4	9	1	2	2	0	0	0	.222
19 years		**2120**	**7555**	**1175**	**2150**	**321**	**49**	**358**	**1430**	**.285**

WORLD SERIES

Year	Team	G	AB	R	H	D	T	HR	RBI	AVE.
1947	NY (A)	6	19	2	3	0	0	1	2	.158
1949	NY	4	16	2	1	0	0	0	1	.063
1950	NY	4	15	2	3	0	0	1	2	.200
1951	NY	6	23	4	6	1	0	0	0	.261
1952	NY	7	28	2	6	1	0	2	3	.214
1953	NY	6	21	3	9	1	0	1	4	.429
1955	NY	7	24	5	10	1	0	1	2	.417
1956	NY	7	25	5	9	2	0	3	10	.360
1957	NY	7	25	5	8	1	0	1	2	.320
1958	NY	7	27	3	6	3	0	0	2	.222
1960	NY	7	22	6	7	0	0	1	8	.318
1961	NY	4	11	2	3	0	0	1	3	.273
1962	NY	2	2	0	0	0	0	0	0	.000
1963	NY	1	1	0	0	0	0	0	0	.000
14 years		**75**	**259**	**41**	**71**	**10**	**0**	**12**	**39**	**.274**

James Leroy Bottomley

Born April 23, 1900, in Oglesby, Illinois; died December 11, 1959, in St. Louis, Missouri. 6', 175 lbs., bats left, throws left. Years in minor leagues: 3; Major League debut: August 18, 1922; Years in Major Leagues: 16. Elected to Hall of Fame: 1974. Nickname: Sunny Jim — because he had a sunny disposition that made him popular with fans and attractive to women.

Jim Bottomley was known as the man with the big smile and the cap cocked crookedly on his head. He was also one of baseball's best first basemen who had some incredible years — and some incredible games — in his career.

His playing days paralleled those of another first baseman, Lou Gehrig, and he was a teammate of another great star, Rogers Hornsby. Had he played in a different era, he might have received much more fanfare because of his remarkable achievements than he got when he was accomplishing them. He led the National League in hits once, with 227 in 1925; in doubles twice, with 44 in 1925 and 40 in 1926; and in runs batted in twice, with 120 in 1926 and 136 in 1928. He hit over .300 nine times, including .371 one year, .367 another year and .348 in yet another year. He drove in more than 100 runs six years in a row and finished with a lifetime batting average of .310. He is one of four players in baseball history to twice have games in which he got six hits in six at-bats. In one of them, on September 16, 1924, he set a Major League record by driving in 12 runs, belting two home runs (one a grand slam), three singles and a double.

Though he never won a batting title, he had a year in which he came about as close as is humanly possible. In 1931, he finished third with an average of .3482. Teammate Chick Hafey won the title with .3489 and the Giants Bill Terry finished second with .3486 in what is still the closest batting title race in baseball history.

Year	Team	G	AB	R	H	D	T	HR	RBI	AVE.
1922	StL (N)	37	151	29	49	8	5	5	35	.325
1923	StL	134	523	79	194	34	14	8	94	.371
1924	Stl	137	528	87	167	31	12	14	111	.316
1925	StL	153	619	92	227	44	12	21	128	.367
1926	StL	154	603	98	180	40	14	19	120	.299
1927	StL	152	574	95	174	31	15	19	124	.303
1928	StL	149	576	123	187	42	20	31	136	.325
1929	StL	146	560	108	176	31	12	29	137	.314
1930	StL	131	487	92	148	33	7	15	97	.304
1931	StL	108	382	73	133	34	5	9	75	.348
1932	StL	91	311	45	92	16	3	11	48	.296
1933	Cin	145	549	57	137	23	9	13	83	.250
1934	Cin	142	556	72	158	21	11	11	78	.284
1935	Cin	107	399	44	103	21	1	1	49	.258
1936	StL (A)	140	544	72	162	39	11	12	95	.298
1937	StL	65	109	11	26	7	0	1	12	.239
16 years		1991	7471	1177	2313	465	151	219	1422	.310

Transactions: Dec. 17, 1932: Traded to Cincinnati for Emil Crabtree and Ownie Carroll. March 21, 1936: Traded to St. Louis Browns for Johnny Burnett.

WORLD SERIES

Year	Team	G	AB	R	H	D	T	HR	RBI	AVE.
1926	StL	7	29	4	10	3	0	0	5	.345
1928	StL	4	14	1	3	0	1	1	3	.214
1930	StL	6	22	1	1	1	0	0	0	.045
1931	StL	7	25	2	4	1	0	0	2	.160
4 years		24	90	8	18	5	1	1	10	.200

Louis Boudreau

Born July 17, 1917, in Harvey, Illinois. 5'11", 190 lbs., bats right, throws right. Years in minor leagues: 2; Major League debut: September 9, 1938; Years in Major Leagues: 15. Elected to Hall of Fame: 1970. Nickname: The Boy Manager — because he became manager of the Cleveland Indians at the age of 24.

Lou Boudreau is probably best known for being the youngest player-manager in baseball history. He was 24 in 1942 when he was named manager of the Cleveland Indians for whom he also played shortstop. He also achieved managerial fame for devising the "Ted Williams shift" in which the shortstop moved over to the right side of the infield and the third baseman moved over toward the second base bag, leaving the left side of the infield unprotected. Williams, a lefthanded batter, was a dead pull hitter. Boudreau experienced some great games and great seasons with the Indians. He won the batting title in 1944 with a .327 average, but didn't win it in 1948 when he hit .355. However, the Indians won the pennant that year as Boudreau drove in 106 runs and scored 116. In a one-game playoff against the Red Sox to determine the American League champion, Boudreau got four hits in four at-bats, including two home runs.

He had four seasons in which he hit more than 40 doubles, leading the league three times, and had a lifetime batting average of .295. Boudreau, who played in 1,207 games as a player-manager, was the last full-time player-manager until Pete Rose played the dual role for the Cincinnati Reds more than 40 years later. He was also an excellent fielder, topping all American League shortstops in fielding in eight out of nine years, beginning in 1940.

Boudreau is the only man to play for and manage two professional sports teams. In 1938 and 1939, he played for and coached the Hammond, Indiana, professional basketball team, where one of his teammates was John Wooden, who rose to greatness as coach of the UCLA basketball championship teams of the 1960s and '70s.

Year	Team	G	AB	R	H	D	T	HR	RBI	AVE.
1938	Cleve	1	1	0	0	0	0	0	0	.000
1939	Cleve	53	225	42	58	15	4	0	19	.258
1940	Cleve	155	627	97	185	46	10	9	101	.295
1941	Cleve	148	579	95	149	45	8	10	56	.257
1942	Cleve	147	506	57	143	18	10	2	58	.283
1943	Cleve	152	539	69	154	32	7	3	67	.286
1944	Cleve	150	584	91	191	45	5	3	67	.327
1945	Cleve	97	346	50	106	24	1	3	48	.306
1946	Cleve	140	515	51	151	30	6	6	62	.293
1947	Cleve	150	538	79	165	45	3	4	67	.307
1948	Cleve	152	560	116	199	34	6	18	106	.355
1949	Cleve	134	475	53	135	20	3	4	60	.284
1950	Cleve	81	260	23	70	13	2	1	29	.269
1951	Bos (A)	82	273	37	73	18	1	5	47	.267
1952	Bos	4	2	1	0	0	0	0	2	.000
15 years		**1646**	**6030**	**861**	**1779**	**385**	**66**	**68**	**789**	**.295**

WORLD SERIES

Year	Team	G	AB	R	H	D	T	HR	RBI	AVE.
1948	Cleve	6	22	1	6	0	0	0	3	.273

Roger Philip Bresnahan

Born June 11, 1879, in Toledo, Ohio; died December 4, 1944, in Toledo, Ohio. 5'8", 180 lbs., bats right, throws right. Years in minor leagues: 2; Major League debut: August 27, 1897; Years in Major Leagues: 17. Elected to Hall of Fame: 1945. Nickname: The Duke of Tralee — because Bresnahan, a native of Toledo, Ohio, liked to tell people he was born in Tralee, Ireland.

Roger Bresnahan was a versatile, innovative ballplayer who was undefeated as a Major League pitcher (4–0) and went on to become one of the game's finest catchers. For several years Bresnahan teamed with Christy Mathewson to form one of baseball's all-time greatest battery combinations. He was also a favorite of manager John McGraw, who managed him one year with Baltimore and then grabbed him the next year when he took over the helm of the New York Giants.

Bresnahan was McGraw's leadoff man — most unusual for a catcher — but Bresnahan had unusual speed and had the kind of daring style that appealed to McGraw. In 1907, Bresnahan introduced what is now a staple for catchers from the Major Leagues all the way down to Little League: shin guards. He is also believed to be the first ballplayer to wear a batting helmet. He experimented with one after getting beaned, but did not wear it for very long.

Bresnahan managed the St. Louis Cardinals from 1909 through 1912 and the Chicago Cubs in 1915. Proof of his remarkable versatility: He played all nine positions during his 17-year Major League career: catcher, 974 games; outfield, 281; third base, 42; first base, 33; second base, 28; pitcher, 9, shortstop, 8.

Year	Team	G	AB	R	H	D	T	HR	RBI	AVE.
1897	Wash (N)	6	16	1	6	0	0	0	3	.375
1900	Chi (N)	2	2	0	0	0	0	0	0	.000
1901	Balt (A)	86	293	40	77	9	9	1	32	.263
1902	Balt-NY (N)	116	413	47	116	22	9	5	56	.281
1903	NY	113	406	87	142	30	8	4	55	.350
1904	NY	109	402	81	114	22	7	5	33	.284
1905	NY	104	331	58	100	18	3	0	46	.302
1906	NY	124	405	69	114	22	4	0	43	.281
1907	NY	110	328	57	83	9	7	4	38	.253
1908	NY	140	449	70	127	25	3	1	54	.283
1909	StL (N)	72	234	27	57	4	1	0	23	.244
1910	StL	88	234	35	65	15	3	0	27	.278
1911	StL	81	227	22	63	17	8	3	41	.278
1912	StL	48	108	8	36	7	2	1	15	.333
1913	Chi (N)	68	161	20	37	5	2	1	21	.230
1914	Chi	86	248	42	69	10	4	0	24	.278
1915	Chi	77	221	19	45	8	1	1	19	.204
17 years		1430	4478	683	1251	223	71	26	530	.279

Transactions: Dec. 12, 1908: Traded to St. Louis Cardinals for Admiral Schiel, Bugs Raymond and Red Murray. June 8, 1913: Sold to Chicago Cubs.

WORLD SERIES

Year	Team	G	AB	R	H	D	T	HR	RBI	AVE.
1905	NY (N)	5	16	3	5	2	0	0	1	.313

George Howard Brett

Born May 15, 1953, in Moundsville, West Virginia. 6', 185 lbs., bats left, throws right. Years in minor leagues: 3; Major League debut: August 2, 1973; Years in Major Leagues: 21. Elected to Hall of Fame: 1999. Nickname: None.

George Brett was one of the best clutch hitters of his era. He batted over .300 in 11 seasons and is the only player in baseball history to win batting titles in three decades. He led the American League with a .333 average in 1976, then hit .390 in 1980 and .329 in 1990. The .390 batting average was the highest since Ted Williams hit .406 in 1941. Only Tony Gwynn of San Diego has surpassed it, but his .394 average was in the strike-shortened 1994 season. In 1980, he also drove in 118 runs in 117 games, becoming the first person to drive in an average of more than one run per game since Joe DiMaggio did it in 1948. In 1979, Brett became the fifth player in baseball history to have 20 or more doubles, triples and homers in the same season.

Brett was at his best when the stakes were the highest. He holds American League Championship Series records for most triples (4), home runs (9), extra base hits (18), total bases (75) and highest slugging percentage (.728). He hit three home runs in a 1976 playoff game, and in 1980 he homered off the Yankees' Rich Gossage to bring the Royals their first World Series appearance. He spent his entire 21-year-career with the Kansas City Royals and led them to their only two World Series appearances in 1980 and 1985. At the time of his induction into the Hall of Fame, Brett was 13th in all-time hits with 3,154 and fifth in doubles with 665. He is the only player in Major League history to have more than 3,000 hits, more than 300 home runs (317), more than 600 doubles (665), and more than 200 stolen bases (201.)

While he was a consistently good hitter, he was known for incredible streaks. One of his best was from May 8–13, 1986, when Brett got three hits in a game in six consecutive games. No other Major League player has accomplished that. Always colorful and combative, Brett's most famous at-bat came in a 1985 game in Yankee Stadium when he hit one out of the park in the ninth inning for an apparent home run. Yankee manager Billy Martin protested, claiming Brett's bat had too much pine tar on the handle. The umpire agreed, nullifying the home run. An angry Brett charged out of the dugout in his own frenzied protest. His antics, captured on videotape, are a part of baseball folklore. Within a week of the incident, American League president Lee McPhail overrruled the umpire's decision and restored the home run, saying the protest should have been lodged before Brett batted.

Year	Team	G	AB	R	H	D	T	HR	RBI	AVE.
1973	KC	13	40	2	5	2	0	0	0	.125
1974	KC	133	457	49	129	21	5	2	47	.282
1975	KC	159	634	84	195	35	13	11	89	.308
1976	KC	159	645	94	215	34	14	7	67	.333
1977	KC	139	564	105	176	32	13	22	88	.312
1978	KC	128	510	79	150	45	8	9	62	.294
1979	KC	154	645	119	212	42	20	23	107	.329
1980	KC	117	449	87	175	33	9	24	118	.390
1981	KC	89	347	42	109	27	7	6	43	.314
1982	KC	144	552	101	166	32	9	21	82	.301
1983	KC	123	464	90	144	38	2	25	93	.310
1984	KC	104	377	42	107	21	3	13	69	.284
1985	KC	155	550	108	184	38	5	30	112	.335
1986	KC	124	441	70	128	28	4	16	73	.290
1987	KC	115	427	71	124	18	2	22	78	.290
1988	KC	157	589	90	180	42	3	24	103	.306
1989	KC	124	457	67	129	26	3	12	80	.282
1990	KC	142	544	82	179	45	7	14	87	.329
1991	KC	131	505	77	129	40	2	10	61	.255

Year	Team	G	AB	R	H	D	T	HR	RBI	AVE.
1992	KC	152	592	55	169	35	5	7	61	.285
1993	KC	145	560	69	149	31	3	19	75	.266
21 years		2707	10349	1583	3154	665	137	317	1595	.305

DIVISIONAL PLAYOFF SERIES

Year	Team	G	AB	R	H	D	T	HR	RBI	AVE.
1981	KC	3	12	0	2	0	0	0	0	.167

LEAGUE CHAMPIONSHIP SERIES

Year	Team	G	AB	R	H	D	T	HR	RBI	AVE.
1976	KC	5	18	4	8	1	1	1	5	.444
1977	KC	5	20	2	6	0	2	0	2	.300
1978	KC	4	18	7	7	1	1	3	3	.389
1980	KC	3	11	3	3	1	0	2	4	.273
1984	KC	3	13	0	3	0	0	0	0	.231
1985	KC	7	23	6	8	2	0	3	5	.348
6 years		27	103	22	35	5	6	9	19	.340

WORLD SERIES

Year	Team	G	AB	R	H	D	T	HR	RBI	AVE.
1980	KC	6	24	3	9	2	1	1	3	.375
1985	KC	7	27	5	10	1	0	0	1	.370
2 years		13	51	8	19	3	1	1	4	.373

Jack Brickhouse

Broadcaster. Elected to Hall of Fame: 1983.

From 1948 to 1981 Jack Brickhouse was a broadcaster of Chicago baseball games, at one time for both the Cubs and the White Sox. He is primarily remembered as being the television voice of the Chicago Cubs, for whom he worked the longest. But he has the distinction of broadcasting the last pennant-winning victory of any Chicago baseball team. On September 22, 1959, WGN television went on the road — unusual in those days — to do a live broadcast of the White Sox–Cleveland Indian game in which Chicago clinched the American League championship.

Brickhouse made famous the home run call of "back ... back ... back" to describe the distance the ball was traveling and, if it was a Cub homer, he would punctuate his "back ... back ... back" with his trademark "Hey, hey!" Brickhouse began his broadcasting career in Peoria, Illinois, where he worked for six years and became an acquaintance of Bob Elson, a Chicago broadcaster of Cubs and White Sox games. Elson helped Brickhouse get a job with WGN, where he assisted Elson in recreating Cubs and White Sox games. In 1942, Elson went in the Navy, and Brickhouse became WGN's baseball guru. Because of other commitments, WGN dropped baseball temporarily and — ironically — in 1945, when the Cubs won their last pennant, Brickhouse was working elsewhere.

In 1948, he was back at WGN, this time on television, where he stayed for 33 years. His longevity with one team has given him a distinction few can match — being the "voice" of a losing team. From 1947 to 1967, the Cubs finished each season in the second division. To which Brickhouse has said: "Thank God I loved my work."

Louis Clark Brock

Born June 18, 1939, in El Dorado, Arkansas. 5'1", 170 lbs., bats left, throws left. Years in minor leagues: 1; Major League debut: September 10, 1961; Years in Major Leagues: 19. Elected to Hall of Fame: 1985. Nickname: None.

When Lou Brock was traded from the Chicago Cubs to the St. Louis Cardinals in 1964, he hardly looked like the man who was going to replace the great Stan Musial, who had retired at the end of the previous season. He had started his career by getting a base hit off of the Phillies' Hall of Fame pitcher, Robin Roberts, in his first Major League at-bat. But he went hitless in his next 11 at-bats, and his fielding ranged from adventurous to disastrous. He sometimes wore a batting helmet in the outfield to protect himself. In the next two seasons with the Cubs, Brock hit .263 and .258 and was hitting .251 at the time of the trade to the Cardinals, who gave up pitcher Ernie Broglio, who had won 18 and 20 games in previous seasons. It appeared to be one of the worst trades in baseball history.

It was — but only because of a reverse of fortunes. Broglio won only seven more games in his career. Brock went on to help lead the Cardinals to the World Series three times in the next five years. He retired in 1979 as the Major Leagues' all-time greatest base stealer with 938 — a figure since surpassed by Rickey Henderson. Brock hit over .300 eight times, finished with 3,023 hits and had a lifetime batting average of .293. In 1968, he led the National League in doubles with 46 and triples with 14. In 1974, he stole 118 bases, setting the single-season record, also since broken by Henderson. He was at his best in big games. Brock played in the World Series in 1964, 1967 and 1968, and his .391 World Series average is second best for anyone appearing in more than 20 games. He stole a record 14 bases in World Series play. Though Brock hit only 149 home runs in his 19-year career — an average of one every 17 games, he hit four in World Series competition in only 87 at-bats. Brock also did well in All-Star games, appearing in five games and hitting .375.

Year	Team	G	AB	R	H	D	T	HR	RBI	AVE.
1961	Chi (N)	4	11	1	1	0	0	0	0	.091
1962	Chi	123	434	73	114	24	7	9	35	.263
1963	Chi	148	547	79	141	19	11	9	37	.258
1964	Chi-StL	155	634	111	200	30	11	14	58	.315
1965	StL	155	631	107	182	35	8	16	69	.288
1966	StL	156	643	94	183	24	12	15	46	.285
1967	StL	159	689	113	206	32	12	21	76	.299
1968	StL	159	660	92	184	46	14	6	51	.279
1969	StL	157	655	97	195	33	10	12	47	.298
1970	StL	155	664	114	202	29	5	13	57	.304
1971	StL	157	640	126	200	37	7	7	61	.313
1972	StL	153	621	81	193	26	8	3	42	.311
1973	StL	160	650	110	193	29	8	7	63	.297
1974	StL	153	635	105	194	25	7	3	48	.306
1975	StL	136	528	78	163	27	6	3	47	.309
1976	StL	133	498	79	150	24	5	4	67	.301
1977	StL	141	489	63	133	22	6	2	46	.272
1978	StL	92	298	31	66	9	0	0	12	.221
1979	StL	120	405	56	123	15	4	5	38	.304
19 years		**2616**	**10332**	**1610**	**3023**	**486**	**141**	**149**	**900**	**.293**

Transactions: June 15, 1964: Traded to St. Louis Cardinals with pitchers Jack Spring and Paul Toth for pitchers Ernie Broglio and Bobby Shantz and outfielder Doug Clemens.

WORLD SERIES

Year	Team	G	AB	R	H	D	T	HR	RBI	AVE.
1964	StL	7	30	2	9	2	0	1	5	.300
1967	StL	7	29	8	12	2	1	1	3	.414
1968	StL	7	28	6	13	3	1	2	5	.464
3 years		**21**	**87**	**16**	**34**	**7**	**2**	**4**	**13**	**.391**

Bob Broeg

Sportswriter. Elected to Hall of Fame: 1979.

Bob Broeg, sports editor of the *St. Louis Post-Dispatch*, was to St. Louis sportswriting what Harry Caray was to St. Louis sports broadcasting — the authoritative word on the day to day actions of the Cardinals. Broeg began work with the *Post-Dispatch* in 1945, the same year Caray started with KMOX radio, and was promoted to sports editor in 1958.

He became not only famous in his own backyard, St. Louis, but also nationally through columns he wrote for various baseball publications and for the nine books he has written. Baseball is not his only area of expertise. Broeg is the only sportswriter in the country with the credentials to vote for Hall of Fame nominees in baseball, pro football and college football.

Heywood C. Broun

Sportswriter. Elected to the Hall of Fame: 1970.

Heywood Broun was a Harvard student when he quit to take his first newspaper job, with the *New York Morning Telegraph* in 1910 and left two years later to go the *New York Herald-Tribune* where he served in many capacities, including drama critic. His next stop was the *New York World* where he wrote a popular column called "It Seems to Me."

He was a colorful writer and colorful character who, at 6'3" and 250 lbs., was larger than many of the athletes he covered. One of his trademarks was a wide-brimmed hat that, coupled with his size, made him easily recognizable from a distance and in a crowd. He wrote one baseball book, *The Sun Field*, published in 1923, and ten years later founded the Newspaper Guild.

Dennis Joseph Brouthers

Born May 8, 1858, in Sylvan Lake, New York; died August 3, 1932, in East Orange, New Jersey. 6'2", 200 lbs., bats left, throws left. Years in minor leagues: None; Major League debut: June 23, 1879; Years in Major Leagues: 19. Elected to Hall of Fame: 1945. Nickname: Dan — specific reason unknown.

Dan Brouthers was one of baseball's great power hitters prior to the 20th century. Before his retirement, he was involved in almost every level of the game except top management. In fact, after his playing days were over, he served as a scout for the New York Giants and even spent some time as a custodian and night watchman at the Polo Grounds.

As a player, he hit over .300 in 14 consecutive seasons. (Walks were counted as hits in those days.) He scored more than 100 runs in a season seven years in a row, and eight out of nine. Although RBI statistics were incomplete in some of his seasons, it is recorded that he drove in more than 100 runs in a season five times — remarkable considering he only reached "double figures" in home runs three times.

He won five batting titles, and his 1882 and 1883 titles made him the first player in baseball history to win batting championships in consecutive seasons. His home run production — slim by today's standards — was outstanding for his time. Back then, he was not only remembered for the number of home runs he hit, but for how far he hit them.

Year	Team	G	AB	R	H	D	T	HR	RBI	AVE.
1879	Troy	39	168	17	46	13	1	4	17	.274
1880	Troy	3	13	0	2	0	0	0		.154
1881	Buff	65	270	60	86	18	9	8	45	.319

Year	Team	G	AB	R	H	D	T	HR	RBI	AVE.
1882	Buff	84	351	71	129	23	11	6		.368
1883	Buff	98	425	85	159	41	17	3		.374
1884	Buff	94	398	82	130	22	16	14		.327
1885	Buff	98	407	87	146	32	11	7	60	.359
1886	Det	121	489	139	181	40	15	11	72	.370
1887	Det	123	500	152	169	36	20	12	101	.338
1888	Det	129	522	118	160	33	11	9	66	.307
1889	Bos	126	485	105	181	26	9	7	118	.373
1890	Bos	123	464	117	160	36	9	1	97	.345
1891	Bos	130	486	117	170	26	19	5	108	.350
1892	Brklyn	152	588	121	197	30	20	5	124	.335
1893	Brklyn	77	282	57	95	21	11	2	59	.337
1894	Balt	123	525	137	182	39	23	9	128	.347
1895	Balt-Lou	29	120	15	36	12	1	2	20	.300
1896	Phil (N)	57	218	42	75	13	3	1	41	.344
1904	NY (N)	2	5	0	0	0	0	0	0	.000
19 years		**1673**	**6716**	**1523**	**2304**	**461**	**206**	**106**	**1056**	**.343**

Mordecai Peter Centennial Brown

Born October 19, 1876, in Nyesville, Indiana; died February 14, 1948, in Terre Haute, Indiana. 5'10", 175 lbs., bats both, throws right. Years in minor leagues: 2; Major League debut: April 19, 1903. Elected to Hall of Fame: 1949. Nickname: Three Fingers — because he lost part of the index finger (on his pitching hand) in a farm accident as a youth.

He was called "Three Fingers" by the fans because, along with his thumb, that's all he had to grip a baseball. A good portion of the index finger on his right hand was chopped off in his childhood when he accidentally stuck it in a piece of farm machinery. He claimed the injury actually helped him later in his chosen profession because of the break it gave him on his curve ball.

Statistics confirm that the "handicap" certainly didn't hold him back. In his 14-year Major League career, he won 239 games, lost only 129, and had an earned run average of 2.06 — the third best of all time. He started 332 games, completed 272 of them (82 percent) and tossed 57 shutouts. He won 20 games in a season six years in a row and had six seasons in which his earned run average was less than 2.00. He began his career with the St. Louis Cardinals and then played 12 years with the Chicago Cubs, along with brief stops in Cincinnati, St. Louis and Brooklyn. Brown won five World Series games for the Cubs, pitching in the fall classics of 1906, 1907, 1908 and 1910. In World Series competition in 1907 and 1908, he pitched 20 innings without allowing a run.

Brown had some memorable showdowns with Christy Mathewson of the Giants. In one, they each took no-hitters into the ninth inning of a scoreless game. Brown gave up two hits and a run in the ninth to lose, 1–0, as Mathewson preserved his no-hitter. Three years later, Brown, pitching in relief, threw eight innings and beat Mathewson and the Giants, 4–2, in a game that decided the National League pennant. Brown had great control, striking out more than twice as many as he walked during his career.

Year	Team	W-L	ERA	G	IP	H	BB	SO
1903	St.L (N)	9-13	2.60	26	201	231	59	83
1904	Chi (N)	15-10	1.86	26	212.1	155	50	81
1905	Chi	18-12	2.17	30	249	219	44	89
1906	Chi	26-6	1.04	36	277.1	198	61	144
1907	Chi	20-6	1.39	34	233	180	40	107
1908	Chi	29-9	1.47	44	312.1	214	49	103
1909	Chi	27-9	1.31	50	342.2	246	53	172
1910	Chi	25-13	1.86	46	295.1	256	64	143
1911	Chi	21-11	2.80	53	270	267	55	129
1912	Chi	5-6	2.64	15	88.2	92	20	34
1913	Cin (N)	11-12	2.91	39	173.1	174	44	41
1914	StL-Brk	14-11	3.52	35	232.2	235	61	113
1915	Chi (F)	17-8	2.09	35	236.1	189	64	95
1916	Chi (N)	2-3	3.91	12	48.1	52	9	21
14 years		239-129	2.06	481	3172.1	2708	673	1375

Transactions: Dec. 12, 1903: Traded with Jack O'Neill to the Chicago Cubs for Jack Taylor and Larry McLean. Feb. 10, 1916: Sold to Chicago Cubs with Clem Clemens, Mickey Doolan, Bill Fischer, Max Flack, Claude Hendrix, Les Mann, Dykes Potter, Joe Tinker, Rollie Zeider and George McConnell.

WORLD SERIES

Year	Team	W-L	ERA	G	IP	H	BB	SO
1906	Chi (N)	1-2	3.66	3	19.2	14	4	12
1907	Chi	1-0	0.00	1	9	7	1	4
1908	Chi	2-0	0.00	2	11	6	1	5
1910	Chi	1-2	5.00	3	18	23	7	14
4 years		5-4	2.81	9	57.2	50	13	35

Warren Brown

Sportswriter. Elected to Hall of Fame: 1973.

Warren Brown was sports editor of the *Chicago American*, one of the city's afternoon newspapers, in a highly competitive era when Chicago had four thriving daily newspapers: the *American* and the *Daily News* in the afternoon, and the *Tribune* and the *Sun-Times* in the morning.

His writing stretched across five decades, from the era of Ruth and Gehrig to the era of Maris and Mantle, and, in his own backyard, from Hack Wilson to Ernie Banks. His writing was crisp and revealing. He once wrote of Wilson, the Cubs slugging outfielder and notorious drinker, "He went after high balls, on and off the field." Observing the Chicago Cubs and Detroit Tigers in the 1945 World Series, he wrote, "I don't believe either team can win it." In his career of nearly 50 years of covering both the Cubs and the White Sox, he was highly regarded for both his wit and his wisdom.

Jack Buck

Broadcaster. Elected to Hall of Fame: 1987.

Jack Buck has been a broadcaster for the St. Louis Cardinals off and on — mostly on — since 1954 when he teamed up on KMOX radio with Harry Caray. He grew up in Massachusetts, entered the service in World War II and came home a wounded veteran — shot in the shoulder. He then entered Ohio State University where, among other things, he took a football course from legendary coach Woody Hayes so he could learn more about the game. His first baseball broadcasting job was with the Columbus Redbirds in 1950. Three years later, he took over as chief announcer for the Rochester Red Wings, the Cardinals' top farm club. One year after that, Buck was in the Majors where he has remained ever since.

Buck, a master of nonchalance, was a sharp contrast to the often controversial Caray. He was the Cardinals' color commentator from 1954 to 1959, then went to ABC television for a year before returning to St. Louis to work again with Caray through the end of the 1969 season — a stretch in which the Cardinals won three pennants and two World Series championships. After 25 years, Caray left St. Louis in 1970. Buck became the "Voice of the Cardinals," where he has been ever since except for brief stints with NBC and CBS television. His affable personality and comfortable broadcasting style have appealed to television networks. Both ABC and CBS chose him to be their principal announcer when they ventured into the "Game of the Week" format, each for a short time.

He has made a name for himself in other sports as well. Buck was the first man to broadcast an American Football League game in 1960. Buck defends his old-school approach to broadcasting — straight reporting — by saying he valued knowledge over flair, and incorporated that philosophy and style into a broadcasting career of more than 40 years.

Morgan Bulkeley

Born December 26, 1837, in East Haddum, Connecticut; died November 6, 1922, in Hartford, Connecticut. Years in Major Leagues: 1 (National League president). Elected to Hall of Fame: 1937.

Morgan Bulkeley was a highly successful businessman and politician, but his election to baseball's Hall of Fame is unquestionably the most questionable of all the inductees. He was the first president of the National League — certainly an honor — but he attained the position because his name was drawn out of a hat, and he retained the position for only a year, at his request. At the end of that year, 1876, he didn't even attend the league meeting.

His league presidency is only one facet of an enormously successful life that included being president of Aetna Insurance Company, which was founded by his father; being mayor of Hartford, Connecticut, from 1880 to 1888; serving as governor of Connecticut from 1888 to 1893; and serving in the United States Senate from 1905 to 1911. In 1896, he was considered as President William McKinley's running mate and even got 39 votes at the Republican National Convention.

James Paul David Bunning

Born October 23, 1931, in Southgate, Kentucky. 6'3", 190 lbs., bats right, throws right. Years in minor leagues: 6; Major League debut: July 20, 1955; Years in Major Leagues: 17. Elected to Hall of Fame: 1996. Nickname: None.

It took Jim Bunning a long time to make it into the Hall of Fame, perhaps because he played his entire career for teams that always fell short of their potential. The most dramatic example is the 1964 Phillies team that blew a 6½ game lead with 12 games left to play. He spent the majority of his career with the Detroit Tigers and the Phillies, winning more than 100 games and striking out more than 1,000 batters in each league. At the time he retired, Bunning and Cy Young were the only pitchers to hold that distinction. Also at the time he retired, Bunning's 2,885 strikeouts were second only to Walter Johnson on the all-time list.

Bunning, a righthander, had a sweeping motion and a delivery in which he whirled his body in such a way that his glove hand hit the ground after almost every pitch. He had only one 20-win season, with Detroit in 1957, but he won 19 five times, including three years in succession, 1964–66. In 1967, his victory total slipped to 17, but he set a Major League record by losing five games by scores of 1–0.

Bunning is one of two pitchers to throw no-hitters in each league. (The other is Nolan Ryan.) His first came for the Tigers against Boston in 1958. Then on Fathers Day, 1964, Bunning, the father of nine, threw a perfect game against the New York Mets. After his baseball career ended, Bunning turned to politics. He was an unsuccessful candidate for governor of Kentucky but was elected to the U.S. House in 1986.

Year	Team	W-L	ERA	G	IP	H	BB	SO
1955	Det	3-5	6.35	15	51	59	32	37
1956	Det	5-1	3.71	15	53.1	55	28	34
1957	Det	20-8	2.69	45	267.1	214	72	182
1958	Det	14-12	3.52	35	219.2	288	79	177
1959	Det	17-13	3.89	40	249.2	220	75	201
1960	Det	11-14	2.79	36	252	217	64	201
1961	Det	17-11	3.19	38	268	232	71	194
1962	Det	19-10	3.59	41	258	262	74	184

Year	Team	W-L	ERA	G	IP	H	BB	SO
1963	Det	12-13	3.88	39	248.1	245	69	196
1964	Phil	19-8	2.63	41	284.1	248	46	219
1965	Phil	19-9	2.60	39	291	253	62	268
1966	Phil	19-14	2.41	43	314	260	55	252
1967	Phil	17-15	2.29	40	302.1	241	73	253
1968	Pitt	4-14	3.88	27	160	168	48	95
1969	Pitt-LA	13-10	3.69	34	212.1	212	59	157
1970	Phil	10-15	4.11	34	219	233	56	147
1971	Phil	5-12	5.48	29	110	126	37	58
17 years		**224-184**	**3.27**	**591**	**3760.1**	**3433**	**1000**	**2855**

Transactions: Dec. 4, 1963: Traded with catcher Gus Triandos to Philadelphia for infielder Don Demeter and pitcher Jack Hamilton. Dec. 15, 1967: Traded to Pittsburgh for infielder Don Money, pitchers Woodie Fryman and Bill Laxton and minor league pitcher Hal Clem. Aug. 15, 1969: Traded to Los Angeles for minor league outfielder Ron Mitchell, minor league infielder Chuck Coggins and cash.

Si Burick

Sportswriter. Elected to Hall of Fame: 1982.

Si Burick covered the Cincinnati Reds and was at every opening day at Crosley Field and Riverfront Stadium from 1929 until his death in 1986. He was the sports editor of the *Dayton Daily News* for 54 years and was the author of biographies of Dodger manager Walter Alston and Cincinnati skipper Sparky Anderson. When he was elected to the writers' branch of the Hall of Fame in 1982, he became the first sportswriter from a non–Major League city to receive that honor.

Jesse Cail Burkett

Born December 4, 1868, in Wheeling, West Virginia; died May 27, 1953, in Worcester, Massachusetts. 5'8", 155 lbs., bats left, throws left. Years in minor leagues: 3; Major League debut: April 22, 1890; Years in Major Leagues: 16. Elected to Hall of Fame: 1946. Nickname: Crab — because of the disposition he often displayed on the playing field.

Jesse Burkett is not a household word even among the most ardent of baseball fans, but he holds or shares two distinctions that will probably never be equaled:

• He hit over .400 one season and did not win the batting title. Playing for the St. Louis Cardinals in 1899, he hit .402 but lost the batting title to Ed Delahanty of the Phillies who hit .409.

• Burkett, Ty Cobb and Rogers Hornsby are the only players in Major League history who hit over .400 three times.

Burkett was a fiery ballplayer of slight build, and he came by his nickname "Crab" quite naturally. He once was ejected from both games of a doubleheader and was known to punch players who he thought were in his way. Burkett, a leadoff hitter much of his career, was a sensational bunter. He won three batting titles in his 16-year career and missed by one hit having 200-hit seasons in seven consecutive years. By the end of his career, the little guy had 2,873 hits and a lifetime batting average of .341.

Year	Team	G	AB	R	H	D	T	HR	RBI	AVE.
1890	NY (N)	101	401	67	124	23	13	4	60	.309
1892	Cle (N)	42	167	29	45	7	4	0	13	.269
1892	Cle	145	608	119	167	15	14	6	66	.275
1893	Cle	125	511	145	178	25	16	6	82	.348
1894	Cle	125	523	138	187	27	14	8	94	.358
1895	Cle	132	555	149	235	21	15	5	83	.423
1896	Cle	133	586	160	240	27	16	6	72	.410
1897	Cle	128	519	128	199	28	8	2	60	.383
1898	Cle	150	624	115	215	18	9	0	42	.345
1899	StL (N)	141	567	115	228	17	10	7	71	.402
1900	StL	142	560	88	203	14	12	7	68	.363
1901	StL	142	597	139	228	21	17	10	75	.382
1902	StL (A)	137	549	97	168	29	9	5	52	.306
1903	StL	133	514	74	152	20	7	3	40	.296
1904	StL	147	576	72	157	15	9	2	27	.273
1905	Bos (A)	149	573	78	147	13	13	4	47	.257
16 years		**2072**	**8430**	**1713**	**2873**	**320**	**185**	**75**	**952**	**.341**

Transactions: Jan. 16, 1905: Traded to Boston for outfielder George Stone.

Roy Campanella

Born November 19, 1921, in Philadelphia, Pennsylvania; died June 26, 1993, in Woodland Hills, California. 5'9½", 205 lbs., bats right, throws right. Years in minor leagues: 3; Major League debut: April 20, 1948; Years in Major Leagues: 10. Elected to Hall of Fame: 1969. Nickname: Campy—a shortened version of his last name.

Roy Campanella of the Brooklyn Dodgers was one of the two best catchers of his day — the other was Yogi Berra of the New York Yankees. Campanella only played ten years in the Major Leagues because of a tragic auto accident in January of 1958 that left him paralyzed. Campanella was the second black player signed by the Dodgers, following Jackie Robinson. He was a roly-poly athlete with a peppy personality who was an outstanding defensive catcher and a great handler of pitchers. He had some great offensive years, too, but he was not as consistent as a hitter, mixing in some bad years with the good.

In his ten-year career, he played on five pennant winners — in 1949, 1952, 1953, 1955 and 1956. He won the National League's Most Valuable Player Award three times: in 1951 when he hit .325 with 33 home runs and 108 RBIs; in 1953 when he hit .312 and belted 41 home runs with 142 RBIs (the homer and RBI totals were records at the time for a catcher); and 1955 when he hit .318 and had 32 home runs and 107 RBIs. His career total of 242 homers was the most ever for a catcher, and would have been more had his career not ended so abruptly. Campanella was injured in the first playoff game against the Giants in 1951 and was sidelined for the rest of the series. That left the Dodgers without his powerful bat and his ability to handle pitchers, which might have been the biggest factor of all in the Dodgers losing the playoffs on Bobby Thomson's famous home run in the ninth inning of the final game.

Baseball's all-time record crowd, 93,103, packed the Los Angeles Coliseum on May 7, 1959, not to see a game but to honor a man. It was Roy Campanella Night. The tribute was especially significant since Campy never played for the Los Angeles Dodgers. His crippling accident occurred three months before the Dodgers opened their first season in LA.

Year	Team	G	AB	R	H	D	T	HR	RBI	AVE.
1948	Brklyn	83	279	32	72	11	3	9	45	.258
1949	Brklyn	130	436	65	125	22	2	22	82	.287
1950	Brklyn	126	437	70	123	19	3	31	89	.281
1951	Brklyn	143	505	90	164	33	1	33	108	.325
1952	Brklyn	128	468	73	126	18	1	22	97	.269
1953	Brklyn	144	519	103	162	26	3	41	142	.312
1954	Brklyn	111	397	43	82	14	3	19	51	.207
1955	Brklyn	123	446	81	142	20	1	32	107	.318
1956	Brklyn	124	388	39	85	6	1	20	73	.219
1957	Brklyn	103	330	31	80	9	0	13	62	.242
10 years		**1215**	**4205**	**627**	**1161**	**178**	**18**	**242**	**856**	**.276**

WORLD SERIES

Year	Team	G	AB	R	H	D	T	HR	RBI	AVE.
1949	Brklyn	5	15	2	4	1	0	1	2	.267
1952	Brklyn	7	28	0	6	0	0	0	1	.214
1953	Brklyn	6	22	6	6	0	0	1	2	.273
1955	Brklyn	7	27	4	7	3	0	2	4	.259
1956	Brklyn	7	22	2	4	1	0	0	3	.182
5 years		**32**	**114**	**14**	**27**	**5**	**0**	**4**	**12**	**.237**

Buck Canel

Broadcaster. Elected to Hall of Fame: 1985.

Buck Canel was the first broadcaster in the Hall of Fame who worked exclusively for Spanish-speaking stations. He brought baseball to Cuba — and Cubans to baseball — through the airwaves and described the talents of many stars who eventually made it to the Major Leagues — stars such as Minnie Minoso, Camilo Pascuel, Willie Miranda, Sandy Amoros, Pedro Ramos, Mike Cuellar and Zoilo Versalles.

He also did many broadcasts of the World Series and, for this reason, was for a long time the Mel Allen of Spanish radio. Like so many of his broadcasting colleagues in the United States, Canel had a catch-phrase that made him famous: *"No se vayan que esto se pone bueno."* — "Don't go away; this is getting good!"

Harry Caray

Broadcaster. Elected to Hall of Fame: 1989.

Harry Caray became one of the most popular baseball broadcasters in the country because of his hometown rooting style, his penchant for reacting like a fan would to plays on the field and, in his early days, because he was the radio voice that people in half the country associated with baseball.

From 1945, when Caray began broadcasting St. Louis Cardinal games on KMOX in St. Louis, until 1958, when the Giants and Dodgers moved to the West Coast, the Cardinals were the Major Leagues' western-most team (as were the Browns until they moved to Baltimore in 1953). Station KMOX was picked up in cities west and southwest of St. Louis, and Caray became the voice of Major League Baseball for millions of listeners. He stayed with the Cardinals for 25 years, then went to Oakland for a year before coming back to the Midwest to broadcast Chicago White Sox games. He did that for 11 years and then became the voice of the Chicago Cubs. In 1995, Caray observed his 50th year as a baseball announcer. His son, Skip, and grandson, Chip, are also baseball broadcasters.

Caray's trademark "Holy Cow" and his home run call, "It may be … it could be … it is" have become part of the baseball lexicon. He also entertained fans by occasionally broadcasting games from the bleachers and by catching foul balls in a fish net he kept in the broadcast booth with him. He died February 18, 1998.

Rod Carew

Born October 1, 1945, in Gatun, Panama. 6', 182 lbs., bats left, throws right. Years in minor leagues: 3; Major League debut: April 11, 1967; Years in Major Leagues: 19. Elected to Hall of Fame: 1991. Nickname: None.

Rod Carew was a spray hitter who bunted well and used the whole field to rap 3,053 hits in his 19-year Major League career. He won seven batting titles. Only Ty Cobb and Honus Wagner (and later Tony Gwynn) had more, and Stan Musial and Rogers Hornsby also had seven. Carew, who played for the Minnesota Twins and California Angels, was the American League Rookie of the Year in 1967.

He hit over .300 in 15 consecutive seasons and was named to 17 straight All-Star teams. He won four consecutive batting titles between 1972 and 1975.

He won his first batting title in 1969 with a .332 average and also stole home seven times that year, tying Pete Reiser for the Major League record. When he won the first of four straight batting titles in 1972 with a .318 average, he did it without the benefit of a home run — but he had 15 bunt singles. No one else has ever gone homerless and won a batting title. In 1977, Carew hit .388, the highest average since Ted Williams hit for the same average in 1957. Nobody had hit higher than that since Williams hit .406 in 1941. Carew won the American League's Most Valuable Player Award that year, and his 239 hits were the most by any player since 1930.

If there was any downside to Carew's play, it was in the field where he had a reputation of being timid as a second baseman, particularly in making the pivot on the doubleplay. Nobody ever questioned his ability to hit. He finished with a lifetime batting average of .328. Like two other great stars before him, Ernie Banks and Luke Appling, Carew never got the chance to play in a World Series.

Year	Team	G	AB	R	H	D	T	HR	RBI	AVE.
1967	Minn	137	514	66	150	22	7	8	51	.292
1968	Minn	127	461	46	126	27	2	1	42	.273
1969	Minn	123	458	79	152	30	4	8	56	.332
1970	Minn	51	191	27	70	12	3	4	28	.366
1971	Minn	147	577	88	177	16	10	2	48	.307
1972	Minn	142	535	61	170	21	6	0	51	.318
1973	Minn	149	580	98	203	30	11	6	62	.350
1974	Minn	153	599	86	218	30	5	3	55	.364
1975	Minn	143	535	89	192	24	4	14	80	.359
1976	Minn	156	605	97	200	29	12	9	90	.331
1977	Minn	155	616	128	239	38	16	14	100	.388
1978	Minn	152	564	85	188	26	10	5	70	.333
1979	Cal	110	409	78	130	15	3	3	44	.318
1980	Cal	144	540	74	179	34	7	3	59	.331
1981	Cal	93	364	57	111	17	1	2	21	.305
1982	Cal	138	523	88	167	25	5	3	44	.319
1983	Cal	129	472	66	160	24	2	2	44	.339
1984	Cal	93	329	42	97	8	1	3	31	.295
1985	Cal	127	443	69	124	17	3	2	39	.280
19 years		2469	9315	1424	3053	445	112	92	1015	.328

Transactions: Feb. 3, 1979: Traded to California Angels for Ken Landreaux, Dave Engle, Paul Hartzell and Brad Havens.

LEAGUE CHAMPIONSHIP SERIES

Year	Team	G	AB	R	H	D	T	HR	RBI	AVE.
1969	Minn	3	14	0	1	0	0	0	0	.071
1970	Minn	2	2	0	0	0	0	0	0	.000

Year	Team	G	AB	R	H	D	T	HR	RBI	AVE.
1979	Cal	4	17	4	7	3	0	0	1	.412
1982	Cal	5	17	2	3	1	0	0	0	.176
4 years		14	50	6	11	4	0	0	1	.220

Max Carey

Born January 11, 1890, in Terre Haute, Indiana; died May 30, 1976, in Miami Beach, Florida. 5'11", 170 lbs., bats both, throws right. Years in minor leagues: 2; Major League debut: October 3, 1910; Years in Major Leagues: 20. Elected to Hall of Fame: 1961. Nickname: Scoops—possibly because a slick-fielding first baseman of the early 1900s had the same nickname; more likely because of his own great ability to scoop up balls in center field.

Max Carey was one of baseball's first good switch-hitters. It would be difficult to rate his greatest game in the Major Leagues. It might have been in the seventh game of the 1925 World Series when the 35-year-old Pittsburgh center fielder rapped out three doubles and a single off of Walter Johnson to help the Pirates beat the Senators. His World Series batting average that year was .458. Or it might have been either of the two games in August of that year when Carey stole second, third and home in the same inning. Historians might point to July 7, 1922, when Carey got six hits and three walks in an 18-inning game that the Pirates eventually lost to the New York Giants.

Carey was a good hitter—he hit over .300 six times and led the league in triples twice—but he was best known as an outstanding outfielder and great base stealer. He led the National League in stolen bases ten times, which is still a National League record. In 1922, he was only caught twice in 53 steal attempts. Carey led the National League in putouts by an outfielder nine times and retired with a National League record total of 6,363. Willie Mays later broke the record but he had a few more seasons under his belt than Carey.

The fleet-footed outfielder had an interesting start and interesting end to his baseball career. His real name was Maximillian Carnarius. When he was a divinity student in Indiana, he had a chance to play in a professional baseball game that was being played in town. He changed his name to Max Carey to protect his amateur status. When his baseball playing days were over, Carey stayed in baseball and ended his career by managing two women's teams.

Year	Team	G	AB	R	H	D	T	HR	RBI	AVE.
1910	Pitt	2	6	2	3	0	1	0	2	.500
1911	Pitt	129	427	77	110	15	10	5	43	.258
1912	Pitt	150	587	114	177	23	8	5	66	.302
1913	Pitt	154	620	99	172	23	10	5	49	.277
1914	Pitt	156	593	76	144	25	17	1	31	.243
1915	Pitt	140	564	76	143	26	5	3	27	.254
1916	Pitt	154	599	90	158	23	11	7	42	.264

Year	Team	G	AB	R	H	D	T	HR	RBI	AVE.
1917	Pitt	155	588	82	174	21	12	1	51	.296
1918	Pitt	126	468	70	128	14	6	3	48	.274
1919	Pitt	66	244	41	75	10	2	0	9	.307
1920	Pitt	130	485	74	140	18	4	1	35	.289
1921	Pitt	140	521	85	161	34	4	7	56	.309
1922	Pitt	155	629	140	207	28	12	10	70	.329
1923	Pitt	153	610	120	188	32	19	6	63	.308
1924	Pitt	149	599	113	178	30	9	7	55	.297
1925	Pitt	133	542	109	186	39	13	5	44	.343
1926	Pitt-Brk	113	424	64	98	17	6	0	35	.231
1927	Brklyn	144	538	70	143	30	10	1	54	.266
1928	Brklyn	108	296	41	73	11	0	2	19	.247
1929	Brklyn	19	23	2	7	0	0	0	1	.304
20 years		**2476**	**9363**	**1545**	**2665**	**419**	**159**	**69**	**800**	**.285**

Transactions: Aug. 13, 1926: Picked up for waiver price by Brooklyn Dodgers.

WORLD SERIES

Year	Team	G	AB	R	H	D	T	HR	RBI	AVE.
1925	Pitt	7	24	6	11	4	0	0	2	.458

Stephen Norman Carlton

Born December 22, 1944, in Miami, Florida. 6'4", 210 lbs., bats left, throws left. Years in minor leagues: 3; Major League debut: April 12, 1965; Years in Major Leagues: 24. Elected to Hall of Fame: 1994. Nickname: Lefty — because he threw lefthanded.

Steve Carlton had a routine that included not speaking to the press, engaging in pregame meditations — and winning on the field. He pitched in two World Series as a youngster for the St. Louis Cardinals, then more than a decade later led the Philadelphia Phillies to their first National League championship in 40 years. But perhaps the true measure of Carlton's greatness is how well he did on bad teams.

In 1972, the Phillies won only 59 games and finished in last place. Carlton won 27 of them, led the league with a 1.98 earned run average and also was the league leader in strikeouts and innings pitched. He is the only pitcher in baseball history to win the Cy Young award for a last place team. He had some great individual games — striking out 19 Mets in a 1969 outing, but losing the game on two Ron Swoboda home runs — and threw six one-hitters. Carlton broke in with the Cardinals but was traded to the Phillies after the 1971 season, primarily because of a salary dispute with Cardinal owner Gussie Busch. He responded with his 27-win season which included four wins over the Cardinals. Carlton's 100th and 300th career victories were against St. Louis.

He won 20 or more games six times in his career, played on Cardinal pennant winners in 1967 and 1968 and Philadelphia division winners in 1976, 1977, 1978, 1980 and 1983. Carlton won the Cy Young award four times. His 329 wins are the second most for a National League lefthander, behind only Warren Spahn. His lifetime strikeout total — 4,136 — is the most for a lefthander and second overall to Nolan Ryan. Carlton led the National League in innings pitched five times. For many of his years with the Phillies, Carlton had his own personal catcher — Tim McCarver, who had caught him in St. Louis. When both McCarver and Carlton landed on the Phillies, they were a regular battery team for several years.

Year	Team	W-L	ERA	G	IP	H	BB	SO
1965	StL	0-0	2.52	15	25	27	8	21
1966	StL	3-3	3.12	9	52	56	18	25
1967	StL	14-9	2.98	30	93	173	62	168
1968	StL	13-11	2.99	34	232	214	61	162
1969	StL	17-11	2.17	31	236	185	93	210
1970	StL	10-19	3.72	34	254	239	109	193
1971	StL	20-9	3.56	37	273	275	98	172
1972	Phil	27-10	1.97	41	346.1	257	87	310
1973	Phil	13-20	3.90	40	293.1	293	113	223
1974	Phil	16-13	3.22	39	291	249	136	240
1975	Phil	15-14	3.56	37	255	217	104	192
1976	Phil	20-7	3.13	35	252.2	224	72	195
1977	Phil	23-10	2.64	36	283	229	89	198
1978	Phil	16-13	2.84	34	247	228	63	161
1979	Phil	18-11	3.62	35	251	202	89	213
1980	Phil	24-9	2.34	38	304	243	90	286
1981	Phil	13-4	2.42	24	190	152	62	179
1982	Phil	23-11	3.10	38	295.2	253	86	286
1983	Phil	15-16	3.11	37	283.2	277	84	275
1984	Phil	13-7	3.58	33	229	214	79	163
1985	Phil	1-8	3.33	16	92	84	53	48
1986	Phi-SF-Chi	9-14	4.95	32	176.3	196	86	120
1987	Cle-Minn	6-14	5.74	32	152	165	86	91
1988	Minn	0-1	16.76	4	9.2	10	5	5
24 years		**329-244**	**3.22**	**741**	**5216.3**	**4672**	**1833**	**4136**

Transactions: Feb. 25, 1972: Traded to Philadelphia for pitcher Rick Wise.

DIVISIONAL CHAMPIONSHIP SERIES

Year	Team	W-L	ERA	G	IP	H	BB	SO
1980	Phi	0-2	3.86	2	14	14	8	13

LEAGUE CHAMPIONSHIP SERIES

Year	Team	W-L	ERA	G	IP	H	BB	SO
1976	Phil	0-1	5.14	1	7	8	5	6

Year	Team	W-L	ERA	G	IP	H	BB	SO
1977	Phil	0-1	6.94	2	11.2	13	8	6
1978	Phil	1-0	4.00	1	9	8	2	8
1980	Phil	1-0	2.19	2	12.1	11	8	6
1983	Phil	2-0	0.66	2	13.2	13	5	13
5 years		4-2	3.52	8	53.2	53	28	39

WORLD SERIES

Year	Team	W-L	ERA	G	IP	H	BB	SO
1967	StL	0-1	0.00	1	6	3	2	5
1968	StL	0-0	6.75	2	4	7	1	3
1980	Phil	2-0	2.40	2	15	14	9	17
1983	Phil	0-1	2.70	1	6.2	5	3	7
4 years		2-2	2.56	6	31.2	29	15	32

John P. Carmichael

Sportswriter. Elected to Hall of Fame: 1974.

John P. Carmichael was a sportswriter, columnist and sports editor of the *Chicago Daily News* for almost four decades. His popular column, "The Barbershop," provided loads of inside information and tidbits about Chicago sports teams. He was also author and editor of the book *My Greatest Day in Baseball*, a classic in which many stars, from Cy Young and Grover Cleveland Alexander, to Joe DiMaggio and Ted Williams, recounted the greatest moment in their careers.

Herb Carneal

Broadcaster. Elected to Hall of Fame: 1996.

Herb Carneal has been one of the voices of the Minnesota Twins from the time they moved from Washington to the northlands in 1961. As color man, main broadcaster and analyst he has been there to describe the World Series team of 1965 to the world championship teams of 1987 and 1991.

Alexander Cartwright

Born April 17, 1820, in New York, New York; died July 12, 1892, in Honolulu, Hawaii. Baseball pioneer. Elected to Hall of Fame: 1938.

Alexander Cartwright is rightfully referred to as "The Father of Modern

Baseball." He put together the first team, the New York Knickerbockers, in 1845, but perhaps more important he put some organization to the game. The Knickerbockers were a group of volunteer firemen and they lost the historic first game, 23–1, perhaps because Cartwright chose to umpire rather than play. The legend of Abner Doubleday inventing baseball gave way to incontrovertible facts that Cartwright was really the founder. So while the Hall of Fame was established in Cooperstown, Doubleday's hometown, Cartwright's legacy, and not Doubleday's, is honored there. Cartwright had an engineering background and he put it to use to determine the bases should be 90 feet apart in a diamond shape. He also came up with rules that provided for nine inning games, three outs in an inning and nine players in the lineup and on the field. Cartwright, whose family was British, had grown up watching and playing the game of rounders, which uses a ball and has bases. He adopted some of the concepts of rounders in developing baseball, but eliminated the rounders rule of hitting a runner with a thrown ball for an out. Cartwright loved to travel around the country, teaching the new game of baseball wherever he went. Eventually, he moved to Hawaii and he taught the game to school children there.

Orlando Manuel Cepeda

Born September 17, 1937, in Ponce, Puerto Rico. 6'2", 210 lbs., bats right, throws right. Major League debut: April 15, 1958; Years in Major Leagues: 17. Elected to Hall of Fame: 1999. Nicknames: The Baby Bull—a takeoff on the nickname of his father, Perucho "The Bull" Cepeda, a great Puerto Rican ballplayer; also, called Cha-Cha, for his graceful movements around first base.

Orlando Cepeda was one of the great power hitters of the 1960s, helping the San Francisco Giants to their only World Series appearance of the decade and leading the St. Louis Cardinals to two National League championships. He was the Rookie of the Year in 1958 when he hit .312 with 25 home runs and 98 runs batted in. He also led the National League in doubles with 38. In his first seven seasons in the Major Leagues, he averaged 32 home runs, 106 runs batted in with a composite batting average of .306. In 1961, he hit 46 home runs and drove in 142 runs and narrowly missed being named the National League's Most Valuable Player. That honor came in 1967 when he hit .325 for the Cardinals and had 25 homers and 111 runs batted in. Cepeda was the second designated hitter in Major League history, following New York's Ron Blomberg. Cepeda just missed being voted into the Hall of Fame in 1994 when he received 73.6 percent of the votes. A 75 percent vote is required.

Year	Team	G	AB	R	H	D	T	HR	RBI	AVE.
1958	SF	148	603	88	188	38	4	25	96	.312
1959	SF	151	605	92	192	35	4	27	105	.317
1960	SF	151	569	81	169	36	3	24	96	.297
1961	SF	152	585	105	182	28	4	46	142	.311

Year	Team	G	AB	R	H	D	T	HR	RBI	AVE.
1962	SF	162	625	105	191	26	1	35	114	.306
1963	SF	156	579	100	183	33	4	34	97	.316
1964	SF	142	529	75	161	27	2	31	97	.304
1965	SF	33	34	1	6	1	0	1	5	.176
1966	SF-StL	142	501	70	151	26	0	20	73	.301
1967	StL	151	563	91	183	37	0	25	111	.325
1968	StL	157	600	71	149	26	2	16	73	.248
1969	Atl	154	573	74	147	28	2	22	88	.257
1970	Atl	148	567	87	173	33	0	34	111	.305
1971	Atl	71	250	31	69	10	1	14	44	.276
1972	Atl-Oak	31	87	6	25	3	0	4	9	.287
1973	Bos	142	550	51	159	25	0	20	86	.289
1974	Bos	33	107	3	23	5	0	1	18	.215
17 years		2124	7927	1131	2351	417	27	379	1365	.297

Transactions: May 8, 1966: Traded to St. Louis Cardinals for pitcher by Ray Sadecki; March 17, 1969: Traded to Atlanta Braves for catcher Joe Torre; June 19, 1972: Traded to Oakland A's for pitcher Dennis McLain.

LEAGUE CHAMPIONSHIP SERIES

Year	Team	G	AB	R	H	D	T	HR	RBI	AVE.
1969	Atl	3	11	2	5	2	0	1	3	.455

WORLD SERIES

Year	Team	G	AB	R	H	D	T	HR	RBI	AVE.
1962	SF	5	19	1	3	1	0	0	2	.158
1967	StL	7	29	1	3	2	0	0	1	.103
1968	StL	7	28	2	7	0	0	2	6	.250
3 years		19	76	4	13	3	0	2	9	.171

Henry Chadwick

Born October 5, 1824, in Exeter, England; died April 29, 1908, in Brooklyn, New York. Baseball pioneer. Elected to Hall of Fame: 1938.

It is fitting that Henry Chadwick's name is closely aligned with Alexander Cartwright's in baseball history. Both were of British ancestry. In fact, Chadwick was born in England. Both were influenced by two British games: rounders and cricket. Both also became enamored with the American game of baseball, which Cartwright organized and developed, and Chadwick, a New York sportswriter, promoted. Chadwick and Cartwright were enshrined in the Hall of Fame in the same year, 1938. His lasting contribution to the game is his invention of the box score and the method of scoring a game in such a way that each player's contributions are easy to follow and to record. Chadwick worked for several newspapers and then was editor of the *Spalding Baseball Guide* for 20 years. He died of pneumonia several days after catching cold on Opening Day at Ebbetts Field in Brooklyn in 1908. President Theodore Roosevelt called Chadwick the "Father of Baseball."

Frank Chance

Born September 9, 1877, in Fresno, California; died September 15, 1924, in Los Angeles, California. 6', 190 lbs., bats right, throws right. Years in minor leagues: None; Major League debut: April 29, 1898; Years in Major Leagues: 17. Elected to Hall of Fame: 1946. Nickname: The Peerless Leader—from Chicago baseball writer Charles Dryden; because of his ability to lead his baseball team; also known as Husk—short for Husky—a name teammates called him after he got into a barroom fight with James J. Corbett, heavyweight boxing champion.

Frank Chance was a good hitting, good fielding first baseman and a great leader for the Chicago Cubs in the early 1900s. He seemed to be able to rise to the occasion, getting three hits off of Christy Mathewson in a classic Cub-Giant playoff game in 1908 to decide the National League pennant; then outshining Tiger great Ty Cobb by hitting .421 in the World Series; and having an overall World Series batting average of .310, with 10 stolen bases, a Major League record until it was topped by Lou Brock. But it was Chance's skills as a team leader that made him special. He is one of the few members of the Hall of Fame who probably could have earned induction for either his playing or managing ability. He broke into the Major Leagues in 1898, became the Cub team captain in 1904 and replaced ailing Frank Selee as manager on August 1, 1905. Under Chance's leadership, the Cubs became a dynasty. In the next five years, they averaged 106 wins and won four pennants. Chance's 1906 team won 116 games — still a Major League record. The Cubs also won two world championships under Chance — something they haven't done even once since then. He later managed two bad teams — the New York Highlanders and Boston Red Sox — that took some of the glitter off of his overall managerial statistics. Still, his winning percentage was .593.

As a Player

Year	Team	G	AB	R	H	D	T	HR	RBI	AVE.
1898	Chi (N)	53	147	32	42	4	3	1	14	.286
1899	Chi	64	192	37	55	6	2	1	22	.286
1900	Chi	56	151	26	46	8	4	0	13	.305
1901	Chi	69	241	38	67	12	4	0	36	.278
1902	Chi	75	236	40	67	9	4	1	31	.284
1903	Chi	125	441	83	144	24	10	2	81	.327
1904	Chi	124	451	89	140	16	10	6	49	.310
1905	Chi	118	392	92	124	16	12	2	70	.316
1906	Chi	136	474	103	151	24	10	3	71	.319
1907	Chi	111	382	58	112	19	2	1	49	.293
1908	Chi	129	452	65	123	27	4	2	55	.272
1909	Chi	93	324	53	88	16	4	0	46	.272
1910	Chi	88	295	54	88	12	8	0	36	.298
1911	Chi	31	88	23	21	6	3	1	17	.239

Year	Team	G	AB	R	H	D	T	HR	RBI	AVE.
1912	Chi	2	5	2	1	0	0	0	0	.200
1913	NY (A)	11	24	3	5	0	0	0	6	.208
1914	NY (A)	1	0	0	0	0	0	0	0	.000
17 years		1286	4295	798	1274	199	80	20	596	.297

WORLD SERIES

Year	Team	G	AB	R	H	D	T	HR	RBI	AVE.
1906	Chi (N)	6	21	3	5	1	0	0	0	.238
1907	Chi	4	14	3	3	1	0	0	0	.214
1908	Chi	5	19	4	8	0	0	0	2	.421
1910	Chi	5	17	1	6	1	1	0	4	.353
4 years		20	71	11	22	3	1	0	6	.310

AS A MANAGER

Year	Team	W-L	Standing
1905	Chi (N)	40-23	Third
1906	Chi	116-36	First
1907	Chi	107-45	First
1908	Chi	99-55	First
1909	Chi	104-49	Second
1910	Chi	104-50	First
1911	Chi	92-62	Second
1912	Chi	91-59	Third
1913	NY (A)	57-94	Seventh
1914	NY (A)	61-76	Sixth
1923	Bos (A)	61-91	Eighth
Totals		**1597-932**	

WORLD SERIES

Year	Team	W-L
1906	Chi (N)	2-4
1907	Chi	4-0
1908	Chi	4-1
1910	Chi	1-4
4 years		11-9

A.B. Chandler

Born July 14, 1898, in Corydon, Kentucky; died June 15, 1991, in Versailles, Kentucky. Years in Major Leagues: 6 (as commissioner). Elected to Hall of Fame: 1982. Nickname: Happy — because of jovial personality.

Happy Chandler was commissioner of baseball for only six years, but he presided over one of the most turbulent eras of the game and set the stage for the upcoming era which was one of baseball's finest. Chandler, a former governor and senator from Kentucky, replaced a legend, Kenesaw Mountain Landis, in 1945. Chandler's tenure was marked by controversy. In 1946, 18 Major League ballplayers signed with a Mexican League that promised much higher salaries. Chandler responded by banning the players for five years. One of the players, Danny Gardella, sued, and although he did not win, his action threatened baseball's reserve clause and its antitrust status, shaking the very foundation of the game's financial structure. In 1947, he suspended Dodger manager Leo Durocher for a year for his alleged association with gamblers. Dodger general manager Branch Rickey sought and received Chandler's endorsement of integrating baseball, but his support did not sit well with most of the owners. In 1951, Chandler was ousted when he got only 9 of 16 votes from owners. Chandler went back to Kentucky where he was elected governor once again.

Oscar McKinley Charleston

Born October 14, 1896, in Indianapolis, Indiana; died October 5, 1954, in Philadelphia, Pennsylvania. 6'1", 190 lbs., bats left, throws left. Years in minor (Negro) leagues: 39 years; Years in Major Leagues: None. Elected to Hall of Fame: 1976. Nickname: None.

Oscar Charleston could have been the starting center fielder for any Major League team had he ever been given the chance. Instead, he played almost 40 years in the Negro leagues hopscotching around the country, signing with one team after another: Indianapolis, Lincoln, Chicago, St. Louis, Harrisburg, Hilldale, Homestead, Pittsburgh, Philadelphia, Brooklyn and back to Indianapolis. He was a great hitter but was also known for his exceptional speed in the outfield. Although recordkeeping was sketchy in his playing days, Charleston easily topped .300 for a lifetime batting average in nearly 40 years of play. In 1925, playing for Harrisburg, he hit .445. The next season, playing for Hilldale, he hit .396. Charleston played on a Pittsburgh Crawford team that boasted five future Hall of Famers: Charleston, Judy Johnson, Josh Gibson, Satchel Paige and Cool Papa Bell. His true legacy is this: Some who saw him and many of the great Major Leaguers play say that Charleston may have been the greatest ballplayer ever.

Jack Chesbro

Born June 5, 1874, in North Adams, Massachusetts; died November 6, 1931, in Conway, Massachusetts. 5'9", 180 lbs., bats right, throws right. Years in minor leagues: 6; Major League debut: July 12, 1899; Years in Major Leagues: 11. Elected to Hall of Fame: 1946. Nickname: Happy Jack—because of his attitude while working in a mental institution before getting into baseball.

Nobody before or since has had a year like Jack Chesbro had in 1904 for the New York Highlanders (later to be Yankees). Chesbro started 51 games, completed

48, and won 41 of them. The 41 wins is still a Major League record and is one of those rare records that may never be broken. Chesbro had six shutouts and tossed a one-hitter, two-hitter and three-hitter along the way. The Highlanders went into the last day of the season 1½ games behind Boston and were playing Boston in a doubleheader. A sweep would bring the pennant to New York. The Highlanders started Happy Jack Chesbro in the first game. He and Ed Deneen battled to a 2–2 tie going into the top of the ninth. With two outs and a runner on third, a pitch got away from Chesbro and sailed past catcher Red Kleinow. Lou Criger scored what proved to be the winning run, and the Highlanders were eliminated from the pennant race. Chesbro had to accept the role of the goat long past his retirement, despite the 41 wins that had gotten the Highlanders into pennant contention in the first place. Happy Jack had been a great pitcher long before 1904. Between 1901 and 1906, he won 154 games, an average of more than 25 wins a season, including a 28-win season with Pittsburgh before he joined the Highlanders. Chesbro's career was never quite the same after the 1904 wild pitch. He lasted five more years, the last three struggling to be a .500 pitcher, and retired after the 1909 season two wins shy of 200 for his career.

Year	Team	W-L	ERA	G	IP	H	BB	SO
1899	Pitt (N)	6-10	4.11	19	149	165	59	28
1900	Pitt	14-13	3.67	32	215.2	220	79	56
1901	Pitt	21-10	2.38	36	287.2	261	52	129
1902	Pitt	28-6	2.17	35	286.1	242	62	136
1903	NY (A)	21-15	2.77	40	324.2	300	74	147
1904	NY	41-12	1.82	55	454.2	338	88	239
1905	NY	19-15	2.20	41	303.1	262	71	156
1906	NY	24-16	2.96	49	325	314	75	152
1907	NY	10-10	2.53	30	206	192	46	78
1908	NY	14-20	2.93	45	289	271	67	124
1909	NY-Bos (A)	0-5	6.14	10	55.2	77	17	20
11 years		198-132	2.68	392	2897	2642	690	1265

Transactions: January 1900: Traded with Paddy Fox, John O'Brien, Art Madison and $25,000 from Pittsburgh to Louisville for Honus Wagner, Deacon Phillipe, Walt Woods, Rube Waddell, Icebox Chamberlain, Chief Zimmer, Tacks Latimer, Claude Ritchey, Fred Clarke, Tommy Leach, Mike Kelly, Conny Doyle and Tom Massitt. (Part of an arrangement whereby the assets of Louisville were being tranferred to Pittsburgh because the Louisville franchise was disbanding. Chesbro later was back with Pittsburgh.) Sept. 11, 1909: Picked up by Boston for waiver price.

Nestor Chylak

Born May 11, 1922, in Peckville, Pennsylvania; died February 17, 1982, in Dunmore, Pennsylvania. Years in Major Leagues: 25 (as an umpire). Elected to Hall of Fame: 1999.

Nestor Chylak was an American League umpire for 25 years who was known for his knowledge of the rules and his ability to keep a game moving. He was especially well respected for his work behind the plate. Chylak worked six All-Star games, three American League Championship Series and three World Series during his career. He is one of the few modern umpires who made it to the Major Leagues without going through an umpiring school. He worked in the minor leagues for seven years before being hired by the American League in 1954. He retired after suffering a slight stroke in 1978 and served as an assistant supervisor of umpires through the 1981 season.

Fred Clifford Clarke

Born October 3, 1872, in Winterset, Iowa; died August 14, 1960, in Winfield, Kansas. 5'10", 165 lbs., bats left, throws right. Years in minor leagues: 4; Major League debut: June 30, 1894; Years in Major Leagues: 21. Elected to Hall of Fame: 1945. Nickname: Cap — short for captain or manager.

Like Frank Chance of the Cubs, his contemporary, Fred Clarke, could have made it to the Hall of Fame as either a player or a manager. He got four singles and a triple in his Major League debut with Louisville, who lost the game to Philadelphia, 13–6. That remains the only time in Major League baseball history that anyone went 5-for-5 in a debut. Louisville only got one other hit that day. Clarke once hit over .400 and didn't win the batting title. In 1897, he hit .406 but Willie Keeler had a .432 average. He hit over .300 11 times and also had 506 stolen bases. He was a fleet-footed left fielder with an exceptionally strong throwing arm. Clarke had four assists in one game and ten putouts in another. After managing Louisville for three years, Clarke took over as manager of the Pirates in 1900. He came over to Pittsburgh in a huge deal that helped Louisville purge its roster as the National League was reduced from 12 to 8 teams. Clarke's Pirate team finished second in 1900 and then won three straight pennants. His Pirate team won 110 games in 1909, third most in baseball history, and then beat the Detroit Tigers in the World Series. His winning percentage as a manager was .576, better than many great managers' stats (Leo Durocher's was .540) but a shade lower than that of his chief rival. Chance with the Cubs had a .593 winning percentage.

As a Player

Year	Team	G	AB	R	H	D	T	HR	RBI	AVE.
1894	Lou (N)	75	310	54	83	11	7	7	48	.268
1895	Lou	132	550	96	191	21	5	4	82	.347
1896	Lou	131	517	96	168	15	18	9	79	.325
1897	Lou	128	518	120	202	30	13	6	67	.390
1898	Lou	149	599	116	184	23	12	3	47	.307
1899	Lou	148	602	122	206	23	9	5	70	.342

Year	Team	G	AB	R	H	D	T	HR	RBI	AVE.
1900	Pitt	106	399	84	110	15	12	3	32	.276
1901	Pitt	129	527	118	171	24	15	6	60	.324
1902	Pitt	113	459	103	145	27	14	2	53	.316
1903	Pitt	104	427	88	150	32	15	5	70	.351
1904	Pitt	72	278	51	85	7	11	0	25	.306
1905	Pitt	141	525	95	157	18	15	2	51	.299
1906	Pitt	118	417	69	129	14	13	1	39	.309
1907	Pitt	148	501	97	145	18	13	2	59	.289
1908	Pitt	151	551	83	146	18	15	2	53	.265
1909	Pitt	152	550	97	158	16	11	3	68	.287
1910	Pitt	123	429	57	113	23	9	2	63	.263
1911	Pitt	110	392	73	127	25	13	5	49	.324
1913	Pitt	9	13	0	1	1	0	0	0	.077
1914	Pitt	2	2	0	0	0	0	0	0	.000
1915	Pitt	1	2	0	1	0	0	0	0	.500
21 years		**2242**	**8568**	**1619**	**2672**	**361**	**220**	**67**	**1015**	**.315**

Transactions: January 1900: Traded with Paddy Fox, John O'Brien, Art Madison and $25,000 from Pittsburgh to Louisville for Honus Wagner, Deacon Phillipe, Walt Woods, Rube Waddell, Icebox Chamberlain, Chief Zimmer, Tacks Latimer, Claude Richey, Fred Clarke, Tommy Leach, Mike Kelly, Conny Doyle and Tom Massitt. (Part of an arrangement whereby the assets of Louisville were being tranferred to Pittsburgh because the Louisville franchise was disbanding.)

WORLD SERIES

Year	Team	G	AB	R	H	D	T	HR	RBI	AVE.
1903	Pitt	8	34	3	9	2	1	0	2	.265
1909	Pitt	7	19	7	4	0	0	2	7	.211
2 years		**15**	**53**	**10**	**13**	**2**	**1**	**2**	**9**	**.245**

AS A MANAGER

Year	Team	W-L	Standing
1897	Lou	35-52	Ninth
1898	Lou	70-81	Ninth
1899	Lou	75-77	Ninth
1900	Pitt	79-60	Second
1901	Pitt	90-49	First
1902	Pitt	103-36	First
1903	Pitt	91-49	First
1904	Pitt	87-66	Fourth
1905	Pitt	96-57	Second
1906	Pitt	93-60	Third
1907	Pitt	91-63	Second
1908	Pitt	98-56	Second
1909	Pitt	110-42	First

Year	Team	W-L	Standing
1910	Pitt	86-67	Third
1911	Pitt	85-69	Third
1912	Pitt	93-58	Second
1913	Pitt	78-71	Fourth
1914	Pitt	69-85	Seventh
1915	Pitt	73-81	Fifth
19 years		**1602-1179**	

WORLD SERIES

Year	Team	W-L
1903	Pitt	3-5
1909	Pitt	4-3
2 years		**7-8**

John Gibson Clarkson

Born July 1, 1861, in Cambridge, Massachusetts; died February 4, 1909, in Cambridge, Massachusetts; 5'10", 160 lbs., bats right, throws right. Years in minor leagues: 3; Major League debut: May 2, 1882; Years in Major Leagues: 11. Elected to Hall of Fame: 1963. Nickname: None.

John Clarkson wasn't a big man, even for his day, and he didn't have any overpowering pitches. But his manager, Cap Anson, said Clarkson had an amazing ability to know exactly what pitch a hitter couldn't hit — and to throw that pitch.

He threw several varieties of curve balls and had a "drop pitch" that kept batters continually off balance. He used these pitches and knowledge of hitters to win 327 games in just 12 seasons.

Clarkson's biggest weakness was that he was moody and needed constant coddling by his manager and teammates. When Clarkson died of pneumonia, at the age of 48, many who knew him believed he was insane.

Year	Team	W-L	ERA	G	IP	H	BB	SO
1882	Wor (N)	1-2	4.50	3	24	49	2	3
1884	Chi (N)	10-3	2.14	14	118	94	25	102
1885	Chi	53-16	1.85	70	623	497	97	318
1886	Chi	35-17	2.41	55	466.2	419	86	340
1887	Chi	38-21	3.08	60	523	513	92	237
1888	Bos (N)	33-20	2.76	54	483.1	448	119	223
1889	Bos	49-19	2.73	73	620	589	203	284
1890	Bos	26-18	3.27	44	383	370	140	138
1891	Bos	33-19	2.79	55	460.2	435	154	141
1892	Bos-Cle	25-16	2.48	45	389	350	132	139
1893	Cleve	16-17	4.45	36	295	358	95	62
1894	Cleve	8-9	4.42	22	150.2	173	46	28
12 years		**327-177**	**2.81**	**531**	**4536.1**	**4295**	**1191**	**2015**

Roberto Walker Clemente

Born August 18, 1934, in Carolina, Puerto Rico; died December 31, 1972, in San Juan, Puerto Rico. 5'11", 185 lbs., bats right, throws right. Years in minor leagues: 1; Major League debut: April 17, 1955; Years in Major Leagues: 18. Elected to Hall of Fame: 1973. Nickname: Arriba — "Let's go" — is what Latin American fans called him with affection; Also, sometimes called "Bob" — an Americanization of "Roberto" which he did not like.

Roberto Clemente was a great ballplayer who could do it all well: hit, run, and field. The Pittsburgh Pirate right fielder hit over .300 13 times, had a .317 lifetime batting average and hit safely in all 14 World Series games in which he appeared. He got his 3,000th hit on September 30, 1972. Three months later, he was killed in a plane crash while on a mercy mission of delivering food and clothing to earthquake victims in Nicaragua. Clemente won the National League batting title in 1961, 1964, 1965 and 1967. He was the National League's Most Valuable Player in 1966. He was an outstanding defensive outfielder who led the league in assists 5 times and won 12 straight Gold Glove awards. In 1958, he threw out 22 runners and topped that with 27 assists in 1961.

For most of his career, Clemente complained he didn't get the credit he deserved. He had the misfortune of playing in a small-market city, Pittsburgh, for his entire career, while stars such as Willie Mays and Mickey Mantle played in the mega-market of New York. Ironically, a few months after his death, he got the recognition that was so important to him in life. He was elected to the Hall of Fame in a special ballot in 1973, as the five-year waiting period rule was waived.

Year	Team	G	AB	R	H	D	T	HR	RBI	AVE.
1955	Pitt	124	474	48	121	23	11	5	47	.255
1956	Pitt	147	543	66	169	30	7	7	60	.311
1957	Pitt	111	451	42	114	17	7	4	30	.253
1958	Pitt	140	519	69	150	24	10	6	50	.289
1959	Pitt	105	432	60	128	17	7	4	50	.296
1960	Pitt	144	570	89	179	22	6	16	94	.314
1961	Pitt	146	572	100	201	30	10	23	89	.351
1962	Pitt	144	538	95	168	28	9	10	74	.312
1963	Pitt	152	600	77	192	23	8	17	76	.320
1964	Pitt	155	622	95	211	40	7	12	87	.339
1965	Pitt	152	589	91	194	21	14	10	65	.329
1966	Pitt	154	638	105	202	31	11	29	119	.317
1967	Pitt	147	585	103	209	26	10	23	110	.357
1968	Pitt	132	502	74	146	18	12	18	57	.291
1969	Pitt	138	507	87	175	20	12	19	91	.345
1970	Pitt	108	412	65	145	22	10	14	60	.352
1971	Pitt	132	522	82	178	29	8	13	86	.341
1972	Pitt	102	378	68	118	19	7	10	60	.312
18 years		2433	9454	1416	3000	440	166	240	1305	.317

LEAGUE CHAMPIONSHIP SERIES

Year	Team	G	AB	R	H	D	T	HR	RBI	AVE.
1970	Pitt	3	14	1	3	0	0	0	1	.214
1971	Pitt	4	18	2	6	0	0	0	4	.333
1972	Pitt	5	17	1	4	1	0	1	2	.235
3 years		12	49	4	13	1	0	1	7	.265

WORLD SERIES

Year	Team	G	AB	R	H	D	T	HR	RBI	AVE.
1960	Pitt	7	29	1	9	0	0	0	3	.310
1971	Pitt	7	29	3	12	2	1	2	4	.414
2 years		14	58	4	21	2	1	2	7	.362

Tyrus Raymond Cobb

Born December 18, 1886, in Narrows, Georgia; died July 17, 1961, in Atlanta, Georgia. 6'1", 175 lbs., bats left, throws right. Years in minor leagues: 3; Major League debut: Aug. 30, 1905; Years in Major Leagues: 22. Elected to Hall of Fame: 1936. Nickname: The Georgia Peach — strictly a newspaper nickname, first used by Detroit Free-Press *sportswriter Joe H. Jackson in 1906, referring to his home state and certainly not a reference to his personality.*

Perhaps the best testimony to Ty Cobb's greatness is that when he was elected to the Hall of Fame in 1936, he received more votes than Babe Ruth, who was also elected — and those voting had seen them both play. He is not only one of the greatest players of all time but probably also the game's most fierce competitor. One of the legendary stories that followed Cobb over the years is that he beat up and killed an irate fan behind the stands after a Tiger game. Recent research has cast doubts on that story, but nobody doubted it for 60 years because it fit Cobb's personality.

In 1912, Cobb went after a fan in the stands in New York and was suspended by the league. His Detroit teammates backed him and refused to play a game against the Philadelphia A's if Cobb could not play. Detroit management fielded a team of amateurs literally picked off the street to play the game. The A's won, 24–2.

In an old-timers game in 1956, when Cobb was 70 years old, he asked the catcher to back up a little in case Cobb, with his shaky hands, might let loose with the bat. The catcher complied, upon which Cobb laid down a bunt in front of the plate. His action at the age of 70 was based on the same motivation that caused him, as a little boy, to once walk a tightrope that was stretched across the main street of his hometown of Royston, Georgia. Reflecting on that incident years later, Cobb said he saw no point in losing if there was a chance to win. He carried that philosophy with him the rest of his life.

When he retired in 1928, Cobb held 43 Major League records. Many have been topped over the years, but one that seems safe is his lifetime batting average of .367. He led the American League in hitting 12 times, in slugging percentage 8 times, in total hits 7 times, and in stolen bases 6 times — including 96 in 1915, a record that stood for nearly 50 years. He led the league in doubles 3 times and triples 4 times. In his best year, 1911, Cobb hit .420, thanks to 248 hits. He also scored 147 runs, drove in 144 and stole 83 bases.

While he is remembered for his fiery temper and for his great ability as a ballplayer, Cobb was also second-to-none in being wise with money. When he first started drawing decent pay from the Tigers, he decided to invest in a couple of small companies that he thought showed great growth potential — General Motors and Coca-Cola. As a result, Cobb was probably baseball's first millionaire.

Year	Team	G	AB	R	H	D	T	HR	RBI	AVE.
1905	Det	41	150	19	36	6	0	1	15	.240
1906	Det	98	350	45	112	13	7	1	41	.320
1907	Det	150	605	97	212	29	15	5	116	.350
1908	Det	150	581	88	188	36	20	4	108	.324
1909	Det	156	573	116	216	33	10	9	107	.377
1910	Det	140	509	106	196	36	13	8	91	.385
1911	Det	146	591	147	248	47	24	8	144	.420
1912	Det	140	553	119	227	30	23	7	90	.410
1913	Det	122	428	70	167	18	16	4	67	.390
1914	Det	97	345	69	127	22	11	2	57	.368
1915	Det	156	563	144	208	31	13	3	99	.369
1916	Det	145	542	113	201	31	10	5	68	.371
1917	Det	152	588	107	225	44	23	7	102	.383
1918	Det	111	421	83	161	19	14	3	64	.382
1919	Det	124	497	92	191	36	13	1	70	.384
1920	Det	112	428	86	143	28	8	2	63	.334
1921	Det	128	507	124	197	37	16	12	101	.389
1922	Det	137	526	99	211	42	16	4	99	.401
1923	Det	145	556	103	189	40	7	6	88	.340
1924	Det	155	625	115	211	38	10	4	74	.338
1925	Det	121	415	97	157	31	12	12	102	.378
1926	Det	79	233	48	79	18	5	4	62	.339
1927	Phil (A)	134	490	104	175	32	7	5	93	.357
1928	Phil (A)	95	353	54	114	27	4	1	40	.323
22 years		3034	11429	2245	4191	724	297	118	1961	.367

WORLD SERIES

Year	Team	G	AB	R	H	D	T	HR	RBI	AVE.
1907	Det	5	20	1	4	0	1	0	1	.200
1908	Det	5	19	3	7	1	0	0	4	.368
1909	Det	7	26	3	6	3	0	0	6	.231
3 years		17	65	7	17	4	1	0	11	.262

Gordon Cobbledick

Sportswriter. Elected to Hall of Fame: 1977.

Gordon Cobbledick was on the staff of the *Cleveland Plain Dealer* for parts of six decades. He started as a sportswriter in 1928, served as a war correspondent during World War II, and then served as sports editor from 1947 until his retirement in 1964. He was also a correspondent for *The Sporting News*.

Cobbledick covered the integrating of the American League when Larry Doby joined the Cleveland Indians in 1947, to be joined the next year by Satchel Paige in the Indians' world championship year. In 1954, Cobbledick covered an Indian team led by Doby and others that won 111 games, an American League record until the New York Yankees won 114 games in 1998.

Gordon Stanley Cochrane

Born April 6, 1903, in Bridgewater, Massachusetts; died June 28, 1962, in Lake Forest, Illinois. 5'10", 180 lbs., bats left, throws right. Years in minor leagues: 2; Major League debut: April 14, 1925; Years in Major Leagues: 13. Elected to Hall of Fame: 1947. Nickname: Mickey, given to him by a minor league manager because of his Scotch-Irish background. Also Black Mike — because of his dark hair and complexion.

Mickey Cochrane was one of the best-hitting catchers of all time, but his career was cut short by a near-fatal beaning. He had a lifetime batting average of .320 — the best career mark for any catcher. He was such a good hitter that he usually batted second in the lineup — most unusual for a catcher.

Cochrane led the Philadelphia A's to pennants in 1929, 1930 and 1931 and, as player manager, led the Detroit Tigers to pennants in 1934 and 1935 — five pennants in seven years. Cochrane was a fiery competitor who was playing for Portland in the Pacific Coast League in 1924 when the Philadelphia A's needed a catcher. Portland, struggling financially, wanted $100,000 for Cochrane. Connie Mack bought the whole Portland franchise for $120,000. Cochrane immediately became a team leader who handled pitchers well and hit with authority. With pitchers like Lefty Grove on the mound and Cochrane behind the plate, the A's won pennants in 1929, 1930 and 1931 with Cochrane hitting .331, .357 and .349, respectively.

After the 1933 season, Mack, trying desperately to recover from the Great Depression, sold Cochrane to the Detroit Tigers for $100,000. Cochrane became a player-manager at the age of 31. The Tigers responded by winning pennants in 1934 and 1935. In the 1935 World Series, Cochrane singled and later scored the winning run in the ninth inning for the victorious Tigers. He won the American League's Most Valuable Player Award for two different teams — the A's in 1928 and the Tigers in 1934. On May 25, 1937, Cochrane was batting against the Yankees' Bump Hadley. With a 3 and 1 count, Mickey leaned in, Hadley rared back and fired an inside pitch that Cochrane didn't see until it was too late. The ball hit him in the temple. He was unconscious for 10 days and never batted again. The next year he was replaced as manager. In the at-bat before he was beaned, Cochrane hit a home run. That hit put his average over .300 for the year and put him in an elite class of ballplayers — those who homered in their last official at-bat in the Major Leagues.

Year	Team	G	AB	R	H	D	T	HR	RBI	AVE.
1925	Phil (A)	134	420	69	139	21	5	6	55	.331
1926	Phil	120	370	50	101	8	9	8	47	.273
1927	Phil	126	432	80	146	20	6	12	80	.338
1928	Phil	131	468	92	137	26	12	10	57	.293
1929	Phil	135	514	113	170	37	8	7	95	.331
1930	Phil	130	487	110	174	42	5	10	85	.357
1931	Phil	122	459	87	160	31	6	17	89	.349
1932	Phil	139	518	118	152	35	4	23	112	.293
1933	Phil	130	429	104	138	30	4	15	60	.322
1934	Det	129	437	74	140	32	1	2	76	.320
1935	Det	115	411	93	131	33	3	5	47	.319
1936	Det	44	126	24	34	8	0	2	17	.270
1937	Det	27	98	27	30	10	1	2	12	.306
13 years		1482	5169	1041	1652	333	64	119	832	.320

Transactions: Traded to Detroit Tigers for Johnny Pasek and $100,000.

WORLD SERIES

Year	Team	G	AB	R	H	D	T	HR	RBI	AVE.
1929	Phil (A)	5	15	5	6	1	0	0	0	.400
1930	Phil	6	18	5	4	1	0	2	3	.222
1931	Phil	7	25	2	4	0	0	0	1	.160
1934	Phil	7	28	2	6	1	0	0	1	.214
1935	Phil	6	24	3	7	1	0	0	1	.292
5 years		31	110	17	27	4	0	2	6	.245

Ritter Collett

Sportswriter. Elected to Hall of Fame: 1991.

Ritter Collett worked for the *Dayton Journal-Herald* and *Dayton Daily News* for almost 45 years. He was sports editor for each of those newspapers at different points in his career. His "beat" was the Cincinnati Reds.

At his Hall of Fame induction in 1992, Collett said he had covered 6 owners, 19 managers and more than 700 players during that time. The Reds made it to the World Series six times. Collett started his career with the *Dayton Journal* in 1946 and was sports editor of the *Dayton Daily News* when he retired in 1991.

Phil Collier

Sportswriter. Elected to Hall of Fame: 1990.

Phil Collier had his first newspaper job at the age of 13 when he worked as a sports statistician for the *Baytown (Texas) Sun*. After military service in World War II and schooling at Texas Christian University, he went to work for the *San Diego Union* in 1953. For the next 40 years, he covered the Dodgers, Angels and Padres. When he was elected to the Hall of Fame in 1990, he was cited for covering more than 6,000 Major League games for the *San Diego Union*. He also wrote for *The Sporting News* and *Sports Illustrated* and served a term as president of the Baseball Writers Association of America.

Edward Trowbridge Collins Sr.

Born May 2, 1887, in Millerton, New York; died March 25, 1951, in Boston, Massachusetts. 5'9", 175 lbs., bats left, throws right. Years in minor leagues: None; Major League debut: September 17, 1906; Years in Major Leagues: 25. Elected to Hall of Fame: 1939. Nickname: Cocky—because of his aggressive style of play and his personality.

Eddie Collins was a terrific ballplayer with a domineering personality and an aggressive style that did not always make him the most popular player—but he had few peers. He played for 25 seasons and sprayed 3,309 hits from a batting style in which he choked up on the bat and slapped the ball to all fields. He had ten seasons in which he hit over .340 and was the pivot man in Connie Mack's "$100,000 infield" that helped the A's win four pennants in five years between 1910 and 1914.

Collins was an outstanding base runner. He stole 67 bases in 1909, 81 in 1910 and 62 in 1912. Collins is one of only three players in baseball history to steal six bases in a game (the others are Otis Nixon and Eric Young), and he did it twice in the same month—on September 11 and 22, 1912. His 743 career stolen bases rank him fourth all-time, behind Rickey Henderson, Lou Brock and Ty Cobb, but in his day, Cobb was his only rival. Collins also stole 14 bases in World Series play, a record later matched by Brock. After the 1914 World Series, in which the A's lost to the Miracle Boston Braves, Collins was sold to the Chicago White Sox. He played on Chicago's 1917 and 1919 pennant winners and endured the Black Sox scandal in which eight of his teammates conspired to throw the 1919 World Series to the Cincinnati Reds. Collins was also an exceptional fielder, leading the league in fielding nine times. He still holds the all-time record for chances accepted at second base.

When his playing days were over, Collins was hired as general manager of the Boston Red Sox, a position he held from 1933 until his death in 1951. He helped build the Red Sox from also-rans to pennant contenders, signing such players as Bobby Doerr and Ted Williams.

Year	Team	G	AB	R	H	D	T	HR	RBI	AVE.
1906	Phil (A)	6	15	2	3	0	0	0	0	.200
1907	Phil	14	20	0	5	0	0	0	2	.250
1908	Phil	102	330	39	90	18	7	1	40	.273
1909	Phil	153	572	104	98	30	10	3	56	.346
1910	Phil	153	583	81	188	16	15	3	81	.322
1911	Phil	132	493	92	180	22	13	3	73	.365
1912	Phil	153	543	137	189	25	11	0	64	.348
1913	Phil	148	534	125	184	23	13	3	73	.345
1914	Phil	152	526	122	181	23	14	2	85	.344
1915	Chi (A)	155	521	118	173	22	10	4	77	.332
1916	Chi	155	545	87	168	14	17	0	52	.308
1917	Chi	156	564	91	163	18	12	0	67	.289
1918	Chi	97	330	51	91	8	2	2	30	.276
1919	Chi	140	518	87	165	19	7	4	80	.319
1920	Chi	153	601	115	222	37	13	3	75	.369
1921	Chi	139	526	79	177	20	10	2	58	.337
1922	Chi	154	598	92	194	20	12	1	69	.324
1923	Chi	145	505	89	182	22	5	5	67	.360
1924	Chi	152	556	108	194	27	7	6	86	.349
1925	Chi	118	425	80	147	26	3	3	80	.346
1926	Chi	106	375	66	129	32	4	1	62	.344
1927	Phil (A)	95	226	50	76	12	1	1	15	.336
1928	Phil	36	33	3	10	3	0	0	7	.303
1929	Phil	9	7	0	0	0	0	0	0	.000
1930	Phil	3	2	1	1	0	0	0	0	.500
25 years		2826	9948	1819	3309	437	186	47	1299	.333

Transactions: Dec. 8, 1914: Sold to Chicago White Sox for $50,000

WORLD SERIES

Year	Team	G	AB	R	H	D	T	HR	RBI	AVE.
1910	Phil (A)	5	21	5	9	4	0	0	3	.429
1911	Phil	6	21	4	6	1	0	0	1	.286
1913	Phil	5	19	5	8	0	2	0	3	.421
1914	Phil	4	14	0	3	0	0	0	1	.214
1917	Chi (A)	6	22	4	9	1	0	0	2	.409
1919	Chi (A)	8	31	2	7	1	0	0	1	.226
6 years		34	128	20	42	7	2	0	11	.328

James Joseph Collins

Born January 16, 1870, in Buffalo, New York; died March 6, 1943, in Buffalo, New York. 5'7", 160 lbs., bats right, throws right. Years in minor leagues: 2; Major League debut: April 18, 1895; Years in Major Leagues: 14. Elected to Hall of Fame: 1945. Nickname: None.

Jimmy Collins was the best third baseman of his day, revolutionizing how the position should be played. Collins started doing things that are considered routine today: barehand pickups, playing off the bag, and moving in or back before the pitch. He got his big break because of some fielding flukes in a game between his Louisville club and the Baltimore Orioles in 1895. The Orioles, with such speedsters as Wee Willie Keeler, laid down seven consecutive bunts that were mishandled by Louisville third baseman Walter Preston. Louisville's manager, John McGraw (later to be a Hall of Fame Major League manager) brought in his center fielder — Collins — to try his hand at third base. He remained there the rest of his career. In reliving that first game several years later, Collins said that after he made the switch to third base, the next four Oriole batters all bunted, and he threw them all out. In 1900, he handled 600 putouts and assists, which is still a record.

Collins was good hitter, too, and led the National League in home runs in 1897 with 15. He hit over .300 five times and drove in 132 runs in 1897. In the early 1900s he became a player-manager and led his Boston club to the American League championship in 1903. When his Boston team beat the Pirates, five games to three, Collins became the first manager to win a World Series.

Year	Team	G	AB	R	H	D	T	HR	RBI	AVE.
1895	Bos-Lou (N)	107	411	75	112	20	5	7	57	.273
1896	Bos (N)	84	304	48	90	10	9	1	46	.296
1897	Bos	134	529	103	183	28	13	6	132	.346
1898	Bos	152	597	107	196	35	5	15	111	.328
1899	Bos	151	599	98	166	28	11	5	92	.277
1900	Bos	142	586	104	178	25	5	6	95	.304
1901	Bos (A)	138	564	108	187	42	16	6	94	.332
1902	Bos	108	429	71	138	21	10	6	61	.322
1903	Bos	130	540	88	160	33	17	5	72	.296
1904	Bos	156	631	85	168	33	13	3	67	.271
1905	Bos	131	508	66	140	26	5	4	65	.276
1906	Bos	37	142	17	39	8	4	1	16	.275
1907	Bos-Phil (A)	141	523	51	146	29	1	0	45	.279
1908	Phil	115	433	34	94	14	3	0	30	.217
14 years		**1726**	**6796**	**1055**	**1997**	**352**	**117**	**65**	**983**	**.294**

Transactions: June 7, 1907: Traded to Philadelphia for Jack Knight.

WORLD SERIES

Year	Team	G	AB	R	H	D	T	HR	RBI	AVE.
1903	Bos (A)	8	36	5	9	1	2	0	1	.250

Earle Combs

Born May 14, 1899, in Pebworth, Kentucky; died July 21, 1976, in Richmond, Kentucky. 6', 185 lbs., bats left, throws right. Years in minor leagues: 2; Major League debut: April 16, 1924; Years in Major Leagues: 12. Elected to Hall of Fame: 1970. Nickname: The Kentucky Colonel — a reference to his home state;

and the Waiter—a reference to his ability to get on base and wait for Babe Ruth or Lou Gehrig to drive him in.

Earle Combs was the leadoff hitter on some of the greatest baseball teams of all-time—the Yankee teams that featured Babe Ruth and Lou Gehrig in the heart of the lineup. Combs was a mild-mannered man who did not smoke or drink and did not use profanity. He knew his role and seemed undisturbed that others were getting bigger headlines. In his best years, he averaged 270 hits and walks, getting on base and in scoring position for the Yankee powerhouses.

He scored 100 runs or more from 1925 through 1932. In 1927, when Babe Ruth hit 60 home runs, leadoff man Combs hit .356 with 231 hits and scored 137 runs, many of them on Ruth home runs or in front of Gehrig, who hit 47. In 1931, when Gehrig, the cleanup hitter, set an American League record with 184 RBIs, Combs scored 120 runs. His best run-scoring year, though, was in 1932 when he scored 143. Combs was a versatile hitter who used his speed to get a lot of bunt hits—and a lot of triples. He led the American League three times in triples and had a lifetime batting average of .325. He was also effective in World Series play, hitting .350 in four World Series appearances.

Combs fractured his skull when he crashed into the left field wall in St. Louis in 1934, cutting short his career. He played one more year, then spent some time in the coaching ranks with the Yankees, St. Louis Browns, Boston Red Sox and Philadelphia Phillies. In his native Kentucky, he also served as banking commissioner.

Year	Team	G	AB	R	H	D	T	HR	RBI	AVE.
1924	NY (A)	24	35	10	14	5	0	0	2	.400
1925	NY	150	593	117	203	36	13	3	61	.342
1926	NY	145	606	113	181	31	12	8	56	.299
1927	NY	152	648	137	231	36	23	6	64	.356
1928	NY	149	626	118	194	33	21	7	56	.310
1929	NY	142	586	119	202	33	15	3	65	.345
1930	NY	137	532	129	183	30	22	7	82	.344
1931	NY	138	563	120	179	31	13	5	58	.318
1932	NY	144	591	143	190	32	10	9	65	.321
1933	NY	122	417	86	125	22	16	5	64	.300
1934	NY	63	251	47	80	13	5	2	25	.319
1935	NY	89	298	47	84	7	4	3	35	.282
12 years		1455	5746	1186	1866	309	154	58	633	.325

WORLD SERIES

Year	Team									
1926	NY	7	28	3	10	2	0	0	2	.357
1927	NY	4	16	6	5	0	0	0	2	.313
1928	NY	1	0	0	0	0	0	0	1	.000
1932	NY	4	16	8	6	2	0	1	4	.375
4 years		16	60	17	21	4	0	1	9	.350

Charles Comiskey

Born August 15, 1859, in Chicago, Illinois; died October 26, 1931, in Eagle River, Wisconsin. Years in Major Leagues: 50 (as player, manager and owner). Elected to Hall of Fame: 1939. Nickname: The Old Roman — coined by Hugh Keough, a Chicago sportswriter and believed to be a reference to Comiskey's striking facial features; also, Commy — a derivation of his last name.

Charles Comiskey was a mediocre baseball player but managed four pennant winners at St. Louis before the turn of the century and, as owner of the Chicago White Sox, saw his team win five American League pennants. Comiskey's image has been tarnished by books and movies about the Black Sox Scandal of 1919 in which he is depicted as an ungrateful tightwad whom the players rebelled against when they agreed to fix the World Series. An objective look at Comiskey's career shows that he made many lasting contributions to baseball, including, with Ban Johnson, helping to form the American League. Johnson was the league's first president. Comiskey also established a franchise ownership in the White Sox that stayed in his family for nearly 60 years.

As a player in the 1880s, he is credited with being the first first baseman to play off the bag and have the pitcher cover first on certain plays. While he was known to be a charitable giver, he was equally notorious for underpaying his players. When Eddie Collins signed with the White Sox in 1915, his $15,000 salary was about twice as much as any other White Sox player. When eight of the players conspired with gamblers to throw the 1919 World Series, it was a reaction to Comiskey's stingy dealings with them, but the episode broke his heart. He suspected something was wrong after the White Sox lost the first two games and he urged his old friend Ban Johnson to halt the series. Johnson didn't, and the fix continued. The ballpark in Chicago still bears the name of the man who founded the team.

John Bertrand Conlan

Born December 6, 1899, in Chicago, Illinois; died April 1, 1989, in Scottsdale, Arizona. 5'7", 160 lbs. Years in Major Leagues: 24 (as National League umpire). Elected to Hall of Fame: 1974. Nickname: Jocko — given to him by a Rochester, New York, sportswriter when Conlan played for Rochester in the 1920s. The reason for the nickname is not clear but Conlan said he hoped it was not because people thought of him as a "bench jockey."

Jocko Conlan was a reserve outfielder for the Chicago White Sox in 1935 when Red Ormsby, an American League umpire, was overcome by heat, and had to leave the game, which was being played in St. Louis. Pressed for a replacement, White Sox manager Jimmy Dykes and Browns manager Rogers Hornsby asked Conlan to give it a try, and Jocko agreed.

He did an adequate job — even calling teammate Luke Appling out on a close play at third. He decided to give umpiring a try full-time and spent five years in the minor leagues learning his craft. He umpired in the National League for 24 years and was highly respected for the way he called a game and kept control of it. He also became well known for his polka-dot bow tie, the chest protector he wore outside of his coat, and for his banter with the ballplayers during the course of a game. He umpired in the World Series six times and participated in six All-Star games and four playoffs in which the pennant was at stake.

Thomas H. Connolly

Born December 31, 1870, in Manchester, England; died April 28, 1961, in Natick, Massachusetts. 5'7", 170 lbs. Years in Major Leagues: 56 (33 as umpire; 23 as supervisor of umpires). Elected to Hall of Fame: 1953. Nickname: "Mr."—preceding his last name; not really a nickname but a measure of respect from the ballplayers.

Tom Connolly was born in England, came to America at age 15, and took a liking to the game Americans played — baseball. He became a National League umpire in 1898 but quit in 1900 in a dispute with league management. In 1901, American League president Ban Johnson hired him, a move that started a career of more than 50 years for "Mr. Connolly," as the ballplayers called him with respect.

Connolly preferred to be low-key in his approach and believed that umpires should not be spectacles on the field. He dressed formally, wearing stiff collars and having a tie held in place with a stick pin. He once went ten years without ejecting anyone, but players and managers alike held him in respect for the way he controlled a game and for his knowledge of the rules.

After umpiring for 33 years, he retired and went to work as supervisor of American League umpires for another 23 years. Among his accomplishments:

• He umpired the first American League game: Chicago beat Cleveland 8–2 on April 24, 1901. It is certain that it was the first league game since all others were rained out that day.

• He umpired in the first World Series in 1903.

• He and Bill Klem were the first two umpires elected to the Hall of Fame, both in 1953.

Roger Connor

Born July 1, 1857, in Waterbury, Connecticut; died January 4, 1931, in Waterbury, Connecticut. 6'2", 210 lbs., bats left, throws left. Years in minor leagues: None; Major League debut: May 1, 1880; Years in Major Leagues: 18. Elected to Hall of Fame: 1976. Nickname: Dear Old Roger — attributed to men who found one of his home run balls out in the street and, inexplicably, took up a collection for "dear old Roger."

Roger Connor was the Babe Ruth of 19th century baseball, hitting more home runs than anyone—until Babe Ruth. His 136 home runs were baseball's best until Ruth surpassed that total in 1921. Connor's real specialty was triples. He could run well for a big man and he legged out 233 triples in his career, a mark surpassed only by the likes of Sam Crawford, Ty Cobb, Honus Wagner and Jake Beckley.

Two of Connnor's greatest games occurred on May 9, 1888, when he hit three home runs in a game and on June 1, 1895, when he got six hits in six at-bats in one game. He hit over .300 12 times with a high of .371 in 1885.

An oddity of his career: Though he was the home run leader of his time, he only led the league once, with 13 in 1890. In 1898, he not only played for his hometown Waterbury team—he owned it.

Year	Team	G	AB	R	H	D	T	HR	RBI	AVE.
1880	Tro (N)	83	340	53	113	18	8	3		.332
1881	Tro	85	367	55	107	17	6	2	31	.292
1882	Tro	81	349	65	115	22	18	4	42	.330
1883	NY (N)	98	409	80	146	28	15	1		.357
1884	NY	116	477	98	151	28	4	4		.317
1885	NY	110	455	102	169	23	15	1		.371
1886	NY	118	485	105	172	29	20	7	71	.355
1887	NY	127	471	113	134	26	22	17	104	.285
1888	NY	134	481	98	140	15	17	14	71	.291
1889	NY	131	496	117	157	32	17	13	130	.317
1890	NY (P)	123	484	134	180	25	15	13	103	.372
1891	NY (N)	129	479	112	139	29	13	6	94	.290
1892	Phil (N)	155	564	123	166	37	11	12	73	.294
1893	NY (N)	135	511	111	158	25	8	11	105	.309
1894	NY-StL (N)	121	462	93	146	35	25	8	93	.316
1895	StL	104	402	78	131	29	9	8	77	.326
1896	StL	126	483	71	137	21	9	11	72	.284
1897	StL	22	83	13	19	3	1	1	12	.229
18 years		**1998**	**7798**	**1621**	**2480**	**442**	**233**	**136**	**1077**	**.318**

Stanley Anthony Coveleski

Born July 13, 1890, in Shamokin, Pennsylvania; died March 20, 1984, in South Bend, Indiana. 5'9", 178 lbs., bats right, throws right. Years in minor leagues: 8; Major League debut: September 10, 1912; Years in Major Leagues: 14. Elected to Hall of Fame: 1969. Nickname: None.

Stan Coveleski often made it look easy. The little righthander for the Cleveland Indians and Washington Senators won 20 games or more in five different seasons, four in a row with the Indians and then with the Senators in their pennant winning year of 1925.

Coveleski was a spitball pitcher who didn't throw hard but beat opponents with finesse. It didn't take him long, either. He didn't walk many batters and he had many games in which he threw less than 100 pitches. He said the trick was to get batters to swing at the first pitch. His greatest moments in baseball occurred in the 1920 World Series in which the Indians took on the Dodgers. Coveleski won three games by scores of 3–1, 5–1 and 3–0 for an 0.67 earned run average.

In 1925, Coveleski was 20–5 with the Senators, including 13 straight wins. He finished with 215 career wins, an excellent total considering he got a late start. He was 27 years old when he made his Major League debut. Coveleski's older brother, Harry, also pitched in the Major Leagues.

Year	Team	W-L	ERA	G	IP	H	BB	SO
1912	Phil (A)	2-1	3.43	5	21	18	4	9
1916	Cleve	15-13	3.41	45	232	247	58	76
1917	Cleve	19-14	1.81	45	298.1	202	94	133
1918	Cleve	22-13	1.82	38	311	261	76	87
1919	Cleve	24-12	2.52	43	296	286	60	118
1920	Cleve	24-14	2.49	41	315	284	65	133
1921	Cleve	23-13	3.36	43	315.2	341	84	99
1922	Cleve	17-14	3.32	35	276.2	292	64	98
1923	Cleve	13-14	2.76	33	228	251	42	54
1924	Cleve	15-16	4.04	37	240.1	286	73	58
1925	Wash	20-5	2.84	32	241	230	73	58
1926	Wash	14-11	3.12	36	245.1	272	81	50
1927	Wash	2-1	3.14	5	14.1	13	8	3
1928	NY (A)	5-1	5.74	12	58	72	20	5
14 years		**215-142**	**2.88**	**450**	**3092.2**	**3055**	**802**	**981**

Transactions: Dec. 12, 1924: Traded to Washington Senators for Byron Spence and Carr Smith.

WORLD SERIES

Year	Team	W-L	ERA	G	IP	H	BB	SO
1920	Cleve	3-0	0,67	3	27	15	2	8
1925	Wash	0-2	3.77	2	14.1	16	5	3
2 years		**3-2**	**1.74**	**5**	**41.1**	**31**	**7**	**11**

Samuel Crawford

Born April 18, 1880, in Wahoo, Nebraska; died June 15, 1968, in Hollywood, California. 6', 190 lbs., bats left, throws left. Years in minor leagues: 1; Major League debut: September 10, 1899; Years in Major Leagues: 19; Elected to Hall of Fame: 1957. Nickname: Wahoo Sam—a reference to his birthplace.

Ed Barrow, who managed Babe Ruth in Boston and was his general manager in New York, knew a good hitter when he saw one. And he said Detroit Tiger outfielder Sam Crawford hit a ball harder than anyone he had ever seen in the dead-ball era. While he only hit 97 home runs in his 19-year career, he hit 312 triples, which is still the Major League record, and also hit 457 doubles. He needed 36 more hits to have 3,000—not a milestone in those days—because he could have easily gotten them. Two years after he retired from the Major Leagues, he hit .360 in the Pacific Coast League. Crawford played right field, next to Ty Cobb, and hit behind him in the lineup. The two were not friends on or off the field but contributed to each other's greatness. Cobb crossed the plate 2,245 times in his career and a lot of those were the result of Crawford's bat. Similarly, Crawford drove in 1,525 runs—and many of those were Cobb dashing across the plate.

Barrow called Crawford the Lou Gehrig of his day, referring to his ability to hit the ball. But there is another comparison to Gehrig that fits. Gehrig played much of his career in the shadow of Ruth while Crawford played side by side with Cobb. That may be one of the reasons it took Crawford so long to get into the Hall of Fame, considering his awesome skills. Cobb was elected in 1936, Crawford in 1957. And although the two men barely spoke to each other in their playing days, Cobb campaigned vigorously for Crawford to be in the Hall of Fame. When Wahoo Sam was finally elected, he was living in a beach cabin in California with an outdoor shower and no telephone—the simple life that he preferred.

Year	Team	G	AB	R	H	D	T	HR	RBI	AVE.
1899	Cin	31	127	25	39	2	8	1	20	.307
1900	Cin	101	389	68	104	14	15	7	59	.267
1901	Cin	131	515	91	170	22	16	16	104	.330
1902	Cin	140	555	94	185	16	23	3	78	.333
1903	Det	137	550	88	184	23	25	4	89	.335
1904	Det	150	571	49	143	21	17	2	73	.250
1905	Det	154	575	73	171	40	10	6	75	.297
1906	Det	145	563	65	166	25	16	2	72	.295
1907	Det	144	582	102	188	34	17	4	81	.323
1908	Det	152	591	102	184	33	16	7	80	.311
1909	Det	156	589	83	185	35	14	6	97	.314
1910	Det	154	588	83	170	26	19	5	120	.289
1911	Det	146	574	109	217	36	14	7	115	.378
1912	Det	149	581	81	189	30	21	4	109	.325
1913	Det	153	610	78	183	32	23	9	83	.316
1914	Det	157	582	74	193	22	26	8	104	.314
1915	Det	156	612	81	183	31	19	4	112	.299
1916	Det	100	322	41	92	11	13	0	42	.286
1917	Det	61	104	6	18	4	0	2	12	.173
19 years		2517	9580	1393	2964	457	312	97	1525	.309

WORLD SERIES

Year	Team	G	AB	R	H	D	T	HR	RBI	AVE.
1907	Det	5	21	1	5	1	0	0	2	.238
1908	Det	5	21	2	5	1	0	0	1	.238
1909	Det	7	28	4	7	3	0	1	3	.250
3 years		17	70	7	17	5	0	1	6	.243

Joseph Edward Cronin

Born October 12, 1906, in San Francisco, California; died September 7, 1984, in Osterville, Massachusetts. 6', 187 lbs., bats right, throws right. Years in minor leagues: 3; Major League debut: April 29, 1926; Years in Major Leagues: 20. Elected to Hall of Fame: 1956. Nickname: None.

Joe Cronin is one of four shortstops in baseball history to score 100 runs and drive in 100 runs in the same season—and he did it four times. The only other shortstops to accomplish that feat were Honus Wagner (who did it three times), Nomar Gareiaparra and Alex Rodriguez. Cronin achieved success as a player, manager, general manager and American League president in a career that lasted close to 60 years. He broke in with the Washington Senators in 1928 and two years later was the American League's Most Valuable Player with his .346 batting average and 126 runs batted in.

He was named player-manager of the Senators in 1933, at the age of 26, and under his guidance the Senators won their last pennant. (About a decade later, Lou Boudreau piloted the Indians at age 24, the youngest ever, but was 31 when the Indians won the pennant in 1948.) Cronin married the boss's daughter. The boss was Clark Griffith, who in 1934 had the chance to trade his son-in-law to Boston for one player and $225,000. Reluctantly, Griffith called Cronin to tell him of the possibility. Cronin urged him to make the deal.

Cronin continued his successful career with the Red Sox. In 1943, he set a record when he hit five home runs as a pinch hitter, two of them grand slams. He guided the Red Sox to a pennant in 1946. When he retired as a player, he served as the Red Sox general manager for 11 years, ushering in Major League players such as Carl Yastrzemski. Then Cronin became president of the American League and was its chairman at the time of his death in 1984.

Year	Team	G	AB	R	H	D	T	HR	RBI	AVE.
1926	Pitt	38	83	9	22	2	2	0	11	.265
1927	Pitt	12	22	2	5	1	0	0	3	.227
1928	Wash	63	227	23	55	10	4	0	25	.242
1929	Wash	145	494	72	139	29	8	8	61	.281
1930	Wash	154	587	127	203	41	9	13	126	.346
1931	Wash	156	611	103	187	44	13	12	126	.306

Year	Team	G	AB	R	H	D	T	HR	RBI	AVE.
1932	Wash	143	557	95	177	43	18	6	116	.318
1933	Wash	152	602	89	186	45	11	5	118	.309
1934	Wash	125	504	68	143	30	9	7	101	.284
1935	Bos (A)	144	556	70	164	37	14	9	95	.295
1936	Bos	81	295	36	83	22	4	2	43	.281
1937	Bos	148	570	102	175	40	4	18	110	.307
1938	Bos	143	530	98	172	51	5	17	94	.325
1939	Bos	143	520	97	160	33	3	19	107	.308
1940	Bos	149	548	104	156	35	6	24	111	.285
1941	Bos	143	518	98	161	38	8	16	95	.311
1942	Bos	45	79	7	24	3	0	4	24	.304
1943	Bos	59	77	8	24	4	0	5	29	.312
1944	Bos	76	191	24	46	7	0	5	28	.241
1945	Bos	3	8	1	3	0	0	0	1	.375
20 years		**2124**	**7579**	**1233**	**2285**	**515**	**118**	**170**	**1424**	**.301**

Transactions: Oct. 26, 1934: Traded to Boston for Lyn Lary and $225,000.

WORLD SERIES

Year	Team	G	AB	R	H	D	T	HR	RBI	AVE.
1933	Wash	5	22	1	7	0	0	0	2	.318

William Arthur Cummings

Born October 17, 1848, in Ware, Massachusetts; died May 17, 1924, in Toledo, Ohio. 5'9", 120 lbs. Baseball pioneer. Years in minor leagues: 4; Years in Major Leagues: 2. Elected to Hall of Fame: 1939. Nickname: Candy—19th century slang, meaning "best."

Candy Cummings pitched in the National Association, predecessor to the National League, and in the National League for a total of only two years and had a lifetime record of more losses than wins. He is in the Hall of Fame because he is credited with developing the curveball, an idea that came to him while watching people throw clam shells into the ocean. It is now believed that many pitchers in Cummings' day experimented with a curveball without calling it that, or perhaps without even realizing what they were doing. The difference with Cummings was that Henry Chadwick saw him pitch, and Chadwick was baseball's first historian. He spread the word, and Cummings' reputation took off.

He pitched so much that he hurt his arm, bringing an end to his baseball career. When his pitching days were over, he served as president of the International Association, baseball's first minor league. Then he went home, opened a paint store and operated it until four years before his death. Had Henry Chadwick come across someone else in his travels, perhaps no one would know about Candy Cummings today. But Chadwick did see him, and Cummings is in the Hall of Fame.

Year	Team	W-L	ERA	G	IP	H	BB	SO
1876	Htfd (N)	16-8	1.67	24	216	215	14	26
1877	Cin (N)	5-14	4.34	19	115.2	219	13	11
2 years		21-22	2.78	43	331.2	434	27	37

Hazen Shirley Cuyler

Born August 30, 1899, in Harrisville, Michigan; died February 11, 1950, in Ann Arbor, Michigan. 5'11", 185 lbs., bats right, throws right. Years in minor leagues: 3; Major League debut: September 29, 1921; Years in Major Leagues: 18. Elected to Hall of Fame: 1968. Nickname: KiKi—pronounced like "Cuy-Cuy," a shortening of his last name and that's actually what it was, derived from teammates calling "Cuy ... Cuy" when they wanted him to catch a fly ball.

Kiki Cuyler was "the other outfielder" with the Waner brothers in Pittsburgh for the first few years of his career until a run-in with his manager, Donie Bush, prompted him to be sent to the Chicago Cubs, where he was a star for years. He broke in with the Pirates in 1924 and hit .354. He followed that with .357 in 1925 and his hit parade included 45 doubles, 26 triples and 17 home runs. Ten of his hits that year were consecutive—a record at the time—and he drove in 102 runs while scoring 144.

The Pirates beat the Washington Senators, four games to three, in the 1925 World Series, with Cuyler banging a bases-loaded, eighth-inning double off Walter Johnson to drive in the winning runs. He "slumped" to .321 in 1926 but led the league in runs scored and in stolen bases. In 1927, KiKi was part of the Pittsburgh powerhouse that won the National League pennant. But during the season, manager Bush said he wanted Cuyler to bat second instead of his usual third. Cuyler balked at the idea; the two men exchanged harsh words; and Bush benched his star hitter. Cuyler appeared in only 85 games in 1927, was benched for the entire World Series and was shipped to the Cubs after the World Series. Cuyler hit .360 for the pennant-winning Cubs in 1929.

Cuyler batted over .300 ten times in his career, and four of those times he hit over .350. His lifetime batting average was .321.

Year	Team	G	AB	R	H	D	T	HR	RBI	AVE.
1921	Pitt	1	3	0	0	0	0	0	0	.000
1922	Pitt	1	0	0	0	0	0	0	0	.000
1923	Pitt	11	40	4	10	1	1	0	2	.250
1924	Pitt	117	466	94	165	27	16	9	85	.354
1925	Pitt	153	617	144	220	43	26	17	102	.357
1926	Pitt	157	614	113	197	31	15	8	92	.321
1927	Pitt	85	285	60	88	13	7	3	31	.309
1928	Chi (N)	133	499	92	142	25	9	17	79	.285
1929	Chi	139	509	111	183	29	7	15	102	.360
1930	Chi	156	642	155	228	50	17	13	134	.355

Year	Team	G	AB	R	H	D	T	HR	RBI	AVE.
1931	Chi	154	613	110	202	37	12	9	88	.330
1932	Chi	110	446	58	130	19	9	10	77	.291
1933	Chi	70	262	37	83	13	3	5	35	.317
1934	Chi	142	559	80	189	42	8	6	69	.338
1935	Chi-Cin	107	380	58	98	13	4	6	40	.258
1936	Cin	144	567	96	185	29	11	7	74	.326
1937	Cin	117	406	48	110	12	4	0	32	.271
1938	Brklyn	82	253	45	69	10	8	2	23	.273
18 years		**1879**	**7161**	**1305**	**2299**	**394**	**157**	**127**	**1065**	**.321**

Transactions: Nov. 28, 1927: Traded to Chicago Cubs for Sparky Adams and Pete Scott.

WORLD SERIES

Year	Team	G	AB	R	H	D	T	HR	RBI	AVE.
1925	Pitt	7	26	3	7	3	0	1	6	.269
1929	Chi	5	20	4	6	1	0	0	4	.300
1930	Chi	4	18	2	5	1	1	1	2	.278
3 years		**16**	**64**	**9**	**18**	**5**	**1**	**2**	**12**	**.281**

Raymond Emmett Dandridge Sr.

Born August 13, 1913, in Richmond, Virginia; died February 12, 1994, in Palm Bay, Florida. 5'7", 175 lbs., bats right, throws right. Years in minor leagues (Negro Leagues): 17; Years in Major Leagues: None. Elected to Hall of Fame: 1987. Nickname: Dandy—a takeoff on his last name but also a description of how he played third base.

Ray Dandridge was built like a fireplug, but those who saw him play say he could match Brooks Robinson or anybody else defensively at third base. He began his career in 1933 with the Detroit Stars and went on to play with the Newark Dodgers and Eagles, the New York Cubans and a team in Vera Cruz, Mexico. In 1949, when he was managing the New York Cubans, he got a call from a New York Giant scout, telling him he might have a shot at the Major Leagues if he still wanted it. Dandridge reported to the Minneapolis Millers, the Giants' top farm team, but that's as close as he got to the Majors. The Giants were willing to integrate, but they decided to go with some of their younger players. Thus, Monte Irvin and Willie Mays got their chance and Dandridge, who was in his late 30s, stayed behind where he won the Most Valuable Player Award, playing for the Millers in 1950 at the age of 37.

Dandridge was a good hitter, consistently hitting over .300 and saving some of his best years for the end of his career. But fans got their money's worth watching him field his position. Short, stocky and bowlegged, he didn't look the part that he played—"a third base Houdini" as one writer called him. A joke of his era made reference to his bow legs: A train would have a better chance of going through him than a ground ball.

Dan Daniel

Sportswriter. Elected to Hall of Fame: 1972.

Dan Daniel was a fixture in New York sportswriting for well over half a century and was still writing at the time of his death in 1981 at the age of 91.

He was known for not only his knowledge but his opinions and he gave both freely in his "Ask Daniel" feature column in the *New York World-Telegram* during that newspaper's heyday. He also wrote for many years for both *Baseball Magazine* and *The Sporting News*.

His real name was Daniel Moskowitz. When he didn't get a byline early in his career because he had a Jewish last name, he decided his first name would be all right for a last name, too.

George Stacey Davis

Born August 23, 1870, in Cohoes, New York; died October 17, 1940, in Philadelphia, Pennsylvania. 5'9", 180 lbs., bats both, throws right. Years in minor leagues: Unknown; Major League debut: April 19, 1890; Years in Major Leagues: 20. Elected to Hall of Fame: 1998. Nickname: None.

George Davis was a switch-hitting infielder for several ball clubs in the 1890s and early 1900s. Playing in the heart of the dead-ball era, he hit over .300 for nine seasons in a row with a high of .362 for New York in 1893. In 1897, he hit .358, drove in 134 runs and scored 114. In 1906 he helped the Chicago White Sox to the American League championship and to a World Series victory over the crosstown rival Chicago Cubs. The World Series win was a stunning upset. Frank Chance's Cubs had won 116 games during the regular season. The White Sox were known as the "Hitless Wonders." Davis, with a .277 average, was second highest in a lineup that featured no .280 hitters.

Davis hit .308 in the six-game World Series. Three of his four hits were doubles. He scored four runs and drove in six—three in the final game as the White Sox won the series, four games to two.

When he retired in 1909, his 2,688 hits were the most ever by a switch hitter. His lifetime batting average was .297.

Year	Team	G	AB	R	H	D	T	HR	RBI	AVE.
1890	Cleve (N)	136	526	98	139	22	9	6	73	.264
1891	Cleve	136	570	115	165	35	12	3	89	.289
1892	Cleve	144	597	95	144	27	12	5	82	.241
1893	NY (N)	133	549	112	195	22	27	11	119	.355
1894	NY	122	477	120	168	26	19	8	91	.352
1895	NY	110	430	108	146	36	9	5	101	.340
1896	NY	124	494	98	158	25	12	6	99	.320
1897	NY	130	519	114	183	31	10	10	134	.358

Year	Team	G	AB	R	H	D	T	HR	RBI	AVE.
1898	NY	121	486	80	149	20	5	2	86	.307
1899	NY	108	416	68	140	21	5	1	57	.337
1900	NY	114	426	69	136	20	4	3	61	.319
1901	NY	130	491	69	148	26	7	7	65	.301
1902	Chi (A)	132	485	76	145	27	7	3	93	.299
1903	NY (N)	4	15	2	4	0	0	0	1	.267
1904	Chi (A)	152	563	75	142	27	15	1	69	.252
1905	Chi	157	550	74	153	28	3	1	55	.278
1906	Chi	133	484	63	134	26	6	0	80	.277
1907	Chi	132	466	59	111	16	2	1	52	.238
1908	Chi	128	419	41	91	14	1	0	26	.217
1909	Chi	28	68	5	9	1	0	0	2	.132
20 years		2368	9031	1539	2688	450	165	73	1435	.297

WORLD SERIES

Year	Team	G	AB	R	H	D	T	HR	RBI	AVE.
1906	Chi (A)	3	13	4	4	3	0	0	6	.308

Leon Day

Born October 30, 1916, in Alexandria, Virginia; died in 1995. 5'10", 180 lbs., bats right, throws right. Years in minor leagues (Negro and Mexican leagues): 20; Years in Major Leagues: None. Elected to Hall of Fame: 1995. Nickname: None.

Leon Day was another of the outstanding players in the Negro leagues who never got a chance in the Major Leagues. For 20 years, he was a great pitcher. In 1937, he was 13–0 for the Newark Eagles. Three years later, he was 12–1 while pitching for Venezuela. In 1941, he set a record in a Puerto Rican League game when he struck out 19. The next year, he set a Negro League record when he fanned 18 in a game. Before he pitched in the Puerto Rican League in 1941, Day had quite a year for Newark. He was the opening day pitcher, then played center field for most of the season when the regular center fielder was drafted into the armed services, then played second base when the regular second baseman was injured.

The pitching staff suffered with Day out of the rotation but he was not an easy out with a bat in his hands. He was a consistent .300 hitter throughout his career and was often used as a pinch hitter. He was in the service in 1944 and 1945 but rejoined the Newark club in 1946 and threw a no-hitter on opening day. He went on to lead the league in strikeouts, innings pitched and complete games. Day was elected to the Hall of Fame in 1995 but died a few months before the induction ceremonies.

Jay Hannah Dean

Born January 16, 1911, in Lucas, Arkansas; died July 17, 1974, in Reno, Nevada; 6'3", 203 lbs., bats right, throws right. Years in minor leagues: 3; Major League debut: September 28, 1930; Years in Major Leagues: 12. Elected to Hall of Fame: 1953. Nickname: Dizzy—Reportedly referred to as that "dizzy rookie" by White Sox manager Lena Blackbourne when Dean was beating the White Sox in an exhibition game in 1928 but surely reinforced by Dean's eccentric behavior during his Major League career.

Dizzy Dean is remembered by one generation of fans as one of baseball's zaniest announcers, fracturing the English language but providing constant entertainment from the broadcast booth. An earlier generation remembers him as a brash, arrogant pitcher for the St. Louis Cardinals who lived by a slogan he made up: "It ain't braggin' if you can do it." Dean averaged 24 wins a season for his first five full seasons in the Major Leagues. He was 30–7 in 1934, and no National League pitcher since then has won 30 games. He led the league in strikeouts 4 times and had a 17-strikeout game that was the league record for 31 years.

He suffered a broken toe in the 1937 All-Star Game when he was struck by a line drive off the bat of Cleveland's Earl Averill. He tried to come back too soon from the injury and hurt his arm while altering his pitching delivery. He was never the same after that and was traded to the Chicago Cubs the next year where he finessed his way to a 7–1 record and another World Series appearance. (He won two games for the Cardinals in the 1934 Series and brother Paul also won two.) His effectiveness gradually dwindled and he retired after the 1941 season but was lured out of retirement in 1947 to pitch for the St. Louis Browns in a publicity stunt. Dean never disappointed anyone in a publicity stunt and he didn't on this day, blanking the White Sox over four innings.

He won 150 games in 12 seasons, but 102 of those came in four years, and he had 134 at the age of 26 when he got hurt in the All-Star game. Dean reportedly gave interviews to three sportswriters from three different cities on the same day, and told them different birthdates, different birthplaces and altered several other facts about his life. He explained later: "They all wanted exclusives." Si Johnson, his roommate for a year in St. Louis, talked of how Dean could stay out all night and still pitch a great game the next day. As for his attitude, Johnson said, "He popped off, but he could back it up." He was, to be sure, one of baseball's most colorful characters.

Year	Team	W-L	ERA	G	IP	H	BB	SO
1930	StL (N)	1-0	1.00	1	9	3	3	5
1932	StL	18-15	3.30	46	286	280	102	191
1933	StL	20-18	3.04	48	293	279	64	199
1934	StL	30-7	2.66	50	311.2	288	75	195
1935	StL	28-12	3.11	50	324.1	326	82	182
1936	StL	24-13	3.17	51	315	310	53	195

Year	Team	W–L	ERA	G	IP	H	BB	SO
1937	StL	13-10	2.69	27	197.1	206	33	120
1938	Chi (N)	7-1	1.81	13	74.2	63	8	22
1939	Chi	6-4	3.36	19	96.1	98	17	27
1940	Chi	3-3	5.17	10	54	68	20	18
1941	Chi	0-0	18.00	1	1	3	0	1
1947	StL (A)	0-0	0.00	1	4	3	1	0
12 years		**150-83**	**3.03**	**317**	**1966.1**	**1927**	**458**	**1155**

Transactions: April 16, 1938: Traded to Chicago Cubs for Curt Davis, Clyde Shoun, Tuck Stainback and $185,000.

WORLD SERIES

Year	Team	W–L	ERA	G	IP	H	BB	SO
1934	StL (N)	2-1	1.73	3	26	20	5	17
1938	Chi (A)	0-1	6.48	2	8.1	8	1	2
2 years		**2-2**	**2.88**	**5**	**34.1**	**28**	**6**	**19**

Edward James Delahanty

Born October 31, 1867, in Cleveland, Ohio; died July 2, 1903, in Fort Erie, Ontario; 6'1", 170 lbs., bats right, throws right; Years in minor leagues: 2; Major League debut: 1888; Years in Major Leagues: 16. Elected to Hall of Fame: 1945. Nickname: Big Ed—not so much because of his size but because of his enormous power with a bat in his hand.

Ed Delahanty was one of the most feared sluggers of the 1890s and early 1900s—on and off the field. He was one of five brothers to play Major League baseball, and his accomplishments are outstanding. Delahanty remains the only player in baseball history to lead both leagues in hitting—.408 with Philadelphia in the National League in 1899 and .376 for Washington in the American League in 1902. He got six hits in a game twice: on June 2, 1890, playing for Cleveland when he knocked four singles, a double and a triple; and on June 16, 1894, with Philadelphia, when he had a double and five singles.

Delahanty hit four home runs in a game on July 13, 1896—a game Philadelphia lost, 9–8. He had two seasons in which he hit over .400, and in one of those he finished fourth in the batting race. He is one of only eight players in baseball history to have two .400 seasons. From 1891 to 1895, he played in a Philadelphia outfield with Billy Hamilton and Sam Thompson—baseball's first Hall of Fame outfield. Big Ed once went 9-for-9 in a doubleheader and had 10 straight hits altogether. His career batting average of .346 is fourth best, behind Ty Cobb, Rogers Hornsby and Shoeless Joe Jackson.

Despite his outstanding career, he is probably more famous for the way he died than for anything he did on the playing field. In the summer of 1903, he was suspended by the Washington Senators for drinking. He boarded a train and as it headed up the East Coast, Delahanty began terrorizing passengers with a razor. The conductor put him off the train on the Canadian side of Niagara Falls where he was last seen staggering on the tracks. His body was found a week later.

Year	Team	G	AB	R	H	D	T	HR	RBI	AVE.
1888	Phil-N	74	290	40	66	12	2	1	31	.228
1889	Phil	56	246	37	72	13	3	0	27	.293
1890	Cleve-P	115	517	107	154	26	13	3	64	.298
1891	Phil-N	128	543	92	132	19	9	5	86	.243
1892	Phil	123	477	79	146	30	21	6	91	.306
1893	Phil	132	595	145	219	35	18	19	146	.368
1894	Phil	114	489	147	199	39	18	4	131	.407
1895	Phil	116	480	149	194	49	10	11	106	.404
1896	Phil	123	499	131	198	44	17	13	126	.397
1897	Phil	129	530	109	200	40	15	5	96	.377
1898	Phil	144	548	115	183	36	9	4	92	.344
1899	Phil	146	581	135	238	55	9	9	137	.410
1900	Phil	131	539	82	174	32	10	2	109	.323
1901	Phil	139	542	106	192	38	16	8	108	.354
1902	Wash	123	473	103	178	43	14	10	93	.376
1903	Wash	42	156	22	52	11	1	1	21	.333
16 years		**1835**	**7505**	**1599**	**2597**	**522**	**185**	**101**	**1464**	**.346**

William Malcolm Dickey

Born June 6, 1907, in Bastrop, Louisiana; died November 12, 1993, in Little Rock, Arkansas. 6'1", 185 lbs., bats left, throws right. Years in minor leagues: 6; Major League debut: August 15, 1928; Years in Major Leagues: 17. Elected to Hall of Fame: 1954. Nickname: None

In Bill Dickey's day, the great debate was who was the greatest catcher: Mickey Cochrane or Bill Dickey, a question to which there is no right answer. Dickey was a great ballplayer who had the good fortune of playing on some great teams.

He hit over .300 in 10 of his first 11 seasons in the Majors, including .362 in 1936, still a record for catchers. For 13 straight years, from 1929 to 1941, he caught 100 or more games, still a record, though it was tied by Johnny Bench more than 30 years later.

He was elected to the American League All-Star team 11 times—and All-Stars weren't even picked in the first five years he was a regular. He retired with a lifetime batting average of .313. Dickey went in the service in 1943, missing part of that season as well as the '44 and '45 seasons. He returned in 1946 and, shortly after the season started, was named to replace Joe McCarthy as manager. Dickey didn't do badly—the Yankees were 57–48 under his direction—but he was replaced in the same season by Johnny Neun.

After his playing career was over, Dickey stuck with the Yankees long enough to help groom a catcher as his successor: Yogi Berra. Both wore uniform number 8, but no one else will—the Yankees have retired the number.

Year	Team	G	AB	R	H	D	T	HR	RBI	AVE.
1928	NY (A)	10	15	1	3	1	1	0	2	.200
1929	NY	130	447	60	145	30	6	10	66	.324
1930	NY	109	366	55	124	25	7	5	65	.339
1931	NY	130	477	65	156	17	10	6	78	.327
1932	NY	108	423	66	131	20	4	15	84	.310
1933	NY	130	478	58	152	24	8	14	97	.318
1934	NY	104	395	56	127	24	4	12	72	.322
1935	NY	120	448	54	125	26	6	14	81	.279
1936	NY	112	423	99	153	26	8	22	107	.362
1937	NY	140	530	87	176	35	2	29	133	.332
1938	NY	132	454	84	142	27	4	27	115	.313
1939	NY	128	480	98	145	23	3	24	105	.302
1940	NY	106	372	45	92	11	1	9	54	.247
1941	NY	109	348	35	99	15	5	7	71	.284
1942	NY	82	268	28	79	13	1	2	38	.295
1943	NY	85	242	29	85	18	2	4	33	.351
1946	NY	54	134	10	35	8	0	2	10	.261
17 years		1789	6300	930	1969	343	72	202	1210	.313

WORLD SERIES

Year	Team	G	AB	R	H	D	T	HR	RBI	AVE.
1932	NY (A)	4	16	2	7	0	0	0	4	.438
1936	NY	6	25	5	3	0	0	1	5	.120
1937	NY	5	19	3	4	0	1	0	3	.211
1938	NY	4	15	2	6	0	0	1	2	.400
1939	NY	4	15	2	4	0	0	2	5	.267
1941	NY	5	18	3	3	1	0	0	1	.167
1942	NY	5	19	1	5	0	0	0	0	.263
1943	NY	5	18	1	5	0	0	1	4	.278
8 years		38	145	19	37	1	1	5	24	.255

Martin Dihigo

Born May 25, 1906, in Matanzas, Cuba; died May 20, 1971, in Cienfuegos, Cuba. 6'3", 220 lbs., bats both, throws right. Years in minor leagues (Negro League, Cuban League, Mexican League): 23; Years in Major Leagues: None. Elected to Hall of Fame: 1977. Nickname: El Maestro—the maestro, because of his leadership skills as both a player and a manager.

Martin Dihigo is the only man in baseball history to be elected to the Halls of Fame in the United States, Cuba and Mexico. What's more, he probably could have been elected as either a pitcher or a hitter because he was superb at both. He played for 23 years for the Cuban Stars, the Homestead Grays, Baltimore Black Sox, Stars of Cuba, New York Cubans and the Hilldale Giants. He batted .421 and .370 in 1926 and 1927, respectively, for the Cuban Stars, and .386 in 1929 for the

Hilldale Giants. From 1937 to 1944, he played in the Mexican League where he pitched most of the time and had a 119–57 record; he also had a batting average of .317 during that same time period. In 1938, he was 18–2 with an earned run average of 0.90, and he won the batting title with a .387 average. That was how he spent his summers.

In the winters, he played in Cuba for almost his entire career and had a lifetime batting average of .291 and a pitching record of 115–60. Hall of Famer Johnny Mize saw Dihigo play and marveled at his ability and versatility, telling friends he was the greatest player he had ever seen because he could play every position, could run and could hit from either side of the plate. Mize batted behind Dihigo and was humbled when pitchers walked Dihigo to get to him. Dihigo retired after the 1946 season, at the age of 40—one year before young Jackie Robinson broke the color barrier in the Major Leagues, opening the door for black stars of the future to have the opportunity that Dihigo was denied.

Joseph Paul DiMaggio

Born November 25, 1914, in Martinez, California. 6'2", 193 lbs., bats right, throws right. Years in minor leagues: 4; Major League debut: May 3, 1936; Years in Major Leagues: 13. Elected to Hall of Fame: 1955. Nickname: Joltin' Joe—a name writers gave him in 1939 because of his amazing hitting, and popularized in a song titled "Joltin' Joe DiMaggio"; also, the Yankee Clipper—because of his grace on the ballfield; also, Joe D, a shortening of his name.

Joe DiMaggio, the graceful center fielder for the New York Yankees, is rated as one of baseball's greatest players. His 56-game hitting streak in 1941 is one of those records that may never be broken. The closest anyone has come to matching it is Pete Rose with his 44-game streak in 1978—which means Rose would have had to hit safely in each game for about two more weeks to catch DiMaggio. The 56-game hitting streak was snapped in Cleveland on July 17 by pitchers Al Smith and Jim Bagby—and by third baseman Ken Keltner who made two terrific plays. The crowd in Cleveland that night was 67,468—the largest crowd ever to see a night game. The next day, DiMaggio started another streak and this one lasted 17 games. The two streaks combined gave him hits in 73 out of 74 games—three games short of half a season. In 1933, three years before he joined the Yankees, DiMaggio gave a hint of his future stardom when he hit safely in 61 consecutive games for the San Francisco Seals.

Joltin' Joe won the batting championship twice and was a three-time winner of the Most Valuable Player Award, including 1941 when he beat out Ted Williams for the honor, even though Williams hit .406. DiMaggio had a lifetime batting average of .325, and he averaged 118 RBIs per year in his 13-year career. In four different seasons, he averaged better than one RBI per game. For his career, he averaged an RBI every 1.13 games. He led the American League in home runs twice. DiMaggio played on Yankee pennant winners and World Series champions in each of his first four years in the Major Leagues and played on ten pennant winners altogether. He was elected to the All-Star team every year he was in the Major Leagues. DiMaggio, who joined the Yankees in 1936, filled part of the void left in the hearts of Yankee fans by the departure of Babe Ruth two years earlier. When DiMaggio retired, he was replaced in center field by Mickey Mantle. His career statistics are awesome, and would have been even better, but DiMaggio lost three years when he was in his prime because of service in the armed forces. When he retired in 1951, Frank Lane, general manager of the Chicago White Sox, said every team in the league would suffer financially with Joltin' Joe's departure. Lane estimated DiMaggio's presence brought an additional 5,000 fans to the ballpark in every city.

He was married for a year to actress Marilyn Monroe. Though it didn't last long, it was a highly publicized romance because of the special popularity of both husband and wife. After her death in 1962, DiMaggio arranged to have roses put at her graveside on a regular basis for 20 years. A job far removed from baseball kept DiMaggio in the limelight. To a generation of fans who never saw him play, DiMaggio became well known as the spokesman for the "Mr. Coffee" coffee maker, a job he held for many years. The Yankee Clipper had two brothers—Dom and Vince—who each played in the Major Leagues.

Year	Team	G	AB	R	H	D	T	HR	RBI	AVE.
1936	NY (A)	138	637	132	206	44	15	29	125	.323
1937	NY	151	621	151	215	35	15	46	167	.346
1938	NY	145	599	129	194	32	13	32	140	.324
1939	NY	120	462	108	176	32	6	30	126	.381
1940	NY	132	508	93	179	28	9	31	133	.352
1941	NY	139	541	122	193	43	11	30	125	.357
1942	NY	154	610	123	186	29	13	21	114	.305
1946	NY	132	503	81	146	20	8	25	95	.290
1947	NY	141	534	97	168	31	10	20	97	.315
1948	NY	153	594	110	190	26	11	39	155	.320
1949	NY	76	272	58	94	14	6	14	67	.346
1950	NY	139	525	114	158	33	10	32	122	.301
1951	NY	116	415	72	109	22	4	12	71	.263
13 years		1736	6821	1390	2214	389	131	361	1537	.325

WORLD SERIES

Year	Team	G	AB	R	H	D	T	HR	RBI	AVE.
1936	NY (A)	6	26	3	9	3	0	0	3	.346
1937	NY	5	22	2	6	0	0	1	4	.273
1938	NY	4	15	4	4	0	0	1	2	.267
1939	NY	4	16	3	5	0	0	1	3	.313
1941	NY	5	19	1	5	0	0	0	1	.263
1942	NY	5	21	3	7	0	0	0	3	.333
1947	NY	7	26	4	6	0	0	2	5	.213
1949	NY	5	18	2	2	0	0	1	2	.111
1950	NY	4	13	2	4	1	0	1	2	.308
1951	NY	6	23	3	6	2	0	1	5	.261
10 years		51	199	27	54	6	0	8	30	.271

Lawrence Eugene Doby

Born December 13, 1923, in Camden, South Carolina; 6'1", 180 lbs., bats left, throws right. Years in minor leagues: 5; Major League debut: July 5, 1948; Years in Major Leagues: 13. Elected to Hall of Fame: 1998. Nickname: None.

Larry Doby was the first black player in the American League, entering Major League baseball three months after Jackie Robinson broke the racial threshold in the National League in 1947. Doby never got the same recognition as Robinson—simply because he was the second and not the first—yet he endured the same kind of pressure and hardships in paving the way for other black players. Ironically, 31 years later, when he was named manager of the Chicago White Sox, he was once again the second black man to become a Major League manager. Another Robinson—Frank Robinson—was first to do it.

Doby had a stellar career with the Cleveland Indians, helping them to two World Series appearances and a World Series championship in 1948, his second full year in the Majors. Doby broke in as a second baseman but was moved to center field where he played the rest of his career. When he made the transition, he was helped by former Cleveland great Tris Speaker. When the Indians won the pennant in 1948, it was their first championship since Speaker's Indians won in 1920. Doby was the first black player to lead the league in home runs, and he did it twice, hitting 32 in both 1952 and 1954. He hit more than 20 home runs eight years in a row and had five seasons with more than 100 RBIs.

He had tremendous power and hit some memorable home runs. He is one of five players to hit a ball out of the old Griffith Stadium in Washington. In 1948, his home run off Johnny Sain of the Braves won a World Series game for the Indians, and his pinch-hit homer in the 1954 All-Star Game provided the winning runs for the American League in an 11–9 slugfest.

Year	Team	G	AB	R	H	D	T	HR	RBI	AVE.
1947	Cleve	29	32	3	5	1	0	0	2	.156
1948	Cleve	121	439	83	132	23	9	14	66	.301
1949	Cleve	147	547	106	153	25	3	24	85	.280
1950	Cleve	142	503	110	164	25	5	25	102	.326
1951	Cleve	134	447	84	132	27	5	20	69	.295
1952	Cleve	140	519	104	143	26	8	32	104	.276
1953	Cleve	149	513	92	135	18	5	29	102	.263
1954	Cleve	153	577	94	157	18	4	32	126	.272
1955	Cleve	131	491	91	143	17	5	26	75	.291
1956	Chi (A)	140	504	89	135	22	3	24	102	.268
1957	Chi	119	416	57	120	27	2	14	79	.288
1958	Cleve	89	247	41	70	10	1	13	45	.283
1959	Det-Chi (A)	39	113	6	26	4	2	0	12	.230
13 years		**1533**	**5348**	**960**	**1515**	**243**	**52**	**253**	**969**	**.283**

Transactions: Oct. 25, 1955: Traded to Chicago for Jim Busby and Chico Carresquel. Dec. 3, 1957: Traded with Jack Harshman, Russ Heman and Jim

Marshall to Baltimore for Tito Francona, Ray Moore and Billy Goodman. April 1, 1958: Traded with Don Ferrarese to Cleveland for Buddy Daley, Dick Williams and Gene Woodling. March 21, 1959: Traded to Detroit for Tito Francona. May 13, 1959: Sold to Chicago for $30,000.

WORLD SERIES

Year	Team	G	AB	R	H	D	T	HR	RBI	AVE.
1948	Cleve	6	22	1	7	1	0	1	2	.318
1954	Cleve	4	16	0	2	0	0	0	0	.125
2 years		**10**	**38**	**1**	**9**	**1**	**0**	**1**	**2**	**.237**

Robert Pershing Doerr

Born April 7, 1918, in Los Angeles, California. 5'11", 175 lbs., bats right, throws right. Years in minor leagues: 3; Major League debut: April 20, 1937; Years in Major Leagues: 14. Elected to Hall of Fame: 1986. Nickname: None.

Bobby Doerr was one of the best second basemen of his generation, and he was signed by someone who knew a good second baseman when he saw one: Eddie Collins. Collins, perhaps baseball's greatest second baseman, was the general manager of the Boston Red Sox when he heard about Doerr. He flew out to San Diego to watch Bobby play in a minor league game and returned to Boston with two players in mind: Doerr and a tall, skinny kid named Ted Williams. He signed them both.

Doerr was a great fielder, but he was no slouch with a bat, either. He had a lifetime batting average of .288 and drove in 100 runs or more six times in his career, with a high of 120 in 1950. In 1944, Doerr hit .325 and won the Most Valuable Player Award. He played in one World Series and nine All-Star games.

Doerr played on great Boston teams of the late 1940s that never quite seemed to have enough pitching to get over the hump. The Red Sox did win a pennant in 1946 but lost to the Cardinals in the World Series. A great clutch hitter, Doerr hit .409 in his only World Series, and twice in his career he got the only hit off Bob Feller or else the great Cleveland pitcher would have had five no-hitters. Doerr was a great fielder, one of the quickest ever on the double-play pivot, and he had good range and a strong arm. In 1948, he accepted 414 chances, going almost three months without an error.

Year	Team	G	AB	R	H	D	T	HR	RBI	AVE.
1937	Bos (A)	55	147	22	33	5	1	2	14	.224
1938	Bos	145	509	70	147	26	7	5	80	.289
1939	Bos	127	525	75	167	28	2	12	73	.318
1940	Bos	151	595	87	173	37	10	22	105	.291
1941	Bos	132	500	74	141	28	4	16	93	.282
1942	Bos	144	545	71	158	35	5	15	102	.290

Year	Team	G	AB	R	H	D	T	HR	RBI	AVE.
1943	Bos	155	604	78	163	32	3	16	75	.270
1944	Bos	125	468	95	152	30	10	15	81	.325
1946	Bos	151	583	95	158	34	9	18	116	.271
1947	Bos	146	561	79	145	23	10	17	95	.258
1948	Bos	140	527	94	150	23	6	27	111	.285
1949	Bos	139	541	91	167	30	9	18	109	.309
1950	Bos	149	586	103	172	29	11	27	120	.294
1951	Bos	106	402	60	116	21	2	13	73	.289
14 years		1865	7093	1094	2042	381	89	223	1247	.288

WORLD SERIES

Year	Team	G	AB	R	H	D	T	HR	RBI	AVE.
1946	Bos	6	22	1	9	1	0	1	3	.409

John Drebinger

Sportswriter. Elected to Hall of Fame: 1973.

John Drebinger was a sportswriter for the *New York Times* for parts of four decades and covered many of baseball's most historic moments. Drebinger was there to report on the 10-run inning of the Philadelphia A's that sunk the Chicago Cubs in the 1929 World Series. He witnessed the first All-Star game in Chicago in 1933, was there for Lou Gehrig's farewell to baseball in 1939, for DiMaggio's hitting streak in 1941, for Bobby Thomson's home run that gave the Giants the pennant in 1951 and for the Brooklyn Dodgers one and only World Series championship in 1955. He had a descriptive style that captured the excitement of the moment and yet conveyed the facts in meticulous detail.

Charles Dryden

Sportswriter. Elected to Hall of Fame: 1965.

Charles Dryden was a sportswriter for the *Chicago Tribune* in early 1900s and was the fourth writer to earn Hall of Fame recognition. Only J.G. Taylor Spink, Ring Lardner and Hugh Fullerton achieved the honor ahead of him.

One of Dryden's claims to fame is coining a phrase that has stood the test of time. Covering a game in New York on July 13, 1906, Dryden watched the White Sox have a big inning largely because of walks and New York errors. The next day, the *Tribune* called the White Sox "The Hitless Wonders"—a name that stuck for the team that went on to win the American League pennant.

Donald Scott Drysdale

Born July 23, 1936, in Van Nuys, California; died July 3, 1993, in Montreal, Canada. 6'6", 208 lbs., bats right, throws right. Years in minor leagues: 2; Major League debut: April 17, 1956; Years in Major Leagues: 14. Elected to Hall of Fame: 1984, Nickname: Big D—because of his size.

Former National League infielder Daryl Spencer tells about playing third base in a game when big Don Drysdale was pitching for the Dodgers. He ran the count to 3-and-0 on Cincinnati's Frank Robinson and then got the signal to intentionally walk him. He did, by whistling the next pitch past Robinson's head. Drysdale never passed up an opportunity to let a batter know who was boss. He hit 154 batters in his career, an average of 1 every 22 innings, which is a Major League record.

Drysdale had an imposing delivery in which he whirled around on the mound and fired the ball sidearmed from such an angle that it looked like it was coming from third base. In 14 seasons with the Brooklyn and Los Angeles Dodgers, Drysdale won 209 games and had a lifetime earned run average of 2.95. He led the National League in strikeouts three times. He won 25 games and the Cy Young Award in 1962, but his most remarkable feat came six years later when he threw six consecutive shutouts on his way to 58 consecutive scoreless innings. Remarkably he only won 14 games that year.

For a decade, Drysdale teamed with lefthander Sandy Koufax to form one of the greatest pitching duos in baseball history. Drysdale could also hit. Twice in his career he hit seven home runs in a season. His ability with a bat allowed him to stay in games when other pitchers would have been lifted for a pinch hitter.

Year	Team	W-L	ERA	G	IP	H	BB	SO
1956	Brklyn	5-5	2.64	25	99	95	31	55
1957	Brklyn	17-9	2.69	34	221	197	61	148
1958	LA	12-13	4.17	44	211.2	214	72	131
1959	LA	17-13	3.46	44	270.2	237	93	242
1960	LA	15-14	2.84	41	269	214	72	246
1961	LA	13-10	3.69	40	244	236	83	182
1962	LA	25-9	2.83	43	314.1	272	78	232
1963	LA	19-17	2.63	42	315.1	287	57	251
1964	LA	18-16	2.18	40	321.1	242	68	237
1965	LA	23-12	2.77	44	308.1	270	66	210
1966	LA	13-16	3.42	40	273.2	279	45	177
1967	LA	13-16	2.74	38	282	269	60	196
1968	LA	14-12	2.15	31	239	201	56	155
1969	LA	5-4	4.43	12	63	71	13	24
14 years		209-166	2.95	518	3432.1	3084	855	2486

WORLD SERIES

Year	Team	W-L	ERA	G	IP	H	BB	SO
1956	Brklyn	0-0	9.00	1	2	2	1	1
1959	LA	1-0	1.29	1	7	11	4	5
1963	LA	1-0	0.00	1	9	3	1	9
1965	LA	1-1	3.86	2	11.2	12	3	15
1966	LA	0-2	4.50	2	10	8	3	6
5 years		3-3	2.95	7	39.2	36	12	36

James Dudley

Broadcaster. Elected to Hall of Fame: 1997.

Jimmy Dudley broadcast Cleveland Indians games over WERE radio from 1948 through 1967. The Indians won the American League pennant and the World Series during Dudley's first year and won another championship in 1954 before going on a long dry spell that did not end until long after Dudley retired.

He began his broadcasting career with WCHV radio in Charlottesville, Virginia, in 1937, and worked at radio stations in Washington, Syracuse, Pittsburgh and Chicago before settling in with the Cleveland station where he stayed until after the 1967 season. He was the voice of the 1969 Seattle Pilots.

Dudley teamed with Jack Graney, Tom Manning, Harry Jones, Ed Edwards, Bob Neal and Herb Score over the years. He was behind the microphone in 1956 when Score, then a pitcher for the Indians, was hit in the eye by a line drive hit by Yankee infielder Gil McDougald. Score pitched for a few years after that but was never the same and eventually moved into the broadcast booth as one of Dudley's partners. Like many announcers, Dudley had a trademark expression—his sign-off to Indian fans all over Ohio: "Lots o' good luck, ya hear?"

Hugh Duffy

Born November 26, 1866, in River Point, Rhode Island; died October 19, 1954, in Allston, Massachusetts. 5'7", 168 lbs., bats right, throws right. Years in minor leagues: 3; Major League debut: 1888; Years in Major Leagues: 17. Elected to Hall of Fame: 1945. Nickname: None.

Hugh Duffy was a little man who packed a wallop. He was so little that his first manager, Cap Anson, reportedly said, "Where's the rest of you?" when he first saw him. As for the wallop, little Hugh hit 18 home runs in one season—an unheard of total back in his day. His .438 batting average in 1894—a statistic he did not know until official league figures were published four months later—is still the all-time record. He finished his 17-year career with a lifetime batting average of .328.

He scouted for the Red Sox for a while after he retired as a player and was the pride of Boston for half a century. The fans loved it when he took the field and hit the ball during batting practice in 1953—at the age of 86.

Hitting wasn't his only strong suit. He was a fleet-footed outfielder who teamed with Hall of Famer Tommy McCarthy to create a great defensive outfield tandem. He also stole 599 bases in his career.

Year	Team	G	AB	R	H	D	T	HR	RBI	AVE.
1888	Chi (N)	71	298	60	84	10	4	7	41	.282
1889	Chi (N)	136	584	144	172	21	7	12	89	.295
1890	Chi (P)	138	596	161	191	36	16	7	82	.320
1891	Bos (A)	127	536	134	180	20	8	8	108	.336
1892	Bos (N)	147	612	125	184	28	12	5	81	.301
1893	Bos	131	560	147	203	23	7	6	118	.363
1894	Bos	125	539	161	237	51	15	18	145	.438
1895	Bos	130	531	110	187	30	6	9	100	.352
1896	Bos	131	527	97	158	16	8	5	112	.300
1897	Bos	134	550	130	187	25	10	11	129	.340
1898	Bos	152	568	97	169	13	3	8	108	.298
1899	Bos	147	588	103	164	29	7	5	102	.279
1900	Bos	55	181	27	55	5	4	2	31	.304
1901	Mil (A)	79	285	40	86	15	9	2	45	.302
1904	Phil (N)	18	46	10	13	1	1	0	5	.283
1905	Phil	15	40	7	12	2	1	0	3	.300
1906	Phil	1	1	0	0	0	0	0	0	.000
17 years		1737	7042	1553	2282	325	118	105	1299	.328

Leo Ernest Durocher

Born July 27, 1905, in West Springfield, Massachusetts; died October 7, 1991, in Palm Springs, California. 5'10", 160 lbs., bats right, throws right. Years in minor leagues: 4; Major League debut: October 2, 1925; Years in Major Leagues 41 (17 as player; 24 as manager). Elected to Hall of Fame: 1994. Nickname: The Lip—because of his argumentative style with umpires, opposing players and managers and league officials.

Leo Durocher was a brash, colorful, competitive player and manager who was always closely associated with his famous line, "Nice guys finish last." As a player, his highest average was .286 and his lifetime batting average was .247. His baseball career spanned a long enough time that he played with Babe Ruth and managed Willie Mays. He gained his Hall of Fame credentials as a manager, winning 2,008 games with the Dodgers, 1939–1946, 1948; Giants, 1949–1955; Cubs, 1966–1972, and Astros, 1972–1973. His win total is seventh best among all managers.

Durocher won pennants with the 1941 Dodgers, 1951 Giants and 1954 Giants, and each had a uniqueness. His Dodger club won 100 games; the '51 Giants were propelled into the World Series on Bobby Thomson's home run against the Dodgers in the third game of a playoff series; and the '54 Giants swept a Cleveland Indian team in the World Series after the Indians had won 111 games in the regular season. Durocher was not always careful about the company he kept. In 1947, Commissioner Happy Chandler suspended him for a year because of his alleged association with gamblers. He returned to manage the Dodgers in 1948 and was fired. The next season he was back again, this time with Brooklyn's biggest rival, the Giants.

Durocher was regarded as someone who did an ordinary job with an ordinary team but was great when his team had a chance to be the champion. One of his prize pupils was Willie Mays, who as a scared rookie in 1951, had a weeks-long horrible slump. Durocher stuck with him, telling him, "You're my center fielder," and Mays reached stardom under Leo's helm.

Durocher also did well with the Cubs. When he took over in 1966, he declared, "This is not an eighth-place team." The Cubs responded by finishing 10th. They gradually improved under Durocher and in 1969 were on their way to a championship until the Mets overtook them in September. Durocher's combative style may have delayed his election to the Hall of Fame, which came in 1994, three years after his death.

As a Manager

Year	Team	Record	Standing
1939	Brklyn	84-69	Third
1940	Brklyn	88-65	Second
1941	Brklyn	100-54	First
1942	Brklyn	104-50	First
1943	Brklyn	81-72	Third
1944	Brklyn	63-91	Seventh
1945	Brklyn	87-67	Third
1946	Brklyn	96-60	Second
1948	Brklyn	37-38	Fifth
1948	NY (N)	41-38	Fifth
1949	NY	73-81	Fifth
1950	NY	86-68	Third
1951	NY	98-59	First
1952	NY	92-62	Second
1953	NY	70-84	Fifth
1954	NY	97-57	First
1955	NY	80-74	Third
1966	Chi (N)	59-103	Tenth
1967	Chi	87-74	Third
1968	Chi	84-78	Third
1969	Chi	92-70	Second
1970	Chi	84-78	Second
1971	Chi	83-79	Third
1972	Chi	46-44	Fourth
1972	Hous	16-15	Second
1973	Hous	82-80	Fourth
24 years		**2008-1710**	

WORLD SERIES

Year	Team	W–L
1941	Brklyn	1–4
1951	NY (N)	2–4
1954	NY	4–0
3 years		**7–8**

Joseph Durso

Sportswriter. Elected to Hall of Fame: 1995.

Joseph Durso made his mark as a sportswriter and columnist for the *New York Times* for three decades in which he covered the rises and falls of the both the Yankees and the Mets many times. He was on the front lines writing about baseball's expansion, labor disputes, and many of its greatest moments.

Bob Elson

Broadcaster. Elected to Hall of Fame: 1979.

Bob Elson was known for his no-nonsense, factual reporting of Chicago sports events for more than 50 years. He was the voice of the Chicago White Sox on WCFL radio and helped groom other great broadcasters such as Hall of Famer Jack Brickhouse.

William Evans

Born February 10, 1884, in Chicago, Illinois; died January 23, 1956, in Miami, Florida. 5'11", 205 lbs. Umpire. Elected to Hall of Fame: 1973.

At age 22, Billy Evans was the youngest man ever to umpire in the Major Leagues. He worked in the days when umpires often were attacked because of their calls. He was involved in a celebrated fight with Ty Cobb when Cobb went after him under the stands in Washington after a game. The Detroit star nearly choked Evans to death. Despite these episodes, Evans developed a rapport with players over the years and eventually earned a reputation for handling games with decisiveness and yet dignity. When he quit umpiring in 1927, he became president of the Southern Association. Later he was general manager of both the Cleveland Indians and the Detroit Tigers and director of the Boston Red Sox farm system.

He had many milestones as an umpire, including being behind the plate when Walter Johnson made his pitching debut; working six no-hitters; and working Babe Ruth's 60th home run game.

John Joseph Evers

Born July 21, 1881, in Troy, New York; died March 28, 1947, in Albany, New York. 5'9", 140 lbs., bats left, throws right. Years in minor leagues: 1; Major League debut: September 1, 1902; Years in Major Leagues: 18. Elected to Hall of Fame: 1946. Nickname: The Crab—at first because of the crab-like way he gripped a bat, but later because of his mean attitude and fiery temper.

Johnny Evers was the middle man in the Chicago Cubs double play combination of Tinker to Evers to Chance, made famous by a Franklin P. Adams poem. Evers was a stickler on rules. Once, he told umpire Hank O'Day he was wrong for not ruling a runner on first base out for not touching second on a hit in which a game-winning run scored. A few weeks later, on September 23, 1908, Fred Merkle was on first for the Giants and failed to touch second when a winning run scored ahead of him on a hit. Evers got the ball, touched second, and O'Day called Merkle out. The game, which ended in a tie, had to be replayed at the end of the season with the pennant at stake. The Cubs won, and Merkle had to live with the "boner" label for the rest of his life. In 1914, Evers was one of the key players in leading the rise of the "Miracle Braves" to the National League pennant and World Series championship over the A's.

Evers managed the Cubs in 1913 and in 1921, and the White Sox in 1924. With the Braves in 1914, he teamed with shortstop Rabbit Marinville to form another outstanding double-play combination. Evers achieved his fame with the Cubs but won the Most Valuable Player Award with the Braves.

Year	Team	G	AB	R	H	D	T	HR	RBI	AVE.
1902	Chi (N)	26	89	7	20	0	0	0	2	.225
1903	Chi	124	464	70	136	27	7	0	52	.293
1904	Chi	152	532	49	141	14	7	0	47	.265
1905	Chi	99	340	44	94	11	2	1	37	.276
1906	Chi	154	533	65	136	17	6	1	51	.255
1907	Chi	151	508	66	127	18	4	2	51	.250
1908	Chi	126	416	83	125	19	6	0	37	.300
1909	Chi	127	463	88	122	19	6	1	24	.263
1910	Chi	125	433	87	114	11	7	0	28	.263
1911	Chi	46	155	29	35	4	3	0	7	.226
1912	Chi	143	478	73	163	23	11	1	63	.341
1913	Chi	135	444	81	126	20	5	3	49	.284
1914	Bos (N)	139	491	81	137	20	3	1	40	.279
1915	Bos	83	278	38	73	4	1	1	22	.263
1916	Bos	71	241	33	52	4	1	0	15	.216
1917	Bos-Phil	80	266	25	57	5	1	1	12	.214
1922	Chi (A)	1	3	0	0	0	0	0	1	.000
1929	Bos (N)	1	0	0	0	0	0	0	0	.000
18 years		**1783**	**6134**	**919**	**1658**	**216**	**70**	**12**	**538**	**.270**

Transactions: February 1914: Traded to Boston for Bill Sweeney and cash. July 12, 1917: Sold to Philadelphia for waiver price.

WORLD SERIES

Year	Team	G	AB	R	H	D	T	HR	RBI	AVE.
1906	Chi (N)	6	20	2	3	1	0	0	1	.150
1907	Chi	5	20	2	7	2	0	0	1	.350
1908	Chi	5	20	5	7	1	0	0	2	.350
1914	Bos (N)	4	16	2	7	0	0	0	2	.438
4 years		19	76	11	24	4	0	0	6	.316

William Ewing

Born October 27, 1859, in Cincinnati, Ohio; died October 20, 1906, in Cincinnati, Ohio. 5'10", 188 lbs., bats right, throws right. Years in minor leagues: 4; Major League debut: September 9, 1880; Years in Major Leagues: 18. Elected to Hall of Fame: 1939. Nickname: Buck—a name bestowed upon him in boyhood for reasons unknown.

Buck Ewing was not only considered the best catcher of the 19th century, but some, including the renowned *Spalding Baseball Guide*, called him the best catcher in baseball's first half-century. In 1919, a publication called the *Reach Guide* listed Ewing as one of the three greatest players of all time, along with Ty Cobb and Honus Wagner.

He is remembered best for his defensive prowess as a catcher, displaying a remarkable ability to throw runners out from his squatting position behind the plate. Modern players such as Johnny Bench could accomplish this but it was unheard of in Ewing's era.

He was an outstanding hitter as well. Ewing hit over .300 in 11 seasons and had a lifetime batting average of .311. He was also versatile, with the ability to play all nine positions, which he did in 1893. He was also a great base stealer, another trait not usually associated with a catcher. After his playing days were over, he was a successful manager with his hometown Cincinnati Red Stockings and the New York Giants.

Year	Team	G	AB	R	H	D	T	HR	RBI	AVE.
1880	Troy (N)	13	45	1	8	1	0	0		.178
1881	Troy	67	272	40	68	14	7	0	25	.250
1882	Troy	74	328	67	89	16	11	2	29	.271
1883	NY (N)	88	376	90	114	11	13	10		.303
1884	NY	94	382	90	106	15	20	3		.277
1885	NY	81	342	81	104	15	12	6		.304
1886	NY	73	275	59	85	11	7	4	31	.309
1887	NY	77	318	83	97	17	13	6	44	.305
1888	NY	103	415	83	127	18	15	6	58	.306
1889	NY	99	407	91	133	23	13	4	87	.327
1890	NY (P)	83	352	98	119	19	15	8	72	.338
1891	NY (N)	14	49	8	17	2	1	0	18	.347

Year	Team	G	AB	R	H	D	T	HR	RBI	AVE.
1892	NY	105	393	58	122	10	15	7	76	.310
1893	Cleve (N)	116	500	117	172	28	15	6	122	.344
1894	Cleve	53	211	32	53	12	4	2	39	.251
1895	Cin (N)	105	434	90	138	24	13	5	94	.318
1896	Cin	69	263	41	73	14	4	1	38	.278
1897	Cin	1	1	0	0	0	0	0	0	.000
18 years		1315	5363	1129	1625	250	178	70	732	.311

Urban Clarence Faber

Born September 6, 1888, in Cascade, Iowa; died September 25, 1976, in Chicago, Illinois. 6'1", 195 lbs., bats both, throws right. Years in minor leagues: 6; Major League debut: April 17, 1914; Years in Major Leagues: 20. Elected to Hall of Fame: 1964. Nickname: Red—for his hair color.

Red Faber, the last of the legal spitball pitchers, pitched 20 years for the Chicago White Sox, who finished in the second division in 15 of those years. Despite the lack of support, Faber managed to win 254 games and had only six losing seasons.

In 1917, he pitched for a good White Sox team, the last team in Chicago to win a World Series. Faber was instrumental in the Series, beating the Giants three times. He had an injured ankle and was unable to pitch in the 1919 World Series, the one in which eight of his teammates conspired with gamblers to lose. In 1921, the White Sox, dismantled by the banning of eight of their players after the Black Sox scandal, finished in seventh place. Faber won 25 games for that team and led the American League with his 2.47 earned run average.

Faber served in the Navy during World War I and missed most of the 1918 season. When he rejoined the White Sox in 1919, he was out of shape and underweight. He won only 11 games. His time in the service, coupled with the downslide of the White Sox after the Black Sox scandal, probably prevented Faber from being a 300-game winner. Another factor: He spent six years in the minor leagues, despite winning 20 games in each of his last two minor league seasons.

Year	Team	W-L	ERA	G	IP	H	BB	SO
1914	Chi (A)	10-9	2.65	40	181.1	154	64	88
1915	Chi	24-14	2.55	50	299.2	264	99	182
1916	Chi	17-9	2.02	35	205.1	167	61	87
1917	Chi	16-13	1.92	41	248	224	85	84
1918	Chi	4-1	1.23	11	80.2	70	23	26
1919	Chi	11-9	3.83	25	162.1	185	45	45
1920	Chi	23-13	2.99	40	319	332	88	108
1921	Chi	25-15	2.47	43	330.2	293	87	124
1922	Chi	21-17	2.80	43	353	334	83	148
1923	Chi	14-11	3.41	32	232.1	233	62	91
1924	Chi	9-11	3.85	21	161.1	173	58	47

Year	Team	W-L	ERA	G	IP	H	BB	SO
1925	Chi	12-11	3.78	34	238	266	59	71
1926	Chi	15-8	3.56	27	184.2	203	57	65
1927	Chi	4-7	4.55	18	110.2	131	41	39
1928	Chi	13-9	3.75	27	201.1	223	68	43
1929	Chi	13-13	3.88	31	234	241	61	68
1930	Chi	8-13	4.21	29	169	188	49	62
1931	Chi	10-14	3.82	44	184	210	57	49
1932	Chi	2-11	3.74	42	106	123	38	26
1933	Chi	3-4	3.44	36	86.1	92	28	18
20 years		**254-212**	**3.15**	**669**	**4087.2**	**4106**	**1213**	**1471**

Charles Feeney

Sportswriter. Elected to Hall of Fame: 1996.

Charley Feeney covered Major League baseball for newspapers in New York and Pittsburgh for 41 years. He was with the *Long Island Star Journal* from 1946 to 1963, covering the Giants' miracle finish in 1951 on Bobby Thomson's playoff home run against the Dodgers, their four-game sweep of the Cleveland Indians in the 1954 World Series and their farewell to the Polo Grounds and New York in 1957 before their move to San Francisco.

He was on the Pittsburgh Pirate beat for the *Pittsburgh Post-Gazette* from 1966 through 1986, covering great players such as Roberto Clemente and Willie Stargell and the fabulous 1979 Pittsburgh team, led by an aging Stargell, that won the World Series.

Robert William Andrew Feller

Born November 3, 1918, in Van Meter, Iowa. 6', 180 lbs., bats right, throws right. Years in minor leagues: None; Major League debut: July 19, 1936; Years in Major Leagues: 18. Elected to Hall of Fame: 1962. Nickname: Rapid Robert—a reference to his fastball; also, The Heater from Van Meter—a reference to his fastball and to his hometown.

Bob Feller said he could remember sitting in a high school classroom and how his answer would be different than those of his classmates when asked: How did you spend your summer vacation? Feller's answer in 1936: I pitched for the Cleveland Indians.

His fastball was the standard from which all other fastballs were measured, and his results were magnificent. At the age of 17, he struck out 15 in his Major League debut against the St. Louis Browns, and later that same year he set the American League record with 17 strikeouts in a game against the Philadelphia A's. When the season was over, he went back to high school. In 1938, he broke his own record when he fanned 18. He led the American League in strikeouts seven times, and in 1946 he struck out 348 batters to establish a new Major League record.

Feller won 266 games in a career cut short by military service that kept him away for three full seasons and part of a fourth. That kept him from winning 300 games and accumulating lifetime strikeout records that would have given future stars like Sandy Koufax, Steve Carlton and Nolan Ryan much harder totals to surpass. Feller tossed three no-hitters in his career, a record in his time, later topped by Koufax and Ryan. But a record nobody has touched: Feller threw 12 one-hitters. One of his no-hitters was on opening day in 1940 against the Chicago White Sox. He lost a heartbreaking 1-0 decision to Johnny Sain of the Boston Braves in the first game of the 1948 World Series. The only run of the game was scored by Phil Masi moments after the Indians were certain Feller had picked him off second base. Feller pitched in one other World Series game in 1948 but did not make an appearance when the Indians returned to the World Series in 1954 and was therefore winless in Series play.

Year	Team	W-L	ERA	G	IP	H	BB	SO
1936	Cleve	5-3	3.34	14	62	52	47	76
1937	Cleve	9-7	3.39	26	148.2	116	106	150
1938	Cleve	17-11	4.08	39	277.2	225	208	240
1939	Cleve	24-9	2.85	39	296.2	227	142	246
1940	Cleve	27-11	2.61	43	320.1	245	118	261
1941	Cleve	25-13	3.15	44	343	284	194	260
1945	Cleve	5-3	2.50	9	72	50	35	59
1946	Cleve	26-15	2.18	48	371.1	277	153	348
1947	Cleve	20-11	2.68	42	299	230	127	196
1948	Cleve	19-15	3.56	44	280.1	255	116	164
1949	Cleve	15-14	3.75	36	211	198	84	108
1950	Cleve	16-11	3.43	35	247	230	103	119
1951	Cleve	22-8	3.50	33	249.2	239	95	111
1952	Cleve	9-13	4.74	30	191.2	219	83	81
1953	Cleve	10-7	3.59	25	175.2	163	60	60
1954	Cleve	13-3	3.09	19	140	127	39	59
1955	Cleve	4-4	3.47	25	83	71	31	25
1956	Cleve	0-4	4.97	19	58	63	23	18
18 years		**266-162**	**3.25**	**570**	**3827**	**3271**	**1764**	**2581**

WORLD SERIES

Year	Team	W-L	ERA	G	IP	H	BB	SO
1948	Cleve	0-2	5.02	2	14.1	10	5	7

Richard Benjamin Ferrell

Born October 12, 1906, in Durham, North Carolina; died July 27, 1995, in Bloomfield, Hills, Michigan. 5'11", 170 lbs., bats right, throws right. Years in minor leagues: 4; Major League debut: April 19, 1929; Years in Major Leagues: 18. Elected to Hall of Fame: 1984. Nickname: None

Rick Ferrell caught more games (1,806) than any other catcher in American League history until Carlton Fisk passed that total 40 years after Ferrell retired. He was an excellent defensive catcher and a good handler of pitchers—and he wasn't bad with the bat, either. Ferrell hit over .300 four times in his 18-year career and had the distinction of catching all nine innings in baseball's first All-Star game in 1933, calling the pitches for Lefty Gomez, Lefty Grove and Alvin Crowder. The American League won, 4–2.

Ferrell caught for the St. Louis Browns, Boston Red Sox and Washington Senators. At Boston and Washington, one of the pitchers he handled was his brother, Wes. When he played against Wes, he hit him pretty well. On April 29, 1931, Wes, pitching for Cleveland, had a no-hitter going against the Browns when Rick hit a groundball to deep short. The shortstop's throw pulled the first baseman off the bag. The official scorer called it an error. Wes always maintained, even years later, that his brother should have been given a hit—quite a concession since the error preserved Wes's no-hitter.

At Washington, Ferrell caught four knuckleball pitchers—and had a record 21 passed balls in one season. Prior to his baseball career, Ferrell was a professional fighter who won 17 of 18 fights.

Year	Team	G	AB	R	H	D	T	HR	RBI	AVE.
1929	StL (A)	64	144	21	33	6	1	0	20	.229
1930	StL	101	314	43	84	18	4	1	41	.268
1931	StL	117	386	47	118	30	4	3	57	.306
1932	StL	126	438	67	138	30	5	2	65	.315
1933	StL-Bos	140	493	58	143	21	4	4	77	.290
1934	Bos (A)	132	437	50	130	29	4	1	48	.297
1935	Bos	133	458	54	138	34	4	3	61	.301
1936	Bos	121	410	59	128	27	5	8	55	.312
1937	Bos-Wash	104	344	39	84	8	0	2	36	.244
1938	Wash	135	411	55	120	24	5	1	58	.292
1939	Wash	87	274	32	77	13	1	0	31	.281
1940	Wash	103	326	35	89	18	2	0	28	.273
1941	Wash-StL	121	387	38	99	19	3	2	36	.256
1942	StL (A)	99	273	20	61	6	1	0	26	.223
1943	StL	74	209	12	50	7	0	0	20	.239
1944	Wash	99	339	14	94	11	1	0	25	.277
1945	Wash	91	286	33	76	12	1	1	38	.266
1947	Wash	37	99	10	30	11	0	0	12	.303
18 years		1884	6028	687	1692	324	45	28	734	.281

Transactions: May 9, 1933: Traded with Lloyd Brown to Boston for Merv Shea and cash. June 11, 1937: Traded with Wes Ferrell and Mel Almada to Washington for Ben Chapman and Bobo Newsom. May 15, 1941: Traded to St. Louis for Vern Kennedy. March 1, 1944: Traded to Washington for Tony Guliani and cash. Guliani announced his retirement; Gene Moore was then sent to St. Louis to complete the deal.

Roland Glen Fingers

Born August 25, 1946, in Steubenville, Ohio. 6'4", 190 lbs., bats right, throws right. Years in minor leagues: 4; Major League debut: September 15, 1968; Years in Major Leagues: 17. Elected to Hall of Fame: 1992. Nickname: Rollie—a shortened version of his first name.

Rollie Fingers was the best relief pitcher in baseball at a time when the relief pitcher's role was becoming a more important factor than ever before. In baseball's early history, starting pitchers were expected to try to go all the way, with relief pitchers being called on to protect a lead, preserve a tie or to keep the game close. For almost the first 100 years of baseball, "saves" weren't even a part of the record keeping. Fingers played in an era when relief pitching became not just a specialty but a necessity. Complete games by starters became the exception rather than the rule as ball clubs developed "short relievers" who sometimes only pitched to a batter or two to "save" the game for the starter. And Rollie Fingers was the best.

His handlebar moustache was his trademark, and closing important games was his legacy. He set a Major League record with his 341 career saves, since surpassed by Lee Smith. He was a major factor in the five division titles won by the Oakland A's and their World Series championship teams of 1972–74. As the A's dominated the World Series he had a hand in eight victories as he won two and saved six. Altogether he was in 16 World Series games for the A's.

Fingers pitched four years for the San Diego Padres and led the National League twice in saves. He became the first relief pitcher to win the Most Valuable Player award and the Cy Young Award—and he did it in the same year, 1981, with the Milwaukee Brewers. The Brewers won the American League championship in 1982 but Fingers missed the World Series because of an arm injury, and Milwaukee lost the series in seven games to the Cardinals. The injury also kept him out of the entire 1983 season.

Year	Team	W-L	ERA	G	IP	H	BB	SO	SAVES
1968	Oak	0-0	27.00	1	1.1	4	1	0	0
1969	Oak	6-7	3.71	60	119	116	41	61	12
1970	Oak	7-9	3.65	45	148	137	48	79	2
1971	Oak	4-6	3.00	48	129	94	30	98	17
1972	Oak	11-9	2.51	65	111.1	85	32	113	21
1973	Oak	7-8	1.92	62	126.2	107	39	110	22
1974	Oak	9-5	2.65	76	119	104	29	95	18
1975	Oak	10-6	2.98	75	126.2	107	39	110	24

Year	Team	W-L	ERA	G	IP	H	BB	SO	SAVES
1976	Oak	13-11	2.47	70	135	118	40	113	20
1977	SD	8-9	3.00	78	132	123	36	113	35
1978	SD	6-13	2.52	67	107	84	29	72	37
1979	SD	9-9	4.50	54	84	91	37	65	13
1980	SD	11-9	2.80	66	103	101	32	69	23
1981	Mil	6-3	1.04	47	78	55	13	61	28
1982	Mil	5-6	2.60	50	79.2	63	20	71	29
1984	Mil	1-2	1.96	33	46	38	13	40	23
1985	Mil	1-6	5.07	47	55	59	19	24	17
17 years		**114-118**	**2.90**	**944**	**1701**	**1474**	**492**	**1299**	**341**

Transactions: Dec. 14, 1976: Signed as free agent with San Diego. Dec. 8, 1980: Traded with Bob Shirley, Gene Tenace and Bob Geren to St. Louis for Terry Kennedy, Steve Swisher, Mike Phillips, John Littlefield, John Urrea, Kim Seaman and Alan Olmstead. Dec. 12, 1980: Traded with Pete Vuckovich and Ted Simmons to Milwaukee for Sixto Lescano, David Green, Larry Sorensen and Dave LaPoint.

DIVISIONAL PLAYOFF SERIES

Year	Team	W-L	ERA	G	IP	H	BB	SO	SAVES
1981	Mil	1-0	3.86	3	4.2	7	1	5	1

LEAGUE CHAMPIONSHIP SERIES

Year	Team	W-L	ERA	G	IP	H	BB	SO	SAVES
1971	Oak	0-0	7.71	2	2.1	2	1	2	0
1972	Oak	1-0	1.69	3	5.1	4	1	3	0
1973	Oak	0-1	1.93	3	4.2	4	2	4	1
1974	Oak	0-0	3.00	2	3	3	1	3	1
1975	Oak	0-1	6.75	1	4	5	1	3	0
5 years		**1-2**	**3.72**	**11**	**19.1**	**18**	**6**	**15**	**2**

WORLD SERIES

Year	Team	W-L	ERA	G	IP	H	BB	SO	SAVES
1972	Oak	1-1	1.74	6	10.1	4	4	11	2
1973	Oak	0-1	0.66	6	13.2	13	4	8	2
1974	Oak	1-0	1.93	4	9.1	8	2	6	2
3 years		**2-2**	**1.35**	**16**	**33.1**	**25**	**10**	**25**	**6**

Elmer Flick

Born January 11, 1876, in Bedford, Ohio; died January 9, 1971, in Bedford, Ohio. 5'8", 160 lbs., bats left, throws right. Years in minor leagues: 2; Major League debut: May 2, 1898; Years in Major Leagues: 13. Elected to Hall of Fame: 1963. Nickname: The Bedford Sheriff—a name given to him by teammates, because of his hometown although the reason for the "sheriff" reference is not known.

Elmer Flick was one of baseball's best hitters at the start of the 20th century. He has the distinction of winning the American League batting title in 1905 with an average of .306 and not winning the National League batting title in 1900 when he hit .378 for the Philadelphia Phillies (Honus Wagner hit .381). He also holds the distinction of being the man Cleveland would not give up when Detroit wanted him—and offered Ty Cobb straight-up in a trade. Flick had good speed, leading the league in triples three years in a row and twice leading the league in stolen bases.

In 1908, he developed a mysterious stomach ailment that caused his weight to drop from 160 to 135. He missed almost the entire season. He tried to come back in 1909 and 1910 but had lost a lot of his strength and speed. At the end of the 1910 season, he retired.

Fifty-three years later, Flick was elected to the Hall of Fame, and upon his induction became its oldest living member. Ironically, considering illness forced such an early retirement, Flick lived longer than players in much better health. He died two days before his 95th birthday in 1971.

Year	Team	G	AB	R	H	D	T	HR	RBI	AVE.
1898	Phil (N)	134	453	84	142	16	14	7	81	.313
1899	Phil	127	485	98	166	22	14	2	98	.342
1900	Phil	138	547	106	207	33	16	11	110	.378
1901	Phil	138	542	112	182	31	17	8	88	.336
1902	Phil-Cleve	121	461	85	137	22	12	2	64	.297
1903	Cleve	142	529	84	158	23	16	2	51	.299
1904	Cleve	150	579	97	177	31	18	6	56	.306
1905	Cleve	131	496	71	152	29	19	4	64	.306
1906	Cleve	157	624	98	194	33	22	1	62	.311
1907	Cleve	147	549	78	166	15	18	3	58	.302
1908	Cleve	9	35	4	8	1	1	0	2	.229
1909	Cleve	66	235	28	60	10	2	0	15	.255
1910	Cleve	24	68	5	18	2	1	1	7	.265
13 years		1484	5603	950	1767	268	170	47	756	.315

Transactions: May 16, 1902: Sold to Cleveland.

Edward Charles Ford

Born October 28, 1928, in New York, New York. 5'10", 181 lbs., bats left, throws left. Years in minor leagues: 4; Major League debut: July 1, 1950; Years in Major Leagues: 16. Elected to Hall of Fame: 1974. Nickname:

*Whitey—because of his light-colored hair; also, Chairman of the Board—
what his catcher, Elston Howard dubbed him because of his dominance on
the mound; also, Slick—which is what his manager Casey Stengel called him
because of his deftness at getting out of jams on and off the field.*

Whitey Ford was the best in his era at winning the big game. He played on
great teams—the New York Yankees of the 1950s and 1960s—and that allowed
him to participate in 11 World Series, where he really showed his stuff.

Ford holds World Series records for most starts, 22; most wins, 10; most
strikeouts, 94; most consecutive scoreless innings, 33⅓; most hits allowed, 134;
most walks, 34; and most losses, 8. Perhaps the most telling statistic is his World
Series earned run average—2.71—against the best in the National League. Ford
came on the scene in the late stages of the 1950 season and compiled a 9–1 record.
He then defeated the Philadelphia Phillies in the fourth and final game of the
World Series. He then spent two years in the military service and returned to
become the premier pitcher in the American League for more than a decade. He
was 18–6 his first year back, then 16–8, 18–7 and 19–6. His win totals fell off the
next few years to 11, 14, 16 and 12, but his winning percentage remained remarkably high.

In 1961, Ford had his best year, winning 25 and, losing only 4. He led the
American League in starts that year with 39 and in innings pitched with 283. It
was also the first year of Casey Stengel's retirement. Stengel conserved Ford's starts,
particularly late in the season. Many thought it was to keep him rested for the
World Series. Others thought Ole Casey was bowing to management's wishes
to not have 20-game winners on the staff—because 20 wins was a magic number
at contract time. Whatever the reason, Ford never won 20 games in his 11 seasons
with Stengel and won 25 and 24 in two of his first three seasons under new
manager Ralph Houk. He won his only Cy Young Award under Houk in 1961.

Year	Team	W-L	ERA	G	IP	H	BB	SO
1950	NY (A)	9-1	2.81	20	112	87	52	59
1953	NY	18-6	3.00	32	207	187	110	110
1954	NY	16-8	2.82	34	210.2	170	101	125
1955	NY	18-7	2.63	39	253.2	188	113	137
1956	NY	19-6	2.47	31	225.2	187	84	141
1957	NY	11-5	2.57	24	129.1	114	53	84
1958	NY	14-7	2.01	30	219.1	174	62	145
1959	NY	16-10	3.04	35	204	194	89	114
1960	NY	12-9	3.08	33	192.2	168	65	85
1961	NY	25-4	3.21	39	283	242	92	209
1962	NY	17-8	2.90	38	257.2	243	69	160
1963	NY	24-7	2.74	38	269.1	240	56	189
1964	NY	17-6	2.13	39	244.2	212	57	172
1965	NY	16-13	3.24	37	244.1	241	50	162
1966	NY	2-5	2.47	22	73	79	24	43
1967	NY	2-4	1.64	7	44	40	9	21
16 years		**236-106**	**2.75**	**498**	**3170.1**	**2766**	**1086**	**1956**

WORLD SERIES

Year	Team	W-L	ERA	G	IP	H	BB	SO
1950	NY (A)	1-0	0.00	1	8.2	7	1	7
1953	NY	0-1	4.50	2	8	9	2	7
1955	NY	2-0	2.12	2	17	13	8	10
1956	NY	1-1	5.25	2	12	14	2	8
1957	NY	1-1	1.13	2	16	11	5	7
1958	NY	0-1	4.11	3	15.1	19	5	16
1960	NY	2-0	0.00	2	18	11	2	8
1961	NY	2-0	0.00	2	14	6	1	7
1962	NY	1-1	4.12	3	19.2	24	4	12
1963	NY	0-2	4.50	2	12	10	3	8
1964	NY	0-1	4.44	1	5.1	8	1	4
11 years		10-8	2.71	22	146	132	34	94

Andrew Foster

Born September 17, 1879, in Calvert, Texas; died December 9, 1930, in Kankakee, Illinois. 6'4", 250 lbs., bats right, throws right. Years in minor leagues: 28 (colored leagues); Years in Major Leagues: None. Elected to Hall of Fame: 1981. Nickname: Rube—bestowed upon him by teammates after he outpitched Rube Waddell and won an exhibition game in 1904.

Rube Foster was a huge man who dominated headlines in the old colored leagues from 1898 to 1926, playing for such teams as the Waco Yellowjackets, Fort Worth Colts, Chicago Union-Giants, Cuban X Giants, Philadelphia Giants, Leland Giants and Chicago American Giants.

In 1904, he beat Rube Waddell of Connie Mack's Philadelphia A's, 5–2, in an exhibition game, earning him the nickname he would carry for the rest of his life. He is also credited with giving Christy Mathewson some tips that turned Matty from a .500 pitcher to one of Major League Baseball's all-time greats. In 1907, he led the Leland Giants to a 110–10 record that included a 46-game winning streak.

Foster excelled in many levels of baseball off the field, which was especially tough for a black man in his day. In 1911, he and a partner bought a ballpark in Chicago from Charles Comiskey and made it the permanent home of the American Giants where he was also the player-manager. Perhaps his greatest legacy is his formation of the Negro National League in 1920. It was the forerunner of the Negro leagues that achieved great success later on. But Foster took ill with a mental ailment and couldn't enjoy what he had started. He died in 1930, never seeing how his idea was to flourish and give black athletes their biggest opportunity for exposure and recognition.

William Foster

Years in minor leagues: 16 (Negro Leagues); Years in Major Leagues: None. Elected to Hall of Fame: 1996. Nickname: Willie—a common derivative of William.

Willie Foster won eight more games in the Negro Leagues than Satchel Paige and was thought to be the best lefthanded pitcher in the leagues. He pitched for 16 years, mostly for the Chicago National Giants, whom he also managed for one year. Foster used a fastball with a lot of zip, a great curveball, a drop pitch and a changeup to baffle opposing hitters. He once pitched a complete game victory in an All-Star game where the opposition included Josh Gibson, Cool Papa Bell and Judy Johnson.

In 1926, he won 26 straight games, including both ends of a doubleheader on the last day of the season to clinch the pennant for Chicago. Then, in the championship series, Foster pitched three complete games, winning two of them—and also relieved in one game. He was 21–3 in 1927.

Foster managed the Chicago team in 1930 and pitched for Kansas City in 1931 before returning to the National Giants. He retired after the 1938 season, nine years before Jackie Robinson broke the color line in Major League Baseball. Foster was the half-brother of Hall of Famer Rube Foster.

Jacob Nelson Fox

Born December 25, 1927, in St. Thomas, Pennsylvania; died December 1, 1975, in Baltimore, Maryland. 5'10", 160 lbs., bats left, throws right. Years in minor leagues: 4; Major League debut: June 8, 1947; Years in Major Leagues: 19. Elected to Hall of Fame: 1997. Nickname: Nellie, Little Nel—both derivatives of his middle name; also, the Mighty Mite, a tribute to his abilities and his size because he looked smaller than his actual height and weight.

Nelson Fox was a sparkplug for the Chicago White Sox in the 1950s whose career statistics are misleading because they don't reflect the role he played on the team. Batting behind speedster Luis Aparicio for many years, Fox often found himself in a position of taking pitches so Aparicio could steal or, after a steal of second, slapping the ball on the ground on the right side to move Aparicio at least to third. So he let good pitches go by and sacrificed himself for the good of the team many times—and still collected 2,663 hits and ended with a lifetime batting average of .288. He choked up on the bat several inches and always had a huge wad of tobacco in his cheek.

In 1959, the Aparicio-Fox one-two tandem was at its finest, and the White Sox won their first American League championship since the Black Sox year of 1919. Fox was the league's Most Valuable Player.

One of the secrets to his success was that, while he never hit with power, he almost always hit. He led the American League in singles seven years in a row, led the league in hits four times, and hardly ever struck out. In a 15-year stretch, the most he ever struck out in a season was 18 times, and his lifetime strikeout to at-bat ratio is the third best in Major League history.

He was a dependable, sure-handed second baseman. For five years, he led all American League second basemen in turning double plays. He was also durable and had a streak of 798 consecutive games played—a record for second basemen at the time—that went from the 1956 season into the 1960 season.

Year	Team	G	AB	R	H	D	T	HR	RBI	AVE.
1947	Phil (A)	7	3	2	0	0	0	0	0	.000
1948	Phil	3	13	0	2	0	0	0	0	.154
1949	Phil	88	247	42	63	6	2	0	21	.255
1950	Chi	130	457	45	113	12	7	0	30	.247
1951	Chi	147	604	93	189	32	12	4	55	.313
1952	Chi	152	648	76	192	25	10	0	39	.296
1953	Chi	154	624	92	178	31	8	3	72	.285
1954	Chi	155	631	111	201	24	8	2	47	.319
1955	Chi	154	636	100	198	28	7	6	59	.311
1956	Chi	154	649	109	192	20	10	4	52	.296
1957	Chi	155	619	110	196	27	8	6	61	.317
1958	Chi	155	623	82	187	21	6	0	49	.300
1959	Chi	156	624	84	191	34	6	2	70	.306
1960	Chi	150	605	85	175	24	10	2	59	.289
1961	Chi	159	606	67	152	11	5	2	51	.251
1962	Chi	157	621	79	166	27	7	2	54	.267
1963	Chi	137	539	54	140	19	0	2	42	.260
1964	Hous	133	442	45	117	12	6	0	28	.265
1965	Hous	21	41	3	11	2	0	0	1	.268
19 years		**2367**	**9232**	**1279**	**2663**	**355**	**112**	**35**	**790**	**.288**

Transactions: Oct. 4, 1949: Traded to Chicago for Joe Tipton. Dec. 10, 1963: Traded to Houston for Jim Golden, Danny Murphy and cash.

WORLD SERIES

Year	Team	G	AB	R	H	D	T	HR	RBI	AVE.
1959	Chi (A)	6	24	4	9	3	0	0	0	.375

James Emory Foxx

Born October 22, 1907, in Sudlersville, Maryland; died July 21, 1967, in Miami, Florida. 5'11", 190 lbs., bats right, throws right. Years in minor leagues: 1; Major League debut: May 1, 1925; Years in Major Leagues: 20. Elected to Hall of Fame: 1951. Nickname: Double X—a reference to the spelling of his last name.

Jimmie Foxx was one of baseball's great power hitters. In 1932 he hit 58 home runs which still ranks as tied for fifth best, behind Mark McGwire (70), Sammy Sosa (66), Roger Maris (61) and Babe Ruth (60). Hank Greenberg in 1938 and McGwire in 1997 also hit 58.

Foxx missed being the best ever by a few inches and a little bad luck. In that 1932 season, he hit five balls off a right field screen in St. Louis and three balls off a left field screen in Cleveland. Neither screen, which extended above the wall, was there when Ruth played. In addition, Foxx hit two home runs that were erased by rainouts. He hit .364 and had 169 RBIs in earning his first Most Valuable Player Award.

He won the MVP Award again the next year when he captured the Triple Crown with 48 home runs, 163 runs batted in and a .356 average. On July 2, 1933, Foxx hit two home runs in the first game of a doubleheader. Then he hit two home runs, a triple and a double in the second game—coming amazingly close to hitting six homers for the day. In 1938, he won his third MVP Award and narrowly missed his second Triple Crown. His .349 batting average and 175 RBIs were both tops, but his 50 home runs were second to Greenberg's 58.

Foxx broke in as a catcher at the age of 17 and got a hit in his first game while pinch hitting for Lefty Grove. The A's already had a pretty good catcher—Mickey Cochrane—so Foxx moved to first base and stayed there the rest of his career. When the A's won the pennant three years in a row, from 1929 through 1931, Double X contributed 100 home runs and 394 RBIs. He finished with 534 career home runs—second only to Babe Ruth for many years. He hit 30 or more home runs 12 years in a row, a Major League record. During that same stretch, from 1929 through 1940, he drove in 100 runs or more each year. A generous man and a big spender in his playing days, he wound up broke. Foxx died in 1967 after choking on a piece of meat in a restaurant in Miami.

Year	Team	G	AB	R	H	D	T	HR	RBI	AVE.
1925	Phil (A)	10	9	2	6	1	0	0	0	.667
1926	Phil	26	32	8	10	2	1	0	5	.313
1927	Phil	61	130	23	42	6	5	3	20	.323
1928	Phil	118	400	85	131	29	10	13	79	.327
1929	Phil	149	517	123	183	23	9	33	118	.354
1930	Phil	153	562	127	188	33	13	37	156	.335
1931	Phil	139	515	93	150	32	10	30	120	.291
1932	Phil	154	585	151	213	33	9	58	169	.361
1933	Phil	149	573	125	204	37	9	48	163	.356
1934	Phil	150	539	120	280	28	6	44	130	.334
1935	Phil	147	535	118	185	33	7	36	115	.346
1936	Bos (A)	155	585	130	198	32	8	41	143	.338
1937	Bos	150	569	111	162	24	6	36	127	.285
1938	Bos	149	565	139	197	33	9	50	175	.349
1939	Bos	124	467	130	168	31	10	35	105	.360
1940	Bos	144	515	106	153	30	4	36	119	.297
1941	Bos	135	487	87	146	27	8	19	105	.300
1942	Bos-Chi (N)	100	305	43	69	12	0	8	33	.226
1944	Chi	15	20	0	1	1	0	0	2	.050
1945	Phil (N)	89	224	30	60	11	1	7	38	.268
20 years		**2317**	**8134**	**1751**	**2646**	**458**	**125**	**534**	**1922**	**.325**

Transactions: Dec. 10, 1935: Traded with Johnny Marcum to Boston for Gordon Rhodes, George Savino and $150,000. June 1, 1942: Sold to Chicago for waiver price.

WORLD SERIES

Year	Team	G	AB	R	H	D	T	HR	RBI	AVE.
1929	Phil (A)	5	20	5	7	1	0	2	5	.350
1930	Phil	6	21	3	7	2	1	1	3	.333
1931	Phil	7	23	3	8	0	0	1	3	.348
3 years		18	64	11	22	3	1	4	11	.344

Ford C. Frick

Born December 19, 1894, in Wawaka, Indiana; died April 8, 1978, in Bronxville, New York. Years in Major Leagues: 31 (National League president and Commissioner). Elected to Hall of Fame: 1970.

Ford Frick was a sportswriter and broadcaster before formally entering baseball front office work. He became the National League's public relations director in 1934, a position he held for less than a year before being named National League president. He served in that capacity for 17 years and then was selected to replace Happy Chandler as commissioner.

When Frick became baseball's top man, the "western" teams were in St. Louis. During his tenure, the Giants and Dodgers moved from New York to California and baseball underwent great geographic changes and expansion, bringing Major League Baseball to Minneapolis–St. Paul, Houston, Milwaukee, Baltimore, Anaheim and Atlanta. Frick is probably best remembered for his "asterisk" decision—ruling in 1961 that if Roger Maris broke Babe Ruth's single season home run record in more than 154 games, it would be noted with a separate entry in the record books. His intention was that both records would be duly noted. But Frick had been a longtime buddy of Ruth's and he was criticized for trying to protect Ruth's record at the expense of Maris.

Ironically, while Frick's name is linked with the asterisk in baseball folklore, he claimed he never suggested the use of an asterisk, that New York sportswriter Dick Young mentioned it in jest. Frick's edict that separate entries for the Ruth and Maris home run records has prevailed. An asterisk has never been used in official record books. As National League president, he stood firmly behind Branch Rickey's decision to bring Jackie Robinson into the Major Leagues and threatened to ban anyone who attempted to interfere with integration of the game. Perhaps his lasting contribution to the game is one of the least known facts about him. When he was president of the National League, city officials in Cooperstown, New York, sought his suggestions on how the city could celebrate the anniversary of its part in the formation of baseball. Frick suggested they start a baseball museum. They agreed, and built the Hall of Fame.

Frank Francis Frisch

Born September 9, 1898, in New York, New York; died March 12, 1973, in Wilmington, Delaware. 5'10", 185 lbs., bats both, throws right. Years in minor leagues: None; Major League debut: June 14, 1919; Years in Major Leagues: 19. Elected to Hall of Fame: 1947. Nickname: The Fordham Flash— because he came directly from Fordham University to the Major Leagues where he was almost immediately successful.

Frankie Frisch was one of the greatest second basemen of all-time. He played 19 years, had 2,880 hits and had a lifetime batting average of .316. As a player-manager for the St. Louis Cardinals, he led the "Gashouse Gang" with Dizzy Dean and company that won the 1934 National League pennant and World Series. He went from Fordham University to the Major Leagues without a stop in between. In 19 years, he played on eight National League champions, including four straight with the Giants between 1921 and 1924. In addition, his team finished in second place six years, giving him 14 of 19 seasons when his club finished either first or second.

In 1927, he was traded by the Giants to the St. Louis Cardinals for Rogers Hornsby in a trade that shocked fans of both teams. Frisch played on Cardinal pennant winners in 1928 and 1930 and in 1931. He was the National League MVP in 1931. His most satisfying year, though, was 1934, when he both played and managed one of baseball's rowdiest, most fun-loving teams: the Cardinals' "Gashouse Gang." Frisch was a great clutch hitter. He homered and singled in baseball's first All-Star game at Comiskey Park in Chicago in 1933. In the 1934 All-Star Game at the Polo Grounds, Frisch was the leadoff hitter for the National League and hit Lefty Grove's first pitch out of the park. In Game 7 of the 1934 World Series against Detroit, Frisch slammed a bases-loaded double to help lead the Cardinals to victory. He held the record for most hits in World Series play until Yogi Berra topped him almost 30 years later.

Frisch holds another distinction from that 1934 World Series. He is the only manager who was ever ordered by the commissioner to remove a player from a game. Commissioner Kenesaw Mountain Landis told Frisch to remove Joe Medwick, the Cardinal left fielder, after Detroit fans pelted him with fruit and other objects. Frisch was an intense ballplayer but he knew how to have fun, too. Once when protesting a call by umpire Beans Reardon, Frisch fell to the ground as if he had fainted. Reardon looked down at him and said, "If you're not dead, you're out of the game." In 1973, he was badly hurt in an automobile accident and died a month later. He was 74.

Year	Team	G	AB	R	H	D	T	HR	RBI	AVE.
1919	NY (N)	54	190	21	43	3	2	2	24	.226
1920	NY	110	440	57	123	10	10	4	77	.280
1921	NY	153	618	121	211	31	17	8	100	.341
1922	NY	132	514	101	168	16	13	5	51	.327
1923	NY	151	641	116	223	32	10	12	111	.348

Year	Team	G	AB	R	H	D	T	HR	RBI	AVE.
1924	NY	145	603	121	198	33	15	7	69	.328
1925	NY	120	502	89	166	26	6	11	48	.331
1926	NY	135	545	75	171	29	4	5	44	.314
1927	StL (N)	153	617	112	208	31	11	10	78	.337
1928	StL	141	547	107	164	29	9	10	86	.300
1929	StL	138	527	93	176	40	12	5	74	.334
1930	StL	133	540	121	187	46	9	10	114	.346
1931	StL	131	518	96	161	24	4	4	82	.311
1932	StL	115	486	59	142	26	2	3	60	.292
1933	StL	147	585	74	177	32	6	4	66	.303
1934	StL	140	550	74	168	30	6	3	75	.305
1935	StL	103	354	52	104	16	2	1	55	.294
1936	StL	93	303	40	83	10	0	1	26	.274
1937	StL	17	32	3	7	2	0	0	4	.219
19 years		**2311**	**9112**	**1532**	**2880**	**466**	**138**	**105**	**1244**	**.316**

Transactions: Dec. 20, 1926: Traded with Jimmy Ring to St. Louis Cardinals for Rogers Hornsby.

World Series

Year	Team	G	AB	R	H	D	T	HR	RBI	AVE.
1921	NY (N)	8	30	5	9	0	1	0	1	.300
1922	NY	5	17	3	8	1	0	0	2	.471
1923	NY	6	25	2	10	0	1	0	1	.400
1924	NY	7	30	1	10	4	1	0	0	.333
1928	StL (N)	4	13	1	3	0	0	0	1	.231
1930	StL	6	27	0	5	2	0	0	0	.208
1931	StL	7	27	2	7	2	0	0	1	.259
1934	StL	7	31	2	6	1	0	0	4	.194
8 years		**50**	**197**	**16**	**58**	**10**	**3**	**0**	**10**	**.294**

Hugh Fullerton

Sportswriter. Elected to Hall of Fame: 1964.

Hugh Fullerton was a highly respected sportswriter for the *Chicago Herald Examiner* who was a central figure in discovering that the Chicago White Sox conspired with gamblers to fix the 1919 World Series.

Fullerton loved baseball and disdained anything that brought a bad name to the game. He heard rumors of a possible fix and discussed the possibilities with his hotel roommate, former great pitcher Christy Mathewson, who had been hired to cover the World Series for the *New York World*. They sat together in the press-box and circled every questionable play on their scorecards. When the series was over, Fullerton took a short vacation, then wrote an article so explosive that Chicago papers refused to print it. Eventually, he sold a watered down version to the *New*

York Evening World. Published on December 15, 1920, it warned of baseball being run by gamblers, with specific reference to the 1919 World Series. Fullerton was scorned by baseball purists, other writers who wouldn't touch the story and by well-respected baseball publications that ridiculed him. But, in the end, he was proven to be right.

James Galvin

Born December 25, 1856, in St. Louis, Missouri; died March 7, 1902, in Pittsburgh, Pennsylvania. 5'8", 190 lbs., bats right, throws right. Nickname: Pud—short for pudding, which is what he made of hitters, opposing players said.

Pud Galvin, baseball's first 300-game winner, was the Walter Johnson of the 19th century. In fact, only Walter Johnson threw more innings than Galvin's 5,959, and only five pitchers in baseball history have won more games than Galvin's 361. He pitched two no-hitters, and one of them followed a one-hitter he threw.

Galvin pitched in an era when clubs had two-man pitching staffs so a lot was expected, and the stocky little righthander with the handlebar moustache and blazing fastball delivered. Pitching for Buffalo in 1884, he stopped Providence's 20-game winning streak with a 2–0 shutout. He won 46 games in both 1883 and 1884, pitching 656 innings in '84. In an 1886 game, he walked three consecutive batters and yet there was never more than one base runner and there was nobody on when the inning ended—because he only faced three batters. How? He picked each base runner off first base.

Though some of his numbers are astonishing, he never got the rave reviews of the men who followed him in the 20th century: Johnson, Cy Young, Grover Cleveland Alexander, Christy Mathewson and others. Galvin was elected to the Hall of Fame in 1965, 73 years after he retired from baseball, and 63 years after his death.

Year	Team	W-L	ERA	G	IP	H	BB	SO
1879	Buff (N)	37-27	2.28	66	593	585	31	136
1880	Buff	20-37	2.21	58	458.2	528	32	128
1881	Buff	29-24	2.37	56	474	546	46	136
1882	Buff	28-23	3.17	52	445.1	476	40	162
1883	Buff	46-29	2.72	76	656.1	676	50	279
1884	Buff	46-22	1.99	72	636.1	566	63	369
1885	Buff-Pitt	16-26	3.99	44	372.1	453	44	120
1886	Pitt (AA)	29-21	2.67	50	434.2	457	75	72
1887	Pitt (N)	28-21	3.21	49	440.2	490	67	76
1888	Pitt	23-25	2.65	50	437.1	446	53	107
1889	Pitt	23-16	4.17	41	341	392	78	77
1890	Pitt (P)	12-13	4.35	26	217	275	49	35
1891	Pitt (N)	14-13	2.88	33	246.1	256	62	46
1892	Pitt-StL (N)	10-13	2.92	24	188	206	54	56
14 years		361-310	2.87	697	5959	6352	744	1799

Joseph Garagiola

Broadcaster. Elected to Hall of Fame: 1991.

Joe Garagiola was a catcher for the St. Louis Cardinals, Pittsburgh Pirates, Chicago Cubs and New York Giants in a nine-year career in which he had a life-time batting average of .257. After his baseball career was over, he made a good living making fun of himself as a ballplayer—but in truth, he had some great moments. He had three hits and two RBIs in a playoff game against the Brook-lyn Dodgers in 1946, helping the Cardinals win. The Cards went on to the World Series against the Red Sox in which Garagiola got six hits, including four in one game.

Garagiola began his broadcasting career in 1955 and published his first book, *Baseball Is a Funny Game*, in 1960, which brought him to national attention. He was a broadcast partner of Harry Caray with the Cardinals from 1955 to 1961, when he joined NBC's broadcast team where he remained through the end of 1988. He replaced Mel Allen on New York Yankee broadcasts in 1965 and continued there for four years until he became host of the popular *Today* television program in 1969 where he stayed until 1973. Garagiola grew up with Yogi Berra. He helped develop the Berra legend for "Yogi-speak" because of the many Berra stories he has told on the air and in speeches over the years.

Henry Louis Gehrig

Born June 19, 1903, in New York, New York; died June 2, 1941, in Riverdale, New York. 6'1", 212 lbs., bats left, throws left. Years in minor leagues: 3; Major League debut: June 1, 1925; Years in Major Leagues: 15. Elected to Hall of Fame: 1939. Nickname: The Iron Horse—the name of a long-running loco-motive, in reference to Gehrig's durability.

Lou Gehrig played in 2,130 games before being struck down by an illness that proved to be fatal. The consecutive games streak remained a record for more than half a century until Cal Ripken, Jr., of the Baltimore Orioles broke it. Gehrig's endurance was phenomenal, but so was his run production, particularly consid-ering he often came up with nobody on base. Consider: In 1927, Babe Ruth set the home run record when he hit 60, driving in 164 runs. But Gehrig won the RBI title that year with 175, an astounding total considering Ruth cleared the bases 60 times ahead of him. In 1931, Gehrig drove in 184 runs, which is still the Amer-ican League record. He drove in more than 150 runs seven times, and had 100 or more RBIs in 13 consecutive seasons. On June 3, 1932, in a game at Philadelphia, Gehrig became the first player in the 20th century to hit four home runs in one game. His 23 career grand slams remains a Major League record.

Gehrig often found himself playing second-fiddle to Ruth, on and off the field. In 1928, Gehrig hit .545 in the World Series; Ruth hit .625. In 1932, he hit a long home run in the World Series at Wrigley Field against the Cubs—just after Ruth hit one where legend has it that he called his shot. In 1927, Gehrig won the Most Valuable Player Award, earning $6,000 a year while Ruth earned $80,000. In 1934, Gehrig won the Triple Crown (one of two in his career) but finished fifth in the MVP voting. He won his second MVP Award in 1936. He finished his career with 1,991 RBIs, third all time behind Ruth and Henry Aaron. Gehrig played with many injuries in keeping his consecutive-game streak alive for 14 years. On May 2, 1939, he removed himself from the lineup before a game in Detroit after struggling in spring training and the first month of the season. Two years and one month later, he died of a rare muscular disease called amyotropic lateral sclerosis. There is still no cure for the ailment which today is often referred to as "Lou Gehrig's Disease."

Year	Team	G	AB	R	H	D	T	HR	RBI	AVE.
1923	NY	13	26	6	11	4	1	1	9	.423
1924	NY	10	12	2	6	1	0	0	5	.500
1925	NY (A)	126	437	73	129	23	10	20	68	.295
1926	NY	155	572	135	179	47	20	16	107	.313
1927	NY	155	584	149	218	52	18	47	175	.373
1928	NY	154	562	139	210	47	13	27	142	.374
1929	NY	154	553	127	166	33	9	35	126	.300
1930	NY	154	581	143	220	42	17	41	174	.379
1931	NY	155	619	163	211	31	15	46	184	.341
1932	NY	156	596	138	208	42	9	34	151	.349
1933	NY	152	593	138	198	41	12	32	139	.334
1934	NY	154	579	128	210	40	6	49	165	.363
1935	NY	149	535	125	176	26	10	30	119	.329
1936	NY	155	579	167	205	37	7	49	152	.354
1937	NY	157	569	138	200	37	9	37	159	.351
1938	NY	157	576	115	170	32	6	29	114	.295
1939	NY	8	28	2	4	0	0	0	1	.143
17 years		2164	8001	1888	2721	535	162	493	1990	.340

WORLD SERIES

Year	Team	G	AB	R	H	D	T	HR	RBI	AVE.
1926	NY (A)	7	23	1	8	2	0	0	3	.348
1927	NY	4	13	2	4	1	2	0	5	.308
1928	NY	4	11	5	6	1	0	4	9	.545
1932	NY	4	17	9	9	1	0	3	8	.529
1936	NY	6	24	5	7	1	0	2	7	.292
1937	NY	5	17	4	5	1	1	1	3	.294
1938	NY	4	14	4	4	0	0	0	0	.286
7 years		34	119	30	43	7	3	10	35	.361

Charles Leonard Gehringer

Born May 11, 1903, in Fowlerville, Michigan; died January 21, 1993, in Bloomfield, Hills, Michigan. 5'11", 180 lbs., bats left, throws right. Years in minor leagues: 1; Major League debut: September 22, 1924; Years in Major Leagues: 19. Elected to Hall of Fame: 1949. Nickname: Mechanical Man— because he seemed to do everything flawlessly, like a machine.

Charlie Gehringer was a quiet, unassuming ballplayer who racked up consistently big numbers but sought no fanfare. Mickey Cochrane, his manager at Detroit, said, "He says 'hello' on opening day, 'good-bye' on closing day—and hits .350 in between."

Gehringer had a stretch in his 19-year career where he hit over .300 in 13 of 14 seasons—and the year he fell below .300, he hit .298. The lefthanded batter sprayed the ball all over the park and occasionally hit a home run. He hit over 40 doubles in seven seasons, including 50 in 1934 and 60 in 1936. He was great at getting on base, walking 1,185 times in his career while striking out only 372 times. He finished his career with 2,839 hits and a lifetime batting average of .320. His ability to get on base paid off in run production. Gehringer scored more than 100 runs in 12 seasons with a high of 144 in 1930. He hit .371 in 1937 and captured the American League's Most Valuable Player Award.

He was a graceful, sure-handed second baseman who led the league in fielding average nine times and in assists seven times at his position. After his retirement from playing, he returned to the Tigers to serve as general manager for two years and served as a club vice president for seven years after that.

Year	Team	G	AB	R	H	D	T	HR	RBI	AVE.
1924	Det	5	13	2	6	0	0	0	1	.462
1925	Det	8	18	3	3	0	0	0	0	.167
1926	Det	123	459	62	127	19	17	1	48	.277
1927	Det	133	508	110	161	29	11	4	61	.317
1928	Det	154	603	108	193	29	16	6	74	.320
1929	Det	155	634	131	215	45	19	13	106	.339
1930	Det	154	610	144	201	47	15	16	98	.330
1931	Det	101	383	67	119	24	5	4	53	.311
1932	Det	152	618	112	184	44	11	19	107	.298
1933	Det	155	628	103	204	42	6	12	105	.325
1934	Det	154	601	134	214	50	7	11	127	.356
1935	Det	150	610	123	201	32	8	19	108	.330
1936	Det	154	641	144	227	60	12	15	116	.354
1937	Det	144	564	133	209	40	1	14	96	.371
1938	Det	152	568	133	174	32	5	20	107	.306
1939	Det	118	406	86	132	29	6	16	86	.325
1940	Det	139	515	108	161	33	3	10	81	.313
1941	Det	127	436	65	96	19	4	3	46	.220
1942	Det	45	45	6	12	0	0	1	7	.267
19 years		**2323**	**8860**	**1774**	**2839**	**574**	**146**	**184**	**1427**	**.320**

WORLD SERIES

Year	Team	G	AB	R	H	D	T	HR	RBI	AVE.
1934	Det	7	29	5	11	1	0	1	2	.379
1935	Det	6	24	4	9	3	0	0	4	.375
1940	Det	6	28	3	6	0	0	0	1	.214
3 years		19	81	12	20	4	0	1	7	.321

Joshua Gibson

Born December 21, 1911, in Buena Vista, Georgia; died January 20, 1947, in Pittsburgh, Pennsylvania. 6'2", 220 lbs., bats right, throws right. Years in minor leagues (Negro Leagues): 17; Years in Major Leagues: None. Elected to Hall of Fame: 1972. Nickname: Boxer—what teammates called him in his early days because they said he caught pop-ups like he was wearing a boxing glove instead of a mitt.

Josh Gibson was the Babe Ruth of the Negro leagues, hitting mammoth home runs—and a lot of them. Teammate Cool Papa Bell claimed that in one season Gibson hit 72 home runs for the Homestead Grays team. He played for the Homestead Grays and Pittsburgh Crawfords from 1930 to 1946. For the Crawfords, he won home run titles in 1932, 1934 and 1936. He played in Central America for a year and then returned to be the home run champion for the Homestead team in 1938 and 1939 and won the batting title in 1940 with a .440 average.

Legend has it that Gibson hit a ball at the Polo Grounds in New York that went out of the park between the upper deck and lower deck and landed on a moving train across the street. He played in Puerto Rico in 1941 and won the batting title and Most Valuable Player Award. Upon returning to the United States, he won home run titles in 1942, 1943 and 1946, plus a batting title in 1943.

Gibson's life was sometimes tragic off the field. His wife died in the childbirth of twins. In the 1940s, he suffered from headaches and depression, and doctors discovered that he had a brain tumor. He died in 1947 at the age of 35, three months before Jackie Robinson became the first black player in the Major Leagues.

Robert Gibson

Born November 9, 1935, in Omaha, Nebraska. 6'1", 193 lbs., bats right, throws right. Years in Major Leagues: 17. Elected to Hall of Fame: 1981. Nickname: Hoot—a reference to a cowboy actor, Edmund Gibson, whose nickname was Hoot.

Bob Gibson was a fiery competitor who was one of the best in an era of great pitchers. His 1968 season was his best: A 22–9 record with an incredible 1.12 earned run average, the lowest earned run average for a starting pitcher in National League history. He had 13 shutouts (five of them in succession) and 268 strikeouts. Gibson won both the Cy Young Award and the Most Valuable Player Award that year. He had five seasons in which he won 20 games or more on his way to 251 Major League wins.

In 1967, he missed a big part of the season after he was struck by a line drive off the bat of Roberto Clemente and broke his leg. He came back at the end of the year and won three games for the Cardinals against Boston in the World Series.

Gibson was 7–2 in World Series play (seven complete games) with a 1.89 earned run average. He struck out 17 Detroit Tigers in the first game of the 1968 World Series, a new strikeout record, and recorded seven consecutive World Series wins as the Cardinals played the Yankees in 1964, the Red Sox in 1967 and the Tigers in 1968. He had 92 strikeouts in 81 innings in World Series play. Gibson was an excellent fielder and a good hitter. In the seventh game of the 1968 World Series, he homered off Boston's Jim Lonborg to help his own cause in a 7–2 victory. Many ballplayers have participated successfully in other sports, but Gibson is the only Hall of Famer to have also played for the Harlem Globetrotters basketball team.

Year	Team	W-L	ERA	G	IP	H	BB	SO
1959	StL	3-5	3.33	13	75.2	77	39	48
1960	StL	3-6	5.61	27	86.2	97	48	69
1961	StL	13-12	3.24	35	211.1	186	119	166
1962	StL	15-13	2.85	32	233.2	174	95	208
1963	StL	18-9	3.39	36	254.2	224	96	204
1964	StL	19-12	3.01	40	287.1	250	86	245
1965	StL	20-12	3.07	38	299	243	103	270
1966	StL	21-12	2.44	35	280.1	210	78	225
1967	StL	13-7	2.98	24	175.1	151	40	147
1968	StL	22-9	1.12	34	304.2	198	62	268
1969	StL	20-13	2.18	35	314	251	95	269
1970	StL	23-7	3.12	34	294	262	88	274
1971	StL	16-13	3.04	31	246	215	76	185
1972	StL	19-11	2.46	34	278	226	88	208
1973	StL	12-10	2.77	25	195	159	57	142
1974	StL	11-13	3.83	33	240	236	104	129
1975	StL	3-10	5.04	22	109	120	62	60
17 years		251-174	2.91	528	3884.2	3279	1336	3117

WORLD SERIES

Year	Team	W-L	ERA	G	IP	H	BB	SO
1964	StL	2-1	3.00	3	27	23	8	31
1967	StL	3-0	1.00	3	27	14	5	26
1968	StL	2-1	1.67	3	27	18	4	35
3 years		7-2	1.89	9	81	55	17	92

Warren Giles

Born May 28, 1896, in Tiskilwa, Illinois; died February 7, 1979, in Cincinnati, Ohio. Years in Major Leagues: 32 years (as club president and league president). Elected to Hall of Fame: 1979.

Warren Giles spent 50 years in professional baseball, as president of the Moline, Illinois, minor league club, general manager of the St. Louis Cardinal farm team in Syracuse, president of the Cincinnati Reds, and president of the National League during an era that is often called the Golden Age of baseball. During his tenure as National League president, the number of black and Latin American ballplayers increased significantly and many—such as Willie Mays, Hank Aaron and Roberto Clemente—became great stars.

He was a young stockholder of the Moline club in the 3-I League when he began making suggestions at a stockholders meeting. Soon, he was told if he knew so much, why didn't he run the club. And they elected him president. He was in his early 20s at the time, and that was the start of a career that lasted more than 50 years.

He took over as president of the Cincinnati Reds in 1937, at a time when the Reds were cellar dwellers. Two years later, the Reds were in the World Series. Giles presided over the National League during its first great periods of expansion and westward movement. The Braves moved from Boston to Milwaukee to Atlanta. The Giants and Dodgers moved to San Francisco and Los Angeles, and franchises were added in Houston, San Diego and New York.

Vernon Louis Gomez

Born November 26, 1910, in Rodeo, California; died February 17, 1989, in Larkspur, California. 6'2", 178 lbs., bats left, throws left. Years in minor leagues: 2; Major League debut: April 29, 1930; Years in Major Leagues: 14. Elected to Hall of Fame: 1972. Nickname: Lefty—a reference to his throwing arm; also Goofy, a reference to his disposition.

Lefty Gomez was a high-kicking, fun-loving pitcher for the New York Yankees at a time when the Yankees dominated the American League. He was well aware of his good fortune. It is said that he taught his children to pray, saying "God bless Mommy, God bless Daddy—and God bless Babe Ruth."

He said the secret to his success was "clean living and a fast outfield." He won 194 games in 14 seasons and had four 20-win seasons, including a 26–5 mark in 1934. He led the American League in strikeouts four times. He won 21 and 24 games in his first two full seasons with the Yankees. He led the league twice in won-loss percentage and twice had the best earned run average.

Gomez was at his best in clutch situations. The Yankees won seven American League pennants with Gomez leading the way. He was 6–0 in World Series play, the best record for any pitcher in the postseason. One thing Gomez couldn't do very well was hit. He and Babe Ruth had a standard bet at the start of each season that Lefty wouldn't get 10 hits during the year. One year, Gomez went 4-for-4 on opening day—and still lost the bet. Ironically, Gomez got a base hit to drive in the American League's first run in the 1933 All-Star game at Comiskey Park in Chicago—the first All-Star Game—to help the American League win, 4–2. Gomez was the winning pitcher.

Year	Team	W-L	ERA	G	IP	H	BB	SO
1930	NY (A)	2-5	5.55	15	60	66	28	22
1931	NY	21-9	2.63	40	243	206	85	150
1932	NY	24-7	4.21	37	265.1	266	105	176
1933	NY	16-10	3.18	35	234.2	218	106	163
1934	NY	26-5	2.33	38	281.2	223	96	158
1935	NY	12-15	3.18	34	246	223	86	138
1936	NY	13-7	4.39	31	188.2	184	122	105
1937	NY	21-11	2.33	34	278.1	233	93	194
1938	NY	18-12	3.35	32	239	239	99	129
1939	NY	12-8	3.41	26	198	173	84	102
1940	NY	3-3	6.59	9	27.1	37	18	14
1941	NY	15-5	3.74	23	156.1	151	103	76
1942	NY	6-4	4.28	13	80	67	65	41
1943	Wash	0-1	5.79	1	4.2	4	5	0
14 years		**189-102**	**3.34**	**368**	**2503**	**2290**	**1095**	**1468**

WORLD SERIES

Year	Team	W-L	ERA	G	IP	H	BB	SO
1932	NY (A)	1-0	1.00	1	9	9	1	8
1936	NY	2-0	4.70	2	15.1	14	11	9
1937	NY	2-0	1.50	2	18	16	2	8
1938	NY	1-0	3.86	1	7	9	1	5
1939	NY	0-0	9.00	1	1	3	0	1
5 years		**6-0**	**2.86**	**7**	**50.1**	**51**	**15**	**31**

Leon Allen Goslin

Born October 16, 1900, in Salem, New Jersey; died May 15, 1971, in Bridgeton, New Jersey. 5'1", 185 lbs., bats left, throws right. Years in minor leagues: 2; Major League debut: September 16, 1921; Years in Major Leagues: 18. Elected to Hall of Fame: 1968. Nickname: Goose—an unflattering reference to his nose, given to him by a Washington sportswriter during his rookie year.

Goose Goslin was the best hitter in the history of the Washington Senators. Statistics show how much he meant to the ball club. The Senators were traditionally a bad team—the doormat of the American League for much of their existence. But when Goslin played for them, they won their only three pennants. He is the only man in baseball history to have played in every World Series game that his team ever played of those players whose teams were in more than one series.

He hit over .300 in his first seven full seasons. His first big year was 1924 when he hit .344 and drove in 129 runs as Washington won its first pennant. In the 1924 World Series—the only one the Senators ever won—Goslin got six straight hits. In 1925, the Senators were in the World Series again, with Goslin hitting .334 and driving in 113 runs. The Washington left fielder continued his dominance of American League pitching with averages of .334 and .354 in 1926 and 1927. In 1928, he won the batting title by .001 over the Browns' Heinie Manusch with a .379 mark. The Senators played the Browns on the last day of the 1928 season and, going into his last at-bat, Goslin had the batting title wrapped up—if he didn't make an out. The first two pitches to him were called strikes, and he argued vehemently on each, trying to get thrown out of the game. His ploy didn't work, and he eventually singled to sew up the title.

Success seemed to follow him wherever he went. Goslin was traded to the lowly St. Louis Browns, who climed to fifth place in 1931. He returned to the Senators in time to help them win their third pennant in 1933. Then he was shipped to Detroit, who hadn't won a championship since 1909. The Tigers were the American League champs in both 1934 and 1935.

In all, Goslin had 11 seasons in which he hit .300 or better and also 11 seasons when he drove in 100 or more runs. Playing in an era dominated by the Yankees with Babe Ruth, Lou Gehrig and company, Goslin played on two teams other than the Yankees that managed to win 5 pennants in 12 years.

Year	Team	G	AB	R	H	D	T	HR	RBI	AVE.
1921	Wash	14	50	8	13	1	1	1	6	.260
1922	Wash	101	358	44	116	19	7	3	53	.324
1923	Wash	150	600	86	180	29	18	9	99	.300
1924	Wash	154	579	100	199	30	17	12	129	.344
1925	Wash	150	601	116	201	34	20	18	113	.334
1926	Wash	147	567	105	201	26	15	17	108	.354
1927	Wash	148	581	96	194	37	15	13	120	.334
1928	Wash	135	456	80	173	36	10	17	102	.379
1929	Wash	145	553	82	159	28	7	18	91	.288
1930	Wash-StL	148	584	115	180	36	12	37	138	.308
1931	StL (A)	151	591	114	194	42	10	24	105	.328
1932	StL	150	572	88	171	28	9	17	104	.299
1933	Wash	132	549	97	163	35	10	10	64	.297
1934	Det	151	614	106	187	38	7	13	100	.305
1935	Det	147	590	88	172	34	6	9	109	.292
1936	Det	147	572	122	180	33	8	24	125	.315
1937	Det	79	181	30	43	11	1	4	35	.238
1938	Wash	38	57	6	9	3	0	2	8	.158
18 years		**2287**	**8655**	**1483**	**2735**	**500**	**173**	**248**	**1609**	**.316**

Transactions: June 13, 1930: Traded to St. Louis for General Crowder and Heinie Manush. Dec. 14, 1932: Traded to Washington with Fred Schulte and Lefty Stewart for Sammy West, Carl Reynolds, Lloyd Brown and $20,000. Dec. 20, 1933: Traded to Detroit for John Stone.

WORLD SERIES

Year	Team	G	AB	R	H	D	T	HR	RBI	AVE.
1924	Wash	7	32	4	11	1	0	3	7	.344
1925	Wash	7	26	6	8	1	0	3	5	.308
1933	Wash	5	20	2	5	1	0	1	1	.250
1934 *	Det	7	29	2	7	1	0	0	2	.241
1935	Det	6	22	2	6	1	0	0	3	.273
5 years		**32**	**129**	**16**	**37**	**5**	**0**	**7**	**18**	**.287**

Curt Gowdy

Broadcaster. Elected to Hall of Fame: 1984.

For two decades, Curt Gowdy was one of the best-known broadcasters in America. He was behind the microphone for the World Series for 12 years, was host of the weekly television program *American Sportsman* for 20 years, and was a broadcaster for Super Bowls, NCAA basketball championships and Olympic games.

Early on, he teamed with Mel Allen on Yankee broadcasts but was best known in baseball circles as the radio voice of the Boston Red Sox from 1951 to 1965. He joined NBC in 1966 and did *Game of the Week* broadcasts as well as every All-Star game and World Series through 1975. During this time period, his was one of the most recognizable voices in America.

Frank Graham

Sportswriter. Elected to Hall of Fame: 1971.

Frank Graham was a longtime New York sportswriter and columnist for several newspapers and was also sportseditor of *Look* magazine. Graham was part of the flamboyant era of sportswriting where colorful language and heavy doses of opinion were a part of the recipe in the sports pages of New York newspapers. Yet his style was crisp, clear and concise.

He was not shy about offering an opinion from time to time. When night baseball was introduced in the Major Leagues, Graham lamented to his readers that baseball had gone the way of wrestling and belly dancing to make a buck. He once described his job as one in which he took the reader to places where a fan's ticket wouldn't admit him.

Henry Benjamin Greenberg

Born January 1, 1911, in New York, New York; died September 4, 1986, in Beverly Hills, California. 6'3", 215 lbs., bats right, throws right. Years in minor leagues: 5; Major League debut: September 14, 1930; Years in Major Leagues: 13. Elected to Hall of Fame: 1965. Nickname: Hammerin' Hank—because of his ability to hit the long ball.

Hank Greenberg was a slugging first baseman and outfielder for the Detroit Tigers who put up some great numbers in a short period of time. He played only nine full seasons, losing two full seasons and most of two others to World War II, and was sidelined most of the 1936 season with a broken wrist.

He made the most of the time he had. Greenberg led the American League in home runs four times, including 1938 when he hit 58. Only two righthanded batters have ever hit more. He also led the league in RBIs four times, including 1937 when he drove in 183. Only Lou Gehrig with 184 and Hack Wilson with 190 ever drove in more. The two-time American League MVP entered the armed forces in May of 1941 and did not return to baseball until the end of the 1945 season, missing four full years. In the last game of the 1945 season, Greenberg hit a ninth-inning, grand slam home run to put the Tigers into World Series. He then slammed two home runs to help the Tigers beat the Cubs.

When he was young, the Yankees made an offer for Greenberg's services but he turned it down because the Yankees already had a pretty good first baseman: Lou Gehrig. He won his first Most Valuable Player award in 1935 when he drove in 170 runs and led the Tigers to their second straight pennant. Five years later, he was Most Valuable Player again when he hit 50 doubles, 41 homers, drove in 150 runs and led the Tigers to their third pennant in seven years. After his playing days were over, he served as vice president and general manager of the Cleveland Indians for Bill Veeck and then teamed with Veeck again as a vice president of the Chicago White Sox.

Year	Team	G	AB	R	H	D	T	HR	RBI	AVE.
1930	Det	1	1	0	0	0	0	0	0	.000
1933	Det	117	449	59	135	33	3	12	87	.301
1934	Det	153	593	118	201	63	7	26	139	.339
1935	Det	152	619	121	203	46	16	36	170	.328
1936	Det	12	46	10	16	6	2	1	16	.348
1937	Det	154	594	137	200	49	14	40	183	.337
1938	Det	155	556	144	175	23	4	58	146	.315
1939	Det	138	500	112	156	42	7	33	112	.312
1940	Det	148	573	129	195	50	8	41	150	.340
1941	Det	19	67	12	18	5	1	2	12	.269
1945	Det	78	270	47	84	20	2	13	60	.311
1946	Det	142	523	91	145	29	5	44	127	.277
1947	Pitt	125	402	71	100	13	2	25	74	.249
13 years		**1394**	**5193**	**1051**	**1628**	**379**	**71**	**331**	**1276**	**.313**

Transactions: Jan. 18, 1947: Sold to Pittsburgh for $75,000.

WORLD SERIES

Year	Team	G	AB	R	H	D	T	HR	RBI	AVE.
1934	Det	7	28	4	9	2	1	1	7	.321
1935	Det	2	6	1	1	0	0	1	2	.167
1940	Det	7	28	5	10	2	1	1	6	.357
1945	Det	7	23	7	7	3	0	2	7	.304
4 years		23	85	17	27	8	2	5	22	.318

Clark Calvin Griffith

Born November 20, 1869, in Nevada, Missouri; died October 27, 1955, in Washington, D.C. 5'8", 156 lbs., bats right, throws right. Major League debut: April 11, 1891; Years in Major Leagues: 64 (as player, manager and owner). Elected to Hall of Fame: 1946. Nickname: The Old Fox—because of how clever he was, as a pitcher, at finding ways to scuff up the ball.

Clark Griffith was elected to the Hall of Fame for his contributions as a baseball executive, but he could have made it as a pitcher. Using his "dinky-dinky" pitch and scuffing the ball whenever he could get away with it, Griffith won 240 games in a 20-year career that included six straight seasons with 20 or more wins. He managed the Chicago White Sox to the American League's first pennant in 1901 and then went to the New York Highlanders (later to be the Yankees) where he was fired after a little more than two seasons. He then managed Cincinnati for three years before moving to Washington where he managed the Senators for a couple of years, all the time buying more stock in the ball club. He became president of the Senators in 1920.

The Senators had their most successful times in the 1920s and 1930s. They won their only three pennants in 1924, 1925 and 1933, but even with the success, Griffith was always struggling to make ends meet. In 1934, he sold his star shortstop, his manager and his son-in-law—all of whom were Joe Cronin—so he could pick up $225,000 to keep the Senators going.

In his later years, Griffith was responsible for signing many Latin American ballplayers, helping to open the door for a generation of stars from countries south of the U.S. borders. He also initiated the custom of having a president throw out the first ball on opening day. His friendship with presidents helped the Senators stay in Washington even when times were tough. His political ties also helped baseball steer clear of antitrust legislation in Congress.

Year	Team	W-L	ERA	G	IP	H	BB	SO
1891	StL-Bos	17-7	3.74	34	226.1	242	73	88
1893	Chi (N)	1-1	5.03	4	19.2	24	5	9
1894	Chi	21-11	4.92	36	261.1	328	85	71
1895	Chi	25-13	3.93	42	353	434	91	79
1896	Chi	22-13	3.54	36	317.2	370	70	81

Year	Team	W-L	ERA	G	IP	H	BB	SO
1897	Chi	21-19	3.72	41	343.2	410	86	102
1898	Chi	26-10	1.88	38	325.2	305	64	97
1899	Chi	22-13	2.79	38	319.2	329	65	73
1900	Chi	14-13	3.05	30	248	245	51	61
1901	Chi (A)	24-7	2.67	35	266.2	275	50	67
1902	Chi	25-9	4.19	28	212.2	247	47	51
1903	NY (A)	14-11	2.70	25	213	201	33	69
1904	NY	7-5	2.87	16	100.1	91	16	36
1905	NY	9-6	1.67	25	102.2	82	15	46
1906	NY	2-2	3.02	17	59.2	58	15	16
1907	NY	0-0	8.64	4	8.1	15	6	5
1909	Cin	0-1	6.00	1	6	11	2	3
1910	Cin	0-0	0.00	0	0	0	0	0
1912	Wash	0-0	0.00	1	0	1	0	0
1913	Wash	0-0	0.00	1	1	1	0	0
1914	Wash	0-0	0.00	1	1	1	0	1
21 years		**240-141**	**3.31**	**453**	**3386.1**	**3670**	**774**	**955**

Burleigh Arland Grimes

Born August 18, 1893, in Emerald, Wisconsin; died December 6, 1985, in Clear Lake, Wisconsin. 5'10", 185 lbs., bats right, throws right. Years in minor leagues: 5; Major League debut: September 10, 1916; Years in Major Leagues: 19. Elected to Hall of Fame: 1964. Nickname: Old Stubblebeard—because he never shaved on the day he was pitching.

Burleigh Grimes was a tough competitor who won 270 games, pitching for seven teams in a 19-year Major League career. He was the last of the legal spitball pitchers, and the brushback pitch was a regular part of his repertoire. The spitball was actually banned in 1920 but 17 pitchers who were already using it were allowed to continue. Grimes went 14 more years, retiring after the 1934 season. He won 20 games or more in five seasons and had a string of 13 straight wins as a starter for the Giants in 1927. He pitched more than 300 innings in five seasons and led the National League in innings pitched three times.

He helped the Dodgers win the pennant in 1920 and later was with two Cardinal pennant winners. Pitching for the Cardinals in the 1931 World Series, Grimes had a no-hitter for seven innings against a Philadelphia A's team that had Jimmy Foxx, Mickey Cochrane and Al Simmons in its lineup and Lefty Grove on the mound. Grimes had a one-hitter with two out in the ninth inning when Simmons touched him for a two-run homer. He finished with a 5–2 two-hitter. Later in that same World Series, he pitched eight innings of shutout ball while agonizing with what turned out to be appendicitis. Grimes was a prominent figure in a World Series game that produced many "firsts." Pitching for Brooklyn in 1920, he gave up the first grand slam home run in Series history to Cleveland's Elmer Smith. Later in the same game, Grimes gave up a homer to Jim Bagby, the first home run by a pitcher in Series history. Clarence Mitchell, who relieved Grimes, came to bat and smashed a line drive to second baseman Bill Wambsganss, who made a couple of tags en route to an unassisted triple play. Grimes was known to intentionally walk batters by throwing four brushback pitches. He could help his own cause with a bat in his hands. Grimes had a lifetime batting average of .248.

Year	Team	W-L	ERA	G	IP	H	BB	SO
1916	Pitt	2-3	2.36	6	45.2	40	10	20
1917	Pitt	3-16	3.53	37	194	186	70	72
1918	Brklyn	19-9	2.14	41	269.2	210	76	113
1919	Brklyn	10-11	3.47	25	181.1	179	60	82
1920	Brklyn	23-11	2.22	40	303.2	271	67	131
1921	Brklyn	22-13	2.83	37	302.1	313	76	136
1922	Brklyn	17-14	4.76	36	259	324	84	99
1923	Brklyn	21-18	3.58	39	327	356	100	119
1924	Brklyn	22-13	3.82	38	310.2	351	91	135
1925	Brklyn	12-19	5.04	33	246.2	305	102	73
1926	Brklyn	12-13	3.71	30	225.1	238	88	64
1927	NY (N)	19-8	3.54	39	259.2	274	87	102
1928	Pitt	25-14	2.99	48	330.2	311	77	97
1929	Pitt	17-7	3.13	33	232.2	245	70	62
1930	Bos-StL	16-11	4.07	33	201.1	246	65	73
1931	StL (N)	17-9	3.65	29	212.1	240	59	67
1932	Chi (N)	6-11	4.78	30	141.1	174	50	36
1933	Chi-StL	3-7	3.78	21	83.1	86	37	16
1934	StL-Pitt-NY	4-5	6.11	22	53	63	26	15
19 years		**270-212**	**3.53**	**617**	**4179.2**	**4412**	**1295**	**1512**

Transactions: Jan. 9, 1918: Traded with Chuck Ward and Al Mamaux to Brooklyn for Casey Stengel and George Cutshaw. Jan. 9, 1927: Traded to New York for Butch Henline as part of a three-team trade with Brooklyn, New York and Philadelphia. Feb. 11, 1928: Traded to Pittsburgh for Vic Aldredge. April 9, 1930: Traded to Boston for Percy Jones and cash. June 16, 1930: Traded to St. Louis for Fred Frankhouse and Bill Sherdel. December 1931: Traded to Chicago for Bud Teachout and Hack Wilson. Aug. 4, 1933: Sold to St. Louis for waiver price. May 15, 1934: Sold to Pittsburgh on waiver price. May 26, 1934: Sold to New York Yankees.

WORLD SERIES

Year	Team	W-L	ERA	G	IP	H	BB	SO
1920	Brklyn	1-2	4.19	3	19.1	23	9	4
1930	StL (N)	0-2	3.71	2	17	10	6	13
1931	StL	2-0	2.04	2	17.2	9	9	11
1932	Chi (N)	0-0	23.63	2	2.2	7	2	0
4 years		**3-4**	**4.29**	**7**	**56.2**	**49**	**26**	**28**

Robert Moses Grove

Born March 6, 1900, in Lonaconing, Maryland; died May 22, 1975, in Norwalk, Ohio. 6'3", 204 lbs., bats left, throws left. Years in minor leagues: 5; Major League debut: April 14, 1925; Years in Major Leagues: 17. Elected to Hall of Fame: 1947. Nickname: Lefty—because he threw and batted lefthanded.

Lefty Grove is the only pitcher in baseball history to win 300 games and also have more than twice as many wins as losses. He was 300–141. His winning percentage of .680 is the fourth best. He led the American League in wins four times and had eight seasons in which he won 20 games or more. He led the league in strikeouts seven times and in earned run average eight times. His best year was 1931—the third consecutive year in which his Philadelphia A's played in the World Series—when Grove was 31–4 and at one point won 16 straight games. He was the league's Most Valuable Player. In 1930 and 1931, Grove was 59–9, a winning percentage of .867. Grove had a legendary temper, particularly after he lost a tough game, and he displayed it by kicking lockers in between games of a doubleheader in August 1931. It was his next start after having won 16 consecutive games. Grove lost 1–0 to the St. Louis Browns with the only run scoring on an error. The A's won the second game 10–0, but their run production came too late to help Grove, who fell one short of tying the American League record of 17 straight wins held by Walter Johnson and Joe Wood.

Grove was responsible for putting an end to another record streak. When he beat the Yankees 7–0 in August of 1933, it snapped a streak in which New York had gone 308 straight games without being shut out. He played the last seven years of his career with the Boston Red Sox after Connie Mack unloaded him and several other superstars in a Depression-era move to get some cash. Grove pitched respectably for the Red Sox, winning 20 games once, and going 15–4 in 1939 but struggled the next two years, when he was past 40 years old. He won seven games in each of those years, just enough to reach the 300-win mark.

Year	Team	W-L	ERA	G	IP	H	BB	SO
1925	Phil (A)	10-13	4.75	45	197	207	131	116
1926	Phil	13-13	2.51	45	258	227	101	194
1927	Phil	20-12	3.29	51	262.1	251	79	174
1928	Phil	24-8	2.58	39	261.2	228	64	183
1929	Phil	20-6	2.81	42	275.1	278	81	170
1930	Phil	28-5	2.54	50	291	273	60	209
1931	Phil	31-4	2.06	41	288.2	249	62	175
1932	Phil	25-10	2.84	44	291.2	269	79	188
1933	Phil	24-8	3.20	45	275.1	280	83	114
1934	Bos (A)	8-8	6.50	22	109.1	149	32	43
1935	Bos	20-12	2.70	35	273	269	65	121
1936	Bos	17-12	2.81	35	253.1	237	65	130
1937	Bos	17-9	3.02	32	262	269	83	153

Year	Team	W-L	ERA	G	IP	H	BB	SO
1938	Bos	14-4	3.08	24	163.2	169	52	99
1939	Bos	15-4	2.54	23	191	180	58	81
1940	Bos	7-6	3.99	22	153.1	159	50	62
1941	Bos	7-7	4.37	21	134	155	42	54
17 years		**300-141**	**3.06**	**616**	**3940.2**	**3849**	**1187**	**2266**

Transactions: Dec. 12, 1933: Traded with Rube Walberg and Max Bishop to Boston for Bob Kline, Rabbit Warstler and $125,000.

WORLD SERIES

Year	Team	W-L	ERA	G	IP	H	BB	SO
1929	Phil (A)	0-0	0.00	2	6.1	3	1	10
1930	Phil	2-1	1.42	3	19	15	3	10
1931	Phil	2-1	2.42	3	26	28	2	16
3 years		**4-2**	**1.75**	**8**	**51.1**	**46**	**6**	**36**

Charles James Hafey

Born February 12, 1904, in Berkley, California; died July 2, 1973, in Calistoga, California. 6'1", 185 lbs., bats right, throws right. Years in minor leagues: 2; Major League debut: August 28, 1924; Years in Major Leagues: 13. Elected to Hall of Fame: 1971. Nickname: Chick—Believed to be short for Charles; Hafey himself did not know the origin.

Chick Hafey was one of the original players in the original farm system designed by St. Louis Cardinals general manager Branch Rickey, who pioneered the feeder system to bring ballplayers up to the Major League level. Hafey was a consistently good hitter whose career was marred by constant health problems. Hafey had poor eyesight caused by a chronic sinus condition that eventually cut short his career. His eye condition changed from time to time, forcing him to have three different pairs of glasses.

His lifetime batting average of .317 is deceiving. He had a six-year stretch where the lowest he hit was .329. Teammate Jim Bottomley said Hafey hit the ball so hard, you could hear the seams crack. Hafey became involved in one of the National League's most celebrated salary disputes that eventually led to him being traded from the Cardinals to the Cincinnati Reds. Prior to the 1928 season Hafey signed a three-year contract that started at $7,000 and called for increases to $8,000 and $9,000 in the next two years.

He then proceeded to have his three finest years, hitting .337 in 1928 with 27 home runs and 111 RBIs in 1928; .338 with 29 home runs and 125 RBIs in 1929; and .336 with 26 home runs and 107 RBIs in 1930. In 1929, Hafey set a National League record when he got ten straight hits. He asked Rickey for $15,000 in 1931 and missed part of spring training while negotiations went on. He had to settle for $12,500 minus pay that was deducted for the time he needed to work out to get in shape. He wound up making $10,400, being docked $2,100 for the time he missed. Hafey won the 1931 batting title in the National League's closest race. He finished with an average of .3489, beating out the Giants' Bill Terry, who hit .3486, and Hafey's teammate Jim Bottomley, who hit .3482. Hafey asked Rickey for $17,000 for the 1932 season, including the $2,100 he had lost from the year before. Instead, he got a $500 raise and was traded to Cincinnati at the start of the season. He hit .344 for the Reds in 1932 and the next year was the starting left fielder for the National League in the first All-Star game. But health problems started to wear him down. By 1936, he was weak enough that he had to sit out the entire season. He returned in 1937, played in 89 games, and then retired.

Year	Team	G	AB	R	H	D	T	HR	RBI	AVE.
1924	StL (N)	24	91	10	23	5	2	2	22	.292
1925	StL	93	358	36	108	25	2	5	57	.302
1926	StL	78	225	30	61	19	2	4	38	.271
1927	StL	103	346	62	114	26	5	18	63	.329
1928	StL	138	520	101	175	46	6	27	111	.337
1929	StL	134	517	101	175	47	9	29	125	.338
1930	StL	120	446	108	150	39	12	26	107	.336
1931	StL	122	450	94	157	35	8	16	95	.349
1932	Cin	83	253	34	87	19	3	2	36	.344
1933	Cin	144	568	77	172	34	6	7	62	.303
1934	Cin	140	535	75	157	29	6	18	67	.293
1935	Cin	15	59	10	20	6	1	1	9	.339
1937	Cin	89	257	39	67	11	5	9	41	.261
13 years		**1283**	**4625**	**777**	**1466**	**341**	**67**	**164**	**833**	**.317**

Transactions: April 11, 1932: Traded to Cincinnnati for Harvey Hendrick, Benny Frey and cash.

WORLD SERIES

Year	Team	G	AB	R	H	D	T	HR	RBI	AVE.
1926	StL (N)	7	27	2	5	2	0	0	0	.185
1928	StL	4	15	0	3	0	0	0	0	.200
1930	StL	6	22	2	6	5	0	0	2	.273
1931	StL	6	24	1	4	0	0	0	0	.167
4 years		**23**	**88**	**5**	**18**	**7**	**0**	**0**	**2**	**.205**

Jesse Joseph Haines

Born July 22, 1893, in Clayton, Ohio; died August 5, 1978, in Dayton, Ohio. 6', 190 lbs., bats right, throws right. Years in minor leagues: 7; Major League debut: July 20, 1918; Years in Major Leagues: 19. Elected to Hall of Fame: 1970. Nickname: Pop—because of his silver-gray hair late in his career.

Jesse Haines alternated a super fastball with a deceiving knuckleball to win 210 games for the St. Louis Cardinals—the most for any Cardinal pitcher until Bob Gibson came along. He helped the Cardinals to the World Series five times, but had to sit out the 1931 Series with a broken wrist caused by a line drive off the bat of Brooklyn's Babe Herman.

Haines had two memorable moments in the 1926 World Series. He shut out the Yankees in his first start and also won his second start. In his third start, he was locked in a 3–3 tie when he developed a blister on his pitching hand. He was relieved by aging Grover Cleveland Alexander with the bases loaded and two outs in the seventh inning. Alexander struck out Tony Lazzeri and the Cardinals went on to win. Haines thought his greatest World Series win came in 1930 when he beat Lefty Grove and a Philadelphia A's team that featured Jimmie Foxx and Mickey Cochrane. Haines won that one, 3–1. He was just a so-so pitcher until he learned how to throw a knuckeball and then learned how to keep batters off balance by mixing it with his blazing fastball. With that formula, he threw a no-hitter against Boston in 1924. He pitched until he was 44 years old, served a short stint as a pitching coach for the Dodgers and then went back home to Montgomery County, Ohio, where he was elected to six terms as county auditor.

Year	Team	W-L	ERA	G	IP	H	BB	SO
1918	Cin	0-0	1.80	1	5	5	1	2
1920	StL	13-20	2.98	47	301.2	303	80	120
1921	StL	18-12	3.50	37	244.1	261	56	84
1922	StL	11-9	3.84	29	183	207	45	62
1923	StL	20-13	3.11	37	266	283	75	73
1924	StL	8-19	4.41	35	222.2	275	66	69
1925	StL	13-14	4.57	29	207	234	52	63
1926	StL	13-4	3.25	33	183	186	48	46
1927	StL	24-10	2.72	38	300.2	273	77	89
1928	StL	20-8	3.18	33	240.1	238	72	77
1929	StL	13-10	5.71	28	179.2	230	73	59
1930	StL	13-8	4.30	29	182	215	54	68
1931	StL	12-3	3.02	19	122.1	134	28	27
1932	StL	3-5	4.75	20	85.1	116	16	27
1933	StL	9-6	2.50	32	115.1	113	37	37
1934	StL	4-4	3.50	37	90	86	19	17
1935	StL	6-5	3.59	30	115.1	110	28	24
1936	StL	7-5	3.90	25	99.1	110	21	19
1937	StL	3-3	4.52	16	65.2	81	23	18
19 years		**210-158**	**3.64**	**555**	**3208.2**	**3460**	**871**	**981**

WORLD SERIES

Year	Team	W-L	ERA	G	IP	H	BB	SO
1926	StL	2-0	1.08	3	16.2	13	9	5
1928	StL	0-1	4.50	1	6	6	3	3
1930	StL	1-0	1.00	1	9	4	4	2
1934	StL	0-0	0.00	1	.2	1	0	2
4 years		**3-1**	**1.67**	**6**	**32.1**	**24**	**16**	**12**

Milo Hamilton

Broadcaster. Elected to Hall of Fame: 1992.

Milo Hamilton's career includes stints broadcasting the St. Louis Browns in their last year and the Atlanta Braves in their first. He served his longest tenure in Atlanta but also broadcast for both Chicago teams, Pittsburgh and Houston. People all over the South heard his radio call of Henry Aaron's 715th home run, breaking Babe Ruth's record, in 1974.

William Robert Hamilton

Born February 16, 1866, in Newark, New Jersey; died December 16, 1940, in Worcester, Massachusetts. 5'6", 165 lbs., bats left, throws right. Years in minor leagues: 1; Major League debut: 1888 (exact date unknown); Years in Major Leagues: 14. Elected to Hall of Fame: 1961. Nickname: Sliding Billy—in recognition of the head-first slide that helped make him a great base stealer.

Billy Hamilton is the only Major League player to end his career with more runs scored (1,690) than games played (1,578). Hamilton twice stole more than 100 bases in a season—117 in 1889 for Kansas City and 115 two years later—and finished with 937 stolen bases. All of those totals surpass Ty Cobb's numbers, and Hamilton protested until his death in 1940 that he, and not Cobb, was the greatest base stealer. One of the reasons he wasn't recognized was that Hamilton played at a time when runners were credited with stolen bases if they advanced a base on a sacrifice fly or advanced two bases on a single. He had a lifetime batting average of .344. He hit .399 in 1894 and finished fourth in the batting race behind Hugh Duffy, Sam Thompson and Ed Delahanty.

Year	Team	G	AB	R	H	D	T	HR	RBI	AVE.
1888	KC (AA)	35	129	21	34	4	4	0	11	.264
1889	KC	137	534	144	161	17	12	3	77	.301
1890	Phil (N)	123	496	133	161	13	9	2	49	.325
1891	Phil	133	527	141	179	23	7	2	60	.340
1892	Phil	139	554	131	183	21	7	3	53	.330
1893	Phil	82	355	110	135	22	7	5	44	.380
1894	Phil	131	559	196	223	25	15	4	87	.399
1895	Phil	123	517	166	201	22	6	7	74	.389
1896	Bos (N)	131	523	152	191	24	9	3	52	.365
1897	Bos	127	507	152	174	17	5	3	61	.343
1898	Bos	110	417	110	154	16	5	3	50	.369
1899	Bos	84	297	63	92	7	1	1	33	.310
1900	Bos	136	520	102	173	20	5	1	47	.333
1901	Bos	102	349	70	102	11	2	3	38	.292
14 years		**1593**	**6284**	**1692**	**2163**	**242**	**94**	**40**	**736**	**.344**

Edward Hugh Hanlon

Born August 27, 1857, in Montville, Connecticut; died April 14, 1937, in Baltimore, Maryland. 5'9", 170 lbs., bats left, throws right. Years in minor leagues: 4; Major League debut: May 1, 1880; Years in Major Leagues: 27 (as player and manager). Elected to Hall of Fame: 1996. Nickname: Ned, origin unknown; also, Foxy Ned, because of all the strategies he used in managing a ball club.

Ned Hanlon was the most innovative manager of the 1890s and early 1900s, and his bizarre methods worked. In a nine-year stretch, his teams finished first five times, second three times and third once. At the end of his 19-year career, Hanlon's teams had won 1,315 games and lost 1,165, a winning percentage of .530.

Hanlon took over a Baltimore team that finished twelfth in 1892. They improved from twelfth to eighth in 1893, but Hanlon decided some drastic changes were necessary. Prior to the 1894 season, he ordered his team to go south to practice for a few weeks before the season started. Critics carped at him, but the training time gave his team the time not only to get into shape, but to practice plays they would use during the season. It wasn't long before other teams followed Hanlon's example, and now "spring training" is a part of every Major League team's preparation for the season. Among Hanlon's other innovations: using righthanded hitters against lefthanded pitchers and vice versa; having defensive players cover for one another when one of them got caught out of position; hiring a groundskeeper to keep the field in shape; and sending a base runner while the batter was swinging at a pitch—the "hit and run." Among those who played for him, learned from him and later managed were Connie Mack, Hugh Jennings, John McGraw, Miller Huggins, Kid Gleason and Wilbert Robinson.

Hanlon managed Pittsburgh in 1889, jumped to Players League in 1890, then went back to National League in 1891. He won three pennants with Baltimore from 1892 to 1894, and won pennants with Brooklyn in 1899 and 1900. He was not above trying to figure out any way he could to win a ball game, including stretching the rules. He is believed to have ordered that a cement block be buried just below the surface of the field in front of home plate in Baltimore. He then taught his players to swing down on the ball so that it would hit the hard surface and bounce high enough for the batter to make it to first base safely. Those types of high bouncing hits are still known today as "Baltimore chops."

Year	Team	Record	Standing
1889	Pittsburgh	26–19	Fifth
1890	Pittsburgh	60–68	Sixth
1891	Pittsburgh	31–47	Eighth
1892	Baltimore	45–85	Twelfth
1893	Baltimore	60–70	Eighth
1894	Baltimore	89–39	First
1895	Baltimore	87–43	First

Year	Team	Record	Standing
1896	Baltimore	90-39	First
1897	Baltimore	90-40	Second
1898	Baltimore	96-53	Second
1899	Brooklyn	101-47	First
1900	Brooklyn	82-54	First
1901	Brooklyn	79-57	Third
1902	Brooklyn	75-63	Second
1903	Brooklyn	70-66	Fifth
1904	Brooklyn	56-97	Sixth
1905	Brooklyn	48-104	Eighth
1906	Cincinnati	64-87	Sixth
1907	Cincinnati	66-87	Sixth
19 years		**1315-1165**	

Will Harridge

Born October 16, 1883, in Chicago, Illinois; died April 9, 1971, in Evanston, Illinois. Baseball executive. Years in Major Leagues: 48 years (as American League secretary, president). Elected to Hall of Fame: 1972

As a Wabash Railroad ticket agent, Will Harridge was responsible for handling travel arrangements for all American League teams as well as umpires. He became acquainted with American League president Ban Johnson, who hired him in 1911 as his private secretary. Harridge stayed employed by the American League for the next 48 years.

He became the league's secretary in 1927 and in 1931 took the top job when league president Ernest Barnard died suddenly. He served in that capacity for 28 years and then served in the newly created position of chairman of the board.

Harridge was a proponent of the All-Star game and supported Chicago sportswriter Arch Ward's idea for the game to be played as part of the Century of Progress Exhibition in 1933. He was not an early proponent of night baseball, but later advocated it when he realized how beneficial it was for families who wanted to go to the ball game. Harridge was league president on July 5, 1947, when Larry Doby became the first black player to appear in an American League game.

Stanley Raymond Harris

Born November 8, 1896, in Port Jervis, New York; died November 8, 1977, in Bethesda, Maryland. 5'9", 156 lbs., bats right, throws right. Years in Major Leagues: 33 years (as player and manager). Elected to Hall of Fame: 1975. Nickname: Bucky—a name he earned in his youth playing basketball when his coach said he shook off defenders like a bucking bronco; also, The Boy Wonder, for winning the pennant his first two years as a manager.

Bucky Harris is the only man in baseball history to lead two different teams to championships in his first year of managing them—and the championships were 23 years apart. As a rookie manager, he piloted the 1924 Washington Senators to a pennant. In 1947, he took over as manager of the New York Yankees and they won the pennant. Both the 1924 Senators and 1947 Yankees won the World Series, too, putting Harris in the record books for that accomplishment as well.

Harris was a second baseman for the Senators and the Detroit Tigers for 12 years, compiling a lifetime batting average of .274. In 1924, at the age of 27, he became the player-manager of the Senators. They won their first pennant ever and went on to win the World Series, thanks in great part to Harris's bat. He drove in both runs in the sixth game as the Senators beat the Giants, 2–1, and drove in three runs the next day when they Senators won the series with a 4–3 win in game seven. Washington won the pennant in Harris's second year at the helm, too, but lost to an awesome Pittsburgh Pirate team that featured four Hall of Famers in their starting lineup—Pie Traynor, KiKi Cuyler and Paul and Lloyd Waner. In his 29-year managerial career, Harris developed a reputation for getting the most of his players, and he often didn't have much to work with. He managed the Senators from 1924 to 1928 and again from 1935 to 1942 and from 1950 to 1954. He also managed Detroit from 1929 to 1933, quitting because he felt he had gone as far as he could with his players and thought a new manager could succeed with what he had developed. Mickey Cochrane, took over and the Tigers won the pennant the next two years.

Harris managed the Red Sox for a year, 1934, the Phillies for part of a season, 1943, the Yankees in 1947 and 1948, followed by his second stint with the Senators and then taking another stab with the Tigers in 1955 and 1956. His 1947 Yankee team won the World Series. His 1948 Yankees went down to the last weekend of the season before the Indians won it all. The Yankees fired Harris and hired Casey Stengel to replace him.

Harris ranks third all time in wins with 2,159. But because of the caliber of teams he was called on to try to salvage, he also ranks second in losses with 2,219.

Year	Team	Record	Standing
1924	Wash	92-62	First
1925	Wash	96-55	First
1926	Wash	81-69	Fourth
1927	Wash	85-69	Third
1928	Wash	75-78	Fourth
1929	Det	70-84	Sixth
1930	Det	75-79	Fifth
1931	Det	61-93	Seventh
1932	Det	76-75	Fifth
1933	Det	73-79	Fifth
1934	Bos (A)	76-76	Fourth

Year	Team	Record	Standing
1935	Wash	67-86	Sixth
1936	Wash	82-71	Fourth
1937	Wash	73-80	Sixth
1938	Wash	75-76	Fifth
1939	Wash	65-87	Sixth
1940	Wash	64-90	Seventh
1941	Wash	70-84	Sixth
1942	Wash	62-89	Seventh
1943	Phil	40-53	Fifth
1947	NY (A)	97-57	First
1948	NY	94-60	Third
1950	Wash	67-87	Fifth
1951	Wash	62-92	Seventh
1952	Wash	78-76	Fifth
1953	Wash	76-76	Fifth
1954	Wash	66-88	Sixth
1955	Det	79-75	Fifth
1956	Det	82-72	Fifth
29 years		**2159-2219**	

WORLD SERIES

Year	Team	Record
1924	Wash	4-3
1925	Wash	3-4
1947	NY (A)	4-3
3 years		**11-10**

Charles Leo Hartnett

Born December 20, 1900, in Woonsocket, Rhode Island; died December 20, 1972, in Park Ridge, Illinois. 6'1", 195 lbs., bats right, throws right; Years in minor leagues: 1; Major League debut: April 12, 1922; Years in Major Leagues: 20. Elected to Hall of Fame: 1955. Nickname: Gabby—dubbed by a sportswriter during his rookie year with the Cubs because of his constant chatter, an unusual trait for a rookie; also, Old Tomato Face, because of how his face became extremely red when he laughed.

Gabby Hartnett is best known for his "Homer in the Gloamin" that he hit on September 28, 1938, off of Pitttsburgh's ace reliever Mace Brown with two out in the bottom of the ninth inning. The homer, in the twilight at Wrigley Field, broke a 5–5 tie and catapulted the Cubs into first place and they went on to win the pennant. That was the hit that secured his place in history. But Hartnett liked to remind people that he was a footnote to another famous baseball happening. He was behind the plate, calling the pitches in the 1934 All-Star Game when the

Giants' Carl Hubbell struck out Babe Ruth, Lou Gehrig, Jimmie Foxx, Al Simmons and Joe Cronin in succession.

He was indirectly involved in yet another baseball historic moment. He was the Cubs catcher in the 1932 World Series when Babe Ruth supposedly called his shot by pointing to the center field bleachers and then hitting one there off Cub hurler Charlie Root. Hartnett, the person closest to Ruth when the incident occurred, said Ruth was simply responding to the Cub bench, which had been razzing him. Hartnett said Ruth put one finger in the air and told the Cub bench jockeys, "it only takes one."

Hartnett started the first five All-Star games for the National League. He played 20 seasons with the Cubs and had a lifetime batting average of .297. When he retired, his 236 career homers were the most ever by a catcher. He was the National League's Most Valuable Player in 1935 when he hit .344. He hit over .300 five times, including his high of .354 in 1937. His homer to beat the Pirates in 1938 was particularly dramatic because the Cubs and Pirates were starting a three-game series that would decide the pennant. Hartnett's homer came in the bottom of the ninth inning of the first game. The umpires had told both teams that with the darkness setting in, the ninth inning would be the last. Hartnett's homer came on an 0-and-2 pitch. Gabby had taken over as Cub manager earlier that season and had helped lift them from a 6½ game deficit to the championship. Hartnett played on four Cub pennant winners, but neither he nor his teammates could do enough to bring a World Series championship to Wrigley Field.

Year	Team	G	AB	R	H	D	T	HR	RBI	AVE.
1922	Chi (N)	31	72	4	14	1	1	0	4	.194
1923	Chi	85	231	28	62	12	2	8	39	.268
1924	Chi	111	354	56	106	17	7	16	67	.299
1925	Chi	117	398	61	115	28	3	24	67	.289
1926	Chi	93	284	35	78	25	3	8	41	.275
1927	Chi	127	449	56	132	32	5	10	80	.294
1928	Chi	120	388	61	117	26	9	14	57	.302
1929	Chi	25	22	2	6	2	1	1	9	.273
1930	Chi	141	508	84	172	31	3	37	122	.339
1931	Chi	116	380	53	107	32	1	8	70	.282
1932	Chi	121	406	52	110	25	3	12	52	.271
1933	Chi	140	490	55	135	21	4	16	88	.276
1934	Chi	130	438	58	131	21	1	22	90	.299
1935	Chi	116	413	67	142	32	6	13	91	.344
1936	Chi	121	424	49	130	25	6	7	64	.307
1937	Chi	110	356	47	126	21	6	12	82	.354
1938	Chi	88	299	40	82	19	1	10	59	.274
1939	Chi	97	306	36	85	18	2	12	59	.278
1940	Chi	37	64	3	17	3	0	1	12	.266
1941	NY (N)	64	150	20	45	5	0	5	26	.300
20 years		1990	6432	867	1912	396	64	236	1179	.297

WORLD SERIES

Year	Team	G	AB	R	H	D	T	HR	RBI	AVE.
1929	Chi (N)	3	3	0	0	0	0	0	0	.000
1932	Chi	4	16	2	5	2	0	1	1	.313
1935	Chi	6	24	1	7	0	0	1	2	.292
1938	Chi	3	11	0	1	0	1	0	0	.091
4 years		16	54	3	13	2	1	2	3	.241

Ernest Harwell

Broadcaster. Elected to Hall of Fame: 1981.

Ernie Harwell began his Major League broadcasting career covering the Brooklyn Dodgers in 1948 and moved over to cover the Giants in 1950. He was on the air when Bobby Thomson hit "the shot heard around the world" in the 1951 playoffs against the Dodgers. In 1954, Harwell left New York for Baltimore and was part of the original broadcast team for the Orioles. In 1960 he moved to Detroit to become the voice of the Tigers, the beginning of a longtime mutual love affair between the announcer and the Tiger fans.

In 1991, Harwell was fired, triggering a massive reaction from thousands of Tiger fans who protested his dismissal. He languished a year on CBS Radio, broadcasting baseball. Not long after that, the Tigers were sold and the new owners brought Harwell back.

Harry Edwin Heilmann

Born August 3, 1894, in San Francisco, California; died July 9, 1951, in Detroit, Michigan. 6'1", 200 lbs., bats right, throws right. Years in minor leagues: 3; Major League debut: May 16, 1914; Years in Major Leagues: 17. Elected to Hall of Fame: 1952. Nickname: Slug—given to him by teammates because of how he could slug the ball; also, Harry the Horse, because of his lack of speed.

Harry Heilmann was a hard-hitting outfielder for the Detroit Tigers who played along side Ty Cobb for most of his career. Though he broke in with the Tigers in 1914, he didn't really develop as a hitter until Cobb, as manager, took him under his wing—something Cobb never did when he played with Heilmann.

Harry the Horse hit .225 in limited action in 1914 and got up as high as .320 in 1919. Cobb took over as player-manager in 1921 and worked with Heilmann on his batting stance, showing him how to better distribute his weight. Heilmann responded by winning batting titles in 1921 with a .393 average; in 1923 with a .403 average; in 1925 with a .393 average; and 1927 with a .398 average. From 1921 through 1927, his lowest average was .346, making him the American League's counterpart to Rogers Hornsby, who was blistering National League pitching.

His emergence as a great hitter also coincided with the end of the dead ball era. He also benefited from hitting behind Cobb, driving in 89 runs or more in 12 of his 17 seasons. In eight of those years, he topped 100 RBIs. In 1925, Heilmann had a torrid September, raising his batting average by 50 points and getting six hits in a season-ending doubleheader to beat out Tris Speaker for the batting title. In 1927, he got seven hits in a season-ending doubleheader to beat out Al Simmons for the title. He was sold to Cincinnati in 1930 and hit .333. He had to sit out the 1931 season because of severe arthritis. He played one more year, then retired with a lifetime batting average of .342. After his playing days were over, Heilmann was a popular play-by-play radio broadcaster for the Tigers. In 1951, Commissioner "Happy" Chandler asked him to be the broadcaster for the All-Star Game, but Heilmann declined because his health was failing. He died the night before the game was played. Six months later, he was elected to the Hall of Fame.

Year	Team	G	AB	R	H	D	T	HR	RBI	AVE.
1914	Det	67	182	25	41	8	1	2	22	.225
1916	Det	136	451	57	127	30	11	2	76	.282
1917	Det	150	556	57	156	22	11	5	86	.281
1918	Det	79	286	34	79	10	6	5	44	.276
1919	Det	140	537	74	172	30	15	8	95	.320
1920	Det	145	543	66	168	28	5	9	89	.309
1921	Det	149	602	114	237	43	14	19	139	.394
1922	Det	118	455	92	162	27	10	21	92	.356
1923	Det	144	524	121	211	44	11	18	115	.403
1924	Det	153	570	107	197	45	16	10	113	.346
1925	Det	150	573	97	225	40	11	13	133	.393
1926	Det	141	502	90	184	41	8	9	103	.367
1927	Det	141	505	103	201	50	9	14	120	.398
1928	Det	151	558	83	183	38	10	14	107	.328
1929	Det	125	453	86	156	41	7	15	120	.344
1930	Cin	142	459	79	153	43	6	19	91	.333
1932	Cin	15	31	3	8	2	0	0	6	.258
17 years		2146	7787	1291	2660	542	151	183	1551	.342

Transactions: Oct. 14, 1929: Sold to Cincinnati Reds.

William Jennings Herman

Born July 7, 1909, in New Albany, Indiana; died September 5, 1992, in West Palm Beach, Florida. 5'11", 195 lbs., bats right, throws right. Years in minor leagues: 4; Major League debut: August 29, 1931; Years in Major Leagues: 15. Elected to Hall of Fame: 1975. Nickname: None.

Billy Herman was a scrappy second baseman who was a tough out and had great hands in the infield. He had five straight seasons in which he had 900 or more chances—which remains a National League record—and led the National League in putouts in seven years.

In 1932, Herman became the Cubs' regular second baseman. With Billy Jurges at shortstop and Charlie Grimm at first base, the double-play combination never made it into a poem like "Tinker to Evers to Chance" but was a solid defensive stronghold for many years. At second base, Herman had a tough act to follow—his predecessor was Rogers Hornsby. Herman hit .314 and the Cubs won the pennant. They won it again in 1935 when he hit .341 and led the National League in hits with 227. Chicago won for a third time in the decade in 1938. In 1941, Herman was shipped to Brooklyn, and the Dodgers won the pennant, as Dodger president Larry McPhail predicted they would when he acquired Herman. He hit over .300 seven times, including a three-year stretch (1935–37) in which he hit .341, .334 and .335. He finished with a .304 lifetime batting average.

He was great in All-Star competition. Herman appeared in 10 All-Star games in a row, and hit .433. After his playing days were over, he had brief stints as manager of the Pittsburgh Pirates and Boston Red Sox.

Year	Team	G	AB	R	H	D	T	HR	RBI	AVE.
1931	Chi (N)	25	98	14	32	7	0	0	16	.327
1932	Chi	154	656	102	206	42	7	1	51	.314
1933	Chi	153	619	82	173	35	2	0	44	.279
1934	Chi	113	456	79	138	21	6	3	42	.303
1935	Chi	154	666	113	227	57	6	7	83	.341
1936	Chi	153	632	101	211	57	7	5	93	.334
1937	Chi	138	564	106	189	35	11	8	65	.335
1938	Chi	152	624	86	173	34	7	1	56	.277
1939	Chi	156	623	111	191	34	18	7	70	.307
1940	Chi	135	558	77	163	24	4	5	57	.292
1941	Chi-Brklyn	144	572	81	163	30	5	3	41	.285
1942	Brklyn	155	571	76	146	34	2	2	52	.256
1943	Brklyn	153	585	76	193	41	2	2	100	.330
1946	Brklyn-Bos	122	436	56	130	31	5	3	50	.298
1947	Pitt	15	47	3	10	4	0	0	6	.213
15 years		**1922**	**7707**	**1163**	**2345**	**486**	**82**	**47**	**839**	**.304**

Transactions: May 6, 1941: Traded to Brooklyn for Johnny Hudson, Charlie Gilbert and $65,000. June 15, 1946: Traded to Boston Braves for Stew Hofferth. Sept. 30, 1946: Traded to Pittsburgh with Elmer Singleton, Stan Wentzel and Whitey Wietelman for Bob Elliott and Hank Camelli.

WORLD SERIES

Year	Team	G	AB	R	H	D	T	HR	RBI	AVE.
1932	Chi (N)	4	18	5	4	1	0	0	1	.222
1935	Chi (N)	6	24	3	8	2	1	1	6	.333
1938	Chi (N)	4	16	1	3	0	0	0	0	.188
1941	Brklyn (N)	4	8	0	1	0	0	0	0	.125
4 years		**18**	**66**	**9**	**16**	**3**	**1**	**1**	**7**	**.242**

Russell Hodges

Broadcaster. Elected to Hall of Fame: 1980.

Russ Hodges delivered the most famous home run call in baseball history on October 3, 1951, when Bobby Thomson's ninth inning home run off of Ralph Branca gave the New York Giants a thrilling come-from-behind victory over Brooklyn in their final playoff game. The result, as Hodges shouted to his audience in an account that has been replayed countless times: "The Giants win the pennant, the Giants win the pennant, the Giants win the pennant, the Giants win the pennant..."

Hodges was a native Kentuckian who did broadcasts for the White Sox, Cubs, Reds, Senators and Yankees before taking on the duties for which he was the most well-known: the voice of the Giants in New York and in San Francisco.

Fans remember his signature shout of "Bye, bye baby" as the likes of Willie Mays, Willie McCovey and Orlando Cepeda rounded the bases after hitting a home run. Hodges broadcast Giants games for 20 years and was still active when he died of a heart attack in 1971.

Thomas Holmes

Sportswriter. Elected to Hall of Fame: 1979.

Tommy Holmes was a familiar sight in the press boxes of Major League ballparks for a half-century. Most of that time he was covering the Brooklyn Dodgers, from their daffy days in the late 1920s and early 1930s through the era in which the Boys of Summer dominated the National League in the early 1950s. Holmes had only one arm, but he did not allow his handicap to get in the way of a successful career. Holmes began that career with the Brooklyn Eagles in 1926 and then joined the staff of the *New York Herald-Tribune*. He was also an author and served as president of the Baseball Writers Association of America in 1947.

Jerome Holtzman

Sportswriter. Elected to Hall of Fame: 1989.

Jerome Holtzman has been a Chicago baseball writer for more than 30 years and has yet to cover the Cubs or White Sox in the World Series. He was a reporter and columnist for the *Chicago Sun-Times* and later for the *Chicago Tribune*. He is a regular contributor to *The Sporting News* and is also the author of several books, including one that is the definitive history of the Chicago Cubs.

Harry Bartholomew Hooper

Born August 24, 1887, in Bell Station, California; died December 18, 1974, in Santa Cruz, California. 5'10", 168 lbs., bats left, throws right. Years in minor leagues: 2; Major League debut: April 16, 1909; Years in Major Leagues: 17. Elected to Hall of Fame: 1971. Nickname: None.

Harry Hooper was part of a great Boston Red Sox outfield that included Tris Speaker and Duffy Lewis that helped the Red Sox to four American League championships and World Series titles in 1912, 1915, 1916 and 1918. He experienced two great World Series moments: making a barehanded catch of a what looked like a home run drive by the Giants' Larry Doyle in the fifth inning of the last game of the 1912 World Series. The Red Sox won, 3–2, in 10 innings. In the 1916 World Series, he hit two home runs against the Philadelphia Phillies, including the game winner off future Hall of Famer Eppa Rixey to break a 4–4 tie in the ninth inning.

He is credited with suggesting to Red Sox manager Ed Barrow in 1919 that if he made pitcher Babe Ruth into an outfielder, he could take advantage of Ruth's power every day. Barrow took him up on his idea. A few years later, Barrow was general manager of the New York Yankees and acquired outfielder Ruth from the Red Sox. Hooper was a great defensive outfielder who perfected a sliding catch that allowed him to jump to his feet and make a throw much faster than if he had dived for the ball.

Year	Team	G	AB	R	H	D	T	HR	RBI	AVE.
1909	Bos (A)	81	255	29	72	3	4	0	12	.282
1910	Bos	155	584	81	156	9	10	2	27	.267
1911	Bos	130	524	93	163	20	6	4	45	.311
1912	Bos	147	590	98	143	20	12	2	53	.242
1913	Bos	148	586	100	169	29	12	4	40	.288
1914	Bos	141	530	85	137	23	15	1	41	.258
1915	Bos	149	566	90	133	20	13	2	51	.235
1916	Bos	151	575	75	156	20	11	1	37	.271
1917	Bos	151	559	89	143	21	11	3	45	.256
1918	Bos	126	474	81	137	26	13	1	44	.289
1919	Bos	128	491	76	131	25	6	3	49	.267
1920	Bos	139	536	91	167	30	17	7	53	.312
1921	Chi (A)	108	419	74	137	26	5	8	58	.327
1922	Chi	152	602	111	183	35	8	11	80	.304
1923	Chi	145	576	87	166	32	4	10	65	.288
1924	Chi	130	476	107	156	27	8	10	62	.328
1925	Chi	127	442	62	117	23	5	6	55	.265
17 years		2308	8785	1429	2466	389	160	75	817	.281

Transactions: March 4, 1921: Traded to Chicago White Sox for Shano Collins and Neimo Leibold.

WORLD SERIES

WORLD SERIES

Year	Team	G	AB	R	H	D	T	HR	RBI	AVE.
1912	Bos (A)	8	31	3	9	2	1	0	2	.290
1915	Bos	5	20	4	7	0	0	2	3	.350
1916	Bos	5	21	6	7	1	1	0	1	.333
1918	Bos	6	20	0	4	0	0	0	0	.200
4 years		24	92	13	27	3	2	2	6	.293

Rogers Hornsby

Born April 27, 1896, in Winters, Texas; died January 5, 1963, in Chicago, Illinois. 5'11", 200 lbs., bats right, throws right. Years in minor leagues: 2; Major League debut: September 10, 1915; Years in Major Leagues: 23. Elected to Hall of Fame: 1942. Nickname: Rajah—a term of royalty and respect and a derivation of Hornsby's first name.

Rogers Hornsby was the greatest hitter in National League history. During one five-year stretch, from 1921 through 1925, he averaged over .400. He won six National League batting titles, and his .424 average in 1924 is the highest season mark for a player in either league in the 20th century. He finished with a lifetime batting average of .358, the highest for any National League player, the best for any righthanded hitter and second highest all-time, behind Ty Cobb.

In the historic 1924 season, Hornsby played in 143 games and got hits in 119 of them. He had 4 four-hit games, 25 three-hit games, 46 two-hit games and 44 games in which he got one hit. Hornsby won seven batting championships, including six in succession, and was voted Most Valuable Player twice. He had over 200 hits in seven seasons, including 250 in 1922. He led the league in hits four times. He also led the league in doubles four times, in triples twice and in home runs twice. He won the Triple Crown twice. He was convinced that success as a hitter depended on good eyesight, and he protected his eyes with some extreme measures. He did not read newspapers and he didn't go to movies for fear the wear and tear would hurt his vision.

Hornsby was also the classic example of how sometimes great ballplayers have difficulty managing because they don't have any players as good as they were. That, coupled with a brusque, overbearing, often irritating personality, led to short stays for him as a manager. He was openly critical of owners and of his players, sometimes embarrassing them with crude remarks about their abilities. In one famous incident, he was once eating dinner with Giant shortstop Doc Farrell when a reporter asked him if the Giants would win the pennant. "Not with him at short-stop," Hornsby replied. That was typical of his bluntness throughout his career, tolerable when he was hitting but not when he was managing. He was a player-manager for the Cardinals and led them (with his bat) to their first World Series championship in 1926. But the Cardinals traded him to the Giants, where he hit

.361, and then the Giants traded him to the Braves. He lasted there a year before he was traded to the Cubs. The Cubs won the pennant in 1929, the year before Hornsby was named their manager. He stayed until mid-season 1932 when he was replaced by Charlie Grimm. The Cubs went on to win the 1932 pennant, but voted not to give Hornsby any share of their World Series bonus.

Year	Team	G	AB	R	H	D	T	HR	RBI	AVE.
1915	StL (N)	18	57	5	14	2	0	0	4	.246
1916	StL	139	495	63	155	17	15	6	65	.313
1917	StL	145	523	86	171	24	17	8	66	.327
1918	StL	115	416	51	117	19	11	5	60	.281
1919	StL	138	512	68	163	15	9	8	71	.318
1920	StL	149	589	96	218	44	20	9	94	.370
1921	StL	154	592	131	235	44	18	21	126	.397
1922	StL	154	623	141	250	46	14	42	141	.401
1923	StL	107	424	89	163	32	10	17	83	.384
1924	StL	143	536	121	227	43	14	25	121	.424
1925	StL	138	504	133	203	41	10	39	143	.403
1926	StL	134	527	96	167	34	5	11	93	.317
1927	NY (N)	155	568	133	205	32	9	26	125	.361
1928	Bos (N)	140	486	99	188	42	7	21	94	.387
1929	Chi (N)	156	602	156	229	47	8	39	149	.380
1930	Chi	42	104	15	32	5	1	2	18	.308
1931	Chi	100	357	64	118	37	1	16	90	.331
1932	Chi	19	58	10	13	2	0	1	7	.224
1933	StL-StL (A)	57	92	11	30	7	0	3	23	.326
1934	StL (A)	24	23	2	7	2	0	1	11	.304
1935	StL	10	24	1	5	3	0	0	3	.208
1936	StL	2	5	1	2	0	0	0	2	.400
1937	StL	20	56	7	18	3	0	1	11	.321
23 years		2259	8173	1579	2930	541	169	301	1584	.358

Transactions: Dec. 20, 1926: Traded to New York Giants for Frankie Frisch and Jimmy Ring. Jan. 10, 1928: Traded to Boston Braves for Shanty Hogan and Jimmy Welsh. Nov. 7, 1928: Traded to Chicago Cubs for Socks Siebold, Percy Jones, Lou Leggett, Freddie Maguire, Bruce Cunningham and $200,000.

World Series

Year	Team	G	AB	R	H	D	T	HR	RBI	AVE.
1926	StL	7	28	2	7	1	0	0	4	.250
1929	Chi	5	21	4	5	1	1	0	1	.238
2 years		12	49	6	12	2	1	0	5	.245

Waite Hoyt

Born September 9, 1899, in Brooklyn, New York; died August 25, 1984, in Cincinnati, Ohio. 5'11", 185 lbs., bats right, throws right. Years in minor

leagues: 3; Major League debut: July 24, 1918; Years in Major Leagues: 21.
Elected to Hall of Fame: 1969. Nickname: Schoolboy—because he signed with
the New York Giants at the age of 15.

Waite Hoyt was an outgoing, confident pitcher who was a mainstay of the
pitching staff of the great Yankee teams in the 1920s. He once said the secret to
success in life is to pitch for the New York Yankees, and his record proves it. He
was signed by the New York Giants at the age of 15, spent three years in the minor
leagues and pitched one inning for the Giants in 1918 before being traded to the
Boston Red Sox. He was 4–6 for Boston in 1919 and 6–6 in 1920 but had one
spectacular performance: In a 13-inning game, Hoyt gave up a hit early in the game,
then threw 11 perfect innings before surrendering another hit. The opponent was
the Yankees, and they liked what they saw. The next year Hoyt was in a Yankee
uniform where he won 19 games in each of the next two years. His best years were
in 1927 and 1928 when he won 22 and 23, respectively.

The Yankees let him go in 1930 and he bounced around with several teams
in the next few years. He settled in as a relief pitcher for the Pirates where he was
15–6 in 1934. Hoyt won 237 games in his career and won six games in the six
World Series he apppeared in with the Yankees. He also appeared in the 1931 World
Series as a member of the Philadelphia A's. In 1921 against the Giants, Hoyt turned
in one of the great pitching performances in World Series history. He pitched three
complete games and allowed two unearned runs, for an earned run average of 0.00
for 27 innings. Unfortunately, one of the unearned runs was the only run scored
in game seven, which Hoyt lost 1–0.

After his playing days were over, the effervescent Hoyt spent 24 years as a
broadcaster of Cincinnati Reds games.

Year	Team	W-L	ERA	G	IP	H	BB	SO
1918	NY (N)	0-0	0.00	1	1	0	0	2
1919	Bos (A)	4-6	3.25	13	105.1	99	22	28
1920	Bos	6-6	4.38	22	121.1	123	47	45
1921	NY (A)	19-13	3.09	43	282.1	301	81	102
1922	NY	19-12	3.43	37	265	271	76	95
1923	NY	17-9	3.02	37	238.2	227	66	60
1924	NY	18-13	3.79	46	247	295	76	71
1925	NY	11-14	4.00	46	243	283	78	86
1926	NY	16-12	3.85	40	217.2	224	62	79
1927	NY	22-7	2.63	36	256.1	242	54	86
1928	NY	23-7	3.36	42	273	279	60	67
1929	NY	10-9	4.24	40	201.2	219	69	57
1930	NY-Det	11-10	4.71	34	183.1	240	56	35
1931	Det–Phil (A)	13-13	4.97	32	203	254	69	40
1932	Brk–NY (N)	6-10	4.35	26	124	141	37	36
1933	Pitt	5-7	2.92	36	117	118	19	44
1934	Pitt	15-6	2.93	48	190.2	184	43	105
1935	Pitt	7-11	3.40	39	164	187	27	63
1936	Pitt	7-5	2.70	22	116.2	115	20	37
1937	Pitt–Brklyn	8-9	3.41	38	195.1	211	36	65

Year	Team	W-L	ERA	G	IP	H	BB	SO
1938	Brklyn	0-3	4.96	6	16.1	24	5	3
21 years		237-182	3.59	674	3762.2	4037	1003	1206

Transactions: Dec. 15, 1920: Traded with Harry Harper, Wally Schang and Mike McNally to New York Yankees for Muddy Ruel, Del Pratt, Sammy Vick and Hank Thormahlen. May 30, 1930: Traded with Mark Koenig to Detroit for Ownie Carroll, Yats Wuestling and Harry Rice. June 30, 1931: Sold to Philadelphia Athletics. November 1932: Sold to Pittsburgh for waiver price.

WORLD SERIES

Year	Team	W-L	ERA	G	IP	H	BB	SO
1921	NY (A)	2-1	0.00	3	27	18	11	18
1922	NY	0-1	1.13	2	8	11	2	4
1923	NY	0-0	15.43	1	2.1	4	1	0
1926	NY	1-1	1.20	2	15	19	1	10
1927	NY	1-0	4.91	1	7.1	8	1	2
1928	NY	2-0	1.50	2	18	14	6	14
1931	Phil (A)	0-1	4.50	1	6	7	0	1
7 years		6-4	1.83	12	83.2	81	22	49

Cal Hubbard

Born October 31, 1900, in Keytesville, Missouri; died October 17, 1977, in St. Petersburg, Florida. 6'2", 265 lbs. Years in Major Leagues: 34 (as American League umpire, assistant supervisor and supervisor of umpires). Elected to Hall of Fame: 1976. Nickname: Big Cal—an obvious one, considering his dimensions.

Cal Hubbard was a huge man who commanded respect as an umpire not only because of his towering presence but because of his knowledge of the rules and his ability to take charge. Hubbard was a great football player who starred as an end and defensive lineman for Centenary College and at Geneva College in Beaver Falls, Pennsylvania, where he was an All-American. He played professional football for the New York Giants and Green Bay Packers where he earned respect for blocking and tackling. He played on four championship teams.

As a young man, he developed a love for learning the rules of the games he participated in and consequently became well aware of the rules of baseball. After serving several years umpiring in the minor leagues, he got the call to the Major Leagues in 1936 and was an outstanding arbiter for the next 16 years.

Between the 1951 and 1952 seasons, Hubbard was injured in a hunting accident when a shotgun pellet grazed his eye and blurred his vision. It forced him to end his umpiring career. The American League hired him to assist Tommy Connolly, a former ump who was the league's supervisor of umpires. When Connolly retired in 1954, Hubbard took over and held that position until his own retirement in 1970. He is the only man ever inducted into the college football, pro football and baseball halls of fame.

Carl Owen Hubbell

Born June 22, 1903, in Carthage, Missouri; died November 21, 1988, in Scottsdale, Arizona. 6', 170 lbs., bats right, throws left. Years in minor leagues: 5; Major League debut: July 26, 1928; Years in Major Leagues: 16. Elected to Hall of Fame: 1947. Nickname: King Carl—a name given to him after his two complete game shutouts in the 1933 World Series; also, The Meal Ticket—because of his ability to win big games.

As the story goes, Gabby Hartnett told his batterymate in the 1934 All-Star Game to just pitch to the American Leaguers like he had all year to his National League opponents. "They won't be able to hit it either," said Gabby. A few minutes later, Carl Hubbell struck out Babe Ruth, Lou Gehrig, Jimmie Foxx, Al Simmons and Joe Cronin in succession.

Hubbell used a baffling screwball and great control to win 253 games in his 16-year career, all with the New York Giants. He averaged less than two walks per nine innings for his career. Between July 17, 1936, and May 31, 1937, Hubbell won 24 straight games, still a Major League record. He threw a no-hitter against the Pittsburgh Pirates in 1929 and a one-hitter against the Dodgers 11 years later. In 1933, he went all the way in an 18-inning, 1–0 win over the St. Louis Cardinals in which he did not issue a single walk. In 1933 Hubbell had one stretch where he pitched 46 consecutive scoreless innings, a record since topped by Don Drysdale and Orel Hershiser. He had 10 shutouts that season with an earned run average of 1.66 and was the National League's Most Valuable Player. In the 1933 World Series, Hubbell beat the Washington Senators twice, 2–1 in 11 innings, and 4–2. All the runs were unearned, and Hubbell pitched all 20 innings.

In 1936 Hubbell earned his second MVP Award with his 26–6 record, once again leading the Giants to a National League championship. The following year, Hubbell compiled his fifth consecutive 20-win season, going 22–8, as the Giants won the pennant once again.

Year	Team	W-L	ERA	G	IP	H	BB	SO
1928	NY (N)	10-6	2.83	20	124	117	21	37
1929	NY	18-11	3.69	39	268	273	67	106
1930	NY	17-12	3.76	37	241.2	263	58	117
1931	NY	14-12	2.66	36	247	213	66	156
1932	NY	18-11	2.50	40	284	260	40	137
1933	NY	23-12	1.66	45	308.2	256	47	156
1934	NY	21-12	2.30	49	313	286	37	118
1935	NY	23-12	3.27	42	302.2	314	49	150
1936	NY	26-6	2.31	42	304	265	57	123
1937	NY	22-8	3.20	39	261.2	261	55	159
1938	NY	13-10	3.07	24	179	171	33	104
1939	NY	11-9	2.75	29	154	150	24	62
1940	NY	11-12	3.65	31	214.1	220	59	86
1941	NY	11-9	3.57	26	164	169	53	75

Year	Team	W-L	ERA	G	IP	H	BB	SO
1942	NY	11-8	3.95	24	157.1	158	34	61
1943	NY	4-4	4.91	12	66	87	24	31
16 years		253-154	2.97	535	3589.1	3463	724	1678

WORLD SERIES

Year	Team	W-L	ERA	G	IP	H	BB	SO
1933	NY (NL)	2-0	0.00	2	20	13	6	15
1936	NY	1-1	2.25	2	16	15	2	10
1937	NY	1-1	3.77	2	14.1	12	4	7
3 years		4-2	1.79	6	50.1	40	12	32

Miller James Huggins

Born March 27, 1880, in Cincinnati, Ohio; died September 25, 1929, in New York City, New York. 5'4", 146 lbs., bats right, throws right. Years in minor leagues: 3; Major League debut: April 15, 1904; Years in Major Leagues: 26 (as player and manager). Elected to Hall of Fame: 1964. Nickname: Hug— short for Huggins.

If ever there was an odd couple in baseball, it was Miller Huggins and Babe Ruth. Huggins, at five foot, four inches, often had to go toe-to-toe with Ruth, the incredible hulk of the New York Yankees during their glory years in the 1920s. Huggins, as manager of the Yankees, argued with Ruth, fined him, suspended him—and won with him. Today, each is memorialized on a monument in Yankee Stadium and each is in the Hall of Fame.

Huggins was a second baseman for Cincinnati and St. Louis in a 13-year playing career and managed the Cardinals for five years. In 1918 the Yankees hired him, and in 1920 Ruth came over from the Boston Red Sox. The Yankees won six pennants in the next eight years and three World Series championships. The 1927 Yankee team is considered to be one of the greatest teams in baseball history, and Huggins was responsible for managing the team on the field, dealing with the antics of the players off the field, and controlling the egos of the players on and off the field. When he contracted blood poisoning and died suddenly in 1929, the Yankees had lost one of the key components of their success.

Huggins had intended for his career to be in law and passed the bar exam after graduating from the University of Cincinnati Law School. He played college baseball and decided to switch careers to play the game he loved. He never practiced law, but his years of managing Babe Ruth are ample proof of his skills as an arbiter.

Year	Team	Record	Standing
1913	StL (N)	51-99	Eighth
1914	StL	81-72	Third
1915	StL	72-81	Sixth
1916	StL	60-93	Seventh
1917	StL	82-70	Third
1918	NY (A)	60-63	Fourth
1919	NY	80-59	Third
1920	NY	95-59	Third
1921	NY	98-55	First
1922	NY	94-60	First
1923	NY	98-54	First
1924	NY	89-63	Second
1925	NY	69-85	Seventh
1926	NY	91-63	First
1927	NY	110-44	First
1928	NY	101-53	First
1929	NY	82-61	Second
17 years		1413-1134	

WORLD SERIES

Year	Team	Record
1921	NY	3-5
1922	NY	0-4
1923	NY	4-2
1926	NY	3-4
1927	NY	4-0
1928	NY	4-0
6 years		18-15

William Hulbert

Baseball executive. Elected to Hall of Fame: 1995.

More than a century after he died, Hulbert was given his rightful place in the Baseball Hall of Fame. He founded the National League and brought civility to what was a rowdy sport, but he purposely did it behind the scenes. That helped the National League take shape, but it also put Hulbert's accomplishments in the background.

He was the owner of the Chicago team when he and other owners got together to discuss the game's problems: infiltration by gamblers, rules that weren't being enforced, inconsistent record keeping, and a generally bad reputation. Hulbert had another problem. He had built his ball club up with players he recruited from the East Coast so he was not well regarded by New England owners. To pacify them, he promoted Hartford owner Morgan Bulkeley, an insurance executive and politician, to be the National League's first president.

Bulkeley had the title and held the position for a year, but did not even attend the league's annual meeting at the end of the year. Hulbert took over as president and promptly kicked three teams out of the league—New York and Philadelphia for failing to complete their 1876 schedules and Cincinnati for selling beer on Sundays. The following year, he became suspicious when the Louisville team began playing poorly after getting off to a great start. His investigation led to four players being banned for life for fixing games. Hulbert also initiated the hiring of umpires by the league and not by the home team, thus starting the practice of having impartial umps at every game. Hulbert was an innovator and a man with a great passion for the game who probably would have done a lot more had he not died of a heart attack in 1882 at the age of 49. He was elected to the Hall of Fame in 1995, 58 years after Bulkeley was enshrined.

James Augustus Hunter

Born April 8, 1946, in Hertford, North Carolina; died September 9, 1999, in Hertford, North Carolina. 6', 195 lbs., bats right, throws right. Years in minor leagues: 1; Major League debut: May 13, 1965; Years in Major Leagues: 15. Elected to Hall of Fame: 1987. Nickname: Catfish—given to him by A's owner Charlie Finley because he didn't think "Jim Hunter" was flashy enough.

Catfish Hunter was a sensational pitcher in high school. When A's scout Clyde Klutz saw him, he called A's owner Charlie Finley and urged him to come to North Carolina to watch the youngster in person. Finley did, and signed him. Hunter was a Major League pitcher at the age of 19. He was 8–8 that first year, 1965, and didn't have a winning season until 1970. Along the way, he did throw a perfect game—on May 8, 1968, against the Minnesota Twins.

Finley had moved the A's from Kansas City to Oakland and was building a dynasty by signing talented, young players like Hunter, Reggie Jackson, Joe Rudi, Sal Bando, and Blue Moon Odom. Hunter won 20 games or more four times in a row—21–11, 21–7, 21–5, 25–12—between 1971 and 1974, helping Oakland to three straight World Series championships. He won the Cy Young Award in 1974. At the end of the 1974 season, Hunter and Finley haggled over a clause in Hunter's contract that called for the owner to give $50,000 to an insurance company for an annuity. When Finley failed to do so, Hunter challenged him. An arbiter ruled in favor of Hunter, said Finley was guilty of a breach of contract and declared Hunter a free agent.

More than 20 teams sent representatives to his North Carolina home, offering him all sorts of cash and deals such as car dealerships and McDonald's franchises. In the end, he signed with the man who originally signed him with the A's: Clyde Klutz, who was now working for the New York Yankees.

Hunter had one big year with the Yankees, 1975, when he won 23 games, and helped them to three American League championships before arm and shoulder problems forced his retirement at the age of 33.

Year	Team	W-L	ERA	G	IP	H	BB	SO
1965	KC	8-8	4.26	32	133	124	46	82
1966	KC	8-11	4.02	30	176.2	158	64	103
1967	KC	13-17	2.81	35	259.2	209	84	196
1968	Oak	13-13	3.35	36	234	210	69	172
1969	Oak	12-15	3.35	38	247	210	85	150
1970	Oak	18-14	3.81	40	262	253	74	178
1971	Oak	21-11	2.96	37	274	225	80	181
1972	Oak	21-7	2.04	38	295	200	70	191
1973	Oak	21-5	3.34	36	256.1	222	69	124
1974	Oak	25-12	2.49	41	318	268	46	143
1975	NY (A)	23-14	2.58	39	328	248	83	177
1976	NY	17-15	3.53	36	298.2	268	68	173
1977	NY	9-9	4.72	22	143	137	47	52
1978	NY	12-6	3.58	21	118	98	35	56
1979	NY	2-9	5.31	19	105	128	34	34
15 years		**224-166**	**3.26**	**500**	**3448.1**	**2958**	**954**	**2012**

Transactions: Dec. 31, 1974: Signed as free agent with New York Yankees.

LEAGUE CHAMPIONSHIP SERIES

Year	Team	W-L	ERA	G	IP	H	BB	SO
1971	Oak	0-1	5.63	1	8	7	2	6
1972	Oak	0-0	1.17	2	15.1	10	5	9
1973	Oak	2-0	1.65	2	16.1	12	5	6
1974	Oak	1-1	4.63	2	11.2	11	2	6
1976	NY (A)	1-1	4.50	2	12	10	1	5
1978	NY	0-0	4.50	1	6	7	3	5
6 years		**4-3**	**3.25**	**10**	**69.1**	**57**	**18**	**37**

WORLD SERIES

Year	Team	W-L	ERA	G	IP	H	BB	SO
1972	Oak	2-0	2.81	3	16	12	6	11
1973	Oak	1-0	2.03	2	13.1	11	4	6
1974	Oak	1-0	1.17	2	7.2	5	2	5
1976	NY (A)	0-1	3.12	1	8.2	10	4	5
1977	NY	0-1	10.38	2	4.1	6	0	1
1978	NY	1-1	4.15	2	13	13	1	5
6 years		**5-3**	**3.29**	**12**	**63**	**57**	**17**	**33**

Robert Hunter

Sportswriter. Elected to Hall of Fame: 1988.

In 1932, budding lawyer Bob Hunter sold his lawbooks for $13 and took a job on the sports desk of the *Los Angeles Post-Record*. A year later he went to work for the *Los Angeles Examiner* and began covering baseball. Fifty-five years later, he was elected to the Hall of Fame after a half-century of covering minor league and Major League baseball.

He once ranked Bobby Thomson's 1951 home run to give the Giants the National League pennant as his biggest thrill, Chuck Dressen as his favorite manager, Joe DiMaggio as the best player he ever saw, and "Jigger" Statz of the old coast league Los Angeles Angels as the best outfielder he ever covered.

Monford Merrill Irvin

Born February 25, 1919, in Columbia, Alaska. 6'2", 195 lbs., bats right, throws right. Years in minor leagues: 12 (11 in Negro Leagues, 1 in minor league); Major League debut: July 8, 1949; Years in Major Leagues: 8. Elected to Hall of Fame: 1973. Nickname: Monte—a short derivation of his first name.

Monte Irvin's best years were in the Negro leagues where he won batting titles for the Newark Eagles with batting averages of .422 in 1940, .396 in 1941 and .398 in 1946. Many thought Irvin would be the man to break the Major League color barrier because of his outstanding years with Newark. But Jackie Robinson got the call from Brooklyn in April 1947 and Larry Doby, Irvin's teammate at Newark, was brought up by the Cleveland Indians in July.

Irvin didn't get his shot until 1949 when, at the age of 30, the New York Giants brought him to the Major Leagues. In 1950, his first full season, he hit .299. A year later, Bobby Thomson hit the miracle home run for the Giants against the Dodgers in the playoffs, but New York wouldn't have gotten that far without Irvin. He hit .312, hit 21 home runs and led the league in runs batted in with 121.

The Giants lost the World Series to the Yankees but Irvin went 4-for-5 in the first game, 3-for-4 in the second game and had a .458 average for the series. He also stole home in one of the games, while Allie Reynolds was on the mound, providing what Irvin called his greatest thrill in baseball. He missed much of the 1952 season with a broken leg but roared back a year later to hit .323. Irvin only played eight years in the Major Leagues because he got such a late start, but finished with a lifetime batting average of .293. He worked for many years as a special assistant to the commissioner of baseball after his playing days were over.

Year	Team	G	AB	R	H	D	T	HR	RBI	AVE.
1949	NY (N)	36	76	7	17	3	2	0	7	.224
1950	NY	110	374	61	112	19	5	15	66	.299
1951	NY	151	558	94	174	19	11	24	121	.312
1952	NY	46	126	10	39	2	1	4	21	.310
1953	NY	124	444	72	146	21	5	21	97	.329
1954	NY	135	432	62	113	13	3	19	64	.262
1955	NY	51	150	16	38	7	1	1	17	.253
1956	Chi (N)	111	339	44	92	13	3	15	50	.272
8 years		764	2499	366	731	97	31	99	443	.293

WORLD SERIES

Year	Team	G	AB	R	H	D	T	HR	RBI	AVE.
1951	NY (N)	6	24	4	11	0	1	0	2	.458
1954	NY	4	9	1	2	1	0	0	2	.222
2 years		10	33	5	13	1	1	0	4	.394

James C. Isaminger

Sportswriter. Elected to Hall of Fame: 1974.

James Isaminger was one of the most respected sportswriters in the first half of the 20th century who is credited as being one of the journalists who helped expose the Black Sox scandal in the 1919 World Series. He began his career with the *Cincinnati Times-Herald*, then worked for 20 years for the *Philadelphia North American* before moving to the *Philadelphia Inquirer* in 1925. He worked there until his death in 1946.

In Philadelphia, he reported on the Connie Mack powerhouse A's teams, one of baseball's earliest dynasties that interrupted the New York Yankees' trips to the World Series by winning three straight championships from 1929 through 1931. He was president of the Baseball Writers Association of America in 1946.

Reginald Martinez Jackson

Born May 18, 1946, in Wyncote, Pennsylvania. 6', 206 lbs., bats left, throws left. Years in minor leagues: 2; Major League debut: June 9, 1967; Years in Major Leagues: 21. Elected to Hall of Fame: 1993. Nickname: Mr. October—because of his amazing ability to get big hits in postseason play.

Reggie Jackson was one of the most dynamic players of his era who was at his best in crucial situations. A .262 lifetime hitter during the regular season, he came to life in the World Series, hitting .357 in 27 games, setting the all-time record for World Series slugging percentage with .755, and hitting 10 home runs in just 98 at-bats. He holds 10 World Series batting records and is tied for 8 other records. But with Reggie, it wasn't just what he did, it's how he did it—with flair and with ego. In 1977, when he joined the New York Yankees after several years in Oakland and one with the Baltimore Orioles, he did not endear himself to teammates when he told the press, "I'm the straw that stirs the drink around here." He also had many run-ins with Yankee manager Billy Martin. In one, Jackson and Martin nearly came to blows in the Yankee dugout, after Martin pulled him from a game because he thought Jackson loafed on a play in right field. Jackson said later he was angry because his manager had embarrassed him—on television.

The Yankees had problems controlling his ego, but with Jackson aboard, they won their first World Series in 15 years in 1977, and they won it again in 1978. In the 1977 World Series, Jackson hit five home runs. Three were in one game—on three pitches. Counting a homer he hit the previous night, Jackson hit four consecutive home runs on four consecutive swings. In 1978, Jackson homered in the game that clinched the Yankee's second straight World Series title. He was a winner and the record shows that he helped his teams be winners, too. In a 12-year stretch from 1971 through 1982, Jackson played for three different teams—and they won 10 division championships. Five wound up being World Series champs. Jackson led or tied for the league lead in home runs four times, drove in more than 100 runs six times, and was the American League's Most Valuable Player in 1973 with his 32 home runs and 117 RBIs. In 1971, he hit a home run in the All-Star game that struck the light tower on the roof of Tiger Stadium in Detroit. He struck out a record 2,597 times in his career, but Jackson always considered that a price a ballplayer had to pay for being a power hitter. His 563 career home runs rank him sixth, behind Hank Aaron, Babe Ruth, Willie Mays, Frank Robinson and Harmon Killebrew.

Year	Team	G	AB	R	H	D	T	HR	RBI	AVE.
1967	KC	35	118	13	21	4	4	1	6	.178
1968	Oak	154	553	82	138	13	6	29	74	.250
1969	Oak	152	549	123	151	36	3	47	118	.275
1970	Oak	149	426	57	101	21	2	23	66	.237
1971	Oak	150	567	87	157	29	3	32	80	.277
1972	Oak	135	499	72	132	25	2	25	75	.265
1973	Oak	151	539	99	158	28	2	32	117	.293
1974	Oak	148	506	90	146	25	1	29	93	.289
1975	Oak	157	593	91	150	39	3	36	104	.253
1976	Balt	134	498	84	138	27	2	27	91	.277
1977	NY (A)	146	525	93	150	39	2	32	110	.286
1978	NY	139	511	82	140	13	5	27	97	.274
1979	NY	131	465	78	138	24	2	29	89	.297
1980	NY	143	514	94	154	22	4	41	111	.300
1981	NY	94	334	33	79	17	1	15	54	.237
1982	Cal	153	530	92	146	17	1	39	101	.275
1983	Cal	116	397	43	77	14	1	14	49	.194
1984	Cal	143	525	67	117	17	2	25	81	.223

Year	Team	G	AB	R	H	D	T	HR	RBI	AVE.
1985	Cal	143	460	64	116	27	0	27	85	.252
1986	Cal	132	419	65	101	12	2	18	58	.241
1987	Oak	115	336	42	74	14	1	15	43	.220
21 years			2820	9864	1551	2584	463	49	563	1702	.262

Transactions: April 2, 1976: Traded with Ken Holtzman and Bill Van Bommell to Baltimore for Don Baylor, Mike Torrez and Paul Mitchell. Nov. 29, 1976: Signed as free agent with New York Yankees. Jan. 22, 1982: Signed as free agent with California Angels.

DIVISION PLAYOFF SERIES

Year	Team	G	AB	R	H	D	T	HR	RBI	AVE.
1981	NY	5	20	4	6	0	0	2	4	.300

LEAGUE CHAMPIONSHIP SERIES

Year	Team	G	AB	R	H	D	T	HR	RBI	AVE.
1971	Oak	3	12	2	4	1	0	2	2	.333
1972	Oak	5	18	1	5	1	0	0	2	.278
1973	Oak	5	21	0	3	0	0	0	0	.143
1974	Oak	4	12	0	2	1	0	0	1	.167
1975	Oak	3	12	1	5	0	0	1	3	.417
1977	NY (A)	5	16	1	2	0	0	0	1	.125
1978	NY	4	13	5	6	1	0	2	6	.462
1980	NY	3	11	1	3	1	0	0	0	.273
1981	NY	2	4	1	0	0	0	0	1	.000
1982	Cal	5	18	2	2	0	0	1	2	.111
10 years		39	137	14	32	5	0	6	18	.234

WORLD SERIES

Year	Team	G	AB	R	H	D	T	HR	RBI	AVE.
1973	Oak	7	29	3	9	3	1	1	6	.310
1974	Oak	5	14	3	4	1	0	1	1	.286
1977	NY (A)	6	20	10	9	1	0	5	8	.450
1978	NY	6	23	2	9	1	0	2	8	.391
1981	NY	3	12	3	4	1	0	1	1	.333
5 years		27	98	21	35	7	1	10	24	.357

Travis Calvin Jackson

Born November 2, 1903, in Waldo, Arkansas; died July 27, 1987, in Waldo, Arkansas. 5'10", 160 lbs., bats right, throws right. Years in minor leagues: 2;

Major League debut: September 27, 1922; Years in Major Leagues: 15. Elected to Hall of Fame: 1982. Nickname: Stonewall—after the Civil War general; also Jax—a shortening of his last name.

Travis Jackson was a great fielding, good hitting shortstop who anchored the infield for John McGraw's New York Giants, helping them to four National League pennants. Jackson had good range in the field and an accurate arm that threw bullets across the infield. He led all National League shortstops in fielding average twice, assists four times and chances three times.

At bat, he hit over .300 six times in his 15-year career, including .327 in 1926 and .339 in 1930. He finished with a lifetime batting average of .291. He drove in more than 90 runs in three different seasons, including 101 in 1934. When he retired, his RBI total of 929 was the most ever by a shortstop.

Year	Team	G	AB	R	H	D	T	HR	RBI	AVE.
1922	NY (N)	3	8	1	0	0	0	0	0	.000
1923	NY	96	327	45	90	12	7	4	37	.275
1924	NY	151	596	81	180	26	8	11	76	.302
1925	NY	112	411	51	117	15	2	9	59	.285
1926	NY	111	385	64	126	24	8	8	51	.327
1927	NY	127	469	67	149	29	4	14	98	.318
1928	NY	150	537	73	145	35	6	14	77	.270
1929	NY	149	551	92	162	21	12	21	94	.294
1930	NY	116	431	70	146	27	8	13	82	.339
1931	NY	145	555	65	172	26	10	5	71	.310
1932	NY	52	195	23	50	17	1	4	38	.256
1933	NY	53	122	11	30	5	0	0	12	.246
1934	NY	137	523	75	140	26	7	16	101	.268
1935	NY	128	511	74	154	20	12	9	80	.301
1936	NY	126	465	41	107	8	1	7	53	.230
15 years		1656	6086	833	1768	291	86	135	929	.291

WORLD SERIES

Year	Team	G	AB	R	H	D	T	HR	RBI	AVE.
1923	NY (N)	1	1	0	0	0	0	0	0	.000
1924	NY	7	27	3	2	0	0	0	1	.074
1933	NY	5	18	3	4	1	0	0	2	.222
1936	NY	6	21	1	4	0	0	0	1	.190
4 years		19	67	7	10	1	0	0	4	.149

Jaime Jarrin

Broadcaster. Elected to Hall of Fame: 1998.

Jaime Jarrin has been the Spanish version of Vin Scully, broadcasting Los Angeles Dodgers baseball games on KWKW, a radio station for Spanish-speaking people, since 1973. The native of Ecuador started out rebroadcasting in Spanish games the Dodgers had already played before moving up to live play-by-play work. He has broadcast 16 World Series for CBS Radio and has served as sports director of KWKW and as vice president of news and sports for Lotus Broadcasting, the parent company of the radio station. He has long been known as the "Spanish Voice of the Dodgers."

Ferguson Arthur Jenkins

Born December 13, 1943, in Chatham, Ontario, Canada. 6'5", 210 lbs., bats right, throws right. Years in minor leagues: 3; Major League debut: September 10, 1965; Years in Major Leagues: 19. Elected to Hall of Fame: 1991. Nickname: Fergie—short for his first name.

Ferguson Jenkins used an easy motion, pinpoint control and durability to win 284 games in his 19-year Major League career, much of it with the Chicago Cubs. He is the only native Canadian in the Hall of Fame.

Jenkins won 20 games or more seven times—including six in a row—and was the National League's Cy Young Award winner in 1971 when he won 24 games and walked only 37 batters in 325 innings, an average of about one walk per every nine innings. He led the Major Leagues in complete games six times and is the only Major League pitcher ever to have more than 3,000 strikeouts and less than 1,000 walks. Like Robin Roberts before him, he played most of his career with teams that did not do well and that may have cost him a shot at being a 300-game winner. In 1968 alone, Jenkins lost five games 1–0 and still managed to win 20 games.

After stumbling to a 14–16 record in 1973, the Cubs traded him to the Texas Rangers, who had lost 105 games. Jenkins won 25 for the Rangers in 1974, more than he had ever won with the Cubs, and was the American League Comeback Player of the Year. In 1980, he was arrested on a drug charge in Toronto, a charge that was later dropped. But the drug stigma stuck with him, in large part because Commissioner Bowie Kuhn suspended him before the charge was dropped. Many believe the drug arrest, though later nullified, cost Jenkins some votes for the Hall of Fame and delayed his entry for several years.

Year	Team	W-L	ERA	G	IP	H	BB	SO
1965	Phil	2-1	2.19	7	12.1	7	2	10
1966	Phil-Chi (N)	6-8	3.32	61	184.1	150	52	150
1967	Chi	20-13	2.80	38	289.1	230	83	236
1968	Chi	20-15	2.63	40	308	255	65	260
1969	Chi	21-15	3.21	43	311	284	71	273
1970	Chi	22-16	3.39	40	313	265	60	274
1971	Chi	24-13	2.77	39	325	304	37	263
1972	Chi	20-12	3.21	36	289	253	62	184
1973	Chi	14-16	3.89	38	271	267	57	170

Year	Team	W-L	ERA	G	IP	H	BB	SO
1974	Tex	25-12	2.83	41	328	286	45	225
1975	Tex	17-18	3.93	37	270	261	56	157
1976	Bos	12-11	3.27	30	209	201	43	142
1977	Bos	10-10	3.68	28	193	190	36	105
1978	Tex	18-8	3.04	34	249	228	41	157
1979	Tex	16-14	4.07	37	259	252	81	164
1980	Tex	12-12	3.77	29	198	190	52	129
1981	Tex	5-8	4.50	19	106	122	40	63
1982	Chi (N)	14-15	3.15	34	217.1	221	68	134
1983	Chi	6-9	4.30	33	167.1	176	46	96
19 years		**284-226**	**3.34**	**664**	**4499.2**	**4142**	**997**	**3192**

Transactions: April 21, 1966: Traded with Adolpho Phillips and John Hern-stein to Chicago Cubs for Larry Jackson and Bob Buhl. Oct. 25, 1973: Traded to Texas Rangers for Bill Madlock and Vic Harris. Nov. 17, 1975: Traded to Boston Red Sox for Juan Beniquez, Steve Barr and Craig Skok. Dec. 14, 1977: Traded to Texas for John Poloni and cash. Dec. 8, 1981: Signed as free agent with Chicago Cubs.

Hugh Ambrose Jennings

Born April 2, 1870, in Pittston, Pennsylvania; died February 1, 1928, in Scranton, Pennsylvania. 5'8", 165 lbs., bats right, throws right. Years in minor leagues: 2; Major League debut: June 1, 1891; Years in Major Leagues: 17. Elected to Hall of Fame: 1945. Nickname: Eee-Yah—derived from a yell of encouragement he gave to his players from the dugout and coaching box.

Hugh Jennings had a winning career in baseball as a player, manager and coach. He was a star shortstop for the Baltimore team that won the league championship in each of Jennings' first three years with the club, 1894–1896. Later, the Detroit Tigers team he managed won the American League championship in 1907 through 1909, his first three years at the helm. Only Ralph Houk with the 1961–1963 Yankees duplicated that feat.

Jennings, who had a law degree from Cornell, quit baseball for a while to study law but later returned to play a few more years. In 1896, he hit .398 and stole 73 bases, a record at the time. One of his specialties was getting hit by pitched balls. In 1896, he led the league in getting hit with pitches with 49, a record that stood for 75 years until Ron Hunt of the New York Mets was whacked 51 times in 1971. Jennings managed the Tigers until 1920, when Ty Cobb took over. He then coached for John McGraw's Giants, and the Giants won the pennant four years in a row.

As a Player

Year	Team	G	AB	R	H	D	T	HR	RBI	AVE.
1891	Louis	90	360	53	105	10	8	1	58	.292
1892	Louis	152	594	65	132	16	4	2	61	.222
1893	Louis-Balt	39	143	12	26	3	0	1	15	.182
1894	Balt	128	501	134	168	28	16	4	109	.335
1895	Balt	131	529	159	204	41	7	4	125	.386
1896	Balt	130	523	125	208	27	9	0	121	.398
1897	Balt	117	439	133	156	26	9	2	79	.355
1898	Balt	143	534	135	175	25	11	1	87	.328
1899	Balt-Brk	69	224	44	67	3	12	0	42	.299
1900	Brklyn	115	441	61	120	18	6	1	69	.272
1901	Phil (N)	82	302	38	83	21	2	1	39	.275
1902	Phil	78	289	31	80	16	3	1	32	.277
1903	Brklyn	6	17	2	4	0	0	0	1	.235
1907	Det	1	4	0	1	1	0	0	0	.250
1909	Det	2	4	1	2	0	0	0	2	.500
1912	Det	1	1	0	0	0	0	0	0	.000
1918	Det	1	1	0	0	0	0	0	0	.000
17 years		**1285**	**4905**	**993**	**1531**	**235**	**87**	**18**	**840**	**.312**

Transactions: February 1901: Sold to Philadelphia Phillies for $3,000.

As a Manager

Year	Team	Record	Standings
1907	Det	92-58	First
1908	Det	90-63	First
1909	Det	98-54	First
1910	Det	86-68	Third
1911	Det	89-65	Second
1912	Det	69-84	Sixth
1913	Det	66-87	Sixth
1914	Det	80-73	Fourth
1915	Det	100-54	Second
1916	Det	87-67	Third
1917	Det	78-75	Fourth
1918	Det	55-71	Seventh
1919	Det	80-60	Fourth
1920	Det	61-93	Seventh
14 years		**1131-972**	

World Series

Year	Team	Record
1907	Det	0-4
1908	Det	1-4
1909	Det	3-4
3 years		**4-12**

Byron Bancroft Johnson

Born January 5, 1864, in Norwalk, Ohio; died March 28, 1931, in St. Louis, Missouri. Baseball executive. Elected to Hall of Fame: 1945. Nickname: Ban— a shortening of his middle name.

Ban Johnson was one of the founders of the American League and was its president for 27 years. He helped create the World Series and headed a three-man commission that oversaw both leagues, which gave him enormous power. Johnson was a graduate of the University of Cincinnati Law School who gave up the law profession early in favor of becoming a newspaper reporter. He became sportseditor of the *Cincinnati Commercial-Gazette* and developed a friendship that not only changed his life but would eventually change baseball forever.

The new friend was Charles Comiskey, manager of the Cincinnati ball club. Together, Johnson and Comiskey started the Western League in 1894, which flourished for six years. In 1900, the men decided to change its name to the American League, as Comiskey and Johnson prepared to mount a challenge to the well-established National League.

The American League operated as a minor league for one year and then placed itself the next year as a competitor to the National League. Johnson was elected as its first president. He ruled the league with an iron hand, banning the sale of liquor at ballparks and instituting policies to cut down on the rough play and rough attitudes of players, coaches and managers. His league did not have the $2,400 salary cap that the well-established National League had, and American League teams were able to raid the rival league for talent. By 1903, the leagues were on so much of an equal status that the first World Series was played. Johnson and Comiskey gradually grew apart. They had a major falling out after the 1919 World Series when Comiskey, owner of the Chicago White Sox, thought Johnson should have canceled the series after the first two games when there were suspicions that something was wrong. It was later determined that eight White Sox players had conspired with gamblers to fix the World Series. The election of Kenesaw Mountain Landis as baseball's first commissioner the following year dissolved most of Johnson's power. He retired in poor health in 1927. One of his lasting legacies is the respect he had for umpires and the authority he gave them to control games, leading to the reduction of boorish activities by players, managers and coaches.

Walter Perry Johnson

Born November 6, 1887, in Humboldt, Kansas; died December 10, 1946, in Washington, D.C. 6'1", 200 lbs., bats right, throws right. Years in minor leagues: None; Major League debut: August 2, 1907; Years in Major Leagues: 21. Elected to Hall of Fame: 1936. Nickname: The Big Train—a reference to his fastball, because trains were the fastest means of transportation in his era; also, Barney, a reference to Barney Oldfield, the race car driver—again, because of the speed of his pitches.

Walter Johnson used a sidearm delivery and a blazing fastball to be one of the most dominant pitchers not only of his time but of all time. Pitching 21 years for usually mediocre Washington Senator teams, Johnson won 416 games. Only Cy Young with 511 has won more. He had 110 shutouts—still the Major League record. He won over 30 games in two consecutive years: 32–12 in 1912 and 36–7 in 1913. He won 20 or more games in 12 seasons, including 10 in a row.

The Big Train had 11 seasons in which his earned run average was under 2.00, and he had the lowest ERA in the league five times. He led the American League in complete games six times, in shutouts seven times and in strikeouts 12 times, including eight years in a row. When he retired in 1927, his 3,508 strikeouts were the Major Leagues' top figure. In 1920 Johnson was 8–10, one of his worst seasons, yet it was the year he threw the only no-hitter of his career.

In 1908, his first full season with the Senators, he threw three shutouts in four days. Two different times in his career, he struck out the side on nine pitches with the bases loaded. In 1913 he won a 15-inning 1–0 game, and five years later he won 1–0 in a game in which he pitched 20 innings. In 1913, Johnson pitched 55⅔ consecutive scoreless innings, a record that stood for 55 years until Don Drysdale broke it in 1968.

Year	Team	W-L	ERA	G	IP	H	BB	SO
1907	Wash	5-9	1.87	14	110.2	98	17	70
1908	Wash	14-14	1.64	36	257.1	194	53	160
1909	Wash	13-25	2.21	40	297	247	84	164
1910	Wash	25-17	1.35	45	373	269	76	313
1911	Wash	25-13	1.89	40	323.1	292	70	207
1912	Wash	32-12	1.39	50	368	259	76	303
1913	Wash	36-7	1.09	47	346	230	38	243
1914	Wash	28-18	1.72	51	371.2	287	74	225
1915	Wash	27-13	1.55	47	336.2	258	56	203
1916	Wash	25-20	1.89	48	371	290	132	228
1917	Wash	23-16	2.30	47	328	259	67	188
1918	Wash	23-13	1.27	39	325	241	70	162
1919	Wash	20-14	1.49	39	290.1	235	51	147
1920	Wash	8-10	3.13	21	143.2	135	27	78
1921	Wash	17-14	3.51	35	264	265	92	143
1922	Wash	15-16	2.99	41	280	283	99	105
1923	Wash	17-12	3.54	43	262	267	69	130
1924	Wash	23-7	2.72	38	277.2	233	77	158
1925	Wash	20-7	3.07	30	229	211	78	108
1926	Wash	15-16	3.61	33	261.2	259	73	125
1927	Wash	5-6	5.10	18	107.2	113	26	48
21 years		416-279	2.17	802	5923.2	4925	1405	3508

WORLD SERIES

Year	Team	W-L	ERA	G	IP	H	BB	SO
1924	Wash	1-2	2.63	3	24	30	11	20
1925	Wash	2-1	2.08	3	26	26	4	15
2 years		**3-3**	**2.34**	**6**	**50**	**56**	**15**	**35**

William Julius Johnson

Born October 26, 1899, in Snow Hill, Maryland; died June 14, 1989, in Wilmington, Delaware. 5'11", 150 lbs., bats right, throws right. Years in minor leagues: 18 (Negro Leagues); Years in Major Leagues: None. Elected to Hall of Fame: 1975. Nickname: Judy—because of his resemblance to Judy Gans, a veteran Negro League player.

Judy Johnson was a great clutch hitter in the Negro leagues who seemed to perform best under pressure, coming up with big hits or spectacular plays at third base when the game was on the line. Those who saw him play say he could field with the best of them, even with Brooks Robinson who is considered the premier fielding third baseman in Major League history. Johnson never got a chance to perform in the Major Leagues. He retired from the Negro leagues ten years before Jackie Robinson made his debut with the Brooklyn Dodgers.

Johnson hit over .300 his first five full seasons in the Negro leagues, 1922–26, then dipped under .300 for two seasons after a serious beaning made him gun-shy at the plate. He then rebounded and hit .390 in 1929. He led his Hilldale team to three straight championships. He then played for the Homestead Grays and Pittsburgh Crawfords. At Pittsburgh, he captained a team where some of his teammates were Satchel Paige, Josh Gibson and Cool Papa Bell, all Hall of Famers. That team won 39, lost 15 and won the Negro National Championship by defeating the New York Cubans in seven games. One of New York's players was Luis Tiant, Sr., whose son would be a star pitcher in the Major Leagues.

After his playing days were over, Johnson worked as a scout for both the Philadelphia A's and Philadelphia Phillies. He recommended that the A's sign a young player named Henry Aaron, but the A's declined because of money problems. Later, as a scout for the Philadelphia Phillies, he was instrumental in the signing of Richie Allen, who developed into one of baseball's best power hitters in the 1960s and 1970s.

Adrian Joss

Born April 12, 1880, in Juneau, Wisconsin; died April 11, 1911, in Toledo, Ohio. 6'3", 185 lbs., bats right, throws right. Years in minor leagues: 2; Major League debut: April 26, 1902; Years in Major Leagues: 9. Elected to Hall of Fame: 1978. Nickname: Addie—short for Adrian

Addie Joss was an outstanding American League pitcher whose career was cut short by a deadly illness. He had some spectacular games and spectacular seasons while he was healthy, though. He won 20 games or more four years in a row, from 1905 through 1908, and had 160 wins in his nine-year career. He was the hardest pitcher in baseball history to reach base on—just 8.7 runners per nine innings. Forty-five of his wins were shutouts, and his lifetime earned run average of 1.88 is second best on the all-time list. Only Ed Walsh had a lower one at 1.82. Fittingly, on October 2, 1908, Joss, of Cleveland, and Walsh, a 40-game winner with the White Sox, engaged in one of the greatest pitching duels in baseball history. Walsh struck out 15 and gave up a run that scored on a wild pitch. Joss threw a perfect game, retiring three pinch hitters in the ninth inning to sew it up. He threw a second no-hitter, also against the White Sox, on April 20, 1910, a game in which only five balls were hit out of the infield on him.

Other outstanding individual efforts: In his Major League debut, on April 26, 1902, pitching for Cleveland, he threw a one-hit shutout against St. Louis, winning 3–0. A few days later, he took a no-hitter into the ninth inning before settling for a two-hitter. In his second season, Joss lost to Rube Waddell of Philadelphia, 2–1, in a game in which each pitcher went the distance in a 14-inning marathon. In 1911, two days after the baseball season opened, Joss took ill and was hospitalized. Two days later, he died of tubercular meningitis. He was 31.

Year	Team	W-L	ERA	G	IP	H	BB	SO
1902	Cleve	17-13	2.77	32	269.1	225	75	106
1903	Cleve	18-13	2.15	32	292.2	239	43	126
1904	Cleve	14-10	1.59	25	192.1	160	30	83
1905	Cleve	20-12	2.01	33	286	246	46	132
1906	Cleve	21-9	1.72	34	282	220	43	106
1907	Cleve	27-11	1.83	42	338.2	279	54	127
1908	Cleve	24-11	1.16	42	325	232	30	130
1909	Cleve	14-13	1.71	33	242.2	198	31	67
1910	Cleve	5-5	2.26	13	107.1	96	18	49
9 years		**160-97**	**1.88**	**286**	**2336**	**1895**	**370**	**926**

Harold Kaese

Sportswriter. Elected to Hall of Fame: 1976.

Harold Kaese got his sportswriting start with the old *Boston Transcript* but won acclaim as a sportswriter and columnist for the *Boston Globe* from 1942 to 1973. He covered all but three years of Ted Williams' career and was there to report on the career of Williams' successor, Carl Yastrzemski, as well. He covered the Red Sox in their pennant winning years of 1946 and 1967 and the Boston Braves (with Spahn and Sain) in their 1948 pennant year. He was elected to the writers' branch of the Hall of Fame in 1976, three years after his retirement and one year after his death.

Albert William Kaline

Born December 19, 1934, in Baltimore, Maryland. 6'2", 184 lbs., bats right, throws right. Years in minor leagues: None; Major League debut: June 25, 1953; Years in Major Leagues: 22. Elected to Hall of Fame: 1980. Nickname: None.

Al Kaline grew up in the Baltimore area before there was a franchise there and at one time had visions of playing for the Washington Senators. But the Detroit Tigers signed him and brought him to the Major Leagues without a single inning of minor league experience. Kaline was not flashy but was smooth in everything he did. He was a consistently good hitter with a picture-perfect swing and was graceful in right field where he had one of the most accurate throwing arms in the American League for two decades.

In 1955, at the age of 20, he led the American League in hits with 200 and won the batting title with a .340 average—and no one younger has accomplished that feat. He hit over .300 in nine seasons. Kaline played 22 seasons and finished with a lifetime batting average of .297. He had 3,007 hits including 399 home runs. His lifetime statistics attest to his consistency. He hit 27 home runs four times in his career, had 29 doubles three times and 28 doubles twice. He was injury prone and yet he had the unique quality of also being durable. He set an American League record by playing in 100 or more games for 20 consecutive years. He won 11 Gold Gloves in right field and had a string of 133 straight games without an error in 1971. He played in 18 All-Star games and one World Series. In 1968, when the Tigers defeated the Cardinals in seven games, Kaline got 11 hits, including two home runs, and hit .379.

Year	Team	G	AB	R	H	D	T	HR	RBI	AVE.
1953	Det	30	28	9	7	0	0	1	2	.250
1954	Det	138	504	42	139	18	3	4	43	.276
1955	Det	152	588	121	200	24	8	27	102	.340
1956	Det	153	617	96	194	32	10	27	128	.314
1957	Det	149	577	83	170	29	4	23	90	.295
1958	Det	146	543	84	170	34	7	16	85	.313
1959	Det	136	511	86	167	19	2	27	94	.327
1960	Det	147	551	77	153	29	4	15	68	.278
1961	Det	153	586	116	190	41	7	19	82	.324
1962	Det	100	398	78	121	16	6	29	94	.304
1963	Det	145	551	89	172	24	3	27	101	.312
1964	Det	146	525	77	154	31	5	17	68	.293
1965	Det	125	399	72	112	18	2	18	72	.281
1966	Det	142	479	85	138	29	1	29	88	.288
1967	Det	131	458	94	141	28	2	25	78	.308
1968	Det	102	327	49	94	14	1	10	53	.287
1969	Det	131	456	74	124	17	0	21	69	.272
1970	Det	131	467	64	130	24	4	16	71	.278
1971	Det	133	405	69	119	19	2	15	54	.294

Year	Team	G	AB	R	H	D	T	HR	RBI	AVE.
1972	Det	106	278	46	87	11	2	10	32	.313
1973	Det	91	310	40	79	13	0	10	45	.255
1974	Det	147	558	71	146	28	2	13	64	.262
22 years		2834	10116	1622	3007	498	75	399	1583	.297

LEAGUE CHAMPIONSHIP SERIES

Year	Team	G	AB	R	H	D	T	HR	RBI	AVE.
1972	Det	5	19	3	5	0	0	1	1	.263

WORLD SERIES

Year	Team	G	AB	R	H	D	T	HR	RBI	AVE.
1968	Det	7	29	6	11	2	0	2	8	.379

Timothy John Keefe

Born January 1, 1857, in Cambridge, Massachusetts; died April 23, 1933, in Cambridge, Massachusetts. 5'10", 185 lbs., bats right, throws right. Years in minor leagues: 1; Major League debut: August 6, 188; Years in Major Leagues: 14. Elected to Hall of Fame: 1964. Nickname: Sir Timothy—a title of respect because of his achievements as a ballplayer.

Tim Keefe was one of the greatest pitchers of the 19th century who is credited with developing the change of pace pitch which today is known as the change up. Pitching for the New York Giants, he teamed with Smiling Mickey Welch to provide the best one-two punch of any starting pitching staff in baseball.

In 1888, Keefe won 19 straight games, a record (for one season) tied by Rube Marquard 24 years later but never surpassed. Keefe's record is tainted only because of a change of rules. He had won eight straight when he was lifted in the second inning of a game in which the Giants were winning 9–0 against Chicago. The thought was to not waste his arm in a game that was locked up early. Because of scoring rules of the day, he was given credit for the win. Later, the rules were changed so that starting pitchers had to pitch five innings to earn a victory.

After that game, Keefe won 10 more in a row to give him 19. In the game that broke the string, also against Chicago, he lost 4–2 with two of the runs against him unearned. (Carl Hubbell holds the all-time record for consecutive wins— 24—over a two-year period.) Keefe won 342 games in a career that lasted only 14 seasons. He was known for his gentlemanly behavior, hardly ever arguing with the umpires. Ironically, when his pitching days were over, Keefe tried umpiring but quit because of players and fans reacting in anger to many of his calls. The kindly gentleman then coached baseball at Harvard, Tufts and Princeton before settling into a successful real estate career.

Year	Team	W-L	ERA	G	IP	H	BB	SO
1880	Troy (N)	6-6	0.86	12	105	71	17	43
1881	Troy	19-27	3.16	46	413	442	88	109
1882	Troy	17-26	2.50	43	375	368	81	116
1883	NY (AA)	41-27	2.41	68	619	486	98	361
1884	NY	37-17	2.29	58	491.2	388	75	323
1885	NY (N)	32-13	1.58	46	398	297	103	230
1886	NY	42-20	2.53	64	540	478	100	291
1887	NY	35-19	3.10	56	478.2	447	108	186
1888	NY	35-12	1.74	51	434.1	316	91	333
1889	NY	28-13	3.31	47	364	310	151	209
1890	NY (P)	17-11	3.38	30	229	228	85	88
1891	NY-Phil (N)	5-11	4.46	19	133.1	155	55	64
1892	Phil	20-16	2.36	39	313.1	264	100	127
1893	Phil	10-7	4.40	22	178	202	79	53
14 years		344-225	2.62	601	5072.1	4452	1231	2533

William Henry Keeler

Born March 3, 1872, in Brooklyn, New York; died January 1, 1923, in Brooklyn, New York. 5'4", 140 lbs., bats left, throws left. Years in minor leagues: 1; Major League debut: September 30, 1892; Years in Major Leagues: 19. Elected to Hall of Fame: 1939. Nickname: Wee Willie—because of his diminutive size.

Wee Willie Keeler was an amazing hitter who sprayed the ball all over the field and was one of the first "place hitters"—bunting when the third baseman and first baseman were back, and swinging away and pushing the ball over their heads when they played in. Playing for John McGraw's Baltimore team from 1894 through 1898, Keeler was among several players who perfected the art of chopping the ball down on the rock-hard infield and then legging out the base hit as the ball bounced high off the dirt. It was a ploy back then. When a batter does it accidentally today, it is still known as a "Baltimore chop."

Keeler explained his theory of hitting in a classic statement that has become part of baseball lore. "Have a clear eye," he said, "and hit 'em where they ain't." He helped his Baltimore team win three straight championships from 1894 through 1896 but saved his best year for 1897. Wee Willie got two hits on April 22 and continued to hit in every game through June 18—44 straight games, a Major League record that held up for 44 years until Joe DiMaggio had his 56-game streak.

Keeler hit .432 in 1897, but lost the batting title to Hugh Duffy who hit .438. The Orioles finished second in 1897 and 1898, then Keeler moved to Brooklyn and played on two more championship teams in 1899 and 1900. At the end of his 19-year career, Keeler had 2,962 hits (3,000 was not a magic number back in those days) and a lifetime batting average of .345, fifth highest in baseball history.

Year	Team	G	AB	R	H	D	T	HR	RBI	AVE.
1892	NY	14	53	7	17	3	0	0	6	.321
1893	NY-Brklyn	27	104	19	33	3	2	2	16	.317
1894	Balt	129	590	165	219	27	22	5	94	.371
1895	Balt	131	565	162	221	24	15	4	78	.391
1896	Balt	127	546	154	214	22	13	4	82	.392
1897	Balt	128	562	147	243	27	19	1	74	.432
1898	Balt	128	564	126	214	10	2	1	44	.379
1899	Brklyn	143	571	140	215	13	14	1	61	.377
1900	Brklyn	137	565	106	208	11	14	4	68	.368
1901	Brklyn	136	589	123	209	16	15	2	43	.355
1902	Brklyn	132	556	86	188	18	7	0	38	.338
1903	NY (A)	132	515	95	164	14	7	0	32	.318
1904	NY	143	543	78	186	14	8	2	40	.343
1905	NY	149	560	81	169	14	4	4	38	.302
1906	NY	152	592	96	180	8	3	2	33	.304
1907	NY	107	423	50	99	5	2	0	17	.234
1908	NY	91	323	38	85	3	1	1	14	.263
1909	NY	99	360	44	95	7	5	1	32	.264
1910	NY (N)	19	10	5	3	0	0	0	0	.300
19 years		**2124**	**8591**	**1722**	**2962**	**239**	**153**	**34**	**810**	**.345**

George Clyde Kell

Born August 23, 1922, in Swifton, Arkansas. 5'10", 170 lbs., bats right, throws right. Years in minor leagues: 2; Major League debut: September 28, 1943; Years in Major Leagues: 15. Elected to Hall of Fame: 1983. Nickname: None.

Many Hall of Famers were destined for greatness from the moment they were spotted by Major League scouts. Such was not the case with George Kell. The Brooklyn Dodgers looked at him and cut him from their minor league roster. After hitting .396 for Lancaster, a Class B minor league team, Connie Mack signed him for the Philadelphia A's but traded him to Detroit after a couple of years.

Kell batted over .300 nine times. His best year was 1949 when he hit .343 and edged out Ted Williams for the American League batting title by a fraction of a point. The following year, he hit .340 and led the league in hits with 218 and in doubles with 56.

Defensively, he was known for his sure-handedness and his accurate arm. He led American League third basemen in assists four times, in fielding percentage seven times and in putouts twice. He also led third basemen in participation in double plays twice.

Year	Team	G	AB	R	H	D	T	HR	RBI	AVE.
1943	Phil (A)	1	5	1	1	0	1	0	1	.200
1944	Phil	139	514	51	138	15	3	0	44	.268
1945	Phil	147	567	50	154	30	3	4	56	.272

Year	Team	G	AB	R	H	D	T	HR	RBI	AVE.
1946	Phil-Det	131	521	70	168	25	10	4	52	.322
1947	Det	152	588	75	188	29	5	5	93	.320
1948	Det	92	368	47	112	24	3	2	44	.304
1949	Det	134	522	97	179	38	9	3	59	.343
1950	Det	157	641	114	218	56	6	8	101	.340
1951	Det	147	598	92	191	36	3	2	59	.319
1952	Det-Bos (A)	114	428	52	133	23	2	7	57	.311
1953	Bos	134	460	68	141	41	2	12	73	.307
1954	Bos-Chi (A)	97	326	40	90	13	0	5	58	.276
1955	Chi	128	429	44	134	24	1	8	81	.312
1956	Chi-Balt	123	425	52	115	22	2	9	48	.271
1957	Balt	99	310	28	92	9	0	9	44	.297
15 years		**1795**	**6702**	**881**	**2054**	**385**	**50**	**78**	**870**	**.306**

Transactions: May 18, 1946: Traded to Detroit for Barney McCosky. June 3, 1952: Traded with Dizzy Trout, Johnny Lipon and Walter Evers to Boston Red Sox for Walt Dropo, Bill Wight, Fred Hatfield, Johnny Pesky and Don Lenhardt. May 23, 1954: Traded to Chicago White Sox for Grady Hatton and $100,000. May 21, 1956: Traded with Bob Nieman, Mike Fornieles and Connie Johnson to Baltimore for Jim Wilson and Dave Philley.

Joseph James Kelley

Born December 9, 1871, in Cambridge, Massachusetts; died August 14, 1943, in Baltimore, Maryland. 5'11", 190 lbs., bats right, throws right. Years in minor leagues: 2; Major League debut: July 27, 1891; Years in Major Leagues: 17. Elected to Hall of Fame: 1971. Nickname: None.

Joe Kelley was a hard-hitting, great fielding outfielder with the Baltimore and Brooklyn teams that were the best in baseball in the 1890s. Kelley hit over .300 for 11 consecutive seasons, but fans remembered him as much for his antics on the field as for his hitting. He often carried a mirror in his pocket or under his cap and would sometimes take it out during the game and look at himself, smoothing his hair and tidying himself up. The fans loved it.

He had his own version of the "hidden ball trick." A left fielder for the Baltimore club, Kelley would hide a ball in tall outfield grass and then, when a ball was hit by him, he would run, pick up the hidden ball and throw it back into the infield—saving time and energy. The ploy was discovered when he threw the hidden ball in at just about the same time the center fielder was throwing in the other ball. But he was more than a showman. Kelley was an outstanding hitter. His high was .393 in 1894 when Baltimore won its first of three consecutive championships. On September 3, 1894, he got nine hits in nine at-bats in a doubleheader—a record no one has come close to matching.

In 1899, he played for Brooklyn and helped win two consecutive championships there. All together, he played on six championship teams in seven years. Later, he had stints as manager at Cincinnati and Boston and was a scout for the New York Yankees.

Year	Team	G	AB	R	H	D	T	HR	RBI	AVE.
1891	Bos	12	45	7	11	1	1	0	3	.244
1892	Pitt–Balt	66	238	29	56	7	7	0	32	.235
1893	Balt	125	502	120	153	27	16	9	76	.305
1894	Balt	129	507	165	199	48	20	6	111	.393
1895	Balt	131	518	148	189	26	19	10	134	.365
1896	Balt	131	519	148	189	31	19	8	100	.364
1897	Balt	131	505	113	183	31	9	5	118	.362
1898	Balt	124	464	71	149	18	15	2	110	.321
1899	Brklyn	143	538	108	175	21	14	6	93	.325
1900	Brklyn	121	454	90	145	23	17	6	91	.319
1901	Brklyn	120	492	77	151	22	12	4	65	.307
1902	Balt–Cin	100	378	74	119	26	9	2	46	.315
1903	Cin	105	383	85	121	22	4	3	45	.316
1904	Cin	123	449	75	126	21	13	0	63	.281
1905	Cin	90	321	43	89	7	6	1	37	.277
1906	Cin	129	465	43	106	19	11	1	53	.228
1907	Bos (N)	73	228	25	59	8	2	2	17	.259
17 years		**1853**	**7006**	**1421**	**2220**	**358**	**194**	**65**	**1194**	**.317**

George Lange Kelly

Born September 10, 1896, in San Francisco, California; died October 13, 1984, in Burlingame, California. 6'3", 195 lbs., bats right, throws right. Years in minor leagues: 2; Major League debut: August 18, 1915; Years in Major Leagues: 16. Elected to Hall of Fame: 1975. Nickname: High Pockets—from sportswriter Damon Runyon because of Kelly's long legs.

High Pockets Kelly had as his greatest supporter in New York Giants manager John McGraw—and McGraw had patience, too. His young first baseman went 0-for-19 when he first came up with the Giants in 1916. By 1920, he was the regular first baseman and led the league in RBIs with 94. He led the league in home runs with 23 in 1921 and had 121 RBIs. He led the league in RBIs again in 1924 with 136. Kelly's timely hitting—the best clutch hitter he ever saw, said McGraw—helped the Giants win four straight National League pennants between 1921 and 1924.

Kelly had six straight seasons of hitting above .300 and had four straight with more than 100 RBIs. The lanky first baseman had some memorable games, too. In September 1923 he had a single, double and three home runs in one game. In 1924 Kelly hit seven homers in six games. Kelly was an outstanding fielder who set National League season records for chances and putouts by a first baseman. He threw across the infield to nail a base runner going to third on an infield out—a play that ended the 1921 World Series.

Year	Team	G	AB	R	H	D	T	HR	RBI	AVE.
1915	NY (N)	17	38	2	6	0	0	1	4	.158
1916	NY	49	76	4	12	2	0	1	3	.158

Year	Team	G	AB	R	H	D	T	HR	RBI	AVE.
1917	NY-Pitt	19	30	2	2	0	1	0	0	.087
1919	NY	32	107	12	31	6	2	1	14	.290
1920	NY	155	590	69	157	22	11	11	94	.266
1921	NY	149	587	95	181	42	9	23	121	.308
1922	NY	151	592	96	194	33	8	17	107	.328
1923	NY	145	560	82	172	23	5	16	103	.307
1924	NY	144	571	91	185	37	9	21	136	.324
1925	NY	147	586	87	181	29	3	20	99	.309
1926	NY	136	499	70	151	24	4	13	80	.303
1927	Cin	61	222	27	60	16	4	5	21	.270
1928	Cin	116	402	46	119	33	7	3	58	.296
1929	Cin	147	577	73	169	45	9	5	103	.293
1930	Cin-Chi (N)	90	354	40	109	16	2	8	54	.308
1932	Brklyn	64	202	23	49	9	1	4	22	.243
16 years		**1622**	**5993**	**819**	**1778**	**337**	**76**	**148**	**1020**	**.297**

Transactions: July 15, 1917: Sold to Pittsburgh Pirates for waiver price. Aug. 4, 1917: Sold to New York Giants for waiver price. Feb. 9, 1927: Traded to Cincinnati for Edd Roush and cash.

WORLD SERIES

Year	Team	G	AB	R	H	D	T	HR	RBI	AVE.
1921	NY (N)	8	30	3	7	1	0	0	3	.233
1922	NY	5	18	0	5	0	0	0	2	.278
1923	NY	6	22	1	4	0	0	0	1	.182
1924	NY	7	31	7	9	1	0	1	4	.290
4 years		**26**	**101**	**11**	**25**	**2**	**0**	**1**	**10**	**.248**

Michael Joseph Kelly

Born December 31, 1857, in Troy, New York; died November 8, 1894, in Boston, Massachusetts. 5'10", 180 lbs., bats right, throws right. Years in minor leagues: None; Major League debut: May 1, 1878; Years in Major Leagues: 16. Elected to Hall of Fame: 1945. Nickname: King—because he was king of the ball diamond—the most colorful character before Babe Ruth, and king of the barrooms, too.

Mike Kelly hit over .300 in eight of his 16 seasons and helped lead the Chicago White Stockings team to five championships in seven years between 1880 and 1886. But he is best remembered for his antics on the field and his knack for doing whatever it took to win a ball game. He once watched from the dugout as a pop foul eluded the Chicago catcher. Kelly yelled to the umpire, "Kelly now catching" and reached out and caught the ball barehanded. It was a legal move under the rules of the day. Soon, rules were changed to include a more formal, less provocative way of announcing a lineup change.

Kelly was a handsome man who modeled for advertising displays and sang and performed on stage in the offseason. In one of his most popular routines, he recited "Casey at the Bat." At the ballpark, he was a crowd pleaser, often arriving in a horse-driven carriage and dressed in silk hat and ascot.

Kelly is credited with being one of the first players to utilize the hit-and-run and to use hand signals behind the plate. He was primarily a catcher and outfielder but played every position during his career. He had a lifetime batting average of .308.

Year	Team	G	AB	R	H	D	T	HR	RBI	AVE.
1878	Cin	60	237	29	67	7	1	0	27	.283
1879	Cin	77	345	78	120	20	12	2	47	.348
1880	Chi (N)	84	344	72	100	17	9	1	60	.291
1881	Chi	82	353	84	114	27	3	2	55	.323
1882	Chi	84	377	81	115	37	4	1	55	.305
1883	Chi	98	428	92	109	28	10	3	61	.255
1884	Chi	108	452	120	160	28	5	13	95	.354
1885	Chi	107	438	124	126	24	7	9	75	.288
1886	Chi	118	451	155	175	32	11	4	79	.388
1887	Bos (N)	116	484	120	156	34	11	8	63	.322
1888	Bos	107	440	85	140	22	11	9	71	.318
1889	Bos	125	507	120	149	41	5	9	78	.294
1890	Bos (P)	89	340	83	111	18	6	4	66	.326
1891	CM-Bos	102	350	65	100	16	7	2	—	.290
1892	Bos (N)	78	281	40	53	7	0	2	41	.189
1893	NY (N)	20	67	9	18	1	0	0	15	.269
16 years		1455	5894	1357	1813	359	102	69	950	.308

Raymond J. Kelly

Sportswriter. Elected to Hall of Fame: 1988.

Ray Kelly was sportseditor of the *New York Times* from 1937 until his retirement in 1958. As a youth, he attended Fordham Prep School where he developed a lifelong friendship with classmate Frank Frisch, who was to become a Hall of Fame baseball player.

He began his newspaper career with the *New York Tribune* in 1920 and joined the *New York Times* in 1922. Before he was done, he had covered the careers of Ruth, Gehrig, DiMaggio and Mantle and had witnessed and written about baseball's expansion westward.

Kelly was known for having an amazing memory, not only recalling names and dates and statistics, but also the page number and page placement of stories that had been published long ago.

John Kieran

Sportswriter. Elected to Hall of Fame: 1973.

John Kieran was an intellectual in the pressbox. He served as one of the experts for the popular radio program *Information Please* for ten years and was author of several books.

He started his sportswriting career with the *New York Times* in 1915, went to the *New York Herald-Tribune* in 1922 but returned to the *Times* in 1927 and started the "Sports of the Times" column. After 17 years, he went to the *New York Sun,* where he was also a columnist. Kieran died in 1981 at the age of 99.

Harmon Clayton Killebrew

Born June 29, 1936, in Payette, Idaho. 6', 200 lbs., bats right, throws right. Years in minor leagues: None; Major League debut: June 23, 1954; Years in Major Leagues: 22. Elected to Hall of Fame: 1984. Nickname: Killer—short for his last name but also a reference to how hard he hit the ball.

Harmon Killebrew hit more home runs—573—than all but four other players in Major League history. His sacrifice bunt total was lower than any one else's in baseball history; in 22 years in the Major Leagues, he never did it. Killebrew had more than 40 home runs in eight different seasons and led the American League in home runs six times. He is third all time in the ratio of home runs to times at bat, trailing Babe Ruth and Ralph Kiner. He never hit 50 home runs, but hit 49 twice, in 1964 and 1969. He has the most home runs by a righthanded batter in the American League.

When Killebrew was first scouted, he was playing semipro ball in the Idaho-Oregon Border League—and hitting .847. He signed with the Washington Senators in 1953. He played with the Senators off and on but did not become a regular until 1959, when he tied Rocky Colavito of Cleveland for the home run title with 42.

He was the American League's Most Valuable Player in 1969 when he hit 49 home runs and had 140 RBIs. In 1965, he helped the Minnesota Twins to their first pennant and hit .286 in the World Series. Killebrew's home run power was awesome, his home run frequency magnificent, but his batting average suffered because of his big swings and slow feet. His lifetime batting average was .256; the highest he ever hit was .288.

Year	Team	G	AB	R	H	D	T	HR	RBI	AVE.
1954	Wash	9	13	1	4	1	0	0	3	.308
1955	Wash	38	80	12	16	1	0	4	7	.200
1956	Wash	44	99	10	22	2	0	5	13	.222
1957	Wash	9	31	4	9	2	0	2	5	.290
1958	Wash	13	31	2	6	0	0	0	2	.194

Year	Team	G	AB	R	H	D	T	HR	RBI	AVE.
1959	Wash	153	546	98	132	20	2	42	105	.242
1960	Wash	124	442	84	122	19	1	31	80	.276
1961	Minn	150	541	94	156	20	7	46	122	.288
1962	Minn	155	552	85	134	21	1	48	126	.243
1963	Minn	142	515	88	133	18	0	45	96	.258
1964	Minn	158	577	95	156	11	1	49	111	.270
1965	Minn	113	401	78	108	16	1	25	75	.269
1966	Minn	162	569	89	160	27	1	39	110	.281
1967	Minn	163	547	105	147	24	1	44	113	.269
1968	Minn	100	295	40	62	7	2	17	40	.210
1969	Minn	162	555	106	153	20	2	49	140	.276
1970	Minn	157	527	96	143	20	1	41	113	.271
1971	Minn	147	500	61	127	19	1	28	119	.254
1972	Minn	139	433	53	100	13	2	26	74	.231
1973	Minn	69	248	29	60	9	1	5	32	.242
1974	Minn	122	333	28	74	7	0	13	54	.222
1975	KC	106	312	25	62	13	0	14	44	.199
22 years		**2435**	**8147**	**1283**	**2086**	**290**	**24**	**573**	**1584**	**.256**

LEAGUE CHAMPIONSHIP SERIES

Year	Team	G	AB	R	H	D	T	HR	RBI	AVE.
1969	Minn	3	8	2	1	1	0	0	0	.125
1970	Minn	3	11	2	3	0	0	2	4	.273
2 years		**6**	**19**	**4**	**4**	**1**	**0**	**2**	**4**	**.211**

WORLD SERIES

Year	Team	G	AB	R	H	D	T	HR	RBI	AVE.
1965	Minn	7	21	2	6	0	0	1	2	.286

Ralph McPherran Kiner

Born October 27, 1922, in Santa Rita, New Mexico. 6'2", 195 lbs., bats right, throws right. Years in minor leagues: 3; Major League debut: April 16, 1946; Years in Major Leagues: 10. Elected to Hall of Fame: 1975. Nickname: None.

Ralph Kiner hit 51 home runs in 1947—just his second full season in the Major Leagues. He hit 23 the year before—his rookie year—and that was good enough to lead the National League. His best home run year was 1949 when he hit 54, fourth highest ever in the National League behind Mark McGwire's 70, Sammy Sosa's 66 and Hack Wilson's 56.

The biggest difference between 1946 and 1947 was the addition of Hank Greenberg as Kiner's teammate on the Pirates. Greenberg, at the end of his great career, served as a mentor to the young Kiner, teaching him the fine points of learning the strike zone. He also hit behind him in the lineup, assuring the young slugger of getting more good pitches to hit. Kiner only played ten years in the Majors but led or tied for the National League lead in home runs in the first seven of those years. He averaged 37 homers and 101 runs batted in per year during his career. In one stretch in 1947, Kiner hit four consecutive home runs, five in two games, six in three games and seven in four games.

His average of 7.1 home runs per 100 at-bats is second only to Babe Ruth. In 1952, Kiner tied with Hank Sauer for the league lead in home runs with 37, but the Pirates finished last. At contract time, general manager Branch Rickey wanted to cut Kiner's salary. Unimpressed with the slugger's statistics, Rickey told him: "We could have finished last without you." Kiner held out, and was traded to the Cubs early in the 1953 season. He finished his career with a brief stay with the Cleveland Indians before starting a second successful career in broadcasting. He was one of the "original Mets," joining their broadcast team in their first year, 1962.

Year	Team	G	AB	R	H	D	T	HR	RBI	AVE.
1946	Pitt	144	502	63	124	17	3	23	81	.247
1947	Pitt	152	565	118	177	23	4	51	127	.313
1948	Pitt	156	555	104	147	19	5	40	123	.265
1949	Pitt	152	549	116	170	19	5	54	127	.310
1950	Pitt	150	547	112	149	21	6	47	118	.272
1951	Pitt	151	531	124	164	31	6	42	109	.309
1952	Pitt	149	516	90	126	17	2	37	87	.244
1953	Pitt-Chi	158	562	100	157	20	3	36	116	.279
1954	Chi	147	557	88	159	36	5	22	73	.285
1955	Cleve	113	321	56	78	13	0	18	54	.243
10 years		**1472**	**5205**	**971**	**1451**	**216**	**39**	**369**	**1015**	**.279**

Transactions: June 4, 1953: Traded to Chicago with Joe Garagiola, Howie Pollet and George Metkovich for Toby Atwell, Bob Schultz, Preston Ward, George Freese, Bob Addis, Gene Hermanski and $150,000. Nov. 16, 1954: Traded to Cleveland for Sam Jones, Gale Wade and $60,000.

Charles Herbert Klein

Born October 7, 1905, in Indianapolis, Indiana; died March 28, 1958, in Indianapolis, Indiana. 6′, 195 lbs., bats left, throws right. Years in minor leagues: 2; Major League debut: July 30, 1928; Years in Major Leagues: 17. Elected to Hall of Fame: 1980. Nickname: None.

Chuck Klein was a powerful lefthanded hitting outfielder for the Philadelphia Phillies who had some great years hitting home runs over the right field wall in the Baker Bowl, 280 feet away. Klein hit only 300 home runs in his career, but he had some outstanding individual years. In 1936, playing for Philadelphia, he hit four home runs in a ten-inning game against Pittsburgh.

The lifetime .320 hitter led the National League with 43 home runs in 1929, his second year in the Majors—and he got some help from his teammates. Klein edged out Mel Ott of the Giants for the homer title by one. The Giants played the Phillies on the last day of the season, and Phillie pitchers walked Ott five times, including once with the bases full, to preserve the home run title for Klein. The 43 home runs were a National League record. In 1930, Klein had one of the greatest seasons overall that any hitter has ever enjoyed. He hit .386, had 40 home runs and 170 RBIs. Not only did he not win the Triple Crown—he didn't lead the league in any of those categories. One other astonishing figure from 1930: Klein had 44 assists in the outfield, still a Major League record.

In 1932, he won the Most Valuable Player Award with his 226 hits, 50 doubles, 38 home runs, 152 runs batted in and .348 average. He won the Triple Crown in 1933 with good numbers but far below his 1932 output in homers and RBIs when he didn't lead in either of those categories. Klein hit .368 with 28 home runs and 120 RBIs. He was sold to the Chicago Cubs after the 1933 season and helped Chicago to the 1935 pennant.

Year	Team	G	AB	R	H	D	T	HR	RBI	AVE.
1928	Phil (N)	64	253	41	91	14	4	11	34	.360
1929	Phil	149	616	126	219	45	6	43	145	.356
1930	Phil	156	648	158	250	59	8	40	170	.386
1931	Phil	148	594	121	200	34	10	31	121	.337
1932	Phil	154	650	152	226	50	15	38	137	.348
1933	Phil	152	606	101	223	44	7	28	120	.368
1934	Chi (N)	115	435	78	131	27	2	20	80	.301
1935	Chi	119	434	71	127	14	4	21	73	.293
1936	Chi-Phil	146	601	102	184	35	7	25	104	.306
1937	Phil	115	406	74	132	20	2	15	57	.325
1938	Phil	129	458	53	113	22	2	8	61	.247
1939	Phil-Pitt	110	317	45	90	18	5	12	56	.284
1940	Phil	116	354	39	77	16	2	7	37	.218
1941	Phil	50	73	6	9	0	0	1	3	.123
1942	Phil	14	14	0	1	0	0	0	0	.071
1943	Phil	12	20	0	2	0	0	0	3	.100
1944	Phil	4	7	1	1	0	0	0	0	.143
17 years		1753	6486	1168	2076	398	74	300	1201	.320

WORLD SERIES

Year	Team	G	AB	R	H	D	T	HR	RBI	AVE.
1935	Chi (N)	5	12	2	4	0	0	1	2	.333

William J. Klem

Born February 22, 1874, in Rochester, New York; died September 1, 1951, in Miami, Florida. 5'7", 157 lbs. Years in Major Leagues: 37 (all as umpire). Elected to Hall of Fame: 1953. Nickname: Catfish—a reference to his big ears and lips, a nickname Klem hated; also, The Great Arbitrator, which appealed to him a lot more.

Bill Klem was regarded as the best umpire in the National League. He certainly set the standard for other umpires, even as to the equipment they wore. National League umpires wore their chest protector inside their coat because Klem wore his inside his coat.

Klem umpired in the National League for 37 years, and stories about him are legendary. Early in his career, he took an action that became his trademark. A player was arguing strenuously with Klem as he marched toward him. Klem drew a line in the dirt in front of him with his shoe and said, "Don't cross that line." For nearly four decades in the National League, players, managers and coaches knew better than to cross that line.

Klem umpired in 18 World Series but was denied the opportunity for several years by Commissioner Kenesaw Mountain Landis, who didn't like Klem's attitude because of two incidents. The ump got into a verbal sparring match with Detroit's Goose Goselin in a hotel lobby during the 1934 World Series. That, plus Klem's admission to Landis that he enjoyed going to track to bet on the horses, caused the commissioner to discipline the veteran umpire. He fined him $50 for the Goselin incident and assigned other umpires to World Series employment as punishment for Klem's gambling admission. In 1940, on the eve of Klem's retirement, Landis bowed to the wishes of National League president Ford Frick, who asked that Klem finalize his career by umpiring in the World Series. Klem was a proud umpire who knew the secret to success in controlling a game: decisiveness. "I never missed one in my heart," he said.

Leonard Koppett

Sportswriter. Elected to Hall of Fame: 1992.

Leonard Koppett covered baseball for several New York newspapers for 27 years. The native of Russia started with the *New York Herald-Tribune* in 1948, went to the *New York Post* six years later, where he remained for nine years before joining the staff of the *New York Times* in 1963.

He covered the entire Casey Stengel era with the Yankees, saw the Dodgers and Giants make their exodus from New York to Los Angeles and San Francisco, helped usher in the Mets, and covered Roger Maris and Mickey Mantle's chase of Babe Ruth's home run record in 1961. Koppett authored nine books, including *The Thinking Man's Guide to Baseball*, and wrote a column for *The Sporting News* for 17 years.

Sanford Koufax

Born December 30, 1935, in Brooklyn, New York. 6'2", 198 lbs., bats right, throws left. Years in minor leagues: None; Major League debut: June 24, 1955; Years in Major Leagues: 12. Elected to Hall of Fame: 1972. Nickname: None.

Sandy Koufax combined a powerful fastball with a jug-handle curve that froze opposing batters, making him one of the most dominant pitchers in the National League for about a decade. He threw four no-hitters, including a perfect game. He shocked the baseball world after the 1966 season when, at the age of 30, coming off a 27-win season, he announced his retirement because of arthritis in his arm that was so painful, he said, it hurt to comb his hair. Koufax struggled early in his career. He was frequently wild, getting himself in jams with bases on balls and then having to "groove" pitches to get them over the plate. After six seasons, he was 36–40 and having a career that didn't seem to be going anywhere.

In the spring of 1961, he worked diligently at getting control of his curve ball so that it could help set up his fastball—and vice versa. He was 18–13 in 1961, his first full season in which he was above .500. In 1962, he was 14–7 with a league-leading earned run average of 2.57. He won the earned run average title the next four seasons, too, reeling off records of 25–5, 19–5, 26–8 and 27–9. From 36–40 in his first six seasons, he was 129–47 in his final six. He struck out 300 or more batters three seasons in a row, becoming the first pitcher to accomplish that, and set the single season strikeout record (since surpassed) of 382 in 1965.

In those last six years, he won five ERA titles, led the National League in strikeouts four times, had four no-hitters, was the Cy Young Award winner three times, and struck out 18 batters in a game twice. In addition, he was the league's Most Valuable Player in 1963. His 27 wins in 1966 are the most by a lefthander in the 20th century (tied by Steve Carlton in 1972). His 11 shutouts in 1966 remain the most by a lefthander in this century. On September 9, 1965, Koufax threw his perfect game against the Chicago Cubs in one of the most remarkable games in baseball history. His mound opponent, Cub lefthander Bob Hendley, threw a one-hitter. The only run of the game scored on a throwing error. Koufax was 4–3 in World Series competition, but his earned run average was 0.95. He allowed ten runs, but only six were earned. When he was inducted into the Hall of Fame at age 36 in 1972, he became its youngest member.

Year	Team	W-L	ERA	G	IP	H	BB	SO
1955	Brklyn	2-2	3.02	12	41.2	33	28	30
1956	Brklyn	2-4	4.91	16	58.2	66	29	30
1957	Brklyn	5-4	3.88	34	104.1	83	51	122
1958	LA	11-11	4.48	40	158.2	132	105	131
1959	LA	8-6	4.05	35	153.1	136	92	173
1960	LA	8-13	3.91	37	175	133	100	197
1961	LA	18-13	3.52	42	255.2	212	96	269
1962	LA	14-7	2.54	28	184.1	134	57	216

Year	Team	W-L	ERA	G	IP	H	BB	SO
1963	LA	25-5	1.88	40	311	214	58	306
1964	LA	19-5	1.74	29	223	154	53	223
1965	LA	26-8	2.04	43	335.2	216	71	382
1966	LA	27-9	1.73	41	323	241	77	317
12 years		165-87	2.76	397	2324.1	1754	817	2396

WORLD SERIES

Year	Team	W-L	ERA	G	IP	H	BB	SO
1959	LA	0-1	1.00	2	9	5	1	7
1963	LA	2-0	1.50	2	18	12	3	23
1965	LA	2-1	0.38	3	24	13	5	29
1966	LA	0-1	1.50	1	6	6	2	2
4 years		4-3	0.95	8	57	36	11	66

Sam Lacy

Sportswriter. Elected to Hall of Fame: 1997.

Sam Lacy was one of the first black members of the Baseball Writers Association of America. He began his newspaper career in the 1920s with the *Washington Tribune* and later became both sportseditor and managing editor. He also worked for the *Chicago Daily Defender*. He then went to Baltimore to become a successful columnist and sportseditor for Afro-American newspapers.

Lacy earned a reputation in the 1940s for his bold crusading for the desegregation of Major League Baseball.

Napoleon Lajoie

Born September 5, 1875, in Woonsocket, Rhode Island; died February 7, 1959, in Daytona Beach, Florida. 6'1", 195 lbs., bats right, throws right. Years in minor leagues: 1; Major League debut: August 12, 1896; Years in Major Leagues: 21. Elected to Hall of Fame: 1937. Nickname: Nap—short for Napoleon; also, Larry—a takeoff on Lajoie.

Nap Lajoie is the only Hall of Famer to have a Major League team named after him. When he was named manager of the Cleveland club in 1905, the team called itself the "Naps" in his honor. They remained the Naps until 1915, when they became the Cleveland Indians.

Lajoie began his career as a second baseman for the Philadelphia Phillies, who signed him in 1896. In 1901, he jumped to the Philadelphia A's of the newly formed American League which did not have the $2,400 salary cap that National League clubs honored. With his new team, he hit .422—still the modern American League high and just two points below Rogers Hornsby's all-time modern batting average record of .424. But the Phillies sued to get him back and the court ruled that if he played for a Philadelphia team, it had to be the Phillies. So the A's traded him to Cleveland.

In 1910, Lajoie and Ty Cobb were locked in a battle for the batting title. In the last few days of the season, Cobb took a commanding lead and went home a few days before the season ended. Lajoie went 8-for-8 in a season-ending doubleheader with the Browns, one of the most brilliant one-day performances of all time, but still lost the title to Cobb, .385 to .384. Seven of the eight hits were bunt singles. Lajoie hit over .300 in 16 of his 21 seasons, and in 10 of those years, he hit over .350. He finished his career with 3,252 hits and a lifetime batting average of .339.

Year	Team	G	AB	R	H	D	T	HR	RBI	AVE.
1896	Phil (N)	39	174	37	57	11	6	4	42	.328
1897	Phil	126	545	107	198	37	25	10	127	.363
1898	Phil	147	610	113	200	40	10	5	127	.328
1899	Phil	72	308	70	117	17	11	5	70	.380
1900	Phil	102	451	95	156	32	12	7	92	.346
1901	Phil (A)	131	543	145	229	48	13	14	125	.422
1902	Phil-Cleve	87	352	81	129	34	5	7	65	.366
1903	Cleve	126	488	90	173	40	13	7	93	.355
1904	Cleve	140	554	92	211	50	14	6	102	.381
1905	Cleve	65	249	29	82	13	2	2	41	.329
1906	Cleve	152	602	88	214	49	7	0	91	.355
1907	Cleve	137	509	53	152	30	6	2	63	.299
1908	Cleve	157	581	77	168	32	6	2	74	.289
1909	Cleve	128	469	56	152	33	7	1	47	.324
1910	Cleve	159	591	92	227	51	7	4	76	.384
1911	Cleve	90	315	36	115	20	1	2	60	.365
1912	Cleve	117	448	66	165	34	4	0	90	.368
1913	Cleve	137	465	67	156	25	2	1	68	.335
1914	Cleve	121	419	37	108	14	3	0	50	.258
1915	Phil (A)	129	490	40	137	24	5	1	61	.280
1916	Phil	113	426	33	105	14	4	2	35	.246
21 years		2475	9589	1504	3252	648	163	82	1599	.339

Transactions: June 1902: Sold to Cleveland Indians. January 1915: Sold to Philadelphia A's for waiver price.

Kenesaw Mountain Landis

Born November 20, 1866, in Millville, Ohio; died November 25, 1944, in Chicago, Illinois. Years in Major Leagues: 23 (as commissioner). Elected to Hall of Fame: 1944. Nickname: None.

Kenesaw Mountain Landis was baseball's first commissioner—and its toughest one. He was elected in 1921, shortly after eight Chicago White Sox players had been acquitted in court of fixing the 1919 World Series. Landis wasn't concerned about the evidence presented in court. He had all the evidence he needed. He imposed lifetime bans on all eight players.

That decision was his most famous, but it was not the only one in which his firm, forthright action had an impact on the game. He learned of a public exchange of unpleasantries between umpire Bill Klem and Detroit outfielder Goose Goselin in a Detroit hotel lobby during the 1934 World Series. Landis did not want his umpires acting like that in public and chose not to use Klem, baseball's most experienced and most respected umpire, in any future World Series. (Klem had not endeared himself to the commissioner another time when he admitted he bet on horses.) Landis relented and allowed Klem to work the 1940 World Series at the urging of National League president Ford Frick because Klem had announced that 1940 would be his last year of umpiring. In the seventh game of the 1934 World Series, St. Louis Cardinal outfielder Joe Medwick was showered with debris thrown by fans in the left field stands. The umpires conferred with Landis, who was in attendance, and he ordered Medwick off the field.

Landis was not a fan of farm systems because he thought it was a way in which ball clubs hid and hoarded talent. In 1938, he used his power of commissioner to order the St. Louis Cardinals to "free" 91 farmhands, and he did the same two years later with the Detroit Tigers. One of the "freed" Cardinals was Pete Reiser, who signed with the Dodgers and was a star with Brooklyn for many years. In 1944, shortly before his death, Landis banned Phillies owner Bill Cox for betting on his own team. He was appointed to the federal bench by President Theodore Roosevelt in 1905, and Judge Landis served notice in that job that he would not tolerate indiscretions. In his most famous decision, Landis fined Standard Oil Co. $29 million in an antitrust case. When he declined to get involved in the Federal League's lawsuit against the American and National leagues, Major League owners took note. When they needed a commissioner, they contacted Judge Landis.

Jack Lang

Sportswriter. Elected to Hall of Fame: 1986. Nickname: Captain Jack—because he organized the first charter flights for sportswriters covering the World Series.

Jack Lang covered Major League baseball in five decades, beginning with the *Long Island Press* in 1946. It folded in 1977, and Lang was hired the next day by the *New York Daily News*. He covered the Brooklyn Dodgers from 1946 until they moved to Los Angeles in 1958, then covered the Yankees from 1958 to 1961, and the New York Mets from their inception in 1962.

He witnessed and wrote about the integration of baseball in 1947, the lone Brooklyn World Series championship team in 1955, the Mantle-Maris home run feats, and the emergence of the Mets from the worst team to a two-time World Series winner.

He also served as the longtime secretary-treasurer of the Baseball Writers Association of America. That gave him the responsibility of sending out the ballots, tallying the results and notifying the winners of the awards for Most Valuable Player, Cy Young Manager of the Year, Rookie of the Year and Hall of Fame.

Ring Lardner

Sportswriter. Elected to Hall of Fame: 1963.

Ring Lardner brought baseball to life for thousands of readers through his fictional stories about the game and through his coverage of Major League baseball, primarily for the *Chicago Tribune* and *The Sporting News*.

Lardner wrote with wit and wisdom and was one of the most beloved writers of his time, which was the early 1900s. He was one of the first writers to suspect the 1919 White Sox of fixing the World Series. He is said to have walked through the train carrying the ball club singing a song parody he made up: "I'm Forever Blowing Ballgames."

Thomas Charles Lasorda

Born September 22, 1927, in Norristown, Pennsylvania; 5'10", 175 lbs., bats left, throws left. Years in minor leagues: 4; Major League debut: August 5, 1954; Years in Major Leagues 39 (as player, scout, coach and manager). Elected to Hall of Fame: 1997. Nickname: El Sorda—a name Lasorda said was never said publicly in his Major League career but was something he was called while he was playing winter ball in Cuba.

Tommy Lasorda didn't win a game as a Major League pitcher but won 1,599 as a Major League manager—all with the Los Angeles Dodgers. With his 20 years as manager of the Dodgers, 1977 to 1996, Lasorda is one of four men to manage one team for 20 years or more—the others are John McGraw, Connie Mack and Lasorda's predecessor with the Dodgers, Walt Alston.

Lasorda pitched in four games for the Dodgers in 1954 and four more in 1955. He was sold to the Kansas City A's where he was 0–4 in 1956, his last year as a Major League pitcher. He signed on as a scout for the Dodgers in 1961 and stayed with the organization for the next 36 years as scout, coach and manager.

Lasorda was known for getting the most out of his players because of the great rapport he had with them. His flamboyant personality also blended well with the celebrity-studded fandom at Dodger Stadium. He also enjoyed bantering with the press. When rookie phenom Fernando Valenzuela was surrounded by the press one day after he had pitched the Dodgers to victory, Lasorda offered to interpret for the lefthander who could speak no English. A writer asked a question, Lasorda spoke some Spanish to Valenzuela and Valenzuela replied. In interpreting it for the media, Lasorda quoted Valenzuela as saying the Dodgers had a great manager.

He then went into a long dissertation listing all the great qualities of the Dodger manager—until the press realized Lasorda was making the whole thing up. The genial skipper won pennants his first two years with the Dodgers—1977 and 1978— and World Series titles in 1981 and 1988.

As a Manager

Year	Team	W-L	Standing
1976	LA	2-2	Second
1977	LA	98-64	First
1978	LA	95-67	First
1979	LA	79-83	Third
1980	LA	92-71	Second
1981	LA	36-21	First (first half)
		27-26	Fourth (second half)
1982	LA	88-74	Second
1983	LA	91-71	First
1984	LA	79-83	Fourth
1985	LA	95-67	First
1986	LA	73-89	Fifth
1987	LA	73-89	Fourth
1988	LA	94-67	First
1989	LA	77-83	Fourth
1990	LA	86-76	Second
1991	LA	93-69	Second
1992	LA	63-99	Sixth
1993	LA	81-81	Fourth
1994	LA	58-56	———- (strike year)
1995	LA	78-66	First
1996	LA	41-35	First
20 years		**1599-1439**	

Division Championship Series

Year	Team	W-L
1981	LA	3-2
1995	LA	0-3
Two years		**3-5**

League Championship Series

Year	Team	W-L
1977	LA	3-1
1978	LA	3-1
1981	LA	3-2
1983	LA	1-3
1985	LA	2-4
1988	LA	4-3
6 years		**16-14**

WORLD SERIES

Year	Team	W-L
1977	LA	2-4
1978	LA	2-4
1981	LA	4-2
1988	LA	4-1
4 years		**12-11**

Earl Lawson

Sportswriter. Elected to Hall of Fame: 1985.

Earl Lawson covered the Reds for the *Cincinnati Post* for 34 years. He began his newspaper career right out of high school, working for the *Cincinnati Times-Star*. He began covering baseball in 1949, joined the *Post* in 1951 and followed the careers of Ted Kluszewski, Frank Robinson, Pete Rose and the Red pennant winners of 1961 and the "Big Red Machine" of the 1970s. He is the author of the book *Cincinnati Seasons*, published in 1987.

Anthony Michael Lazzeri

Born December 6, 1903, in San Francisco, California; died August 6, 1946, in San Francisco, California. 5'11", 170 lbs., bats right, throws right. Years in minor leagues: 4; Major League debut: April 13, 1926; Years in Major Leagues: 14. Elected to Hall of Fame: 1991. Nickname: Poosh 'em Up—a chant from Italian fans, urging Lazzeri the batter to push the ball up—and out of the park

Tony Lazzeri was a quiet, no-nonsense second baseman for some of the greatest teams in baseball history, including the 1927 New York Yankees and Yankee teams a decade later that featured Joe DiMaggio. Lazzeri's accomplishments were often lost in the lofty statistics of his teammates. In 1927, he was third in the league in home runs with 18. Finishing first and second were Babe Ruth with 60 and Lou Gehrig with 47. Lazzeri also had a 60 home run year—1925—his last year in the minor leagues.

He played 14 years in the Major Leagues and drove in more than 100 runs in seven of those seasons. He hit over .300 five times, including .354 in 1929. He helped the Yankees to seven World Series appearances and is remembered for two memorable World Series at-bats.

In one, Lazzeri, a rookie, struck out against an aging Grover Cleveland Alexander, whom the St. Louis Cardinals brought in from the bullpen. It was the seventh inning of the seventh game of the 1926 World Series and the bases were loaded. The Cardinals went on to win the game. In 1936, Lazzeri hit a grand slam home run in the World Series and batted .400. Lazzeri was released by the Yankees after the 1937 season and was signed by the Cubs. He helped the Cubs to a pennant in 1938. On May 24, 1936, he drove in 11 runs in one game, which is still the American League record.

Year	Team	G	AB	R	H	D	T	HR	RBI	AVE.
1926	NY (A)	155	589	79	162	28	14	18	114	.275
1927	NY	153	570	92	176	29 ·	8	18	102	.309
1928	NY	116	404	62	134	30	11	10	82	.332
1929	NY	147	545	101	193	37	11	18	106	.354
1930	NY	143	571	109	173	34	15	9	121	.303
1931	NY	135	484	67	129	27	7	8	83	.267
1932	NY	142	510	79	153	28	16	15	113	.300
1933	NY	139	523	94	154	22	12	18	104	.294
1934	NY	123	438	59	117	24	6	14	67	.267
1935	NY	130	477	72	130	18	6	13	83	.273
1936	NY	150	537	82	154	29	6	14	109	.287
1937	NY	126	446	56	109	21	3	14	70	.244
1938	Chi (N)	54	120	21	32	5	0	5	23	.267
1939	Brk-NY	27	83	13	24	2	0	4	14	.289
14 years		1740	6297	986	1840	334	115	178	1191	.292

WORLD SERIES

Year	Team	G	AB	R	H	D	T	HR	RBI	AVE.
1926	NY (A)	7	26	2	5	1	0	0	3	.192
1927	NY	4	15	1	4	1	0	0	2	.267
1928	NY	4	12	2	3	1	0	0	0	.250
1932	NY	4	17	4	5	0	0	2	5	.294
1936	NY	6	20	4	5	0	0	1	7	.250
1937	NY	5	15	3	6	0	1	1	2	.400
1938	Chi (N)	2	2	0	0	0	0	0	0	.000
7 years		32	107	16	28	3	1	4	14	.262

Robert Granville Lemon

Born September 22, 1920, in San Bernadino, California. 6', 180 lbs., bats left, throws right. Years in minor leagues: 2; Major League debut: September 9, 1941; Years in Major Leagues: 13. Elected to Hall of Fame: 1976. Nickname: None.

Bob Lemon accomplished a lot on the mound in a short period of time. He broke in as a third baseman in the Cleveland organization and was an adequate hitter with good power, but he had trouble making throws. He would throw so hard that the ball would dip and dance around on its way to first. Cleveland decided to make a pitcher out of him. He didn't pitch his first game until he was 26 years old, but it didn't take him long to learn. He won 11 games in that first year as a starter.

The next year, 1948, he was a star. He won 20 games with 10 shutouts, including a no-hitter against the Detroit Tigers. He helped the Indians win the pennant and then won two games in the World Series in which Cleveland defeated the Boston Braves. Lemon's pitches didn't have notorious speed like those of his teammate Bob Feller, but he turned his weakness as a third baseman into a strength on the mound— his pitches had movement. In 1951, he narrowly missed throwing his second non-hitter. In fact, he missed a perfect game by one pitch—one that Vic Wertz of the Tigers hit out of the park in the eighth inning. Lemon's early training as a hitter and an infielder paid off for him in his pitching career. He was a good fielder who helped himself out of jams with his glove, and he hit 37 home runs in his career to help keep himself in ball games. He was frequently used as a pinch hitter. He won 20 or more games seven times and led the American League in wins three times. In the 1954 World Series in which the Indians were swept by the Giants, Lemon pitched the opener, held the Giants to two runs for nine innings but lost the game on Dusty Rhodes' pinch homer in the 10th—a drive that traveled about 260 feet in the Polo Grounds.

When his pitching career was over, he scouted, coached and managed. In the Major Leagues, he managed the Kansas City Royals, Chicago White Sox and New York Yankees twice. He took the Yankees to the World Series in 1978 and again in 1981. He took over the Yankees in 1978 with his club 10½ games behind the Red Sox. The Yankees made an incredible surge, tied the Red Sox for the lead and then beat them in a one-game playoff highlighted by Bucky Dent's home run.

Year	Team	W-L	ERA	G	IP	H	BB	SO
1941	Cleve	0-0	0.00	0	0	0	0	0
1942	Cleve	0-0	0.00	0	0	0	0	0
1946	Cleve	4-5	2.49	32	94	77	68	39
1947	Cleve	11-5	3.44	37	167.1	150	97	65
1948	Cleve	20-14	2.82	43	293.2	231	129	147
1949	Cleve	22-10	2.99	37	279.2	211	137	138
1950	Cleve	23-11	3.84	44	288	281	146	170
1951	Cleve	17-14	3.52	42	263.1	244	124	132
1952	Cleve	22-11	2.50	42	309.2	236	105	131
1953	Cleve	21-15	3.36	41	286.2	283	110	98
1954	Cleve	23-7	2.72	36	258.1	228	92	110
1955	Cleve	18-10	3.88	35	211.1	218	74	100
1956	Cleve	20-14	3.03	39	255.1	230	89	94
1957	Cleve	6-11	4.60	21	117.1	129	64	45
1958	Cleve	0-1	5.33	11	25.1	41	16	8
15 years		207-128	3.23	460	2850	2559	1251	1277

WORLD SERIES

Year	Team	W-L	ERA	G	IP	H	BB	SO
1948	Cleve	2-0	1.65	2	16.1	16	7	6
1954	Cleve	0-2	6.75	2	13.1	16	8	11
2 years		2-2	3.94	4	29.2	32	15	17

Walter Fenner Leonard

Born September 8, 1907, in Rocky Mount, North Carolina; died November 27, 1997, in Rocky Mount, North Carolina. 5'10", 185 lbs., bats left, throws left. Years in minor leagues: 18 (Negro Leagues). Years in Major Leagues: None. Elected to Hall of Fame: 1972. Nickname: Buck—a childhood nickname from a brother who could not pronounce "Buddy," the family's nickname for him.

Buck Leonard was one of the Negro Leagues' greatest hitters. As the hard-hitting first baseman of the Homestead Grays, he teamed with catcher Josh Gibson as the two became the Ruth and Gehrig of black baseball. He played 18 years, beginning with short stints with the Portsmouth Firefighters, Baltimore Stars and Brooklyn Royal Giants in 1933. In 1934, he joined the Homestead club and remained there for the next 17 seasons. With Leonard and Gibson leading the way, the Grays won championships in nine straight years, from 1937 and 1945.

In 1950, St. Louis Browns owner Bill Veeck offered Leonard a spot on the Browns but, at the age of 43, he turned it down. Leonard said later he appreciated the offer and only wished he could have played in the Major Leagues when he was young enough to show what he could do. Instead, he played five years in the Mexican League, retiring at the age of 48.

His unofficial lifetime batting average in the Negro Leagues was .324. In 1948, he led the league with a .395 average. Leonard was also an excellent first baseman, known for digging throws out of the dirt.

Allen Lewis

Sportswriter. Elected to Hall of Fame: 1981.

Allen Lewis covered baseball for the *Philadelphia Inquirer* from 1949 until his retirement in 1979 and then, in retirement, wrote a column for the *Inquirer* from his home in Clearwater, Florida. He served for 12 years as chairman of baseball's Scoring Rules Committee and was recognized as an expert on baseball rules. Lewis covered the Philadelphia Phillies' "Whiz Kids" pennant winners of 1950, then two decades of second-division teams before the Steve Carlton–Mike Schmidt era brought them to the top again in the early 1970s. He wrote for *The Sporting News* for 17 years, covered 24 World Series and saw 10 no-hitters.

Fred Lieb

Sportswriter. Elected to Hall of Fame: 1972

Fred Lieb became one of baseball's great historians through his newspaper articles, columns and especially his books. One of his books, *Baseball as I Have Known*

It, is considered one of the landmark books about the sport. He held card No. 1 in the Baseball Writers Association. Lieb worked for the Philadelphia News Bureau and three New York newspapers before some successful investments allowed him to "retire" in 1934.

For the next 35 years, he wrote a column for *The Sporting News* as well as several books, including team histories of the Detroit Tigers, Boston Red Sox, St. Louis Cardinals, Pittsburgh Pirates, Baltimore Orioles and Philadelphia Phillies.

Frederick Anthony Lindstrom

Born: November 21, 1905, in Chicago, Illinois; died October 4, 1981, in Chicago, Illinois. 5'1", 170 lbs., bats right, throws right. Years in minor leagues: 2; Major League debut: April 15, 1924; Years in Major Leagues: 13. Elected to Hall of Fame: 1976. Nickname: Lindy—a shortening of his last name.

Fred Lindstrom had a love-hate relationship with his manager, John McGraw, but he was a mainstay on some of McGraw's great New York Giant teams, anchoring down the third base position. He was signed right out of high school and played for Toledo at the age of 16. Two years later, as a member of McGraw's Giants, he became the youngest player ever to play in a World Series. In that series, he hit .333 and had four hits in one of the games. He was victimized in the field by two ground balls that hit pebbles and bounced over his head, the last one costing the Giants the ball game and winning the World Series for the Washington Senators.

Lindstrom was at times jovial and at other times moody and contentious. He had expected to be the Giants manager when McGraw retired. When his former roommate Bill Terry was named instead, Lindstrom informed him he wanted to be traded. He got his wish and spent some time with the Cubs, including their 1935 pennant winner, and the Pirates before he retired. He had a lifetime batting average of .311, helped by seven seasons in which he hit over .300. He hit .358 in 1928 and .379 in 1930. Lindstrom spent many years as the Northwestern University baseball coach and then was postmaster in Evanston, Illinois.

Year	Team	G	AB	R	H	D	T	HR	RBI	AVE.
1924	NY (N)	52	79	19	20	3	1	0	4	.253
1925	NY	104	356	43	102	15	12	4	33	.287
1926	NY	140	543	90	164	19	9	9	76	.302
1927	NY	138	562	107	172	36	8	7	58	.306
1928	NY	153	646	99	231	39	9	14	107	.358
1929	NY	130	549	99	175	23	6	15	91	.319
1930	NY	148	609	127	231	39	7	22	106	.379
1931	NY	78	303	38	91	12	6	5	36	.300
1932	NY	144	595	83	161	26	5	15	92	.271
1933	Pitt	138	538	70	167	39	10	5	55	.310

Year	Team	G	AB	R	H	D	T	HR	RBI	AVE.
1934	Pitt	97	383	59	111	24	4	4	49	.290
1935	Chi (N)	90	342	49	94	22	4	3	62	.275
1936	Brklyn	26	106	12	28	4	0	0	10	.264
13 years		1438	5611	895	1747	301	81	103	779	.311

Transactions: Dec. 12, 1932: Traded to Pittsburgh as part of a three-way trade between New York, Pittsburgh and Philadelphia, for Glenn Spencer and Gus Dugas. Nov. 22, 1934: Traded with Larry French to Chicago Cubs for Guy Bush, Jim Weaver and Babe Herman.

WORLD SERIES

Year	Team	G	AB	R	H	D	T	HR	RBI	AVE.
1924	NY (N)	7	30	1	10	2	0	0	4	.333
1935	Chi (N)	4	15	0	3	1	0	0	0	.200
2 years		11	45	1	13	3	0	0	4	.289

John Henry Lloyd

Born April 25, 1884, in Palatka, Florida; died March 19, 1965, in Atlantic City, New Jersey. 5'11", 180 lbs., bats left, throws right. Years in minor leagues: 26 (Negro Leagues); Years in Major Leagues: None. Elected to Hall of Fame: 1977. Nickname: Pop—because of his leadership qualities and, in the later stages of his career, his age compared to other players.

Pop Lloyd was a tremendous hitter and a teacher of hitting who was said to have tutored the best—and beat the rest. He was a well-traveled player—by his own design. "I go where the money is," he said, and he proved it.

He played for the Cuban X Giants for three years, the Leland Giants of Chicago for one year, the Lincoln Giants of New York for three years, the Chicago American Giants for four years and then played and managed, in a 13-year span for the Brooklyn Royal Giants, the Bacharach Giants, the Hilldale Giants and then back with Lincoln.

Many who saw him play say he was the best all-around ballplayer, the black Honus Wagner. He was a big man with huge hands. He was graceful and quick at shortstop and had a picturesque swing at the plate. Lloyd had some outstanding seasons, including 1911 at Lincoln when he had the remarkable batting average of .475. He hit over .400 two other times in his career: .415 in 1923 and .422 in 1924.

Ernesto Natali Lombardi

Born April 6, 1908, in Oakland, California; died September 26, 1977, in Santa Cruz, California. 6'3", 230 lbs., bats right, throws right. Years in minor leagues: 5; Major League debut: April 15, 1931; Years in Major Leagues: 17. Elected to Hall of Fame: 1986. Nickname: Schnozz—because of his ample nose.

Ernie Lombardi is the only catcher in Major League history to win two batting titles. He was tops in the league in 1938 with a .342 average and won the batting championship again in 1942 with a .330 average. In 1938, he was the National League's Most Valuable Player. What made his batting titles especially impressive is that Lombardi didn't have the benefit of any infield hits—he was notoriously slow. Baseball historians John Thorn and Pete Palmer wrote that Lombardi was the slowest of all in the Hall of Fame—including the exhibits.

But the Schnozz could hit. Using a 46-ounce bat and a grip in which his fingers interlocked on the bat, the big guy terrorized National League pitchers because of how hard he hit the ball. Yet he was not much of a home run hitter; his line drives usually stayed in the park.

He had some terrific individual games both at the plate and behind it. He hit four consecutive doubles in consecutive innings in one game and had six consecutive hits in another. Lombardi was the catcher in 1938 when Johnny Vander Meer tossed two straight no-hitters. Lombardi played five years in the minor leagues before Brooklyn brought him up to the Majors in 1931. He played second fiddle to another future Hall of Fame catcher, Al Lopez, but was traded to Cincinnati in 1932. There he starred for a decade and led the Reds to two straight pennants in 1938 and 1939. At the end of his 17-year career, Lombardi had a .306 lifetime batting average.

Year	Team	G	AB	R	H	D	T	HR	RBI	AVE.
1931	Brklyn	73	182	20	54	7	1	4	23	.297
1932	Cin	118	413	43	125	22	9	11	68	.303
1933	Cin	107	350	30	99	21	1	4	47	.283
1934	Cin	132	417	42	127	19	4	9	62	.305
1935	Cin	120	332	36	114	23	3	12	64	.343
1936	Cin	121	387	42	129	23	2	12	68	.333
1937	Cin	120	368	41	123	22	1	9	59	.334
1938	Cin	129	489	60	167	30	1	19	95	.342
1939	Cin	130	450	43	129	26	2	20	85	.287
1940	Cin	109	376	50	120	22	0	14	74	.319
1941	Cin	117	398	33	105	12	1	10	60	.264
1942	Bos (N)	105	309	32	102	14	0	11	46	.330
1943	NY (N)	104	295	19	90	7	0	10	51	.305
1944	NY	117	373	37	95	13	0	10	58	.255
1945	NY	115	368	46	113	7	1	19	70	.307
1946	NY	88	238	19	69	4	1	12	39	.290
1947	NY	48	110	8	31	5	0	4	21	.282
17 years		**1853**	**5855**	**601**	**1792**	**277**	**27**	**190**	**990**	**.306**

Transactions: March 14, 1932: Traded with Babe Herman and Wally Gilbert to Cincinnati for Tony Cuccinello, Joe Stripp and Clyde Sukeforth. Feb. 7, 1942: Sold to Boston Braves. April 27, 1943: Traded to New York Giants for Hugh Poland and Connie Ryan.

WORLD SERIES

Year	Team	G	AB	R	H	D	T	HR	RBI	AVE.
1939	Cin	4	14	0	3	0	0	0	2	.214
1940	Cin	2	3	0	1	1	0	0	0	.333
2 years		**6**	**17**	**0**	**4**	**1**	**0**	**0**	**2**	**.235**

Alfonzo Ramon Lopez

Born August 20, 1908, in Tampa, Florida. 5'11", 165 lbs., bats right, throws right. Years in minor leagues: 4; Major League debut: September 27, 1928; Years in Major Leagues: 36 (as player and manager). Elected to Hall of Fame: 1977. Nickname: Señor—because of his Spanish background.

Al Lopez was a journeyman catcher who played for Brooklyn, Boston, Pittsburgh and Cleveland in a 19-year Major League career. His 1,918 games behind the plate was a Major League record for about 40 years until it was broken by Bob Boone and then Carlton Fisk. But it was Lopez's skills as a manager that earned him a berth in the Hall of Fame. He spent six years as manager of the Cleveland Indians. The Indians finished first once and second five times. He then managed the Chicago White Sox for the next nine years. Chicago finished first once and second five times. That's two first-place finishes and ten second-place finishes in a 15-year span.

Lopez was the only manager to break the New York Yankees' stranglehold on American League championships between 1949 and 1964. His 1954 Cleveland Indians' team won 111 games, an American League record. His 1959 White Sox team won Chicago's first league championship in 40 years. The Indians didn't win another one for 42 years, and Chicago hasn't won another one.

Lopez was a master at handling pitchers during his playing days, and that skill carried over when he became a manager. His 1954 Indian team featured four future Hall of Famers: Bob Lemon, Bob Feller, Hal Newhouser, and Early Wynn. His 1959 White Sox pitching staff was led by Wynn, who won the Cy Young Award with his 22 wins.

AS A MANAGER

Year	Team	Record	Standing
1951	Cleve	93-61	Second
1952	Cleve	93-61	Second
1953	Cleve	92-62	Second
1954	Cleve	111-43	First
1955	Cleve	93-61	Second
1956	Cleve	88-66	Second
1957	Chi (A)	90-64	Second

Year	Team	Record	Standing
1958	Chi	82-72	Second
1959	Chi	94-60	First
1960	Chi	87-67	Third
1961	Chi	86-76	Fourth
1962	Chi	85-77	Fifth
1963	Chi	94-68	Second
1964	Chi	98-64	Second
1965	Chi	95-67	Second
1968	Chi	33-48	Ninth
1969	Chi	8-9	Fourth
17 years		**1422-1026**	

WORLD SERIES

Year	Team	Record
1954	Cleve	0-4
1959	Chi	2-4
2 years		**2-8**

Theodore Amar Lyons

Born December 28, 1900, in Lake Charles, Louisiana; died July 25, 1986, in Sulphur, Louisiana. 5'11", 200 lbs., bats both, throws right. Major League debut: July 2, 1923; Years in Major Leagues: 21. Elected to Hall of Fame: 1955. Nickname: Tex—not widely used but given to him by a sportswriter in the minor leagues who did not know his first name; also Amar, his middle name, which some players called him—and which Lyons detested.

Ted Lyons played 21 years with the same team: the Chicago White Sox, a team which not only never won a pennant but rarely came close. They finished in the second division in 16 of his 21 seasons, yet Lyons won 260 games. Had he played for a better team, and averaged two more wins a year, he would have been a 300-game winner.

Lyons led the American League in wins twice, with a 21–11 record in 1925 and 22–14 mark in 1927. He won more than 20 games a third time, in 1930, when he was 22–15. He led the league in innings pitched twice and in complete games twice. Perhaps his most remarkable feat came in 1942 when he had the American League's lowest earned run average, 2.10, at the age of 41. He also completed all 20 of his starts that year, finishing with a 14–6 record. Lyons had a good knuckleball in addition to the usual assortment of pitches, and despite walking many more batters than he struck out, had a knack for getting the big out when he needed it. This enabled him to finish 75 percent of his starts over the course of his career.

Lyons had some remarkable games in his career. In one, he went all the way in a 21-inning game against Detroit, only to lose it 6–5. In 1926, he threw a no-hitter against the Boston Red Sox. He walked the first batter. The second batter was retired on a great catch in the outfield by Johnny Mostil, after which the base runner was doubled up. Lyons then retired the next 25 batters. Lyons was to the White Sox what Ernie Banks would later be for the Cubs—a great player for a team that never made it to the top, a player who never complained and was always a favorite with the fans. Lyons, in fact, became a "Sunday pitcher" for the White Sox. They tried to arrange to have him pitch Sunday home games because he was such a drawing card.

Year	Team	W-L	ERA	G	IP	H	BB	SO
1923	Chi (A)	2-1	6.35	9	22.2	30	15	6
1924	Chi	12-11	4.87	41	216.1	279	72	52
1925	Chi	21-11	3.26	43	262.2	274	83	45
1926	Chi	18-16	3.01	39	283.2	268	106	51
1927	Chi	22-14	2.84	39	307.2	291	67	71
1928	Chi	15-14	3.98	39	240	276	68	60
1929	Chi	14-20	4.10	37	259.1	276	76	57
1930	Chi	22-15	3.78	42	297.2	331	57	69
1931	Chi	4-6	4.01	22	101	117	33	16
1932	Chi	10-15	3.28	33	230.2	243	71	58
1933	Chi	10-21	4.38	36	228	260	74	74
1934	Chi	11-13	4.87	30	205.1	249	66	53
1935	Chi	15-8	3.02	23	190.2	194	56	54
1936	Chi	10-13	5.14	26	182	227	45	48
1937	Chi	12-7	4.15	22	169.1	182	45	45
1938	Chi	9-11	3.70	23	194.2	238	52	54
1939	Chi	14-6	2.76	21	172.2	162	26	65
1940	Chi	12-8	3.24	22	186.1	188	37	72
1941	Chi	12-10	3.70	22	187.1	199	37	63
1942	Chi	14-6	2.10	20	180.1	167	26	50
1946	Chi	1-4	2.32	5	42.2	38	9	10
21 years		**260-230**	**3.67**	**594**	**4161**	**4489**	**1121**	**1073**

Joseph Vincent McCarthy

Born April 21, 1887, in Philadelphia, Pennsylvania; died January 13, 1978, in Buffalo New York. Years in Major Leagues: 24 (all as manager). Elected to Hall of Fame: 1957. Nickname: Marse Joe—a derivative of "massah" or "master" applied by a sportswriter because of McCarthy's masterful managerial ability.

Joe McCarthy has the highest winning percentage of any manager in baseball history—quite a feat for someone who never played in the big leagues. In 24 years of Major League managing, his teams finished first nine times and second seven times. He became the first manager to win a pennant without having Major

League playing experience when he won with the Cubs in 1929. When he won three years later with the Yankees, he was the first to win pennants in both leagues. McCarthy took over a sixth-place Chicago Cubs team in 1926 and turned it into a pennant winner by 1929. The Cubs lost the World Series to the A's. In 1930, the Cubs failed to repeat, finishing second, and McCarthy resigned with four games remaining in the season. In 1932, when he won with the Yankees, they beat the Cubs with four straight wins in the World Series. He won nine championships overall—eight with the Yankees—and had World Series champions in eight of those nine years. He remained with the Yankees through the 1946 season, then resigned because of ill health. He returned in 1948 to manage the Boston Red Sox from 1948 to 1950 before calling it a career. McCarthy is credited with helping Cub slugger Hack Wilson attain stardom. McCarthy's .614 winning percentage is the all-time record for managers, as is his .698 winning percentage in World Series competition. In 24 years, his teams were never out of the first division.

Year	Team	W-L	Standing
1926	Chi (N)	82-72	Fourth
1927	Chi	85-68	Fourth
1928	Chi	91-63	Third
1929	Chi	98-54	First
1930	Chi	86-64	Second
1931	NY (A)	94-59	Second
1932	NY	107-57	First
1933	NY	91-59	Second
1934	NY	94-60	Second
1935	NY	89-60	Second
1936	NY	102-51	First
1937	NY	102-52	First
1938	NY	99-53	First
1940	NY	88-66	Third
1941	NY	101-53	First
1942	NY	103-51	First
1943	NY	98-56	First
1944	NY	83-71	First
1945	NY	81-71	Fourth
1946	NY	35-22	Second
1948	Bos	96-59	Second
1949	Bos	96-58	Second
1950	Bos	32-30	Fourth
24 years		**2126-1335**	

WORLD SERIES

Year	Team	W-L
1929	Chi (N)	1-4
1932	NY	4-0
1936	NY	4-2
1937	NY	4-1
1938	NY	4-0

Year	Team	W-L
1939	NY	4-0
1941	NY	4-1
1942	NY	1-4
1943	NY	4-1
9 years		**30-13**

Thomas Francis Michael McCarthy

Born July 24, 1864, in South Boston, Massachusetts; died August 5, 1922, in Boston, Massachusetts. 5'7", 170 lbs., bats right, throws right. Years in minor leagues: 1; Major League debut: July 10, 1884; Years in Major Leagues: 13. Elected to Hall of Fame: 1946. Nickname: Little Mac—a combination of his size and the first part of his last name; also, he and outfielder Hugh Duffy were often called "The Heavenly Twins" when they played together for Boston.

Tommy McCarthy was a hard-hitting, great fielding outfielder who starred for the Boston and St. Louis teams of the 1880s and 1890s. He only played nine full seasons but hit over .300 in four them with a high of .350 for St. Louis in 1890. His lifetime batting average was .292. His most productive years were with Boston where he teamed with Hugh Duffy to entertain fans. The two became known as "The Heavenly Twins." McCarthy was an excellent base runner who stole 93 bases in 1888 and 83 in 1890 on his way to a career total of 467. His innovative fielding techniques in the outfield led to some rule changes. McCarthy liked to charge line drives and catch them on the short hop, sometimes fooling umpires into thinking he caught the balls on the fly. He frequently ran in, trapped balls and threw runners out at first. He also developed a technique for juggling a ball while he was running in toward the infield, freezing a base runner who did not know whether the ball would drop or be caught. Years after McCarthy retired, umpire Bill Klem said McCarthy's juggling act led to the infield fly rule.

Year	Team	G	AB	R	H	D	T	HR	RBI	AVE.
1884	Bos (U)	53	209	37	45	3	2	0	--	.215
1885	Bos (N)	40	148	16	27	2	0	0	11	.182
1886	Phil (N)	8	27	6	5	2	1	0	3	.185
1887	StL (AA)	18	70	7	13	4	0	0	6	.186
1888	StL	131	511	107	140	20	3	1	68	.274
1889	StL	140	604	136	176	24	7	2	63	.291
1890	StL	133	548	137	192	28	9	6	--	.350
1891	StL	136	578	127	179	21	8	8	95	.310
1892	Bos	152	603	119	146	18	6	4	63	.242
1893	Bos	116	462	107	160	28	6	5	111	.346
1894	Bos	127	539	118	188	21	8	13	126	.349
1895	Bos	117	452	90	131	13	2	2	73	.290
1896	Brklyn	104	377	62	94	8	6	3	47	.249
13 years		**1275**	**5128**	**1069**	**1496**	**192**	**58**	**44**	**665**	**.292**

Willie Lee McCovey

Born January 10, 1938, in Mobile, Alabama. 6'4", 198 lbs., bats left, throws left; Years in minor leagues: 4; Major League debut: July 30, 1959; Years in Major Leagues: 22. Elected to Hall of Fame: 1986. Nickname: Stretch— because of his height, his long legs and his ability to stretch for a ball while playing first base.

Willie McCovey started his Major League career by hitting two singles and two triples as the Giants beat the Phillies and Robin Roberts, 7–2. That was in 1959, and despite the fact that he didn't get called up until July 30, McCovey won the National League Rookie of the Year Award, hitting .354 with 13 home runs. In 1969, he hit 45 home runs, drove in 126 runs and hit .320 to win the league's Most Valuable Player Award. His 45 intentional walks that year remain the National League record. McCovey led the league in homers three times, in runs scored once and in RBIs two years in a row. In 1968 and 1969, he led the league in both home runs and RBIs—only the fifth player in history to lead those categories two years in a row. The RBI titles are particularly significant since McCovey spent most of his career batting behind Willie Mays and Orlando Cepeda. He holds the National League record for home runs by a left handed batter (521) and for grand slams (18). McCovey spent two and a half seasons with San Diego and half a season with Oakland before returning to the Giants in 1977, when he won another honor—the Comeback Player of the Year Award when, at the age of 39, he batted .280 with 28 home runs. McCovey's most famous at-bat is one in which he made an out. The Yankees were winning 1–0 with two out in the bottom of the ninth inning of the seventh game of the 1962 World Series. Mays had just doubled to put runners on second and third. McCovey swung at a Ralph Terry pitch and hit a screaming line drive that would have surely scored both runs—but it was right at second baseman Bobby Richardson, who leaped up and speared it, salvaging the Yankee victory.

Year	Team	G	AB	R	H	D	T	HR	RBI	AVE.
1959	SF	52	192	32	68	9	5	13	38	.354
1960	SF	101	260	37	62	15	3	13	51	.238
1961	SF	106	328	59	89	12	3	18	50	.271
1962	SF	91	229	41	67	6	1	20	54	.293
1963	SF	152	564	103	158	19	5	44	102	.280
1964	SF	130	364	55	80	14	1	18	54	.220
1965	SF	160	540	93	149	17	4	39	92	.276
1966	SF	150	502	85	148	26	6	36	96	.295
1967	SF	135	456	73	126	17	4	31	91	.276
1968	SF	148	523	81	153	16	4	36	105	.293
1969	SF	149	491	101	157	26	2	45	126	.320
1970	SF	152	495	98	143	39	2	39	126	.289
1971	SF	105	329	45	91	13	0	18	70	.277
1972	SF	81	263	30	56	8	0	14	35	.213

Year	Team	G	AB	R	H	D	T	HR	RBI	AVE.
1973	SF	130	383	52	102	14	3	29	75	.266
1974	SD	128	344	53	87	19	1	22	63	.253
1975	SD	122	413	43	104	17	0	23	68	.252
1976	SD-Oak	82	226	20	46	9	0	7	36	.204
1977	SF	141	478	54	134	21	0	28	86	.280
1978	SF	108	351	32	80	19	2	12	64	.228
1979	SF	117	353	34	88	9	0	15	57	.249
1980	SF	48	113	8	23	8	0	1	16	.204
22 years		**2588**	**8197**	**1229**	**2211**	**353**	**46**	**521**	**1555**	**.270**

Transactions: Oct. 15, 1973: Traded with Bernie Williams to San Diego Padres for Mike Caldwell. Aug. 30, 1976: Sold to Oakland A's. Jan. 6, 1977: Signed with San Francisco as free agent.

LEAGUE CHAMPIONSHIP SERIES

Year	Team	G	AB	R	H	D	T	HR	RBI	AVE.
1971	SF	4	14	2	6	0	0	2	6	.429

WORLD SERIES

Year	Team	G	AB	R	H	D	T	HR	RBI	AVE.
1962	SF	4	15	2	3	0	1	1	1	.200

Arch McDonald

Broadcaster. Elected to Hall of Fame: 1999.

Arch McDonald was the radio voice of the lowly Washington Senators for 22 years. He had a laid-back style and a knack for coming up with phrases that fans loved to hear. He spent five years broadcasting Senators games, then went to New York and was the radio sidekick of Mel Allen on Yankee games for a year. But he returned the following year to Washington where he remained for the next 17 years. McDonald covered Senator teams that didn't win often—and frequently misplayed their way into losses. Many Senator fans heard McDonald lament that the Senators "cut down the old pine tree again."

Joseph Jerome McGinnity

Born March 19, 1871, in Rock Island, Illinois; died November 14, 1929, in Brooklyn, New York. 5'11", 206 lbs., bats right, throws right. Years in minor leagues: 3 years; Major League debut: April 18, 1899; Years in Major Leagues: 10. Elected to Hall of Fame: 1946. Nickname: Iron Man—with two possible meanings; one is his off-season job, as an "iron man" in a foundry, the other because of his remarkable durability on the mound.

Iron Man Joe McGinnity had a remarkable career. He pitched three years in the minor leagues, just 10 years in the Major Leagues, and then 17 more years in the minor leagues. In his 10 seasons in the Majors, he won 247 games—an average of almost 25 wins a season. He won more than 30 games twice and had two seasons in which he topped the 400-inning mark. McGinnity started and won both games of three doubleheaders in 1903 on his way to a 31-win season. He had 44 complete games and his 434 innings pitched that year are still the Major League record. In 1904, he had another great year, with 35 wins in 408 innings.

McGinnity had an underhand delivery in which his hand almost hit the ground. He also kept batters loose with inside pitches, averaging one hit batsman for every 19 hitters—by far the Major League record.

He was the third base coach for the Giants in 1908 when Al Bridwell singled in what appeared to be winning run against the Cubs. But Fred Merkle, the runner on first, headed for the clubhouse before touching second. Johnny Evers got the ball, tagged second, and Merkle was called out. McGinnity always claimed he picked up the game ball and that Evers used a ball supplied by the Cubs bench. After his Major League career ended in 1908, McGinnity continued to pitch in the minors. He won 15 games for Dubuque in 1923 at age 53 and continued to pitch through the end of the 1925 season.

Year	Team	W-L	ERA	G	IP	H	BB	SO
1899	Balt	28-17	2.58	48	380	358	93	74
1900	Brklyn	29-9	2.90	45	347	350	113	93
1901	Balt	26-20	3.56	48	382	412	96	75
1902	Balt-NY (N)	21-18	2.84	44	351.2	341	78	106
1903	NY	31-20	2.43	55	434	391	109	171
1904	NY	35-8	1.61	51	408	307	86	144
1905	NY	21-15	2.87	46	320	289	71	125
1906	NY	27-12	2.25	45	339.2	316	71	105
1907	NY	18-18	3.16	47	310.1	320	58	120
1908	NY	11-7	2.27	37	186	192	37	55
10 years		**247-144**	**2.64**	**466**	**3458.2**	**3276**	**812**	**1068**

WORLD SERIES

Year	Team	W-L	ERA	G	IP	H	BB	SO
1905	NY	1-1	0.00	2	17	10	3	6

William McGowan

Born January 18, 1896, in Wilmington, Delaware; died December 9, 1954, in Silver Spring, Maryland. 5'9", 178 lbs. Years in Major Leagues: 30 (as umpire). Elected to Hall of Fame: 1992. Nickname: Number One—an indication of the respect given to him as an umpire.

Bill McGowan got the attention and respect of ballplayers, managers and coaches by his demeanor on the field. He kept ball games moving along and set the tone for the game by the brisk pace with which he did everything. Connie Mack said he wished he had ballplayers who hustled like Bill McGowan. He was an exceptional umpire behind the plate. Jimmy Dykes, who managed in the American League for two decades, said there were games in which McGowan never "missed" a pitch—meaning he called every pitch correctly.

He used animated gestures to signal "out" or "safe" and often got into spirited discussions with ballplayers. In 1948, he was suspended for throwing his ball-and-strike indicator at Washington pitcher Ray Scarborough, and two years later was suspended again when he refused to tell the press which players he had ejected from the Detroit Tigers bench during a game with the St. Louis Browns. McGowan thought the players were taunting Browns pitcher Satchel Paige. McGowan also had a proud work ethic. He worked every inning of every game for a period of 16½ years—2,541 straight games.

Perhaps his greatest legacy to the game is the umpiring school he started in 1939. His was the second school—George Barr had started one four years earlier—and was the training ground for many umpires who made it to the Major Leagues in the 1940s and 1950s. By the mid–1960s, attendance at an umpire school was practically a requirement for those who wanted to advance in the profession. Like his counterpart Bill Klem in the National League, McGowan set most of the standards for American League umpires. For example, American League umps wore their chest protectors outside their coats for 30 years for no other reason than that's the way McGowan preferred it. Failing health slowed him down at an early age. He died of heart failure in 1954 at the age of 57 and was elected to the Hall of Fame 38 years later.

John Joseph McGraw

Born April 7, 1873, in Truxton, New York; died February 25, 1934, in New Rochelle, New York. Years in Major Leagues: 33 (as manager). Elected to Hall of Fame: 1937. Nickname: Little Napoleon—because of his small size but his commanding presence on a baseball field.

John McGraw was a scrappy ballplayer who made a name for himself in the minor leagues for his willingness to be as daring as he had to be to win. He is credited with inventing the hit-and-run play and was also adept at what came to be called "the Baltimore chop"—hitting a ball into the hard infield dirt with such force that the ball would bounce high up in the air, allowing the runner to beat the throw to first.

McGraw played for the great Baltimore teams of the 1890s with Wee Willie Keeler and Hughie Jennings and hit .300 or better for nine straight years. He was named manager of the Baltimore Orioles in the newly formed American League in 1901 but switched over to the National League's New York Giants the following year. American League president Ban Johnson had lured McGraw into the league, but the feisty McGraw became angry with Johnson for consistently backing umpires in their disputes with players. In his second year in the National League, McGraw's Giants won the National League pennant but did not play in the World Series because McGraw refused to play against a team from Johnson's league. It would be 90 years before another World Series was cancelled.

The Giants won again in 1905 and McGraw allowed the team to play in the World Series. They beat the Philadelphia A's, the first of three world championships McGraw would win. The Giants won ten pennants under McGraw, including four in a row from 1921 to 1924—a record that held up until Casey Stengel's Yankees won five in a row, 1949–1953. While McGraw's aggressive tactics never changed, players' attitudes did—and he became less and less effective as a manager. When he turned over the reins to his first baseman, Bill Terry, in 1932, it broke a long period in which the two men had not spoken to one another. McGraw was the epitome of the rough-and-tumble baseball player as well as the aggressive, smart, brazen manager. He once said he never saw the point of taking a loss philosophically. McGraw's teams won 2,840 games. Only Connie Mack won more.

Year	Team	Record	Standing
1899	Balt	86-62	Fourth
1901	Balt	68-65	Fifth
1902	Balt	28-34	Seventh
1902	NY (N)	25-38	Eighth
1903	NY	84-55	Second
1904	NY	106-47	First
1905	NY	105-48	First
1906	NY	96-56	Second
1907	NY	82-71	Fourth
1908	NY	98-56	Second
1909	NY	92-61	Third
1910	NY	91-63	Second
1911	NY	99-54	First
1912	NY	103-48	First
1913	NY	101-51	First
1914	NY	84-70	Second
1915	NY	69-83	Eighth
1916	NY	86-66	Fourth
1917	NY	98-56	First
1918	NY	71-53	Second
1919	NY	87-53	Second
1920	NY	86-68	Second
1921	NY	94-59	First
1922	NY	93-61	First
1923	NY	95-58	First
1924	NY	93-60	First
1925	NY	86-66	Second
1926	NY	74-77	Fifth
1927	NY	92-62	Third
1928	NY	93-61	Second
1929	NY	84-67	Third

Year	Team	Record	Standing
1930	NY	87-67	Third
1931	NY	85-67	Second
1932	NY	17-23	Eighth
33 years		**2840-1984**	

WORLD SERIES

Year	Team	Record
1905	NY	4-1
1911	NY	2-4
1912	NY	3-4
1913	NY	1-4
1917	NY	2-4
1921	NY	5-3
1922	NY	4-0
1923	NY	2-4
1924	NY	3-4
9 years		**26-28**

Joseph McGuff

Sportswriter. Elected to Hall of Fame: 1984.

Joe McGuff was a sportswriter, sportseditor and columnist for 40 years with the *Kansas City Times* and *Kansas City Star*. He started writing about baseball in Tulsa in 1948, writing about the Tulsa Oilers and continued when he moved to Kansas City in 1950 when his "beat" was the Kansas City Blues minor league team.

In 1955, he became an instant Major League baseball writer when the A's moved to Kansas City. By 1966, he was a columnist and eventually became sports editor of the *Kansas City Star*. He covered 19 All-Star games and was at the scene 30 years for the World Series. He served a term as president of the Baseball Writers Association of America.

Connie Mack

Born December 22, 1862, in East Brookfield, Massachusetts; died February 8, 1956, in Germantown, Pennsylvania. 6'1", 170 lbs., bats right, throws right. Years in minor leagues: 4; Major League debut: October 7, 1886; Years in Major Leagues: 60 (as player and manager). Elected to Hall of Fame: 1937. Nickname: The Tall Tactician—referring to his height and his managerial ability; also Mr. Mack, a title of respect for the elderly statesman of baseball as well as a nickname.

Connie Mack had a nondescript Major League playing career and had just been fired as manager of the Pittsburgh club in the National League when Ban

Johnson hired him to manage the Milwaukee minor league team in the Western League. The move changed his life, because in 1901, Johnson formed a second Major League, the American League and hired Mack to manage the Philadelphia franchise. Thus began a lifelong, roller coaster career with the A's, filled with ups and downs that included championships, a celebrated lawsuit, massive "garage sales" of ballplayers twice to avoid bankruptcy, and a reputation as being one of baseball's greatest early leaders. Mack still has the most wins—and the most losses— of any Major League manager. When Mack started the A's, he raided the existing Philadelphia team for players and won championships in 1902 and 1905. The Phillies had sued over the player raids, and the Pennsylvania Supreme Court ruled that Mack either had to give the players back to the Phillies or trade them. Mack traded them.

It didn't take him long to restock, and the A's won pennants in 1910, 1911, 1913 and 1914 with their "$100,000 infield" of Stuffy McInnis, Eddie Collins, Jack Barry and Frank Baker and the pitching of Chief Bender and Eddie Plank. After the "Miracle Braves" beat the A's in the 1914 World Series, Mack traded or sold most of his stars over the next few years so that he could "restock" once again. He waited 15 years for another pennant, but got it with one of the greatest teams of all time. The A's won pennants in 1929, 1930 and 1931 with teams led by Jimmy Foxx, Al Simmons and Mickey Cochrane and a pitching staff led by the great Lefty Grove.

The Great Depression hit the A's hard and once again, Mack shipped the nucleus of his championship teams elsewhere and the A's never really recovered. They remained mired at the bottom of the American League for the remainder of Mack's career. In straw hat or derby, in business suit and waving a rolled up scorecard, Mack managed the A's for 50 years, quitting at the age of 87. He died in 1956 at the age of 93. Mack's real name was Cornelius McGillicuddy. He changed his name to Connie Mack—so it would fit in a boxscore!

Year	Team	Record	Standing
1894	Pitt	12–10	Seventh
1895	Pitt	71–61	Seventh
1896	Pitt	66–63	Sixth
1901	Phil (A)	74–62	Fourth
1902	Phil	83–53	First
1903	Phil	75–60	Second
1904	Phil	81–70	Fifth
1905	Phil	92–56	First
1906	Phil	78–67	Fourth
1907	Phil	88–57	Second
1908	Phil	68–85	Sixth
1909	Phil	95–58	Second
1910	Phil	102–48	First
1911	Phil	101–50	First
1912	Phil	90–62	Third
1913	Phil	96–57	First
1914	Phil	99–53	First

Year	Team	Record	Standing
1915	Phil	43-109	Eighth
1916	Phil	36-117	Eighth
1917	Phil	55-98	Eighth
1918	Phil	52-76	Eighth
1919	Phil	36-104	Eighth
1920	Phil	48-106	Eighth
1921	Phil	53-100	Eighth
1922	Phil	65-89	Seventh
1923	Phil	69-83	Sixth
1924	Phil	71-81	Fifth
1925	Phil	88-64	Second
1926	Phil	83-67	Third
1927	Phil	91-63	Second
1928	Phil	98-55	Second
1929	Phil	104-46	First
1930	Phil	102-52	First
1931	Phil	107-45	First
1932	Phil	94-60	Second
1933	Phil	79-72	Third
1934	Phil	68-82	Fifth
1935	Phil	58-91	Eighth
1936	Phil	53-100	Eighth
1937	Phil	54-97	Seventh
1938	Phil	53-99	Eighth
1939	Phil	55-97	Seventh
1940	Phil	54-100	Eighth
1941	Phil	64-90	Eighth
1942	Phil	55-99	Eighth
1943	Phil	49-105	Eighth
1944	Phil	72-82	Fifth
1945	Phil	52-98	Eighth
1946	Phil	49-105	Eighth
1947	Phil	78-76	Fifth
1948	Phil	84-70	Fourth
1949	Phil	81-73	Fifth
1950	Phil	52-102	Eighth
53 years		**3776-4025**	

WORLD SERIES

Year	Team	Record
1905	Phil (A)	1-4
1910	Phil	4-1
1911	Phil	4-2
1913	Phil	4-1
1914	Phil	0-4
1929	Phil	4-1
1930	Phil	4-2
1931	Phil	3-4
8 years		**24-19**

William Boyd McKechnie

Born August 7, 1886, in Wilkinsburg, Pennsylvania; died October 29, 1965, in Bradenton, Florida. Years in Major Leagues: 36 (as player and manager). Elected to Hall of Fame: 1962. Nickname: Deacon—because of his gentlemanly manner and the fact that he actually was a deacon in the Methodist church.

Bill McKechnie is the only Major League manager to win pennants with three different teams in the same league: Pittsburgh in 1925, St. Louis in 1928 and Cincinnati in 1939 and 1940. His 1925 Pirate club, with the Waner brothers, Pie Traynor and KiKi Cuyler, won the World Series, as did his 1940 Reds club, despite a late season tragedy when catcher Willard Hershberger committed suicide in his hotel room.

After his success in Pittsburgh, he was hired to manage the Cardinals and won a pennant in his first year in St. Louis, 1928. But the Cards dropped four straight to the Yankees in the World Series. Midway into the 1929 season McKechnie was fired. He hooked on to manage the lowly Boston Braves, who were financially strapped and mired in the second division. It is the only team which failed to win a pennant under McKechnie, but he was named Manager of the Year when Boston finished fifth in 1938. At Boston in 1935, McKechnie managed Babe Ruth in his last Major League season.

McKechnie went from rags to riches when he was hired in 1938 by wealthy Reds owner Powell Crosley to try to rejuvenate the Cincinnati team, which had finished eighth in 1937. In two years, McKechnie had the Reds in the World Series. He was known as a shrewd judge of talent and a master in his knowledge of the game. After he retired as a manager, he signed on as pitching coach of Lou Boudreau's Cleveland Indians. McKechnie worked with veteran Bob Feller, an outfielder-turned-pitcher named Bob Lemon and an aging rookie by the name of Satchel Paige to help win a World Series title for the Indians.

Year	Team	Record	Standing
1915	Nwk (F)	54-45	Sixth
1922	Pitt	53-36	Fifth
1923	Pitt	87-67	Third
1924	Pitt	90-63	Third
1925	Pitt	95-58	First
1926	Pitt	84-69	Third
1928	StL (N)	95-59	First
1929	StL	33-29	Fourth
1930	Bos (N)	70-84	Sixth
1931	Bos	64-90	Seventh
1932	Bos	77-77	Fifth
1933	Bos	83-71	Fourth
1934	Bos	78-73	Fourth
1935	Bos	38-115	Eighth
1936	Bos	71-83	Sixth

Year	Team	Record	Standing
1937	Bos	79-73	Fifth
1938	Cin	82-68	Fourth
1939	Cin	97-57	First
1940	Cin	100-53	First
1941	Cin	88-66	Third
1942	Cin	76-76	Fourth
1943	Cin	87-67	Second
1944	Cin	89-65	Third
1945	Cin	61-93	Seventh
1946	Cin	67-87	Sixth
25 years		1898-1724	

WORLD SERIES

Year	Team	Record
1925	Pitt	4-3
1928	StL	0-4
1939	Cin	0-4
1940	Cin	4-3
4 years		8-14

Lee MacPhail

Baseball executive. Elected to Hall of Fame: 1998.

Lee MacPhail was a second generation baseball executive who presided over some of the most turbulent times in the sport's history. The son of Larry MacPhail grew up with baseball and got a job working in the farm system of his father's Brooklyn Dodger club in 1941. He served overseas in World War II and came back and got a job with his father's New York Yankee ball club. Eventually he was the head of the team's farm system under general manager George Weiss. Together, they helped build a dynasty. The Baltimore Orioles liked what MacPhail did in New York and hired him to put a spark in their organization which had been sputtering under the direction of Paul Richards who was serving as both manager and general manager. When Richards left to be general manager of the new Houston franchise, it created not only the two openings in the jobs he had filled, but many in his coaching staff went with him.

MacPhail rebuilt the Orioles and had them on the verge of greatness when he left after the 1965 season to become administrative assistant to the game's new commissioner, retired Air Force Gen. William Eckert, who had no baseball background. MacPhail's last deal before leaving Baltimore brought Frank Robinson to the Orioles. Robinson won the Triple Crown and the Most Valuable Player award in 1966, and the Orioles won pennants in four of the next six years. In 1966,

MacPhail, who almost 20 years before was Yankee farm director, became the Yankees general manager, a position he held until he became American League president in 1974. During the next 10 years, baseball entered the free-agent era, experienced more expansion, and endured its first strike, in 1981. MacPhail, in his genial, businesslike manner, is credited with helping negotiate a settlement.

As league president, he was also involved with the most controversial decisions of his era involving the outcome of a game. On July 24, 1983, George Brett of the Kansas City Royals hit a two-run homer with two outs in the ninth inning to give the Royals a 5–4 lead over the New York Yankees. Yankee manager Billy Martin argued, saying Brett's bat was illegal because it exceeded the pine tar limit on the handle. Home plate umpire Tim McClelland agreed and ruled that Brett's at-bat was actually the game-ending third out. The Royals protested the ruling. MacPhail reversed the decision, allowed the home run for Brett and ordered the game be resumed where it left off. It was resumed in August with no further scoring.

Leland Stanford MacPhail

Born February 3, 1890, in Cass City, Michigan; died October 1, 1975, in Miami, Florida. Baseball Executive. Elected to Hall of Fame: 1978. Nickname: Larry—a takeoff on his first name.

Larry MacPhail built pennant winners in Cincinnati and Brooklyn, started a dynasty with the New York Yankees and introduced night baseball to the Major Leagues. He was a dreamer and an innovator about the game itself but a realist and shrewd tactician with the teams he led as general manager and in other executive positions.

After several years as a lawyer, president of a tool company and owner of an auto agency, MacPhail bought the Columbus Redbirds minor league team in 1930 and almost immediately instituted his first "first"—travel by air. By 1933, he was in Cincinnati where he was asked to bring a ball club back from the dead. He made some trades, introduced night baseball and had the Reds on their way to the World Series in 1939 and 1940. By the time they got there, MacPhail was on to other challenges: the Brooklyn Dodgers needed help. The Dodgers won the pennant in 1941.

He stayed in Brooklyn long enough to have some celebrated run-ins with manager Leo Durocher. At the end of the 1942 season, MacPhail was part of a partnership that bought the New York Yankees. The Yankees had declined some from their latest glory years of the late 1930s. By 1947, they were back on top, and after the World Series MacPhail retired. But he had helped start a dynasty that saw the Yankees win in 1947, finish behind Cleveland in 1948, then reel off five straight championships before the Indians won again in 1954, then reel off four more championships before the White Sox won in 1959, and then five more championships. MacPhail not only started night baseball while he was in Cincinnati, but also installed lights in Brooklyn and at Yankee Stadium. In the front office, he started pension plans for players, managers, coaches and those affiliated with ball clubs off the field as well.

Mickey Charles Mantle

Born October 20, 1931, in Commerce, Oklahoma; died August 13, 1995, in Dallas, Texas. 6', 201 lbs., bats both, throws right. Years in minor leagues: 2; Major League debut: April 17, 1951; Years in Major Leagues: 18. Elected to Hall of Fame: 1974. Nickname: The Commerce Comet—a nickname given Mantle early in his career, referring to his speed and his hometown; also, The Mick—what he was most often called if a nickname was used at all.

Mickey Mantle was the most powerful switch hitter in baseball history and was one of the most popular Yankees of all time. He was plagued with injuries most of his career, yet his achievements are spectacular. Mantle hit over .300 ten times, topped the 50 homer mark twice, led the American League in home runs four times, in slugging percentage four times and won the Most Valuable Player Award three times—in 1956, 1957 and 1962. In 1956, he won the Triple Crown with his .353 batting average, 52 home runs and 130 runs batted in. Mantle, whose father named him after Hall of Famer Mickey Cochrane, broke in with the Yankees in 1951 as the heir apparent in center field to Joe DiMaggio, who retired at the end of that season. Early in his career, he was considered the fastest man in all of baseball on the base paths, but bad knees slowed him down over the years. His speed helped him be a good defensive outfielder. On October 8, 1956, his long, running catch of a ball hit by Gil Hodges preserved Don Larsen's perfect game.

Mantle was known for his tape-measure home runs. Long before technology was used to measure home run distances, Mantle hit one in Washington's Griffith Stadium in 1953 that was estimated at 565 feet. Four years later, on July 23, 1957, The Mick hit for the cycle against Chicago's Bob Keegan, and his home run came within inches of clearing the roof at Yankee Stadium, a feat that has never been accomplished. Long before Reggie Jackson acquired the nickname of Mr. October, Mantle established some World Series records that have never been broken, including his 18 home runs, 40 RBIs and 42 runs scored.

In 1961, Mantle and teammate Roger Maris went on a season-long chase of Babe Ruth's single-season home run record of 60. Maris hit his 61st on the last day of the season. Once again, Mantle's injuries held him back. Mantle had 54 home runs when his season ended in mid–September.

Year	Team	G	AB	R	H	D	T	HR	RBI	AVE.
1951	NY (A)	96	341	61	91	11	5	13	65	.267
1952	NY	142	549	94	171	37	7	23	87	.311
1953	NY	127	461	105	136	24	3	21	92	.295
1954	NY	146	543	129	163	17	12	27	102	.300
1955	NY	147	517	121	158	25	11	37	99	.306

Year	Team	G	AB	R	H	D	T	HR	RBI	AVE.
1956	NY	150	533	132	188	22	5	52	130	.353
1957	NY	144	474	121	173	28	6	34	94	.365
1958	NY	150	519	127	158	21	1	42	97	.304
1959	NY	144	541	104	154	23	4	31	75	.285
1960	NY	153	527	119	145	17	6	40	94	.275
1961	NY	153	514	132	163	16	6	54	128	.317
1962	NY	123	377	96	121	15	1	30	89	.321
1963	NY	65	172	40	54	8	0	15	35	.314
1964	NY	143	465	92	141	25	2	35	111	.303
1965	NY	122	361	44	92	12	1	19	46	.255
1966	NY	108	333	40	96	12	1	23	56	.288
1967	NY	144	440	63	108	17	0	22	55	.245
1968	NY	144	435	57	103	14	1	18	54	.237
18 years		**2401**	**8102**	**1677**	**2415**	**344**	**72**	**536**	**1509**	**.298**

WORLD SERIES

Year	Team	G	AB	R	H	D	T	HR	RBI	AVE.
1951	NY (A)	2	5	1	1	0	0	0	0	.200
1952	NY	7	29	5	10	1	1	2	3	.345
1953	NY	6	24	3	5	0	0	2	7	.208
1955	NY	3	10	1	2	0	0	1	1	.200
1956	NY	7	24	6	6	1	0	3	4	.250
1957	NY	6	19	3	5	0	0	1	2	.263
1958	NY	7	24	4	6	0	1	2	3	.250
1960	NY	7	25	8	10	1	0	3	11	.400
1961	NY	2	6	0	1	0	0	0	0	.167
1962	NY	7	25	2	3	1	0	0	0	.120
1963	NY	4	15	1	2	0	0	1	1	.133
1964	NY	7	24	8	8	2	0	3	8	.333
12 years		**65**	**230**	**42**	**59**	**6**	**2**	**18**	**40**	**.257**

Henry Emmett Manush

Born July 20, 1901, in Tuscumbia, Alabama; died May 12, 1971, in Sarasota, Florida. 6', 200 lbs., bats left, throws left. Years in minor leagues: 2; Major League debut: April 20, 1923; Years in Major Leagues: 17. Elected to Hall of Fame: 1964. Nickname: Heinie—a crude reference to his German ancestry.

Heinie Manush was a great line drive hitter who had some great teachers. He broke in with the Detroit Tigers in 1923 in an outfield that also featured Ty Cobb and Harry Heilmann. He hit .334.

Manush had some classic battles for the American League batting title. He won it in 1926, but had to get six hits in nine at-bats in a doubleheader on the last day of the season to overtake Babe Ruth. He was traded to the St. Louis Browns in 1928, where he lost the the batting title by one point to Goose Goslin of Washington. The

Browns were playing the Senators that day, and Goslin got the hit that gave him the batting championship in his last at-bat. In 1933, Manush finished second again, hitting .336. Jimmie Foxx won the title for the second straight year, hitting .356. In 1930, he was traded to Washington for Goslin. In the 1933 World Series, Manush was called out on a close play at first. In the argument that ensued, umpire Charlie Moran ejected Manush—a highly unusual gesture in a World Series game.

Years later, Manush said that when he and Moran were arguing toe to toe, he reached over and grabbed Moran's bow tie, which was held around his neck by elastic. Manush pulled the tie back and let go, snapping it against the umpire's neck. Commissioner Kenesaw Mountain Landis saw the ejection but did not see what caused it. But he ordered that henceforth only the commissioner could eject a player. Manush was traded to the Boston Red Sox in 1935 and had stints with Brooklyn and Pittsburgh before retiring with a lifetime batting average of .330.

Year	Team	G	AB	R	H	D	T	HR	RBI	AVE.
1923	Det	109	308	59	103	20	5	4	54	.334
1924	Det	120	422	83	122	24	8	9	68	.289
1925	Det	99	278	46	84	14	3	5	47	.302
1926	Det	136	498	95	188	35	8	14	86	.378
1927	Det	151	593	102	177	31	18	6	90	.298
1928	StL (A)	154	638	104	241	47	20	13	108	.378
1929	StL	142	574	85	204	45	10	6	81	.355
1930	StL-Wash	137	554	100	194	49	12	9	94	.350
1931	Wash	146	616	110	189	41	11	6	70	.307
1932	Wash	149	625	121	214	41	14	14	116	.342
1933	Wash	153	658	115	221	32	17	5	95	.336
1934	Wash	137	556	88	194	42	11	11	89	.349
1935	Wash	119	479	68	131	26	9	4	56	.273
1936	Bos (A)	82	313	43	91	15	5	0	45	.291
1937	Brklyn	132	466	57	155	25	7	4	73	.333
1938	Brklyn-Pitt	32	64	11	16	4	2	0	10	.250
1939	Pitt	10	12	0	0	0	0	0	1	.000
17 years		**2008**	**7654**	**1287**	**2524**	**491**	**160**	**110**	**1183**	**.330**

Transactions: Dec. 2, 1927: Traded with Lu Blue to St. Louis Browns for Chick Galloway, Elam Vanglider and Harry Rice. June 13, 1930: Traded with General Crowder to Washington for Goose Goslin. Dec. 17, 1935: Traded to Boston Red Sox for Carl Reynolds and Roy Johnson. May 1938: Sold to Pittsburgh for waiver price.

World Series

Year	Team	G	AB	R	H	D	T	HR	RBI	AVE.
1933	Wash	5	18	2	2	0	0	0	0	.111

Walter James Vincent Maranville

Born November 11, 1891, in Springfield, Massachusetts; died January 5, 1954, in New York City, New York. 5'5", 155 lbs., bats right, throws right. Years in minor leagues: 2; Major League debut: September 10, 1912; Years in Major Leagues: 23. Elected to Hall of Fame: 1954. Nickname: Rabbit—according to some accounts, because of the size of his ears, which he could wiggle; according to other accounts, because of his antics, such as doing handsprings on the ball field.

Rabbit Maranville was one of the most colorful players of his day—and that "day" lasted almost a quarter of a century in the Major Leagues. His career paralleled Babe Ruth's, and they were teammates with the Boston Bees in the National League when they both retired. Maranville was tiny but was extremely quick in the field. He was making "basket catches" long before Willie Mays made them famous, and he had tremendous range in the field. He was a durable player who appeared in 2,670 games—only Ty Cobb and Eddie Collins played in more.

Maranville was part of the 1914 "Miracle Braves" team that swept the powerful Philadelphia A's in the World Series. A few weeks later, he and some teammates performed in a vaudeville act. That is an apt summation of Maranville's priorities—baseball and fun. Also in 1914, Maranville set the record for most chances handled by a shortstop (broken many times since then) and he and second baseman Johnny Evers led the league in double plays. He loved to needle umpires and keep fans entertained with his constant chatter and his aggressive style of play and his pranks. Though his career batting average was only .258, he scored high on Hall of Fame ballots from the time he was first eligible, meaning that writers who saw him play saw some valuable intangibles that don't show up in statistics sheets. Maranville died on January 5, 1954, and was posthumously elected to the Hall of Fame that same year.

Year	Team	G	AB	R	H	D	T	HR	RBI	AVE.
1912	Bos (N)	26	86	8	18	2	0	0	8	.209
1913	Bos	143	571	68	141	13	8	2	48	.247
1914	Bos	156	586	74	144	23	6	4	78	.246
1915	Bos	149	509	51	124	23	6	2	43	.244
1916	Bos	155	604	79	142	16	13	4	38	.235
1917	Bos	142	561	69	146	19	13	3	43	.260
1918	Bos	11	38	3	12	0	1	0	3	.316
1919	Bos	131	480	44	128	18	10	5	43	.267
1920	Bos	134	493	48	131	19	15	1	43	.266
1921	Pitt	153	612	90	180	25	12	1	70	.294
1922	Pitt	155	672	115	198	26	15	0	63	.295
1923	Pitt	141	581	78	161	19	9	1	41	.277
1924	Pitt	152	594	62	158	33	20	2	71	.266
1925	Chi (N)	75	266	37	62	10	3	0	23	.233
1926	Brklyn	78	234	32	55	8	5	0	24	.235
1927	StL (N)	9	29	0	7	1	0	0	0	.241
1928	StL	112	366	40	88	14	10	1	34	.240

Year	Team	G	AB	R	H	D	T	HR	RBI	AVE.
1929	Bos (N)	146	560	87	159	26	10	0	55	.284
1930	Bos	142	558	85	157	26	8	2	43	.281
1931	Bos	145	562	69	146	22	5	0	33	.260
1932	Bos	149	571	67	134	20	4	0	37	.235
1933	Bos	143	478	46	104	15	4	0	38	.218
1935	Bos	23	67	3	10	2	0	0	5	.149
23 years		2670	10078	1255	2605	380	177	28	884	.258

Transactions: Feb. 23, 1921: Traded to Pittsburgh for Billy Southworth, Fred Nicholson, Walter Barbare and $15,000. Oct. 27, 1954: Traded to Chicago Cubs with Charlie Grimm and Wilbur Cooper for Vic Aldridge, George Grantham and Al Niehaus. Nov. 8, 1925: Sold to Brooklyn for waiver price. Dec. 8, 1928: Sold to Boston Braves.

WORLD SERIES

Year	Team	G	AB	R	H	D	T	HR	RBI	AVE.
1914	Bos (N)	4	13	1	4	0	0	0	3	.308
1928	StL (N)	4	13	2	4	1	0	0	0	.308
2 years		8	26	3	8	1	0	0	3	.308

Juan Antonio Sanchez Marichal

Born October 20, 1938, in Laguna Verda, Dominican Republic. 5'11", 190 lbs., bats right, throws right. Years in minor leagues: 2; Major League debut: July 19, 1960; Years in Major Leagues: 16. Elected to Hall of Fame: 1983. Nickname: The Dominican Dandy—sportwriters' reference to his homeland.

Juan Marichal was the greatest pitcher in the 1960s never to have won a Cy Young Award, the victim of pitching in the same league and in the same era as Sandy Koufax and Bob Gibson. He was the Major Leagues' winningest pitcher from 1963 through 1969, including 1963 when he was 25–8, 1966 when he was 25–6, and 1968 when he was 26–9. He had a stretch where he won 20 or more games in six out of seven seasons. His career totals show 243 wins—a record for Latin American pitchers that stood until Dennis Martinez broke it in 1998—and three times as many strikeouts as walks.

Marichal was a graceful artist with a high leg kick and a delivery that was sometimes sidearm, sometimes three-quarters and sometimes straight overhand. He mixed his pitches to keep hitters off balance and had excellent control. His Major League debut gave opponents a hint of what to expect in years to come: He blanked the Phillies 2–0 on one hit—an eighth inning single by Clay Dalrymple. On June 15, 1963, Marichal threw a no-hitter against the Houston Colt 45s, allowing only two base runners on walks.

His worst day in baseball occurred on August 22, 1965, when he became enraged at Dodger catcher John Roseboro. Marichal was batting and was upset about pitches he thought were purposely too far inside. Roseboro then caught a pitch and fired the ball back to the pitcher with the ball whizzing by Marichal's ear. He accosted Roseboro and hit him with his bat. He was ejected from the game, suspended for nine days and fined $1,750—the largest penalty in National League history.

Year	Team	W-L	ERA	G	IP	H	BB	SO
1960	SF	6-2	2.66	11	81.1	59	28	58
1961	SF	13-10	3.89	29	185	183	48	124
1962	SF	18-11	3.36	37	262.2	233	90	153
1963	SF	25-8	2.41	41	321.1	259	61	248
1964	SF	21-8	2.48	33	269	241	52	206
1965	SF	22-13	2.13	39	295.1	224	46	240
1966	SF	25-6	2.23	37	307.1	228	36	222
1967	SF	14-10	2.76	26	202.1	195	42	166
1968	SF	26-9	2.43	38	325.2	295	46	218
1969	SF	21-11	2.10	37	300	244	54	205
1970	SF	12-10	4.11	34	243	269	48	123
1971	SF	18-11	2.94	37	279	244	56	159
1972	SF	6-16	3.71	25	165	176	46	72
1973	SF	11-15	3.79	34	209	231	37	87
1974	Bos	5-1	4.87	11	57.1	61	14	21
1975	LA (N)	0-1	13.50	2	6	11	5	1
16 years		**243-142**	**2.89**	**471**	**3509.1**	**3153**	**709**	**2303**

Transactions: Dec. 7, 1973: Sold to Boston Red Sox.

LEAGUE CHAMPIONSHIP SERIES

Year	Team	W-L	ERA	G	IP	H	BB	SO
1971	SF	0-1	2.25	1	8	4	0	6

WORLD SERIES

Year	Team	W-L	ERA	G	IP	H	BB	SO
1962	SF	0-0	0.00	1	4	2	2	4

Richard Marquard

Born October 9, 1889, in Cleveland, Ohio; died June 1, 1980, in Baltimore, Maryland. 6'3", 180 lbs., bats right, throws left. Major League debut: September 25, 1908; Years in Major Leagues: 18. Elected to Hall of Fame: 1971. Nickname: Rube—because Marquard reminded a sportswriter of pitcher Rube Waddell—and the nickname stuck.

Rube Marquard is the only Hall of Famer to be notified at sea that he was inducted. He was 81 and on a cruise on the *Queen Elizabeth 2* when he received the news. Later, at a dance, the ship's captain stopped the music to announce the good news to everyone on board, and the dance band played "Take Me Out to the Ball Game."

Marquard was one of the greatest pitchers of the early 1900s. From 1911 through 1913, the tall lefthander won 73 games for the New York Giants, leading them to three consecutive pennants. In 1912, he started the season with 19 consecutive victories—still the Major League record—and would have had 20, a win in relief, except scoring rules of the day dictated that a victory went to the hurler who pitched the most innings. Marquard threw a no-hitter against the Dodgers in 1915 but played for them in 1916 and helped them to the pennant that year and again in 1920. Injuries plagued him after his three big years with the Giants and, except for one 19-win season, he never came close to a 20-win season again.

He was one of the most popular players of his era and was married to actress and singer Blossom Seeley. Together they had a song-and-dance act, but nothing matched his performances on the mound. He had an earned run average of 2.00 or under in three of his five World Series years. His World Series ERA was 1.54 in 1911 and 0.50 in 1912. He finished with 201 career wins.

Year	Team	W-L	ERA	G	IP	H	BB	SO
1908	NY (N)	0-1	3.60	1	5	6	2	2
1909	NY	5-13	2.60	29	173	155	73	109
1910	NY	4-4	4.46	13	70.2	65	40	52
1911	NY	24-7	2.50	45	277.2	221	106	237
1912	NY	26-11	2.57	43	294.2	286	80	175
1913	NY	23-10	2.50	42	288	248	49	151
1914	NY	12-22	3.06	39	268	261	47	92
1915	NY-Brklyn	11-10	4.04	33	193.2	207	38	92
1916	Brklyn	13-6	1.58	36	205	169	38	107
1917	Brklyn	19-12	2.55	37	232.2	200	60	117
1918	Brklyn	9-18	2.64	34	239	231	59	89
1919	Brklyn	3-3	2.29	8	59	54	10	29
1920	Brklyn	10-7	3.23	28	189.2	181	35	89
1921	Cin	17-14	3.39	39	265.2	291	50	88
1922	Bos (N)	11-15	5.09	39	198	255	66	57
1923	Bos	11-14	3.73	38	239	265	65	78
1924	Bos	1-2	3.00	6	36	33	13	10
1925	Bos	2-8	5.75	26	72	105	27	19
18 years		**201-177**	**3.08**	**536**	**3306.2**	**3233**	**858**	**1593**

Transactions: Aug. 31, 1915: Sold to Brooklyn for waiver price. Dec. 15, 1920: Traded to Cincinnati for Dutch Ruether. Feb. 18, 1922: Traded with Larry Kopf to Boston Braves for Jack Scott.

WORLD SERIES

Year	Team	W-L	ERA	G	IP	H	BB	SO
1911	NY (N)	0-1	1.54	3	11.2	9	1	8
1912	NY	2-0	0.50	2	18	14	2	9

Year	Team	W-L	ERA	G	IP	H	BB	SO
1913	NY	0-1	7.00	2	9	10	3	3
1916	Brklyn	0-2	4.91	2	11	12	6	9
1920	Brklyn	0-1	2.00	2	9	7	3	6
5 years		2-5	2.76	11	58.2	52	15	35

Edwin Lee Mathews Jr.

Born October 13, 1931, in Texarkana, Texas. 6'1", 195 lbs., bats left, throws right. Years in minor leagues: 3; Major League debut: April 15, 1952; Years in Major Leagues: 17. Elected to Hall of Fame: 1978. Nickname: None

Eddie Mathews was the most powerful hitting third baseman of his generation. He hit 512 home runs in his career. Among third basemen, only Mike Schmidt has surpassed that. Mathews hit 30 or more home runs nine years in a row and hit more than 40 four times. He saw a lot of good pitches because for most of his career he hit ahead of Henry Aaron. He saw his share of bad pitches, too, leading the league in walks four times. The Mathews-Aaron combination was often compared to the Ruth-Gehrig combination because of its impact in the lineup. The number of home runs they hit as teammates, 863, far surpasses Ruth and Gehrig, who hit 772 while playing together. With Mathews and Aaron anchoring the lineup, the Milwaukee Braves won pennants in 1957 and 1958 and just missed in 1956 and 1959. The Braves beat the Yankees, four games to three, to win their only World Series championship in 1957.

Mathews led the National League in home runs in 1953 with 47 (the record for third basemen at the time) and was the league leader again in 1959 with 46. He was signed by Braves scout Johnny Moore, who sought Mathews out at his high school graduation dance in 1949. He advanced quickly to Boston's Triple-A ball club at Milwaukee where he hit a grand-slam home run in his first at-bat. As a rookie with the Boston Braves, he hit 25 home runs, a rookie record at the time. In September of 1952, he hit three home runs in a game at Brooklyn. No other rookie had ever done that.

Mathews is the only player to have been with the Braves in Boston, Milwaukee and Atlanta, playing for them in their last year in Boston, their first year in Atlanta and 13 years in between in Milwaukee. He ended his career as a part-time player on Detroit's World Series championship team in 1968. Mathews managed the Braves for parts of three seasons, 1972–74.

Year	Team	G	AB	R	H	D	T	HR	RBI	AVE.
1952	Bos (N)	145	528	80	128	23	5	25	58	.242
1953	Mil	157	579	110	175	31	8	47	135	.302
1954	Mil	138	476	96	138	21	4	40	103	.290
1955	Mil	141	499	108	144	23	5	41	101	.289
1956	Mil	151	552	103	150	21	2	37	95	.272

Year	Team	G	AB	R	H	D	T	HR	RBI	AVE.
1957	Mil	148	572	109	167	28	9	32	94	.292
1958	Mil	149	546	97	137	18	1	31	77	.251
1959	Mil	148	594	118	182	16	8	46	114	.306
1960	Mil	153	548	108	152	19	7	39	124	.277
1961	Mil	152	572	103	175	23	6	32	91	.306
1962	Mil	152	536	106	142	25	6	29	90	.265
1963	Mil	158	547	82	144	27	4	23	84	.263
1964	Mil	141	502	83	117	19	1	23	74	.233
1965	Mil	156	546	77	137	23	0	32	95	.251
1966	Atl	134	452	72	113	21	4	16	53	.250
1967	Atl-Det	137	436	53	103	16	2	16	57	.236
1968	Det	31	52	4	11	0	0	3	8	.212
17 years		2391	8537	1509	2315	354	72	512	1453	.271

Transactions: Dec. 31, 1966: Traded with Sandy Alomar and Arnie Umbach to Houston for Dave Nicholson and Bob Bruce. Aug. 17, 1967: Traded to Detroit for Fred Gladding and cash.

WORLD SERIES

Year	Team	G	AB	R	H	D	T	HR	RBI	AVE.
1957	Mil	7	22	4	5	3	0	1	4	.227
1958	Mil	7	25	3	4	2	0	0	3	.160
1968	Det	2	3	0	1	0	0	0	0	.333
3 years		16	50	7	10	5	0	1	7	.200

Christopher Mathewson

Born August 12, 1880, in Factoryville, Pennsylvania; died October 7, 1925, in Saranac, New York. 6'1", 195 lbs., bats right, throws right. Years in minor leagues: 2; Major League debut: July 17, 1900; Years in Major Leagues: 17. Elected to Hall of Fame: 1936. Nickname: Matty—a derivation of his last name; also, Big Six, referring to New York City's most famous fire engine.

Christy Mathewson was one of the greatest pitchers of all time and one of the most popular players of his era. He played many years for John McGraw's New York Giants, leading them to five pennants. He was known as a decent Christian man who didn't smoke or drink and didn't carouse. Being the gentleman that he was, and playing in the giant publicity center of New York, Mathewson became one of baseball's first folk heroes. His lifetime statistics are staggering: 373 wins, third best all time behind Cy Young and Walter Johnson (and tied with Grover Cleveland Alexander); 80 shutouts, third best all time behind Johnson and Alexander; nine seasons of 20 wins or more; four seasons of 30 wins or more, including a National League record of 37 in 1908.

Mathewson was fresh out of Bucknell University (where he sang in the Glee Club) when he entered professional baseball. In his second year, pitching for

Norfolk, he was 20–2—in July—when the New York Giants brought him up. He won 20 games as a Giant rookie in 1901. One of the pitches that made him so tough was his "fade-away," which acted like the modern screwball. He also had a great curveball and excellent control. In 1908, when he won the 37 games, Matty walked only 42 in 391 innings. He had some spectacular individual achievements, none better than his performance in the 1905 World Series against Connie Mack's Philadelphia A's. Mathewson threw three shutouts in six days, allowing only 14 hits and 1 walk.

His overall World Series statistics are phenomenal, and are an indication of how bad his luck could be at times. He posted a World Series earned run average of 1.15, yet had only a 5–5 record to show for it. He lost several games as a result of Giant errors that led to unearned runs. In 1903, he posted an 8–0 mark against the National League champion Pittsburgh Pirates. He won 30 or more games three years in a row between 1903 and 1905, and his earned run average was 1.43 or below in each of those years. After his playing days were over, he managed the Cincinnati Reds for two years and was president of the Boston Braves from 1923 to 1925 but was ill during much of that time. Mathewson served in World War I and injested poison gas, which eventually led to pulmonary tuberculosis and his death at the age of 45.

Year	Team	W-L	ERA	G	IP	H	BB	SO
1900	NY (N)	0-3	4.76	6	34	35	22	15
1901	NY	20-17	2.41	40	336	288	97	221
1902	NY	14-17	2.11	34	276.2	241	73	159
1903	NY	30-13	2.26	45	366.1	321	100	267
1904	NY	33-12	2.03	48	367.2	306	78	212
1905	NY	31-8	1.27	43	339	252	64	206
1906	NY	22-12	2.97	38	266.2	262	77	128
1907	NY	24-13	1.99	41	316	250	53	178
1908	NY	37-11	1.43	56	390.2	285	42	259
1909	NY	25-6	1.14	37	275.1	192	36	149
1910	NY	27-9	1.90	39	318	292	60	184
1911	NY	26-13	1.99	45	307	303	38	141
1912	NY	23-12	2.12	43	310	311	34	134
1913	NY	25-11	2.06	40	306	291	21	93
1914	NY	24-13	3.00	41	312	314	23	80
1915	NY	8-14	3.58	27	186	199	20	57
1916	NY-Cin	4-4	3.01	13	74.2	74	8	19
17 years		373-188	2.13	636	4782	4216	846	2502

Transactions: Dec. 15, 1900: Traded by Cincinnati to New York Giants for Amos Rusie. July 20, 1916: Traded with Edd Roush and Bill McKechnie to Cincinnati for Buck Herzog and Red Killefer.

WORLD SERIES

Year	Team	W-L	ERA	G	IP	H	BB	SO
1905	NY (N)	3-0	0.00	3	27	14	1	18
1911	NY	1-2	2.00	3	27	25	2	13

Year	Team	W-L	ERA	G	IP	H	BB	SO
1912	NY	0-2	1.57	3	28.2	23	5	10
1913	NY	1-1	0.95	2	19	14	2	7
4 years		5-5	1.15	11	101.2	76	10	48

Willie Howard Mays

Born May 6, 1931, in Westfield, Alabama. 5'11", 170 lbs., bats right, throws right. Years in minor leagues: 2; Major League debut: May 25, 1951; Years in Major Leagues: 22. Elected to Hall of Fame: 1979. Nickname: The Say Hey Kid—a name bestowed upon him by writers and broadcasters because of his habit early in his career of saying "Say, Hey," when he didn't know somebody's name.

Willie Mays was one of the best all-around ballplayers of all time. He could do it all: hit, hit with power, run, field and throw. "If he could cook, I would marry him," said his manager, Leo Durocher of the Giants. Mays hit 660 home runs in his careeer, which places him first all time in the National League and third all time overall, behind Henry Aaron (755) and Babe Ruth (714), who hit homers in both leagues. Mays led the National League in home runs four times (hitting over 50 in two seasons), triples three times, runs scored twice, batting average once, slugging percentage five times and stolen bases four times.

He hit over .300 ten times in his career and had a span of 12 consecutive years where he hit .290 or above. He won the National League's Most Valuable Player awards in both 1954 and 1965. On April 30, 1961, Mays hit four home runs in a game at Milwaukee. In the field, he was quick, graceful and colorful. He wore a hat that was too small for him and would fall off as he chased after fly balls, adding to the flair of the spectacular fielding. He won Gold Glove awards in 11 consecutive years and holds the National League records for putouts and chances.

His over-the-shoulder running catch on a 460-foot drive by Vic Wertz in the 1954 World Series is considered one of the greatest catches of all time. After he caught the ball, he whirled and fired the ball back to the infield to double Larry Doby off second base. Mays once hit a ball so hard that Giants announcer Russ Hodges proclaimed, "The only man who could catch that ball just hit it!" Mays was the master of the "basket catch," holding his glove out in front of him and letting the ball drop in. He was hitting .477 for the Minneapolis Millers in 1951 when the Giants brought him up. He began his Major League career with an 0-for-22 slump, but Durocher stuck with him. Mays was one of the sparks that brought the Giants the championship in the famous playoff against the Dodgers. Always a crowd pleaser, Mays hit .307 in 24 All-Star game appearances. Two oddities of his great career: Despite driving in 100 runs or more ten times, he never led the league in RBIs. Also, despite 660 career home runs, Mays failed to homer in 71 World Series at-bats.

Year	Team	G	AB	R	H	D	T	HR	RBI	AVE.
1951	NY (N)	121	464	59	127	22	5	20	68	.274
1952	NY	34	127	17	30	2	4	4	23	.236
1954	NY	151	565	119	195	33	13	41	110	.345
1955	NY	152	580	123	185	18	13	51	127	.319
1956	NY	152	578	101	171	27	8	36	84	.296
1957	NY	152	585	112	195	26	20	35	97	.333
1958	NY	152	600	121	208	33	11	29	96	.347
1959	SF	152	575	125	180	43	5	34	104	.313
1960	SF	151	595	107	190	29	12	29	103	.319
1961	SF	154	572	129	176	32	3	40	123	.308
1962	SF	162	621	130	189	36	5	49	141	.304
1963	SF	157	596	115	187	32	7	38	103	.314
1964	SF	157	578	121	171	21	9	47	111	.296
1965	SF	157	558	118	177	21	3	52	112	.317
1966	SF	152	552	99	159	29	4	37	103	.288
1967	SF	141	486	83	128	22	2	22	70	.263
1968	SF	148	498	84	144	20	5	23	79	.289
1969	SF	117	403	64	114	17	3	13	58	.283
1970	SF	139	478	94	139	15	2	28	83	.291
1971	SF	136	417	82	113	24	5	18	61	.271
1972	SF-NY	88	244	35	61	11	1	8	22	.250
1973	NY (N)	66	209	24	44	10	0	6	25	.211
22 years		**2992**	**10881**	**2062**	**3283**	**523**	**140**	**660**	**1903**	**.302**

Transactions: May 11, 1972: Traded to New York Mets for Charlie Williams and $50,000.

LEAGUE CHAMPIONSHIP SERIES

Year	Team	G	AB	R	H	D	T	HR	RBI	AVE.
1971	SF	4	15	2	4	2	0	1	3	.267
1973	NY (N)	1	3	1	1	0	0	0	1	.333
2 years		**5**	**18**	**3**	**5**	**2**	**0**	**1**	**4**	**.278**

WORLD SERIES

Year	Team	G	AB	R	H	D	T	HR	RBI	AVE.
1951	NY (N)	6	22	1	4	0	0	0	1	.182
1954	NY	4	14	4	4	1	0	0	3	.286
1962	SF	7	28	3	7	2	0	0	1	.250
1973	NY (N)	3	7	1	2	0	0	0	1	.286
4 years		**20**	**71**	**9**	**17**	**3**	**0**	**0**	**6**	**.239**

Tom Meany

Sportswriter. Elected to Hall of Fame: 1975.

Tom Meany made a career of covering baseball and other sports in New York, where he began his career at age 20 with the *Brooklyn Daily Times.* For the next 41 years, he wrote newspaper and magazine articles, columns and many books.

For the majority of his newspaper career, he covered the Brooklyn Dodgers for the *New York World Telegram.* At the time of his death, he was in charge of publicity for the New York Mets and was sports editor of *Collier's* magazine.

Joseph Michael Medwick

Born November 24, 1911, in Carteret, New Jersey; died March 21, 1975, in St. Petersburg, Florida. 5'10", 187 lbs., bats right, throws right. Years in minor Leagues: 2; Major League debut: September 2, 1932; Years in Major Leagues: 17. Nickname: Ducky—because of the way he walked, which some fans and writers thought resembled a waddle.

One of the top sluggers of the 1930s, Joe Medwick was the left fielder on the St. Louis Cardinals' famed Gashouse Gang teams. He was a tough competitor and a brawler, even with his own teammates. But in his prime, he was a great hitter. Medwick is the last National League player to win the Triple Crown, winning it in 1937 with his .374 batting average, 31 home runs and 154 RBIs. Those numbers also earned him the Most Valuable Player Award. Medwick won the National League RBI title three years in a row. The most famous incident of his career occurred on the basepaths. In the sixth inning of the seventh game of the 1934 World Series, Medwick slid hard into third baseman Marv Owen, igniting the hometown Detroit fans in Briggs Stadium. When he took his position in left field the next inning, he was pelted with so much debris that Commissioner Kenesaw Mountain Landis, who was in attendance, ordered Medwick out of the game. Medwick had 11 hits at the time, one short of the World Series record.

He was traded to the Dodgers in June of 1940. A few days later, the Cardinals came to Ebbets Field for a series. Medwick ran into ex-teammate Bob Bowman in a hotel lobby and the two exchanged harsh words. Later, when Medwick batted against Bowman, he was beaned and knocked unconscious. He never seemed to regain his full intensity after the beaning, though he did help Brooklyn win the pennant in 1941. Medwick played several more years and retired with a lifetime batting average of .324.

Year	Team	G	AB	R	H	D	T	HR	RBI	AVE.
1932	StL (N)	26	106	13	37	12	1	2	12	.349
1933	StL	148	595	92	182	40	10	18	98	.306
1934	StL	149	620	110	198	40	18	18	106	.319

Year	Team	G	AB	R	H	D	T	HR	RBI	AVE.
1935	StL	154	634	132	224	46	13	23	126	.353
1936	StL	155	636	115	223	64	13	18	138	.351
1937	StL	156	633	111	237	56	10	31	154	.374
1938	StL	146	590	100	190	47	8	21	122	.322
1939	StL	150	606	98	201	48	8	14	117	.332
1940	StL-Brklyn	143	581	83	175	30	12	17	86	.301
1941	Brklyn	133	538	100	171	33	10	18	88	.318
1942	Brklyn	142	553	69	166	37	4	4	96	.300
1943	Brklyn-NY	126	497	54	138	30	3	5	70	.278
1944	NY (N)	128	490	64	164	24	3	7	85	.337
1945	NY-Bos	92	310	31	90	17	0	3	37	.290
1946	Brklyn	41	77	7	24	4	0	2	18	.312
1947	StL (N)	75	150	19	46	12	0	4	28	.307
1948	StL	20	19	0	4	0	0	0	2	.211
17 years		1984	7635	1198	2471	540	113	205	1383	.324

Transactions: June 12, 1940: Traded with Curt Davis to Brooklyn for Ernie Koy, Carl Doyle, Sam Nahem, Bert Haas and $125,000. July 6, 1943: Sold to New York Giants. June 16, 1945: Traded with Ewald Pyle to Boston Braves for Clyde Kluttz.

WORLD SERIES

Year	Team	G	AB	R	H	D	T	HR	RBI	AVE.
1934	StL	7	29	4	11	0	1	1	5	.379
1941	Brklyn	5	17	1	4	1	0	0	0	.235
2 years		12	46	5	15	1	1	1	5	.326

Sid Mercer

Sportswriter. Elected to Hall of Fame: 1969.

Sid Mercer was a great New York baseball writer whose career spanned the time from Christy Mathewson to Mel Ott. At the heart of his career, he covered John McGraw's Giants and developed a great friendship with the feisty manager until an incident in which his integrity was challenged.

Mercer was with McGraw in 1917 when the manager learned he had been suspended and fined by National League president John K. Tenner for fighting with umpire Bill Byron during a recent game. McGraw reacted with a viscious personal attack on Tenner, which Mercer reported. When Tenner read the article, he threatened to expel McGraw from the league; McGraw therefore denied ever making the statements. Mercer and McGraw did not speak to one another for ten years before reconciling.

Mercer worked for the *St. Louis Post Dispatch* in 1905 before serving a year as road secretary for the St. Louis Browns. He joined the *New York Evening Globe* in 1907 and later joined the *New York Evening Journal*. His next move was to the *New York American*, and he was with the merged *Journal-American* at the time of his death in 1945. He was one of the founders of the Baseball Writers Association of America. Mercer was also acclaimed as a great boxing writer and even detoured off the baseball beat for about two years to concentrate on boxing.

John Robert Mize

Born January 7, 1913, in Demorest, Georgia; died June 2, 1993, in Demorest, Georgia. 6'2", 215 lbs., bats left, throws right. Years in minor leagues: 6; Major League debut: April 16, 1936; Years in Major Leagues: 15. Elected to Hall of Fame: 1981. Nickname: The Big Cat—because of his grace and quick reflexes in playing first base.

Johnny Mize was a star with three Major League teams: the St. Louis Cardinals, New York Giants and New York Yankees. In his first year with the Cardinals, 1936, Mize got off to a great start, with eight doubles, four triples and five home runs in his first 28 hits. He hit .329 for the year. In 1937, he hit .364. In 1938, he hit three home runs in a game for the first time in his career. A week later, he duplicated the feat. In his 15-year career, the Big Cat had six three–home run games. Mize won the National League batting title in 1939 with a .349 average.

He hit over .300 in his first nine seasons. He led the league in home runs four times to go along with his one batting championship. His 51 home runs for the Giants in 1947 remains the National League record for lefthanded batters.

For a big man, he was amazingly graceful around first base. While with the Cardinals, he made two unassisted double plays in the same season and once went 61 consecutive games without an error.

In 1949, after Mize had hit 91 home runs in the previous two seasons for the Giants, manager Leo Durocher decided to go for youth and speed. The Giants peddled Mize to the Yankees, where he played on five straight championship teams. In the 1952 World Series, he hit homers in three straight games, a batting average of .400 and a slugging average of over 1.000—at age 39. He hit 359 home runs in a career that, like many other Major League players, was cut short by three years in the military.

Year	Team	G	AB	R	H	D	T	HR	RBI	AVE.
1936	StL (N)	126	414	76	136	30	8	19	93	.329
1937	StL	145	560	103	204	40	7	25	113	.364
1938	StL	149	531	85	179	34	16	27	102	.337
1939	StL	153	564	104	197	44	14	28	108	.349
1940	StL	155	579	111	182	31	13	43	137	.314
1941	StL	126	473	67	150	39	8	16	100	.317
1942	NY (N)	142	541	97	165	25	7	26	110	.305
1946	NY	101	377	70	127	18	3	22	70	.337
1947	NY	154	586	137	177	26	2	51	138	.302
1948	NY	152	560	110	162	26	4	40	125	.289

Year	Team	G	AB	R	H	D	T	HR	RBI	AVE.
1949	NY-NY (A)	119	411	63	108	16	0	19	64	.263
1950	NY	90	274	43	76	12	0	25	72	.277
1951	NY	113	332	37	86	14	1	10	49	.259
1952	NY	78	81	9	36	9	0	4	29	.263
1953	NY	81	104	6	26	3	0	4	27	.250
15 years		1884	6443	1118	2011	367	83	359	1337	.312

Transactions: Dec. 13, 1934: Sold to Cincinnati Reds (and then returned to St. Louis because of a bad knee). Dec. 11, 1941: Traded to New York Giants for Ken O'Dea, Bill Lohrman, Johnny McCarthy and $50,000. Aug. 22, 1949: Sold to New York Yankees for $40,000.

WORLD SERIES

Year	Team	G	AB	R	H	D	T	HR	RBI	AVE.
1949	NY (A)	2	2	0	2	0	0	0	2	1.000
1950	NY	4	15	0	2	0	0	0	0	.133
1951	NY	4	7	2	2	1	0	0	1	.286
1952	NY	5	15	3	6	1	0	3	6	.400
1953	NY	3	3	0	0	0	0	0	0	.000
5 years		18	42	5	12	2	0	3	9	.286

Joe Leonard Morgan

Born September 19, 1943, in Bonham, Texas. 5'7", 160 lbs., bats left, throws right. Years in minor leagues: 2; Major League debut: September 21, 1963; Years in Major Leagues: 22. Elected to Hall of Fame: 1990. Nickname: Little Joe—called that by some people because of his size.

Joe Morgan was an important cog in the Big Red Machine of the 1970s that brought the Cincinnati Reds to the top of the baseball world. Morgan played for the Reds for eight years. They advanced to the National League Championship Series in five of those years and they never finished lower than second. He was voted the league's Most Valuable Player in both 1975 and 1976. When he left the Reds, he returned to Houston and helped the Astros win their division championship in 1980. In 1982, playing for the San Francisco Giants, his home run on the final day of the season beat the Dodgers and enabled the Atlanta Braves to win the division championship. In 1983, at the age of 39, he helped the Philadelphia Phillies win the pennant.

He was a small man who had the knack of getting the big hit. When he retired in 1984, his 268 home runs were the most ever hit by a second baseman. He also had the record for most games played at that position, as well as most putouts, assists and total chances. His 1,865 career walks are third highest in baseball history, behind Babe Ruth and Ted Williams—an unusual statistic for a man whose lifetime batting average was .271 and who did not hit with power. His ability to get on base paid off. He scored more than 100 runs eight times in his career.

Morgan broke in with the Houston Colt .45s in 1963 and another Hall of Fame second baseman, Nelson Fox, who was winding down his career, took him under his wing. One of the things he taught Morgan was to keep his left arm away from his body when he was batting. That tip led to a famous Morgan trademark at the plate: the flapping of his left elbow as he waited for a pitch—a reminder to himself to keep the left arm free.

Year	Team	G	AB	R	H	D	T	HR	RBI	AVE.
1963	Hous	8	25	5	6	0	1	0	3	.240
1964	Hous	10	37	4	7	0	0	0	0	.189
1965	Hous	157	601	100	163	22	12	14	40	.271
1966	Hous	122	425	60	121	14	8	5	42	.285
1967	Hous	133	494	73	136	27	11	6	42	.275
1968	Hous	10	20	6	5	0	1	0	0	.250
1969	Hous	147	535	94	126	18	5	15	43	.236
1970	Hous	144	548	102	147	28	9	8	52	.268
1971	Hous	160	583	87	149	27	11	13	56	.256
1972	Cin	149	552	122	161	23	4	16	73	.292
1973	Cin	157	576	116	167	35	2	26	82	.290
1974	Cin	149	512	107	150	31	3	22	67	.293
1975	Cin	146	498	107	163	27	6	17	94	.327
1976	Cin	141	472	113	151	30	5	27	111	.320
1977	Cin	153	521	113	150	21	6	22	78	.288
1978	Cin	132	441	68	104	27	0	13	75	.236
1979	Cin	127	436	70	109	26	1	9	32	.250
1980	Hous	141	461	66	112	17	5	11	49	.243
1981	SF	90	308	47	74	16	1	8	31	.240
1982	SF	134	463	68	134	19	4	14	61	.289
1983	Phil	123	404	72	93	20	1	16	59	.230
1984	Oak	117	369	51	90	21	0	6	44	.244
22 years		**2650**	**9281**	**1651**	**2518**	**449**	**96**	**268**	**1134**	**.271**

Transactions: Nov. 29, 1971: Traded with Denis Menke, Jack Billingham, Ed Armbrister and Cesar Geronimo to Cincinnati for Lee May, Tommy Helms and Jimmy Stewart. January 31, 1980: Signed by Houston as free agent. Dec. 14, 1982: Traded to Philadelphia with Al Holland for Mike Krukow, Mark Davis and Charles Penigar. Dec. 13, 1983: Signed by Oakland as free agent.

LEAGUE CHAMPIONSHIP SERIES

Year	Team	G	AB	R	H	D	T	HR	RBI	AVE.
1972	Cin	5	19	5	5	0	0	2	3	.263
1973	Cin	5	20	1	2	1	0	0	1	.100
1975	Cin	3	11	2	3	3	0	0	1	.273
1976	Cin	3	7	2	0	0	0	0	0	.000
1979	Cin	3	11	0	0	0	0	0	0	.000

Year	Team	G	AB	R	H	D	T	HR	RBI	AVE.
1980	Hous	4	13	1	2	1	1	0	0	.154
1983	Phil	4	15	1	1	0	0	0	0	.067
7 years		27	96	12	13	5	1	2	5	.135

WORLD SERIES

Year	Team	G	AB	R	H	D	T	HR	RBI	AVE.
1972	Cin	7	24	4	3	2	0	0	1	.125
1975	Cin	7	27	4	7	1	0	0	3	.259
1976	Cin	4	15	3	5	1	1	1	2	.333
1983	Phil	5	19	3	5	0	1	2	2	.263
4 years		23	85	14	20	4	2	3	8	.235

Edgar Munzel

Sportswriter. Elected to Hall of Fame: 1977.

Edgar Munzel was a sportswriter for the *Chicago Herald-Examiner* and the *Chicago Sun-Times* in a career that began in 1929 and spanned 44 years. He covered more than 9,000 baseball games, mostly as the beat writer for the Cubs and White Sox.

Tim Murnane

Sportswriter. Elected to Hall of Fame: 1978

Tim Murnane was one of the early players of the game, then managed Hall of Famer Harry Wright's Boston team and was also a scout and a minor league president. He got his highest acclaim, however, as sportswriter and later sports editor of the *Boston Globe*.

Bob Murphy

Broadcaster. Elected to Hall of Fame: 1994

Bob Murphy can honestly attest to a career that has featured the best and the worst. Behind the mike, he has worked with some of broadcasting's best: Curt Gowdy in Boston, Ernie Harwell in Boston and Lindsey Nelson and Ralph Kiner in New York. As for the worst, he and Kiner and Nelson described the play-by-play of the original New York Mets in 1962 and stuck with them for many years to come.

Jim Murray

Sportswriter. Elected to Hall of Fame: 1987.

One of the nation's outstanding sportswriters for half a century, Jim Murray is known for his wit, wisdom and perceptions about baseball and most other sports. He is a Pulitzer Prize winner and was elected the country's finest sportswriter 14 times. He is also an inductee into the National Sportscasters and Sportswriters Hall of Fame. He is the author of many books and his column is syndicated in dozens of newspapers, but his home base has been the *Los Angeles Times* for more than 30 years.

Stanley Frank Musial

Born November 21, 1920, in Donora, Pennsylvania. 6', 175 lbs., bats left, throws left. Years in minor leagues: 4; Major League debut: September 17, 1941; Years in Major Leagues: 22. Elected to Hall of Fame: 1969. Nickname: Stan the Man—because he was so well respected not only as a player but as an individual.

Stan Musial was the best hitter of his generation—in the National League. He was a contemporary of Ted Williams in the American League. Together, they set the standard for hitting for two decades. He had a "peek-a-boo" batting stance: a crouch with his head angled in such a way he looked like he was peeking at each pitch. Musial began his career as a pitcher but an injury in the minor leagues caused him to switch to the outfield. Musial hit over .300 in 18 of his 22 Major League seasons—all with the St. Louis Cardinals. He won seven National League batting titles and was the league's Most Valuable Player three times—in 1943, 1946, and 1948—and finished second four times. Musial played in 12 games for the Cardinals in 1941 and then led them to the National League pennant in 1942, 1943, 1944 and 1946. (He didn't play in 1945 because he was in the military.)

In 1948, he had one of the greatest offensive years in baseball history. Musial hit .376 to lead the National League. He also led the league in runs batted in, 131; runs scored, 135; doubles, 46; triples, 18; hits, 230; total bases, 429; and slugging percentage, .702. He hit 39 home runs that year, leaving him one short of winning the Triple Crown. He was never known as a home run hitter but he hit some famous round trippers. One won the 1955 All-Star Game at Milwaukee. A year earlier, he hit five home runs in a doubleheader, tying a record Don Mueller had set in 1951. Musial had 475 career homers.

He won his seventh and last batting title in 1957—at the age of 37—when he hit .351. He hit .330 five years later, at the age of 42. He finished with a lifetime batting average of .331 and was the owner of one of baseball's most remarkable statistics. Of his 3,630 hits, 1,815 were at home and 1,815 were on the road. Had he scored two more runs, that total would have equaled his runs batted in.

At the time of his retirement in 1963, he held 29 National League records and 17 Major League records. One of those records is playing more than 1,000 games at each of two positions: outfield where he began his career, and first base where he ended it.

Year	Team	G	AB	R	H	D	T	HR	RBI	AVE.
1941	StL (N)	12	47	8	20	4	0	1	7	.426
1942	StL	140	467	87	147	32	10	10	72	.315
1943	StL	157	617	108	220	48	20	13	81	.357
1944	StL	146	568	112	197	51	14	12	94	.347
1946	StL	156	624	124	228	50	20	16	103	.365
1947	StL	149	587	113	183	30	13	19	95	.312
1948	StL	155	611	135	230	46	18	39	131	.376
1949	StL	157	612	128	207	41	13	36	123	.338
1950	StL	146	555	105	192	41	7	28	109	.346
1951	StL	152	578	124	205	30	12	32	108	.355
1952	StL	154	578	105	194	42	6	21	91	.336
1953	StL	157	593	127	200	53	9	30	113	.337
1954	StL	153	591	120	195	41	9	35	126	.330
1955	StL	154	562	97	179	30	5	33	108	.319
1956	StL	156	594	87	184	33	6	27	109	.310
1957	StL	134	502	82	176	38	3	29	102	.351
1958	StL	135	472	64	159	35	2	17	62	.337
1959	StL	115	341	37	87	13	2	14	44	.255
1960	StL	116	331	49	91	17	1	17	63	.275
1961	StL	123	372	46	107	22	4	15	70	.288
1962	StL	135	433	57	143	18	1	19	82	.330
1963	StL	124	337	34	86	10	2	12	58	.255
22 years		**3026**	**10972**	**1949**	**3630**	**725**	**177**	**475**	**1951**	**.331**

WORLD SERIES

Year	Team	G	AB	R	H	D	T	HR	RBI	AVE.
1942	StL	5	18	2	4	1	0	0	2	.222
1943	StL	5	18	2	5	0	0	0	0	.278
1944	StL	6	23	2	7	2	0	1	2	.304
1946	StL	7	27	3	6	4	1	0	4	.228
4 years		**23**	**86**	**9**	**22**	**7**	**1**	**1**	**8**	**.256**

Lindsey Nelson

Broadcaster. Elected to Hall of Fame: 1988.

Lindsey Nelson was one of the most popular and well-recognized broadcasters of his generation, covering major events of most every sport. He was NBC's regular announcer for college football, pro basketball and Major League Baseball for many years when he became the play-by-play man for the New York Mets in 1962.

Teamed with Ralph Kiner and Bob Murphy, he did Met broadcasts for 19 years and became almost as well known for his style of dress as for his broadcasts. Nelson had an array of plaid sport coats that he wore to the ballpark.

Nelson also broadcast San Francisco Giant games late in his career. He did play-by-play for Notre Dame football for 13 years and was the television announcer for 26 Cotton Bowl games.

Harold Newhouser

Born May 20, 1921, in Detroit, Michigan. 6'2", 180 lbs., bats left, throws left. Years in minor leagues: 1; Major League debut: September 29, 1939. Years in Major Leagues: 17. Elected to Hall of Fame: 1992. Nickname: Prince Hal— a newspaper nickname bestowed upon him by Detroit writers when he was the dominant pitcher in the American League.

Detroit's Hal Newhouser's accomplishments in 1944 and 1945—a combined record of 54 wins and 18 losses—were downplayed by some critics because they occurred during the war years, when many Major League ballplayers were in the service, replaced by lesser talents. Newhouser silenced the critics by going 26–9 in 1946, the year after the war ended, and two years later he won 21 games. In that three-year period of 1944–46, Newhouser was 80–27. He won the American League's Most Valuable Player Award in 1944 and 1945, the only pitcher to have ever won it two years in a row.

The tall lefthander with the blazing fastball and big curve was a native of Detroit. He won 200 games pitching for the Tigers, but he endured some tough times, too. In 1943, he lost 13 games in a row (six of them in one-run games) on his way to an 8–17 record, his third straight losing season. In 1953, he had shoulder problems that caused the Tigers to release him at the end of the season.

He had one more good year left in him, and he was 7–2 for the great Cleveland Indian team that won 111 games. With his induction into the Hall of Fame in 1992, Newhouser became the fourth pitcher on that 1954 Indian team to be enshrined—the others were Bob Feller, Bob Lemon and Early Wynn. Newhouser led the Tigers to the World Series in 1945, pitching the pennant clincher and then winning two games, against the Cubs.

Year	Team	W-L	ERA	G	IP	H	BB	SO
1939	Det	0–1	5.40	1	5	3	4	4
1940	Det	9–9	4.86	28	133.1	149	76	89
1941	Det	9–11	4.79	33	173	166	137	106
1942	Det	8–14	2.45	38	183.2	137	114	103
1943	Det	8–17	3.04	37	195.2	163	111	144
1944	Det	29–9	2.22	47	312.1	264	102	187
1945	Det	25–9	1.81	40	313.1	239	110	212
1946	Det	26–9	1.94	37	292.1	215	98	275
1947	Det	17–17	2.87	40	285	268	110	176

Year	Team	W-L	ERA	G	IP	H	BB	SO
1948	Det	21-12	3.01	39	272.1	249	99	143
1949	Det	18-11	3.36	38	292	277	111	144
1950	Det	15-13	4.34	35	213.2	232	81	87
1951	Det	6-6	3.92	15	96.1	98	19	37
1952	Det	9-9	3.74	25	154	148	47	57
1953	Det	0-1	7.06	7	21.2	31	8	6
1954	Cleve	7-2	2.51	26	46.2	34	18	25
1955	Cleve	0-0	0.00	2	2.1	1	4	1
17 years		207-150	3.06	488	2992.2	2674	1249	1796

WORLD SERIES

Year	Team	W-L	ERA	G	IP	H	BB	SO
1945	Det	2-1	6.10	3	20.2	25	4	22
1954	Cleve	0-0	0.00	1	0	1	1	0
2 years		2-1	6.53	4	20.2	26	5	22

Charles Augustus Nichols

Born September 14, 1869, in Madison, Wisconsin; died April 11, 1953, in Kansas City, Missouri. 5'10", 180 lbs., bats right, throws right. Years in minor leagues: 3; Major League debut: April 23, 1890; Years in Major Leagues: 15. Elected to Hall of Fame: 1949. Nickname: Kid—because of slender build as a youth.

Kid Nichols won 30 or more games seven years in a row and 20 or more ten years in a row. His streak of 30-win seasons was broken in 1898 when he won 29. Nichols was extremely durable. He worked more than 400 innings in his first five full seasons and 300 or more in six out of the next seven years.

Nichols worked without a windup and was one dimensional: he threw hard and he had no curveball. He ranks seventh in career wins with 360, and fourth in complete games with 533. He completed 95 percent of the games he started.

He was a sensation as a teenager pitching in amateur leagues in Wisconsin. He was signed to a pro contract at the age of 17 and was 18–13 at Kansas City in 1887. The next year, he split his time between Memphis and Kansas City and was 26–11. Though his statistics were great, it was thought he was too young to bring up to the Major Leagues. But after the 1889 season, in which he pitched for Omaha and compiled a 39–8 record with a 1.77 earned run average, there was no holding him back. He was 20 when he made his Major League debut in April of 1890. After his retirement, he opened a motion picture theater with retired Cub shortstop Joe Tinker and later operated bowling alleys.

Year	Team	W-L	ERA	G	IP	H	BB	SO
1890	Bos (N)	27-19	2.21	48	427	374	112	222
1891	Bos	30-17	2.39	52	425.2	413	103	240
1892	Bos	35-16	2.83	53	454	404	121	187
1893	Bos	33-13	3.52	52	425	426	127	94
1894	Bos	32-13	4.75	50	407	488	121	113
1895	Bos	30-14	3.29	48	394	417	82	146
1896	Bos	30-15	2.81	49	375	387	101	102
1897	Bos	30-11	2.64	46	368	362	72	136
1898	Bos	29-12	2.13	50	388	316	85	138
1899	Bos	21-17	2.94	42	349	326	86	109
1900	Bos	13-15	3.07	29	231.1	215	73	54
1901	Bos	18-15	3.22	38	321	306	90	143
1904	StL (N)	21-13	2.02	36	317	268	50	134
1905	StL-Phil	11-11	3.11	24	191	193	46	66
1906	Phil (N)	0-1	9.82	4	11	17	13	1
15 years		**360-202**	**2.94**	**621**	**5084**	**4912**	**1282**	**1885**

Philip Henry Niekro

Born April 1, 1939, in Blaine, Ohio. 6'1", 180 lbs., bats right, throws right. Years in minor leagues: 6; Major League debut: April 15, 1964; Years in Major Leagues: 24. Elected to Hall of Fame: 1997. Nickname: Knucksie—because of his mastery of the knuckleball.

Phil Niekro was the most successful knuckleball pitcher of all time, and his statistics would have been even better except for several factors that worked against him. He won 318 games despite playing most of his career with an Atlanta Braves team that finished last or close to last most of the time. Also, he spent seven years in the minor leagues and was used as a relief pitcher his first two years with the Braves. He was 28 years old when he moved into the starting rotation. Still another factor: When Niekro was pitching, the Braves were shut out 47 times—a Major League record for lack of support for one pitcher.

On the positive side, Niekro won 20 or more games three times: 23 in 1969 when the Braves won a division title; 20 in 1974; and 21 in 1979. In 1982, he was 17–4 with one of two Braves teams that won division titles while Niekro played for them. On August 5, 1973, Niekro tossed a no-hitter against the San Diego Padres. On October 6, 1985, while pitching for the New York Yankees, he beat Toronto, 8–0. It was his 300th win and, at age 46, he became oldest pitcher ever to throw a shutout. He had signed as a free agent with the Yankees and was 16–8 in 1983 at the age of 45.

Niekro holds the record for most wins after the age of 40: 121. He also holds the record for most wild pitches, 200, including six in one game and four in one inning. His brother Joe also pitched in the Major Leagues and won 221 games. Their total of 539 career wins is the most by a brother combination.

Year	Team	W-L	ERA	G	IP	H	BB	SO
1964	Mil (N)	0-0	4.80	10	15	15	7	8
1965	Mil	2-3	2.89	41	74.2	73	26	49
1966	Atl	4-3	4.11	28	50.1	48	23	17
1967	Atl	11-9	1.87	46	207	164	55	129
1968	Atl	14-12	2.59	37	256.2	228	45	140
1969	Atl	23-13	2.57	40	284	235	57	193
1970	Atl	12-18	4.27	34	230	222	68	168
1971	Atl	15-14	2.98	42	269	248	70	173
1972	Atl	16-12	3.06	38	282	254	53	164
1973	Atl	13-10	3.31	42	245	214	89	131
1974	Atl	20-13	2.38	41	302	249	88	195
1975	Atl	15-15	3.20	39	276	285	72	144
1976	Atl	17-11	3.29	38	271	249	101	173
1977	Atl	16-20	4.04	44	330	315	164	262
1978	Atl	19-18	2.88	44	334	295	102	248
1979	Atl	21-20	3.39	44	342	311	113	208
1980	Atl	15-18	3.63	40	275	256	85	176
1981	Atl	7-7	3.11	22	139	120	56	62
1982	Atl	17-4	3.61	35	234.1	225	73	144
1983	Atl	11-10	3.97	34	201.2	212	105	128
1984	NY (A)	16-8	3.09	32	215.2	219	76	136
1985	NY	16-12	4.09	33	220	203	120	149
1986	Cleve	11-11	4.33	34	210	241	95	81
1987	Tor-Cle-Atl	7-13	5.50	26	136	157	22	66
24 years		318-274	3.35	864	5404	5044	1809	3342

Transactions: January 6, 1984: Signed with New York Yankees as free agent.

James Henry O'Rourke

Born August 24, 1852, in Bridgeport, Connecticut; died January 8, 1919, in Bridgeport, Connecticut. 5'8", 185 lbs., bats right, throws right. Years in minor leagues: 4; Major League debut: April 22, 1876; Years in Major Leagues: 19. Elected to Hall of Fame: 1945. Nickname: Orator Jim—because of his highly polished way of speaking, even when arguing with umpires.

When Jim O'Rourke singled to left field on April 22, 1876, he got the first hit in National League history. The league had just been formed and O'Rourke's Boston Red Stockings team was taking on Philadelphia in the first opening day in Major League Baseball history.

O'Rourke played every position at one time or another in his 19-year career and finished with a lifetime batting average of .310. Actually, his career was 18 years plus one game. In 1904, O'Rourke, who had been retired for 11 years, wanted to play again and talked his old friend, John McGraw, into letting him do it. At the age of 52, O'Rourke caught the pennant-clinching game for the New York Giants and got a base hit in one of his four at-bats.

O'Rourke also umpired and served as a minor league president before retiring. He was a graduate of Yale Law School and was infamous for giving lengthy answers to simple questions. But he was also known for his fairness. He once caught in a game between two teams in a league of which he was president. At one point, he argued with the home plate umpire so vigorously that he began swearing. When he realized what he had done, he announced to the crowd that he was fining himself $10.

Year	Team	G	AB	R	H	D	T	HR	RBI	AVE.
1876	Bos (N)	70	312	61	102	17	3	2	43	.327
1877	Bos	61	265	68	96	14	4	0	23	.362
1878	Bos	60	255	44	71	17	7	1	29	.278
1879	Prov (N)	81	362	69	126	19	9	1	46	.348
1880	Bos (N)	86	363	71	100	20	11	6	45	.275
1881	Buff (N)	83	348	71	105	21	7	0	30	.302
1882	Buff	84	370	62	104	15	6	2		.281
1883	Buff	94	436	102	143	29	8	1		.328
1884	Buff	108	467	119	162	33	7	5		.347
1885	NY (N)	112	477	119	143	21	16	5		.300
1886	NY	105	440	106	136	26	6	1	34	.309
1887	NY	103	397	73	113	15	13	3	88	.285
1888	NY	107	409	50	112	16	6	4	50	.274
1889	NY	128	502	89	161	36	7	3	81	.321
1890	NY (P)	111	478	112	172	37	5	9	115	.360
1891	NY (N)	136	555	92	164	28	7	5	95	.295
1892	NY	115	448	62	136	28	5	0	56	.304
1893	Wash (N)	129	547	75	157	22	5	3	95	.287
1904	NY (N)	1	4	1	1	0	0	0	0	.250
19 years		**1774**	**7435**	**1446**	**2304**	**414**	**132**	**51**	**830**	**.310**

Melvin Thomas Ott

Born March 2, 1909, in Gretna, Louisiana; died November 21, 1958, in New Orleans, Louisiana. 5'9", 170 lbs., bats left, throws right. Years in minor leagues: None; Major League debut: April 27, 1926; Years in Major Leagues: 22. Elected to Hall of Fame: 1951. Nickname: Master Melvin, a reference to his age—16—when he signed with the New York Giants.

Mel Ott was a schoolboy catcher when he boarded a train from Louisiana to New York at the age of 16 so that Giants manager John McGraw could take a look at him. McGraw liked what he saw and decided to take the youngster under his wing. McGraw signed him but wanted to keep him with him rather than have minor league coaches and managers interfere with Ott's unorthodox style. (A lefthanded batter, he lifted his right foot when he swung.) Ott played in his first Major League game at age 17, with no minor league experience. Twenty-two years later, he retired as the National League's all-time home run leader.

McGraw changed him from a catcher to an outfielder. Ott replaced the great Ross Youngs in right field for the Giants. Youngs, a career .300 hitter, died in his prime of Bright's disease. McGraw had groomed Ott slowly, playing him in 35 games at age 17, 82 games at age 18 and 124 games at age 19. At age 20, the right field job was his, and he played in 151 games. During the course of his career, he hit more than 30 home runs in eight seasons and led or tied for the league lead in six. It would have been seven except for some chicanery in 1929. On the last day of the season, the Philadelphia Phillies intentionally walked him five times, including once with the bases loaded, so that the Phils' Chuck Klein could win the home run title. In World Series competition, Ott hit four home runs in three years. He had 2,876 lifetime hits. When he retired, Ott had the National League record for home runs, runs scored, runs batted in and walks, records that have all been surpassed.

Ott managed the Giants from 1942 to 1948. He was a kind, polite man who was well-liked. This made him popular with teammates, fans, and even opposing players, but it was not a helpful trait for him as a manager. It is believed that Leo Durocher, then managing the Dodgers, was referring to Ott when he said, "Nice guys finish last." Ott died on November 21, 1958, from injuries he received in a head-on auto accident in Louisiana.

Year	Team	G	AB	R	H	D	T	HR	RBI	AVE.
1926	NY (N)	35	60	7	23	2	0	0	4	.383
1927	NY	82	163	23	46	7	3	1	19	.282
1928	NY	124	435	69	140	26	4	18	77	.322
1929	NY	150	545	138	179	37	2	42	151	.328
1930	NY	148	521	122	182	34	5	25	119	.349
1931	NY	138	497	104	145	23	8	29	115	.292
1932	NY	154	566	119	180	30	8	38	123	.318
1933	NY	152	580	98	164	36	1	23	103	.283
1934	NY	153	582	119	190	29	10	35	135	.326
1935	NY	152	593	113	191	33	6	31	114	.322
1936	NY	150	534	120	175	28	6	33	135	.328
1937	NY	151	545	99	160	28	2	31	95	.294
1938	NY	152	527	116	164	23	6	36	116	.311
1939	NY	125	396	85	122	23	2	27	80	.308
1940	NY	151	536	89	155	27	3	19	79	.289
1941	NY	148	525	89	150	29	0	27	90	.286
1942	NY	152	549	118	162	21	0	30	93	.295
1943	NY	125	380	65	89	12	2	18	47	.234
1944	NY	120	399	91	115	16	4	26	82	.288
1945	NY	135	451	73	139	23	0	21	79	.308
1946	NY	31	68	2	5	1	0	1	4	.074
1947	NY	4	4	0	0	0	0	0	0	.000
22 years		2732	9456	1859	2876	488	72	511	1860	.304

WORLD SERIES

Year	Team	G	AB	R	H	D	T	HR	RBI	AVE.
1933	NY (N)	5	18	3	7	0	0	2	4	.389
1936	NY	6	23	4	7	2	0	1	3	.304
1937	NY	5	20	1	4	0	0	1	3	.200
3 years		16	61	8	18	2	0	4	10	.295

Leroy Robert Paige

Born July 7, 1906, in Mobile, Alabama; died February 19, 1978, in Lebanon, Pennsylvania. 6'2", 180 lbs., bats right, throws right. Years in minor leagues: 22 (Negro Leagues); Major League debut: July 9, 1948; Years in Major Leagues: 6. Elected to Hall of Fame: 1971. Nickname: Satchel—a name he got when, as a child, he worked as a porter on a train and one of his duties was hauling satchels.

Satchel Paige was a 42-year-old rookie, the oldest rookie in Major League history, when he came up with the Cleveland Indians in 1948 and helped them win the American League pennant. Prior to that, he was one of baseball's greatest showmen—and greatest pitchers—but was not allowed to display his talents in the Major Leagues because of his color. He did face Major League competition when the big leaguers barnstormed between seasons. Paige once beat Dizzy Dean 1–0 in one of those barnstorming games. He impressed Dean so much that Diz said if he and Paige were on the same team, they'd win the pennant by the Fourth of July and would go fishing until the World Series began.

Paige had exceptional control. Many ballplayers recall him warming up by using a gum wrapper as an imaginary home plate and firing the ball over the gum wrapper. Paige was a character off the field. He would leave passes for "Mrs. Paige" in every city in the American League and explain it by saying simply, "I am in great demand." Perhaps his most famous saying was the guiding force of his life: "Don't look back. Something may be gaining on you." He came up with the Indians in 1948 and posted a 6–1 record in 21 games with a 2.40 earned run average. He pitched two-thirds of an inning in the World Series and did not allow a base runner. The next season, he was only 4–7 with the Indians but had a respectable earned run average of 3.04.

Then it was on to the St. Louis Browns where he played for Bill Veeck, the same owner who had signed him with the Indians. He toiled three years with the hapless Browns and then retired until 1965 when he pitched an inning for the Kansas City A's as a publicity stunt for owner Charlie Finley. He pitched three scoreless innings, giving up just one hit at the age of 57. Johnny Sain, a Yankee pitcher when Paige was playing, was also a good hitter and was used frequently as a pinch hitter by the Yankees. Sain was nearing the end of his great career and was getting batters out with a terrific curveball. Paige's bread and butter pitch was his fastball, but Sain recalls that when he pinch hit against Satchel, the old master wanted to show that he too had a pretty good curve. Sain said Paige fed him three curveballs, the first one better than average, the second one better than the first and the third one unbelievable. Sain was out on three pitches that he watched dance by him. In the Negro leagues, Paige is said to have pitched more than 10,000 innings, relying on his "hesitation" pitch which he couldn't use in the Major Leagues because it most often resulted in a balk. For several seasons, his catcher in the Negro Leagues was Josh Gibson. They formed not only what might have been the best battery combination in baseball, but many believe the best hitter who ever lived was teamed with the best pitcher who ever lived.

Year	Team	W–L	ERA	G	IP	H	BB	SO
1948	Cleve	6-1	2.48	21	72.2	61	25	45
1949	Cleve	4-7	3.04	31	83	70	33	54
1951	StL (A)	3-4	4.79	23	62	67	29	48
1952	StL	12-10	3.07	46	138	116	57	91
1953	StL	3-9	3.53	57	117.1	114	39	51
1965	KC	0-0	0.00	1	3	1	0	1
6 years		**28-31**	**3.29**	**179**	**476**	**429**	**183**	**290**

World Series

Year	Team	W–L	ERA	G	IP	H	BB	SO
1948	Cleve	0-0	0.00	1	.2	0	0	0

James Alvin Palmer

Born October 15, 1945, in New York City, New York. 6'3", 194 lbs., bats right, throws right. Years in minor leagues: 1; Major League debut: April 17, 1965; Years in Major Leagues: 19. Elected to Hall of Fame: 1990. Nickname: None.

Jim Palmer had a high-kicking, smooth delivery that made his pitching motion look effortless on the mound. He was one of the Major Leagues' dominating pitchers for nearly two decades and won more games in the 1970s—186—than any other pitcher. He won 268 games and was a Cy Young Award winner three times. Nagging injuries that plagued him throughout his career—and sparked numerous arguments with his manager Earl Weaver—probably prevented him from winning 300 games. A back injury reduced his service to nine games in 1967 and forced him to miss the entire 1968 campaign.

When he was healthy, he was incredible. In 1966, Palmer became the youngest pitcher in World Series history to throw a shutout when he beat the Dodgers 6–0 a little over a week before his 21st birthday. The losing pitcher was Sandy Koufax in the last game of his Major League career. Then Palmer's back problems sidelined him for all but nine games the next two years. In 1969, he posted a 16–4 record but was on the disabled list part of that season, too. He made his first start, coming off the disabled list on August 13, and threw a no-hitter against the Oakland A's. The Orioles were on their way to being a dominant team, winning their division in 1969, 1970, 1971, 1973 and 1974. They got to the World Series in 1969, 1970 and 1971, and were back in 1979 and 1983. Palmer is the only pitcher to win a World Series game in three different decades, winning in 1966, 1970 and 1983. His postseason won-loss record is 8–3: 4–1 in league championship play and 4–2 in the World Series.

He won 20 games or more in eight of nine years—two streaks of four years with an off year (7–12 in 1974) in between. He won the Cy Young Award three times, in 1973, 1975, and 1976. His lifetime earned run average was 2.86. In 1971, he and Dave McNally, Mike Cuellar, and Pat Dobson were all 20-game winners, only the second time in baseball history that happened. Palmer pitched 3,948 innings in his career without ever allowing a grand-slam home run.

Year	Team	W-L	ERA	G	IP	H	BB	SO
1965	Bal	5-4	3.72	27	92	75	56	75
1966	Bal	15-10	3.46	30	208.1	176	91	147
1967	Bal	3-1	2.94	9	49	34	20	23
1969	Bal	16-4	2.34	26	181	131	64	123
1970	Bal	20-10	2.71	39	305	263	100	199
1971	Bal	20-9	2.68	37	282	231	106	184
1972	Bal	21-10	2.07	36	274.1	219	70	184
1973	Bal	22-9	2.40	38	296	225	113	158
1974	Bal	7-12	3.27	26	179	176	69	84
1975	Bal	23-11	2.09	39	323	253	80	193
1976	Bal	22-13	2.51	40	315	255	84	159
1977	Bal	20-11	2.91	39	319	263	99	193
1978	Bal	21-12	2.46	38	296	246	97	138
1979	Bal	10-6	3.29	23	156	144	43	67
1980	Bal	16-10	3.98	34	224	238	74	109
1981	Bal	7-8	3.76	22	127	117	46	35
1982	Bal	15-5	3.13	36	227	195	63	103
1983	Bal	5-4	4.23	14	76.2	86	19	34
1984	Bal	0-3	9.17	5	17.2	263	100	199
19 years		**268-152**	**2.86**	**558**	**3948**	**3349**	**1311**	**2212**

League Championship Series

Year	Team	W-L	ERA	G	IP	H	BB	SO
1969	Bal	1-0	2.00	1	9	10	2	4
1970	Bal	1-0	1.00	1	9	7	3	12
1971	Bal	1-0	3.00	1	9	7	3	8
1973	Bal	1-0	1.84	3	14.2	11	8	15
1974	Bal	0-1	1.00	1	9	4	1	4
1979	Bal	0-0	3.00	1	9	7	2	3
6 years		**4-1**	**1.96**	**8**	**59.2**	**46**	**19**	**46**

World Series

Year	Team	W-L	ERA	G	IP	H	BB	SO
1966	Bal	1-0	0.00	1	9	4	3	6
1969	Bal	0-1	6.00	1	6	5	4	5
1970	Bal	1-0	4.60	2	15.2	11	9	9
1971	Bal	1-0	2.65	2	17	15	9	15

Year	Team	W-L	ERA	G	IP	H	BB	SO
1979	Bal	0-1	3.60	2	15	18	5	8
1983	Bal	1-0	0.00	1	2	2	1	1
6 years		4-2	3.20	9	64.2	55	31	44

Herbert Jefferies Pennock

Born February 10, 1894, in Kennett Square, Pennsylvania; died January 30, 1948, in New York City, New York. 6', 160 lbs., bats both, throws left. Years in minor leagues: None; Major League debut: May 14, 1912; Years in Major Leagues: 22. Elected to Hall of Fame: 1948. Nickname: The Knight of Kennett Square—referring to knightly or grand pitching style and to his birthplace.

Many pitchers earned their way into the Hall of Fame by blazing the ball past opposing hitters; Herb Pennock made a career out of frustrating them. Weighing only 160 pounds, he didn't overpower anyone, but he won 240 American League games with an assortment of breaking balls and a lot of finesse. Pennock signed right out of high school with Connie Mack's Philadelphia A's and pitched in the 1914 World Series at the age of 20. But the A's lost that World Series to the "Miracle Braves" and Mack unloaded much of his talent. Pennock went to the Red Sox, where he teamed with a hard-throwing lefthander who also had quite a future— Babe Ruth. In 1923, the Red Sox also decided to shuffle some players, and Pennock wound up with the Yankees.

Helped by the great Yankee lineup, Pennock won 19 or more games four out of the next five years and was a mainstay on the New York pitching staff for a decade. He often gave up more hits than he had innings pitched but managed to wriggle out of jams, partly because he didn't give up a lot of walks. Evidence of Pennock's pitching style: He once tossed an 11-hit shutout for the Yankees. Pennock was at his best in World Series competition. He pitched in four World Series with the Yankees, had a 5–0 record and a 1.95 earned run average. His finest moment was in the third game of the 1927 World Series against the hard-hitting Pittsburgh Pirates with a lineup that featured Pie Traynor and the Waner brothers, Paul and Lloyd.

Pennock took a perfect game into the eighth inning before surrendering a base hit to Traynor after retiring 22 batters in a row. He settled for a three-hitter in a game the Yankees won 8–1. Characteristically, he struck out one and walked none. After his playing days were over, Pennock was vice president and general manager of the Philadelphia Phillies. He was attending a National League meeting in New York when he died at the age of 53.

Year	Team	W-L	ERA	G	IP	H	BB	SO
1912	Phil (A)	1-2	4.50	17	50	48	30	38
1913	Phil	2-1	5.13	14	33.1	30	22	17
1914	Phil	11-4	2.79	28	151.2	136	65	90
1915	Phil-Bos (A)	3-6	6.36	16	58	69	39	31

Year	Team	W-L	ERA	G	IP	H	BB	SO
1916	Bos	0-2	3.04	9	26.2	23	8	12
1917	Bos	5-5	3.31	24	100.2	90	23	35
1919	Bos	16-8	2.71	32	219	223	48	70
1920	Bos	16-13	3.68	37	242.1	244	61	68
1921	Bos	12-14	4.04	32	222.2	268	59	91
1922	Bos	10-17	4.32	32	202	230	74	59
1923	NY	19-6	3.33	35	224.1	235	68	93
1924	NY	21-9	2.83	40	286.1	302	64	101
1925	NY	16-17	2.96	47	277	267	71	88
1926	NY	23-11	3.62	40	266.1	294	43	78
1927	NY	19-8	3.00	34	209.2	225	48	51
1928	NY	17-6	2.56	28	211	215	40	53
1929	NY	9-11	4.90	27	158	205	28	49
1930	NY	11-7	4.32	25	156.1	194	20	46
1931	NY	11-6	4.28	25	189.1	247	30	65
1932	NY	9-5	4.60	22	146.2	191	38	54
1933	NY	7-4	5.54	23	65	96	21	22
1934	Bos (A)	2-0	3.05	30	62	68	16	16
22 years		**240-162**	**3.61**	**617**	**3558.1**	**3900**	**916**	**1227**

Transactions: June 13, 1915: Sold to Boston for waiver price. January 30, 1923: Traded to New York Yankees for Camp Skinner, Norm McMillan, George Murray and $50,000.

WORLD SERIES

Year	Team	W-L	ERA	G	IP	H	BB	SO
1914	Phil (A)	0-0	0.00	1	3	2	2	3
1923	NY (A)	2-0	3.63	3	17.1	19	1	8
1926	NY	2-0	1.23	3	22	13	4	8
1927	NY	1-0	1.00	1	9	3	0	1
1932	NY	0-0	2.25	2	4	2	1	4
5 years		**5-0**	**1.95**	**10**	**55.1**	**39**	**8**	**24**

Gaylord Jackson Perry

Born September 15, 1938, in Williamston, North Carolina. 6'4", 205 lbs., bats right, throws right. Years in minor leagues: 5; Major League debut: April 14, 1962; Years in Major Leagues: 22. Elected to Hall of Fame: 1991. Nickname: None.

Gaylord Perry is the only player in baseball history to win the Cy Young Award in both the American and National leagues. He won it first with the Cleveland Indians in 1972 when he was 24–16 with a 1.92 earned run average. Then in 1978, pitching for the San Diego Padres, he won it again, this time with 21–6 record and 2.72 earned run average. Perry pitched 22 years, won 314 games and had 303 complete games, including a no-hitter he tossed for the San Francisco Giants, a

1–0 victory over the St. Louis Cardinals on September 17, 1968. Perry won 20 or more games five times in his career. He won 240 games when he was past the age of 30—only Cy Young and Warren Spahn topped that mark.

He was best known in his career for his reputation for throwing a spitball, and he took advantage of that reputation in his movements on the mound. Perry would frequently touch the back of his hair, the bill of his cap, his belt buckle, or his shirt sleeve—anything to try to get an edge in his battle of wits with opposing batters. Umpires frequently called time and checked him for foreign substances and once, while pitching for Seattle, he was ejected from a game for throwing a spitter.

But much of the time, Perry was content to try to distract batters. He called it his attempt to lead the league in "psych-outs." Perry was well-traveled, pitching for the Giants, Indians, Texas Rangers, Padres, New York Yankees, Atlanta Braves, Seattle Mariners and Kansas City Royals during his long career. He pitched the most years with the Giants. In 1962, he was a teammate of future Hall of Famers Willie Mays, Willie McCovey, Juan Marichal and Orlando Cepeda. His older brother, Jim, won 215 games in the Major Leagues.

Year	Team	W-L	ERA	G	IP	H	BB	SO
1962	SF	3-1	5.23	13	43	54	14	20
1963	SF	1-6	4.03	31	76	84	29	52
1964	SF	12-11	2.75	44	206.1	179	43	155
1965	SF	8-12	4.19	47	195.2	194	70	170
1966	SF	21-8	2.99	36	255.2	242	40	201
1967	SF	15-17	2.61	39	293	231	84	230
1968	SF	16-15	2.45	39	290.2	240	59	173
1969	SF	19-14	2.49	40	325	290	91	233
1970	SF	23-13	3.20	41	329	292	84	214
1971	SF	16-12	2.76	37	280	255	67	158
1972	Cleve	24-16	1.92	41	343	253	82	234
1973	Cleve	19-19	3.38	41	344	315	115	238
1974	Cleve	21-13	2.52	37	322	230	99	216
1975	Cleve-Tex	18-17	3.24	37	305.2	277	70	233
1976	Tex	15-14	3.24	32	250	232	52	143
1977	Tex	15-12	3.37	34	238	239	56	177
1978	SD	21-6	2.72	37	261	241	66	154
1979	SD	12-11	3.05	32	233	225	67	140
1980	Tex-NY (A)	10-13	3.67	34	206	224	64	135
1981	Atl	8-9	3.93	23	151	182	24	60
1982	Sea	10-12	4.40	32	216.2	245	54	116
1983	Sea-KC (A)	7-14	4.64	30	186.1	214	49	82
22 years		**314-265**	**3.10**	**777**	**5351**	**4938**	**1379**	**3534**

Transactions: Nov. 29, 1971: Traded with Frank Duffy to Cleveland for Sam McDowell. June 13, 1975: Traded to Texas for Jim Bibby, Jackie Brown, Rick Waits and $100,000. January 25, 1978: Traded to San Diego for Dave Tomlin and $125,000. Feb. 15, 1980: Traded to Texas with Tucker Ashford and Joe Carroll for Willie Montanez. Aug. 14, 1980: Traded to New York Yankees for Ken Clay and Marvin Thompson. January 12, 1981: Signed as free agent with Atlanta.

LEAGUE CHAMPIONSHIP SERIES

Year	Team	W-L	ERA	G	IP	H	BB	SO
1971	SF	1-1	6.14	2	14.2	19	3	11

Edward Stewart Plank

Born August 31, 1875, in Gettysburg, Pennsylvania; died February 24, 1926, in Gettysburg, Pennsylvania. 5'11", 175 lbs., bats left, throws left. Years in minor leagues: None; Major League debut: May 13, 1901; Years in Major Leagues: 18. Elected to Hall of Fame: 1946. Nickname: Gettysburg Eddie— because of his hometown.

Eddie Plank is the third winningest lefthander in baseball history with his 327 career wins—only Warren Spahn and Steve Carlton are ahead of him. Plank was one of the mainstays on Connie Mack's Philadelphia A's teams in the early 1900s. He was known for his fidgety mannerisms on the mound, toying with his cap, his shoes, his sleeves—anything to distract batters or make them anxious. This was almost sure to happen against good batters in tough game situations.

Gettysburg Eddie went straight from Gettysburg College to the Major Leagues. He played on six pennant-winning teams but in only four World Series. The A's won the crown in 1902 but there was no World Series. In 1910, the A's won again, but Mack chose to go with righthanders in the World Series and Plank did not make an appearance.

He had some memorable moments when he did pitch in the World Series. In 1905, against the New York Giants, he lost to Christy Mathewson 3–0 in the first game and to Joe McGinnity 1–0 in game four. In 1911, against the Giants again, he was 1–1, including a win against Rube Marquard. In 1913, Plank lost to Mathewson again 3–0 but later beat him 3–1 on a two-hitter. In the 1914 series, he lost 1–0 to Bill James of the Boston Braves. His World Series won-loss record was 2–5 with a 1.32 earned run average. Plank won 20 games or more eight times in his career and ranks fifth all-time in career shutouts with 69.

Year	Team	W-L	ERA	G	IP	H	BB	SO
1901	Phil (A)	17-13	3.31	33	260.2	254	68	90
1902	Phil	20-15	3.30	36	300	319	61	107
1903	Phil	23-16	2.38	43	336	317	65	176
1904	Phil	26-16	2.14	43	357	309	86	201
1905	Phil	25-12	2.26	41	346.2	287	75	210
1906	Phil	19-6	2.25	26	211.2	173	51	108
1907	Phil	24-16	2.20	43	343.2	282	85	183
1908	Phil	14-16	2.17	34	244.2	202	46	135
1909	Phil	19-10	1.70	34	275.1	215	62	132
1910	Phil	16-10	2.01	38	250.1	218	55	123
1911	Phil	23-8	2.10	40	256.2	237	77	149
1912	Phil	26-6	2.22	37	259.2	234	83	110

Year	Team	W-L	ERA	G	IP	H	BB	SO
1913	Phil	18-10	2.60	41	242.2	211	57	151
1914	Phil	15-7	2.87	34	185.1	178	42	110
1915	StL (F)	21-11	2.08	42	268.1	212	54	147
1916	StL (A)	16-15	2.33	37	235.2	203	67	88
1917	StL	5-6	1.79	20	131	105	38	26
17 years		**327-193**	**2.34**	**622**	**4505.1**	**3956**	**1072**	**2246**

Transactions: Feb. 10, 1916: Sold to St. Louis with Babe Borton, Harry Chapman, Doc Crandall, Charlie Deal, Bob Groom, Grover Hartley, Armando Marsans, Ward Miller, Johnny Tobin and Ernie Johnson. January 22, 1918: Traded with Del Pratt and $15,000 to New York Yankees for Les Nunamaker, Fritz Maisel, Nick Cullop, Urban Shocker and Joe Gedeon. (Plank declined to report and retired.)

WORLD SERIES

Year	Team	W-L	ERA	G	IP	H	BB	SO
1905	Phil (A)	0-2	1.59	2	17	14	4	11
1911	Phil	1-1	1.86	2	9.2	6	0	8
1913	Phil	1-1	0.95	2	19	9	3	7
1914	Phil	0-1	1.00	1	9	7	4	6
4 years		**2-5**	**1.32**	**7**	**54.2**	**36**	**11**	**32**

Shirley Povich

Sportswriter. Elected to Hall of Fame: 1975.

Shirley Povich went to work for the *Washington Post* in 1924 and was still writing columns when he died in 1998 at the age of 92. He wrote about all three of the Washington Senators' pennants, and his column "This Morning" was a fixture in the *Post* for nearly 50 years. He was also a regular columnist in *The Sporting News*.

In the 1950s, Povich crusaded for integration in sports, particularly chiding the Washington Redskins. After a Redskins loss to the Cleveland Browns, Povich wrote: "While the Reskins steadfastly refuse to employ black athletes, their end zone was being integrated four times by Jim Brown."

Bob Prince

Broadcaster. Elected to the Hall of Fame: 1986.

Bob Prince, known as "The Gunner" by millions of fans, was the radio voice of the Pittsburgh Pirates for 28 years. His enthusiasm and brashness were loved by listeners in a three-state area who anxiously awaited his fervent declaration after a Pirate victory: "We had 'em all the way."

Charles Gardner Radbourn

Born December 9, 1853, in Rochester, New York; died February 3, 1897, in Bloomington, Illinois. 5'9", 168 lbs., bats right, throws right. Years in minor leagues: 2; Major League debut: May 5, 1881; Years in Major Leagues: 11. Elected to Hall of Fame: 1939. Nickname: Old Hoss—because he was such a workhorse of a pitcher.

It took Old Hoss Radbourn only 11 Major League seasons to post 308 victories because of his incredible ability to pitch with little or no rest. Pitching for Providence in 1884, Radbourn won 60 games—almost one-fifth of his career total—while working 679 innings. During one month of that season, Providence won 20 games and Radbourn had 18 of the victories. The next year, he won 26. He had nine seasons in which he won 20 games or more, including 31 in 1882 and 49 in 1883 before the even more phenomenal 1884 season. He had a good fastball, a lively curve and an early version of a screwball, all of which he threw underhand—and hard—from the 19th century pitching distance of 50 feet.

His career was outstanding because of how often he pitched, but it was also cut short for the same reason. He once told friends he would have trouble lifting his arm above his shoulder even if someone held a $5 bill in that direction. He had six consecutive seasons of pitching 400 innings or more, including two over 600 and two over 500. He had a strikeout-to-walk ratio of more than 2-to-1 even though, when his arm started to fail him, he walked more than he struck out in three out of his last four seasons.

He retired after his 11th season and bought a bar. A few years later, he accidentally shot himself while hunting, practically blinding him in one eye and seriously disfiguring him. He lived in virtual obscurity after that. Baseball's best pitcher for a decade died in seclusion at the age of 43.

Year	Team	W-L	ERA	G	IP	H	BB	SO
1880	Buff	0-0	0.00	0	0	0	0	0
1881	Prov	25-11	2.43	41	325.1	309	64	117
1882	Prov	31-19	2.09	55	474	429	51	201
1883	Prov	49-25	2.05	76	632.1	563	56	315
1884	Prov	60-12	1.38	75	678.2	528	98	441
1885	Prov	26-20	2.20	49	445.2	423	83	154
1886	Bos (N)	27-30	3.00	58	509.1	521	111	218
1887	Bos	24-23	4.55	50	425	505	133	87
1888	Bos	7-16	2.87	24	207	187	45	64
1889	Bos	20-11	3.67	33	277	282	72	99
1890	Bos (P)	27-12	3.31	41	343	352	100	80
1891	Cin (N)	12-12	4.25	26	218	236	62	54
12 years		**308-191**	**2.67**	**528**	**4535.1**	**4335**	**875**	**1830**

Harold Henry Reese

Born July 23, 1918, in Ekron, Kentucky; died August 14, 1999, in Louisville, Kentucky. 5'10", 178 lbs., bats right, throws right. Years in minor leagues: 2; Major League debut: April 23, 1940; Years in Major Leagues: 16. Elected to Hall of Fame: 1984. Nickname: Pee Wee—not because of his small size but because as a youth, he was a marbles champion in Louisville and "Pee Wee" is a type of marble; also, The Little Colonel—in this case it is because of his size, being one of the smallest players on the Louisville Colonels minor league team.

Pee Wee Reese was the captain of the "Boys of Summer" Dodger teams—a steadying influence on a team filled with stars such as Roy Campanella, Jackie Robinson, Duke Snider, Gil Hodges and Don Newcombe. Reese was competitive and consistent and exercised outstanding leadership qualities. Outside of Branch Rickey, he is credited with helping pave the way for Jackie Robinson's acceptance in the Major Leagues after Robinson broke the color line in 1947. Fans in the stands as well as some teammates, opposing players, managers and coaches didn't want Robinson on the same field with them, and it was Reese, a native Southerner, who befriended Jackie and set the example for others to follow.

In his rookie season, 1940, Reese was severely beaned in Chicago in midseason and was out about a week. When he returned to the lineup, he got at least one hit or a walk in 26 straight games, was blanked for a game, and then got a hit or walked in his next 22 games. Reese played 16 seasons with the Dodgers—15 in Brooklyn and one in Los Angeles. During that time, the Dodgers won seven pennants, finished second six times and third twice. Only the New York Yankees had a better record during that time period, and the Dodgers faced the Yankees seven times in the World Series.

Pee Wee excelled as a Dodger leadoff man, setting the table for the power hitters that followed him the lineup. He scored more than 90 runs eight straight years, topping the 100 mark twice, including a league-leading 132 in 1949. Reese finished in the top 10 in voting for the Most Valuable Player Award in eight of his 16 seasons. He, like so many other ballplayers of his era, lost three years to military service.

Year	Team	G	AB	R	H	D	T	HR	RBI	AVE.
1940	Brklyn	84	312	58	85	8	4	5	28	.272
1941	Brklyn	152	595	76	136	23	5	2	46	.229
1942	Brklyn	151	564	87	144	24	5	3	53	.255
1946	Brklyn	152	542	79	154	16	10	5	60	.284
1947	Brklyn	142	476	81	135	24	4	12	73	.284
1948	Brklyn	151	566	96	155	31	4	9	75	.274
1949	Brklyn	155	617	132	172	27	3	16	73	.279
1950	Brklyn	141	531	97	138	21	5	11	52	.260
1951	Brklyn	154	616	94	176	20	8	10	85	.286
1952	Brklyn	149	559	94	152	18	8	6	58	.272
1953	Brklyn	140	524	108	142	25	7	13	61	.271

Year	Team	G	AB	R	H	D	T	HR	RBI	AVE.
1954	Brklyn	141	554	98	171	35	8	10	69	.309
1955	Brklyn	145	553	99	156	29	4	10	61	.282
1956	Brklyn	147	572	85	147	19	2	9	46	.257
1957	Brklyn	103	330	33	74	3	1	1	29	.224
1958	LA	59	147	21	33	7	2	4	17	.224
16 years		2166	8058	1338	2170	330	80	126	885	.269

WORLD SERIES

Year	Team	G	AB	R	H	D	T	HR	RBI	AVE.
1941	Brklyn	5	20	1	4	0	0	0	2	.200
1947	Brklyn	7	23	5	7	1	0	0	4	.304
1949	Brklyn	5	19	2	6	1	0	1	2	.316
1952	Brklyn	7	29	4	10	0	0	1	4	.345
1953	Brklyn	6	24	0	5	0	1	0	0	.208
1955	Brklyn	7	27	5	8	1	0	0	2	.296
1956	Brklyn	7	27	3	6	0	1	0	2	.222
7 years		44	169	20	46	3	2	2	16	.272

Joseph Reichler

Sportswriter. Elected to Hall of Fame: 1980.

Joe Reichler spent 23 years covering baseball and other sports for the Associated Press, but one of his lasting contributions is the creation of the *Baseball Encyclopedia*, the first great compendium of facts, figures and statistics on teams and individuals who have graced the playing fields for more than a century.

Reichler was also author of several books, including *It's Good to Be Alive* with Roy Campanella, *The Game and the Glory*, and *Baseball's Greatest Moments*. He served for a time as director of public relations for the office of the commissioner of baseball.

Edgar Charles Rice

Born February 20, 1890, in Morocco, Indiana; died October 13, 1974, in Rossmor, Maryland. 5'10", 155 lbs., bats left, throws left. Years in minor leagues: 2; Major League debut: August 7, 1915. Elected to Hall of Fame: 1963. Nickname: Sam—acquired because Clark Griffith, when asked by reporters who his latest acquisition was, couldn't think of Rice's first name so he told them it was Sam, and the nickname stuck.

Sam Rice played 19 of his 20 Major League years with the Washington Senators. He was a fleet-footed center fielder who made one of the most spectacular, controversial catches in World Series history. He was also a consistently good hitter who hit over .300 in 13 years of a 15-year stretch. The Senators only went to the World Series three times in their existence and, like Goose Goselin, Rice played on each of those teams.

He had more than 200 hits in six seasons, including 1924, when he put together a 31-game hitting streak, and 1926, when he led the American League with 216 hits each time. In between, in 1925, he hit .350 in leading the Senators to their first World Series and got 12 hits in the World Series, a record since broken by Bobby Richardson.

It was in that World Series that Rice, playing center field, raced back and made a dive into the stands and disappeared from sight in an effort to catch a drive hit by the Pirates' Earl Smith. When he emerged, he held the ball up, signaling he caught it, and umpire Cy Rigler ruled Smith was out. The Pirates protested, not only to the umpires but to Commissioner Kenesaw Mountain Landis, who was attending the game. But the call stood: Rice was credited with the catch. He enjoyed the controversy caused by the catch and, whenever he was asked about it, he would always smile and say, "The umpire said I caught it." At his request, a letter he wrote was opened, after his death, in which he confirmed that he caught the ball. Rice only played in seven games in 1918, a war year, which cost him the opportunity to be part of the exclusive fraternity of players with 3,000 hits. He missed it by 13.

Year	Team	G	AB	R	H	D	T	HR	RBI	AVE.
1915	Wash	4	8	1	3	0	0	0	0	.375
1916	Wash	58	197	26	59	8	3	1	17	.299
1917	Wash	155	586	77	177	25	7	0	69	.302
1918	Wash	7	23	3	8	1	0	0	3	.348
1919	Wash	141	557	80	179	23	9	3	71	.321
1920	Wash	153	624	83	211	29	9	3	80	.338
1921	Wash	143	561	83	185	39	13	4	79	.330
1922	Wash	154	633	91	187	37	13	6	69	.295
1923	Wash	148	595	117	188	35	18	3	75	.316
1924	Wash	154	646	106	227	38	14	1	76	.334
1925	Wash	152	649	111	216	31	13	1	87	.350
1926	Wash	152	641	98	216	32	14	3	76	.337
1927	Wash	142	603	98	179	33	14	2	65	.297
1928	Wash	148	616	95	202	32	15	2	55	.328
1929	Wash	150	616	119	199	39	10	1	62	.323
1930	Wash	147	593	121	207	35	13	1	73	.349
1931	Wash	120	413	81	128	21	8	0	42	.310
1932	Wash	106	288	58	93	16	7	1	34	.323
1933	Wash	73	85	19	25	4	3	1	12	.294
1934	Cleve	97	335	48	98	19	1	1	33	.293
20 years		**2404**	**9269**	**1515**	**2987**	**497**	**184**	**34**	**1077**	**.322**

WORLD SERIES

Year	Team	G	AB	R	H	D	T	HR	RBI	AVE.
1924	Wash	7	29	2	6	0	0	0	1	.207
1925	Wash	7	33	5	12	0	0	0	3	.364
1933	Wash	1	1	0	1	0	0	0	0	1.000
3 years		15	63	7	19	0	0	0	4	.302

Grantland Rice

Sportswriter. Elected to Hall of Fame: 1966.

Grantland Rice is often described as the dean of American sportswriters, not because he was the first, nor because he was the most prolific, but because of the quality of his writing. Not many sportswriters are quoted directly from their works, but Rice is an exception. It was Rice who first wrote, "It's not whether you win or lose but how you play the game." It was Rice who immortalized the backfield of a Notre Dame football team by comparing them to the Four Horsemen of the Apocalypse. And it was Rice who wrote a poem entitled "Game Called" on the day that Babe Ruth died that alluded to a curtain being drawn on a darkened field.

Milton Richman

Sportswriter. Elected to Hall of Fame: 1980.

Milt Richman covered sports for United Press (later United Press International) for 42 years, covering such momentous events as Jackie Robinson's breaking the color line in Major League Baseball, the expansion of baseball first to the West Coast and then to the South and to Canada, the creation of free agency, the escalation of player salaries, and the player strikes.

Richman was an infielder in the St. Louis Browns farm system who turned in his glove for a typewriter. He went to work for UPI in 1944—the only year the Browns ever won a pennant. He rose to become sports editor of the wire service.

Wesley Branch Rickey

Born December 20, 1881, in Lucasville, Ohio; died December 9, 1965, in Columbia, Missouri. Baseball executive. Elected to Hall of Fame: 1967. Nickname: Mahatma—what sportswriters dubbed him because of his habit of philosophizing about the game of baseball.

Branch Rickey was a frustrated ballplayer who became one of baseball's legendary executives. He earned a law degree from the University of Michigan but turned to baseball, instead, for a career. He caught briefly in the Major Leagues—once allowing 13 stolen bases in one game—and managed both the Cardinals and Browns. But his genius was in the front office, where he took actions that changed the game forever. Rickey will always be remembered for breaking the color line in Major League Baseball by carefully selecting the player he thought had what it took: the ability to play at the Major League level and the temperment to take the abuse he was sure to get. Rickey picked Jackie Robinson, as Rickey put it, not because he had the courage to fight back, but because he had the courage not to. When Rickey plucked Robinson from the Dodgers farm club at Montreal and put him in the Major Leagues on April 15, 1947, it opened the door for hundreds of other talented black players to have a shot at the big leagues. Among them were Roy Campanella, Don Newcombe, Joe Black and others who helped the Dodgers win seven pennants in 12 years.

But Rickey put his expertise into the game in many other ways. He introduced the concept of the farm system, in which Major League clubs owned minor league teams where they could groom young players. Rickey was especially successful in St. Louis and Brooklyn. With the Cardinals, he devised the farm system in 1919 and it helped develop the future Cardinal teams that won five pennants in nine years between 1926 and 1934. In 1942, he moved on to the Dodgers and used the farm system there, plus his integration of the game, to make Brooklyn hugely successful. At one time, Rickey alone had 800 players under contract with his Major League team and his farm system.

In the early 1950s, Rickey became general manager of the Pittsburgh Pirates, one of baseball's worst teams. By 1960, Rickey was gone but he had sown the seeds for the Pirates to win the National League pennant and the World Series. Rickey was an innovator—he created Ladies Day and Knothole Days to try to attract women and kids into the ballpark at bargain prices—but he could be stingy, too. After Ralph Kiner led the National League in home runs for the seventh consecutive year, Rickey wanted to cut his pay. He reasoned that the Pirates had finished last with Kiner; they could have done that without him. Late in his career, Rickey broke from the Major League Baseball establishment and tried to start another league, called the Continental League. It failed, but Major League Baseball got the message and began taking steps toward expansion.

Eppa Rixey Jr.

Born May 3, 1891, in Culpepper, Virginia; died February 23, 1963, in Cincinnati, Ohio. 6'5", 210 lbs., bats left, throws left. Years in minor leagues: None; Major League debut: June 21, 1912; Years in Major Leagues: 21; Elected to Hall of Fame: 1968. Nickname: Eppa Jephtha—given to him by a Cincinnati sportswriter who wrote a poem and needed to give Rixey a middle name to fill out a line of the poem; Rixey had no middle name, but many record books list it as Jephtha.

Eppa Rixey is the only Major League player ever scouted and signed by a Major League umpire. He was pitching for the University of Virginia in 1912. His coach was Cy Rigler, who was also a Major League umpire. Rigler signed him to a contract with the Philadelphia Phillies—a practice umpires are now prohibited from doing.

Rixey spent 21 years in the Majors, 13 of them with the Cincinnati Reds. When he retired at the age of 43, he had the most victories of any lefthander in the National League—266—a record he claimed went without much fanfare until Warren Spahn surpassed him in 1959.

He won 20 or more games four times and led the National League in wins in 1922 with 25. He was not a flashy pitcher who got a lot of strikeouts, but more of a finesse hurler, working the ball around. Though he is said to have worked the count to 3-and-2 on many batters, the record shows he only allowed 2.1 walks per every nine innings pitched over 22 years. He went out in style, winning his last six starts in 1933, at the age of 42. Rixey had the misfortune of playing his entire career with the Phillies and Reds, two teams that rarely rose to the top of the heap. So despite his 266 wins, the only category in which he remains in the top 10 in baseball history is losses— 251. Rixey waited 30 years for his election to the Hall of Fame but did not live to be inducted. He died of a heart attack a month after learning he had been elected.

Year	Team	W-L	ERA	G	IP	H	BB	SO
1912	Phil (N)	10-10	2.50	23	162	147	54	59
1913	Phil	9-5	3.12	35	155.2	148	56	75
1914	Phil	2-11	4.37	24	103	124	45	41
1915	Phil	11-12	2.39	29	176.2	163	64	88
1916	Phil	22-10	1.85	38	287	239	74	134
1917	Phil	16-21	2.27	39	281.1	249	67	121
1919	Phil	6-12	3.97	23	154	160	50	63
1920	Cin	11-22	3.48	41	284.1	288	69	109
1921	Cin	19-18	2.78	40	301	324	66	76
1922	Cin	25-13	3.53	40	313.1	337	45	80
1923	Cin	20-15	2.80	42	309	334	65	97
1924	Cin	15-14	2.76	35	238.1	219	47	57
1925	Cin	21-11	2.88	39	287.1	302	47	69
1926	Cin	14-8	3.40	37	233	231	58	61
1927	Cin	12-10	3.48	34	219.2	240	43	42
1928	Cin	19-18	3.43	43	291.1	317	67	58
1929	Cin	10-13	4.16	35	201	235	60	37
1930	Cin	9-13	5.10	32	164	207	47	37
1931	Cin	4-7	3.91	22	126.2	143	30	22
1932	Cin	5-5	2.66	25	111.2	108	16	14
1933	Cin	6-3	3.15	16	94.1	118	12	10
21 years		**266-251**	**3.15**	**692**	**4494.2**	**4633**	**1082**	**1350**

Transactions: Feb. 22, 1921: Traded to Cincinnati for Jimmy Ring and Greasy Neale.

WORLD SERIES

Year	Team	W-L	ERA	G	IP	H	BB	SO
1915	Phil (N)	0-1	4.05	1	6.2	4	2	2

Philip Francis Rizzuto

Born September 25, 1918, in New York City, New York. 5'6", 160 lbs., bats right, throws right. Years in minor leagues: 4; Major League debut: April 15, 1941; Years in Major Leagues: 13. Elected to Hall of Fame: 1994. Nickname: Scooter—given to him by a minor league teammate because of how he covered his territory at shortstop.

Phil Rizzuto was a rangy shortstop with a great glove who helped the Yankees win nine pennants during his 13-year career. They also won the World Series seven times. He finished second in the balloting for Most Valuable Player in 1949 when the Yankees began their amazing streak of winning pennants, missing only twice between 1949 and 1964. Rizzuto lost the MVP to Ted Williams in 1949 but the Scooter had a better year in 1950 and won the MVP. He hit over .300 twice—in his rookie year, 1941, when he hit .307, and in his MVP year when he .324.

At 5 foot, 6 inches, he was one of the smallest Major League players. In the field, he made up for his lack of size with his great speed, enabling him to cover a lot of ground at shortstop, where he played his entire career except for two brief appearances at second base. He once had a string of 289 consecutive chances without an error.

Rizzuto retired after the 1956 season and spent the next 39 years in the broadcast booth, where his call of "Holy Cow" was a sure sign that something exciting was happening in a Yankee game.

Year	Team	G	AB	R	H	D	T	HR	RBI	AVE.
1941	NY (A)	133	515	65	158	20	9	3	46	.307
1942	NY	144	553	79	157	24	7	4	68	.284
1946	NY	126	471	53	121	17	1	2	38	.257
1947	NY	153	549	78	150	26	9	2	60	.273
1948	NY	128	464	65	117	13	2	6	50	.252
1949	NY	153	614	110	169	22	7	5	64	.275
1950	NY	155	617	127	200	36	7	7	66	.324
1951	NY	144	540	87	148	21	6	2	43	.274
1952	NY	152	578	89	147	24	10	2	43	.254
1953	NY	134	413	54	112	21	3	2	54	.271
1954	NY	127	307	47	60	11	0	2	15	.195
1955	NY	81	143	19	37	4	1	1	9	.259
1956	NY	31	52	6	12	0	0	0	6	.231
13 years		1661	5816	877	1588	239	62	38	562	.273

WORLD SERIES

Year	Team	G	AB	R	H	D	T	HR	RBI	AVE.
1941	NY (A)	5	18	0	2	0	0	0	0	.111
1942	NY	5	21	2	8	0	0	1	1	.381
1947	NY	7	26	3	8	1	0	0	2	.308

Year	Team	G	AB	R	H	D	T	HR	RBI	AVE.
1949	NY	5	18	2	3	0	0	0	1	.167
1950	NY	4	14	1	2	0	0	0	0	.143
1951	NY	6	25	5	8	0	0	1	3	.320
1952	NY	7	27	2	4	1	0	0	0	.148
1953	NY	6	19	4	6	1	0	0	0	.316
1955	NY	7	15	2	4	0	0	0	1	.267
9 years		52	183	21	45	3	0	2	8	.246

Robin Evan Roberts

Born September 30, 1926, in Springfield, Illinois. 6'1", 201 lbs., bats both, throws right. Years in minor leagues: 1; Major League debut: June 18, 1948; Years in Major Leagues: 19. Elected to Hall of Fame: 1976. Nickname: None.

Robin Roberts was one of the great pitchers of the 1950s, hampered by the fact that he played for a team—the Philadelphia Phillies—that didn't win many games. After pitching one year in the minor leagues and compiling a 9–1 record, the Phillies brought him up to the Major Leagues. In a spring training game in 1948, the rookie struck out Joe DiMaggio and Phil Rizzuto of the Yankees to serve notice that he was ready. In the 1950 pennant race, the Phillies' ace lefthander Curt Simmons got drafted, depleting the Philadelphia pitching staff. Roberts started three of the Phils' last five games, including the pennant clincher that he won 2–1 in ten innings over Don Newcombe of the Dodgers.

The Phillies then lost four straight to the New York Yankees in the World Series, but Roberts pitched well. He lost the second game 2–1 in 10 innings to Allie Reynolds on a Joe DiMaggio homer in 10th. Roberts led the National League in innings pitched and complete games five times. He won 20 games or more six years in a row for poor Philadelphia teams. His 28 wins in 1952 remain the most in the National League since Dizzy Dean won 30 in 1934.

Roberts had a tremendous fastball and great control. Over his 19-year career, he averaged just 1.7 walks per nine innings. But his only "out" pitch was his blazing fastball. That, combined with his amazing control, allowed batters to dig in on him. He gave up more than 500 home runs in his career, including 46 in 1956, a record at the time. Nearly always rising to the top with teams that rarely rose to the first division, Roberts only had two really sub-par years. He was 10–22 in 1957 and 1–10 in 1961. The low win totals in those two years prevented him from having 300 career wins. He finished with 286, including 42 in the American League toward the end of his career.

Year	Team	W-L	ERA	G	IP	H	BB	SO
1948	Phil	7-9	3.19	20	146.2	148	61	84
1949	Phil	15-15	3.69	43	226.2	229	75	95
1950	Phil	20-11	3.02	40	304.1	282	77	146

Year	Team	W-L	ERA	G	IP	H	BB	SO
1951	Phil	21-15	3.03	44	315	284	64	127
1952	Phil	28-7	2.59	39	330	292	45	148
1953	Phil	23-16	2.75	44	346.2	324	61	198
1954	Phil	23-15	2.97	45	336.2	289	56	185
1955	Phil	23-14	3.28	41	305	292	53	160
1956	Phil	19-18	4.45	43	297.1	328	40	157
1957	Phil	10-22	4.07	39	249.2	246	43	128
1958	Phil	17-14	3.24	35	269.2	270	51	130
1959	Phil	15-17	4.27	35	257.1	267	35	137
1960	Phil	12-16	4.02	35	237.1	256	34	122
1961	Phil	1-10	5.85	26	117	154	23	54
1962	Bal	10-9	2.78	27	191.1	176	41	102
1963	Bal	14-13	3.33	35	251.1	230	40	124
1964	Bal	13-7	2.91	31	204	203	52	109
1965	Bal-Hous	10-9	2.78	30	190.2	171	30	97
1966	Hous-Chi	5-8	4.82	24	112	141	21	54
19	**years**	**286-245**	**3.41**	**676**	**4688.2**	**4582**	**902**	**2357**

Transactions: Oct. 16, 1961: Sold to Baltimore Orioles.

WORLD SERIES

Year	Team	W-L	ERA	G	IP	H	BB	SO
1950	Phil	0-1	1.64	2	11	11	3	5

Brooks Calbert Robinson Jr.

Born May 18, 1937, in Little Rock, Arkansas. 6'1", 180 lbs., bats right, throws right. Years in minor leagues: 2; Major League debut: September 17, 1955; Years in Major Leagues: 23. Elected to Hall of Fame: 1983. Nickname: Vacuum Cleaner—by fans and sportswriters because of his ability to sweep up just about any ball hit toward him.

Brooks Robinson of the Baltimore Orioles was the best fielding third baseman of his era and might have made it to the Hall of Fame on the strength of his fielding alone. But he also had some great years at the plate, notably 1964 when he was the American League's Most Valuable Player with a .317 average, 28 home runs and 118 RBIs. But it was at third base that he was a wizard. Only Pie Traynor might have been better, said Casey Stengel. He holds the Major League record for third basemen for games played; most assists; most chances accepted; most double plays; highest fielding percentage; and most years leading the league in fielding percentage. He won the Gold Glove Award 16 years in a row.

Though his lifetime batting average was .267, he had some sensational streaks. Twice in his career, he got eight straight hits. Though not a power hitter, he hit six grand slams for the Orioles. In league championship series play in 1969, 1970 and 1971, he hit hit .500, .583 and .364, respectively.

He was voted the Most Valuable Player of the 1970 World Series when he put on one of the greatest one-man performances ever. Robinson got nine hits to tie the record for most hits in a five-game series. But it was his play in the field that made his performance so remarkable. He was credited with making six brilliant plays: leaping to catch line drives, diving to snare ground balls and then throwing runners out at first, and charging to pick up bunts and weakly hit balls. It is the only case in baseball history in which a glove was sent to the Hall of Fame after a World Series. Ironically, he made an error on the first ball hit to him in the series. Robinson holds one dubious Major League record: He hit into four triple plays in his career.

Year	Team	G	AB	R	H	D	T	HR	RBI	AVE.
1955	Bal	6	22	0	2	0	0	0	1	.091
1956	Bal	15	44	5	10	4	0	1	1	.227
1957	Bal	50	117	13	28	6	1	2	14	.239
1958	Bal	145	463	31	110	16	3	3	32	.238
1959	Bal	88	313	29	89	15	2	4	24	.284
1960	Bal	152	595	74	175	27	9	14	88	.294
1961	Bal	163	668	89	192	38	7	7	61	.287
1962	Bal	162	634	77	192	29	9	23	86	.303
1963	Bal	161	589	67	148	26	4	11	67	.251
1964	Bal	163	612	82	194	35	3	28	118	.317
1965	Bal	144	559	81	166	25	2	18	80	.297
1966	Bal	157	620	91	167	35	2	23	100	.269
1967	Bal	158	610	88	164	25	5	22	77	.269
1968	Bal	162	608	65	154	36	6	17	75	.253
1969	Bal	156	598	73	140	21	3	23	84	.234
1970	Bal	158	608	84	168	31	4	18	94	.276
1971	Bal	156	589	67	160	21	1	20	92	.272
1972	Bal	153	556	48	139	23	2	8	64	.250
1973	Bal	155	549	53	141	17	2	9	72	.257
1974	Bal	153	553	46	159	27	0	7	59	.288
1975	Bal	144	482	50	97	15	1	6	53	.201
1976	Bal	71	218	16	46	8	2	3	11	.211
1977	Bal	24	47	3	7	2	0	1	4	.149
23 years		**2896**	**10654**	**1232**	**2848**	**482**	**68**	**268**	**1357**	**.267**

LEAGUE CHAMPIONSHIP SERIES

Year	Team	G	AB	R	H	D	T	HR	RBI	AVE.
1969	Bal	3	14	1	7	1	0	0	0	.500
1970	Bal	3	12	4	7	2	0	0	1	.583
1971	Bal	3	11	2	4	1	0	1	3	.364
1973	Bal	5	20	1	5	2	0	0	2	.250
1974	Bal	4	12	1	1	0	0	1	1	.083
5 years		**18**	**69**	**9**	**24**	**6**	**0**	**2**	**7**	**.348**

WORLD SERIES

Year	Team	G	AB	R	H	D	T	HR	RBI	AVE.
1966	Bal	4	14	2	3	0	0	1	1	.214
1969	Bal	5	19	0	1	0	0	0	2	.053
1970	Bal	5	21	5	9	2	0	2	6	.429
1971	Bal	7	22	2	7	0	0	0	5	.318
4 years		21	76	9	20	2	0	3	14	.263

Frank Robinson

Born August 31, 1935, in Beaumont, Texas. 6'1", 194 lbs., bats right, throws right. Years in minor leagues: 3; Major League debut: April 17, 1956; Years in Major Leagues: 21. Elected to Hall of Fame: 1982. Nickname: The Judge—a name applied to him when he headed a "Kangaroo Court" as a member of the Baltimore Orioles.

John "Red" Flaherty, who umpired in the American League for 21 years, said Frank Robinson was the hardest working ballplayer he ever saw. "An umpire can tell when a ballplayer is loafing and Frank Robinson never loafed," he said. Robinson had a great career in the National League—and followed it with a great career in the American League. He was the National League's Rookie of the Year in 1956 when he tied the rookie record with 38 home runs. That same season, at age 20, he was the youngest starter ever in an All-Star game. Five years later, he won the Most Valuable Player Award in leading the Cincinnati Reds to their first pennant in 21 years. In 10 years with the Reds, he hit 324 home runs and drove in more than 1,000 runs.

But in December of 1965, the Reds, thinking Robinson had already peaked, traded him to the Baltimore Orioles. In his first year with Baltimore, he won the Triple Crown with a .316 average, 49 home runs and 122 runs batted in. He was the American League's Most Valuable Player in leading the Orioles to the World Series. He is the only man to capture MVP honors in both leagues. With Robinson leading the way, the Orioles went to the World Series four times in six years.

He hit 586 home runs in his 21-year career. Only Henry Aaron, Babe Ruth and Willie Mays hit more. In 1975, he became baseball's first black manager when he was named player-manager of the Cleveland Indians. In that role, he homered in his first game to help the Indians to a victory. In 1981, he became manager of the San Francisco Giants and the following year was the National League's Manager of the Year as the Giants finished third. He later managed the Orioles.

Year	Team	G	AB	R	H	D	T	HR	RBI	AVE.
1956	Cin	152	572	122	166	27	6	38	83	.290
1957	Cin	150	611	97	197	29	5	29	75	.322
1958	Cin	148	554	90	149	25	6	31	83	.269
1959	Cin	146	540	106	168	31	4	36	125	.311
1960	Cin	139	464	86	138	33	6	31	83	.297

Year	Team	G	AB	R	H	D	T	HR	RBI	AVE.
1961	Cin	153	545	117	176	32	7	37	124	.323
1962	Cin	162	609	134	208	51	2	39	136	.342
1963	Cin	140	482	79	125	19	3	21	91	.259
1964	Cin	156	568	103	174	38	6	29	96	.306
1965	Cin	156	582	109	172	33	5	33	113	.296
1966	Bal	155	576	122	182	34	2	49	122	.316
1967	Bal	129	479	83	149	23	7	30	94	.311
1968	Bal	130	421	69	113	27	1	15	52	.268
1969	Bal	148	539	111	166	19	5	32	100	.308
1970	Bal	132	471	88	144	24	1	25	78	.306
1971	Bal	133	455	82	128	16	2	28	99	.281
1972	LA (N)	103	342	41	86	6	1	19	59	.251
1973	Cal	147	534	85	142	29	0	30	97	.266
1974	Cal-Cleve	144	477	81	117	27	3	22	68	.245
1975	Cleve	49	118	19	28	5	0	9	24	.237
1976	Cleve	36	67	5	15	0	0	3	10	.224
21 years		**2808**	**10006**	**1829**	**2943**	**528**	**72**	**586**	**1812**	**.294**

Transactions: Dec. 9, 1965: Traded to Baltimore for Milt Pappas, Jack Bald-schun and Dick Simpson. Dec. 2, 1971: Traded with Pete Richert to Los Ange-les for Doyle Alexander, Bob O'Brien, Sergio Robles and Royle Stillman. Nov. 28, 1972: Traded with Bill Singer, Mike Strahler, Billy Grabarkewitz and Bobby Valentine to California for Andy Messersmith and Ken McMullen. Sept. 12, 1974: Traded to Cleveland for Ken Suarez, Rusty Torres and cash.

LEAGUE CHAMPIONSHIP SERIES

Year	Team	G	AB	R	H	D	T	HR	RBI	AVE.
1969	Bal	3	12	1	4	2	0	1	2	.333
1970	Bal	3	10	3	2	0	0	1	2	.200
1971	Bal	3	12	2	1	1	0	0	1	.083
3 years		**9**	**34**	**6**	**7**	**3**	**0**	**2**	**5**	**.206**

WORLD SERIES

Year	Team	G	AB	R	H	D	T	HR	RBI	AVE.
1961	Cin	5	15	3	3	2	0	1	4	.200
1966	Bal	4	14	4	4	0	1	2	3	.286
1969	Bal	5	16	2	3	0	0	1	1	.188
1970	Bal	5	22	5	6	0	0	2	4	.273
1971	Bal	7	25	5	7	0	0	2	2	.280
5 years		**26**	**92**	**19**	**23**	**2**	**1**	**8**	**14**	**.250**

Jack Roosevelt Robinson

Born January 31, 1919, in Cairo, Georgia; died October 24, 1972, in Stam-ford, Connecticut. 5'11", 195 lbs., bats right, throws right. Years in minor leagues: 1; Major League debut: April 15, 1947; Years in Major Leagues: 10. Elected to Hall of Fame: 1962. Nickname: Rabbit—a nickname as a fullback for UCLA because of his quickness, a takeoff on jackrabbit; in the Major Leagues, he was simply called Jackie.

When Brooklyn general manager Branch Rickey picked Jackie Robinson as the player to break the color line in Major League Baseball, it wasn't just because of his ability to hit, run and field at the Major League level. It was also because Rickey thought Robinson had the courage *not* to fight back if he was cursed at and berated, not only by fans but by opposing players, coaches and managers. He faced all of that, and more. Major League club owners voted 15–1 against integrating baseball, but Commissioner A.B. "Happy" Chandler was a strong supporter and his will won out. Some of Robinson's own teammates were cool to him, and some opposing teams threatened to boycott games if Robinson played.

Robinson had been a star athlete at UCLA and is the only Major League baseball player to have played in a Rose Bowl game, an All-Star baseball game and a World Series. Rickey was aware of the fact that Robinson had played on integrated teams, and that was a factor in picking him for the Major Leagues. Also, Robinson was passionate about the cause of integration. In the Army, he was court-martialed for refusing to sit in the back of bus (and was subsequently acquitted). Jackie weathered the storms in his travels around the National League and led the way for hundreds of other black ballplayers to make their way to the Major Leagues. He was much more than just a figurehead; he was a great ballplayer. Through all of the controversy of his first year, Robinson was the Rookie of the Year in 1947 and the league's Most Valuable Player two years later when he won the batting title. In his ten-year career, his Dodgers won six pennants and one World Series. Despite being 28 years old when he played his first Major League game, Robinson had the energy and enthusiasm of a youngster. It showed up particularly in his running. Robinson was a gifted base stealer who stole home 19 times in his career, including five times in one season and once in a World Series game.

He hit .297 in his rookie year. For most of that first season, despite all the pressures, Robinson maintained a batting average of over .300 and dipped under it only because of a late season slump that occurred after the Dodgers had clinched the pennant. His speed paid off: Robinson led the league in stolen bases with 29 and was second in runs scored with 125. His presence helped every other National League team at the gate. In some cities, it was standing-room-only when the Dodgers came to town. By season's end, the National League had set an all-time attendance record, surpassing the 1946 total by 750,000. Five National League teams established attendance records, including the Dodgers who drew 1.8 million in cozy Ebbets Field. After 1947, when he just missed hitting .300, Robinson hit over .300 in six of the next nine seasons, finishing with a lifetime batting average of .311. His best year was 1949, his MVP year, when he was batting champion with a .342 average and 124 runs batted in. At the end of the 1956 season, Robinson was traded to the New York Giants and decided to retire. For the next 15 years, he was active in many civil rights causes, never backing away from the cause that had been a driving force in his life. He was 53 when he died of a heart attack in 1972.

Year	Team	G	AB	R	H	D	T	HR	RBI	AVE.
1947	Brklyn	151	590	125	175	31	5	12	48	.297
1948	Brklyn	147	574	108	170	38	8	12	85	.296
1949	Brklyn	156	593	122	203	38	12	16	124	.342
1950	Brklyn	144	518	99	170	39	4	14	81	.328
1951	Brklyn	153	548	106	185	33	7	19	88	.338
1952	Brklyn	149	510	104	157	17	3	19	75	.308
1953	Brklyn	136	484	109	159	34	7	12	95	.329
1954	Brklyn	124	386	62	120	22	4	15	59	.311
1955	Brklyn	105	317	51	81	6	2	8	36	.256
1956	Brklyn	117	357	61	98	15	2	10	43	.275
10 years		**1382**	**4877**	**947**	**1518**	**273**	**54**	**137**	**734**	**.311**

Transactions: Dec. 13, 1956: Traded to New York Giants for Dick Littlefield; trade was cancelled when Robinson retired.

WORLD SERIES

Year	Team	G	AB	R	H	D	T	HR	RBI	AVE.
1947	Brklyn	7	27	3	7	2	0	0	3	.259
1949	Brklyn	5	16	2	3	1	0	0	2	.188
1952	Brklyn	7	23	4	4	0	0	1	2	.174
1953	Brklyn	6	25	3	8	2	0	0	2	.320
1955	Brklyn	6	22	5	4	1	1	0	1	.182
1956	Brklyn	7	24	5	6	1	0	1	2	.250
6 years		**38**	**137**	**22**	**32**	**7**	**1**	**2**	**12**	**.234**

Wilbert Robinson

Born June 2, 1864, in Hudson, Massachusetts; died August 8, 1934, in Atlanta Georgia. 5'8", 215 lbs., bats right, throws right. Years in minor leagues: None; Major League debut: April 18, 1886; Years in Major Leagues: 35 (as player, coach and manager). Elected to Hall of Fame: 1945. Nickname: Uncle Robbie—a term of affection and respect from players he managed.

Wilbert Robinson was a good catcher for Baltimore before 1900 but made his mark as manager of Brooklyn in the National League. He was so revered, in fact, that the team was known as the Robins for many years, in his honor. Robinson was known for getting the most out of his players with a low-key, common sense, often humorous approach to the game. As a pitching coach early in his career, he worked with a young hurler named Rube Marquard and helped him become a Hall of Famer.

He was a coach with John McGraw's Giants for two years, but the two had a falling out over a missed sign in the 1913 World Series. Robinson moved over to Brooklyn, the Giants' arch-rival, where he won two pennants in the next seven years. At Brooklyn, Robinson presided over some of the game's zaniest characters.

He decided to start a "Bonehead Club" in which he fined players for making stupid plays. He became the first victim when he turned in the wrong lineup card at the start of a game. He also once changed first basemen at the last minute when he discovered he couldn't spell the name of the player he wanted to start.

Perhaps his most celebrated feat was when he agreed to try to catch a baseball dropped from an airplane. A grapefruit was dropped instead, and when Uncle Robbie caught it, it splattered all over his chest. Robbie felt all the wet dew on him and, thinking it was blood, thought he had been mortally wounded. Robinson had the longest tenure as manager of Brooklyn until Walter Alston came along in the 1950s and stayed on board for 23 years. As a player, Robinson got seven hits in a nine-inning game in 1892 and drove in 11 runs in the same game. As a manager, in his 19 years and over 2,800 games, his teams won two more games than they lost.

Year	Team	Record	Standing
1902	Bal (A)	22-54	Eighth
1914	Brklyn	75-79	Fifth
1915	Brklyn	80-72	Third
1916	Brklyn	94-60	First
1917	Brklyn	70-81	Seventh
1918	Brklyn	57-69	Fifth
1919	Brklyn	69-71	Fifth
1920	Brklyn	93-61	First
1921	Brklyn	77-75	Fifth
1922	Brklyn	76-78	Sixth
1923	Brklyn	76-78	Sixth
1924	Brklyn	92-62	Second
1925	Brklyn	68-85	Sixth
1926	Brklyn	71-82	Sixth
1927	Brklyn	65-88	Sixth
1928	Brklyn	77-76	Sixth
1929	Brklyn	70-83	Sixth
1930	Brklyn	86-68	Fourth
1931	Brklyn	79-73	Fourth
19 years		**1397-1395**	

WORLD SERIES

Year	Team	Record
1916	Brklyn	1-4
1920	Brklyn	2-5
2 years		**3-9**

Wilbur Rogan

Born in 1893 in Oklahoma City, Oklahoma; died in 1964 in Kansas City, Missouri. 6', 180 lbs., bats right, throws right. Years in minor leagues: 20

(Negro Leagues); Years in Major Leagues: None. Elected to Hall of Fame:
1998. Nickname: Bullet Joe—because of the speed of his pitches.

Bullet Joe Rogan was the best pitcher of his era in the Negro leagues. He was
the ace of the Kansas City Monarchs staff—and cleanup hitter. Rogan's career
began in 1919 and lasted through the 1938 season. His successor with the Monarchs was Satchel Paige, so comparisons were inevitable—much like comparisons
between Nolan Ryan and Bob Feller in the second half of the 20th century.

Chet Brewer, who scouted for the Pittsburgh Pirates after a pitching career
with the Monarchs, said Rogan's curveball was faster than most pitchers' fastball.
One of the things that made Rogan's pitches seem so fast was that he had an excellent palm ball that floated to the plate, keeping batters constantly off-balance.

What made Rogan so tough is that he was a great hitter, too. In a three-year
stretch, Rogan had a won-loss record of 15–6 and hit .337 in 1927, was 9–2 while
hitting .354 in 1928, and hit .344 in 1929, a year in which he pitched occasionally but had no wins or losses.

Another Rogan asset: He developed a pickoff move in which he and his first
baseman had a secret signal—so the first baseman could play off the bag, then make
a break for it to take the pickoff throw. Major League players who saw the move
marveled at it. Rogan was 26 in 1919 when he joined the Monarchs. He pitched
a one-hitter in his first start. During his career, he played every position but catcher
and also managed the Monarchs. He later umpired in the Negro leagues and had
the habit of giving tips to young pitchers between innings.

Edd J. Roush

Born May 8, 1893, in Oakland City, Indiana; died March 21, 1988, in
Bradenton, Florida. 5'11", 175 lbs., bats left, throws left. Years in minor leagues:
5; Major League debut: August 20, 1913; Years in Major Leagues: 18. Elected
to Hall of Fame: 1962. Nickname: None.

Edd Roush was a no-nonsense ballplayer who had contract disputes every year
so he could avoid spring training and sat out an entire season when he didn't get
what he wanted. When he did play, he swung a 48-ounce bat and was considered
the best center fielder of his era. Playing for Cincinnati, he just missed winning
batting titles three years in a row. He was batting champion in 1917 with a .341
mark, was edged out by Zack Wheat in 1918 when he hit .333 to Wheat's .335,
and won it again in 1919 with a .321 mark. Roush averaged .340 over one ten-year
period in his career. His lifetime batting average was .323.

Despite the big bat, Roush was not a power hitter, banging only 68 home runs,
but he was consistent. In 1921 and 1922, he hit .352. In 1923, he hit .351. He had
some classic confrontations with temperamental Giants manager John McGraw,
who had him early in his career, dealt him to Cincinnati when he'd had enough of
Roush's brash attitude, then spent a decade trying to get him back with the Giants.
It was under McGraw's reign that Roush held out the entire 1930 season.

Roush was a frugal man who invested his money wisely in up-and-coming companies like Sears & Roebuck and Procter & Gamble. He also knew how to save money in his playing days. He discovered that if he went to spring training and didn't sign, his return home would be at his expense. So he stayed home and negotiated. Roush is often compared with Tris Speaker who was a contemporary in the American League. Both were great center fielders who got their way with management. When Speaker was traded from Boston to Cleveland, the Red Sox got $55,000 as part of the deal. Speaker threatened to retire if he didn't get $10,000 of the cash, and he got it. In 1930, Roush was upset when the Giants wanted to cut his pay $7,500. He claimed that in all the good years he'd had, he never received a $7,500 raise so he wasn't going to take that kind of cut. The Giants didn't give in, and Roush sat out the season.

Year	Team	G	AB	R	H	D	T	HR	RBI	AVE.
1913	Chi (A)	9	10	2	1	0	0	0	0	.100
1914	Ind (F)	74	166	26	54	8	4	1	30	.325
1915	Nwk (F)	145	551	73	164	20	11	3	60	.298
1916	NY-Cin (N)	108	341	38	91	7	15	0	20	.267
1917	Cin	136	522	82	178	19	14	4	67	.341
1918	Cin	113	435	61	145	18	10	5	62	.333
1919	Cin	133	504	73	162	19	12	4	71	.321
1920	Cin	149	579	81	196	22	16	4	90	.339
1921	Cin	112	418	68	147	27	12	4	71	.352
1922	Cin	49	165	29	58	7	4	1	24	.352
1923	Cin	138	527	88	185	41	18	6	88	.351
1924	Cin	121	483	67	168	23	21	3	72	.348
1925	Cin	134	540	91	183	28	16	8	83	.339
1926	Cin	144	563	95	182	37	10	7	79	.323
1927	NY (N)	140	570	83	173	27	4	7	58	.304
1928	NY	46	163	20	41	5	3	2	13	.252
1929	NY	115	450	76	146	19	7	8	52	.324
1931	Cin	101	376	46	102	12	5	1	41	.271
18 years		**1967**	**7363**	**1099**	**2376**	**339**	**182**	**68**	**981**	**.323**

Transactions: Dec. 23, 1915: Sold to New York Giants for $7,500. July 20, 1916: Traded with Christy Mathewson and Bill McKehnie to Cincinnati for Buck Herzog and Red Killifer. Feb. 8, 1927: Traded to New York Giants for George Kelly and cash.

WORLD SERIES

Year	Team	G	AB	R	H	D	T	HR	RBI	AVE.
1919	Cin	8	28	6	6	2	1	0	7	.214

Charles Herbert Ruffing

Born May 3, 1905, in Granville, Illinois; died February 17, 1986, in Cleveland, Ohio. 6'1", 210 lbs., bats right, throws right. Years in minor leagues: 1;

Major League debut: May 31, 1924; Years in Major Leagues: 22. Elected to Hall of Fame: 1973. Nickname: Red, because of the color of his hair.

Red Ruffing's route to the Hall of Fame as a great pitcher was not exactly a straight line. He never intended to be a pitcher. He was a hard-hitting outfielder in his younger days, but he lost four toes in a mining accident that almost cost him any chance for a career at all in baseball. What it did cost him was the agility to run the bases with speed and without pain. So Ruffing became a pitcher.

He appeared in eight games with the Boston Red Sox in 1924 but had no record. In 1925, his first full season, he was 9–18. The next year he was 6–15. The following year he was 5–13, then he was 10–25. He followed that with a 9–22 year. His five-year won-loss total was 39–93—not exactly Hall of Fame material. The Red Sox traded Ruffing to the New York Yankees in 1930 for outfielder Cedric Durst, who played in 102 games for the Red Sox, hit .245, and retired at the end of the season. For Ruffing, on the other hand, it was as if his career was just beginning. He was 15–8 in 1930. He won 20 or more games for four years in a row between 1936 and 1939, leading the Yankees to six consecutive American League championships. He pitched for the Yankees through 1946, finished up with a year with the White Sox and had a career record of 273 wins and 225 losses. His record with the Yankees was 231–124. He was 7–2 in World Series competition with an earned run average of 2.63. In the opening game of the 1942 World Series, Ruffing had a no-hitter until Terry Moore broke it up with one out in the eighth inning. The Yankees won the game, 7–4. Ruffing had trouble running but he never forgot how to hit. He had a lifetime batting average of .269. and had 521 hits included 36 home runs. He was a frequent pinch hitter for the Yankees.

Year	Team	W-L	ERA	G	IP	H	BB	SO
1924	Bos (A)	0-0	6.65	8	23	29	9	10
1925	Bos	9-18	5.01	37	217.1	253	75	64
1926	Bos	6-15	4.39	37	166	169	68	58
1927	Bos	5-13	4.66	26	158.1	160	87	77
1928	Bos	10-25	3.89	42	289.1	303	96	118
1929	Bos	9-22	4.86	35	244.1	280	118	109
1930	Bos-NY (A)	15-8	4.38	38	221.1	242	68	131
1931	NY	16-14	4.41	37	237	240	87	132
1932	NY	18-7	3.09	35	259	219	115	190
1933	NY	9-14	3.91	35	235	230	93	122
1934	NY	19-11	3.93	36	256.1	232	104	149
1935	NY	16-11	3.12	30	222	201	76	81
1936	NY	20-12	3.85	33	271	274	90	102
1937	NY	20-7	2.98	31	256.1	242	68	131
1938	NY	21-7	3.31	31	247.1	246	82	127
1939	NY	21-7	2.93	28	233.1	211	75	95
1940	NY	15-12	3.38	30	226	218	76	97
1941	NY	15-6	3.54	23	185.2	177	54	60
1942	NY	14-7	3.21	24	193.2	183	41	80

Year	Team	W-L	ERA	G	IP	H	BB	SO
1945	NY	7-3	2.89	11	87.1	85	20	24
1946	NY	5-1	1.77	8	61	37	23	19
1947	Chi (A)	3-5	6.11	9	53	63	11	16
22 years		273-225	3.80	624	4344	4294	1541	1987

Transactions: May 6, 1930: Traded to New York Yankees for Cedric Durst and $50,000.

WORLD SERIES

Year	Team	W-L	ERA	G	IP	H	BB	SO
1932	NY (A)	1-0	4.00	1	9	10	6	10
1936	NY	0-1	4.50	2	14	16	5	12
1937	NY	1-0	1.00	1	9	7	3	8
1938	NY	2-0	1.50	2	18	17	2	11
1939	NY	1-0	1.00	1	9	4	1	4
1941	NY	1-0	1.00	1	9	6	3	5
1942	NY	1-1	4.08	2	17.2	14	7	11
7 years		7-2	2.63	10	85.2	74	27	61

Damon Runyan

Sportswriter. Elected to Hall of Fame: 1967.

Damon Runyan was one of America's most famous writers of the first half of the 20th century who was known for often sarcastic wit. One of his early works was later made into the hugely successful play *Guys and Dolls.*

Runyan began his career as a sportswriter for newspapers in Colorado. Later, as a sportsreporter for the *New York American*, he was the highest paid sportswriter in the country. He is credited with being one of the writers who suspected early on that the 1919 World Series was fixed.

Amos Wilson Rusie

Born May 31, 1871, in Indianapolis, Indiana; died December 6, 1942, in Seattle, Washington. 6'1", 210 lbs., bats right, throws right. Years in minor leagues: None; Major League debut: May 9, 1889; Years in Major Leagues: 10. Elected to Hall of Fame: 1977. Nickname: The Hoosier Thunderbolt— references to his home state and to how hard he could throw a baseball.

Amos Rusie was a righthanded pitcher for the New York Giants in the 1890s who threw the ball so hard, he caused a rule change. The pitcher's mound was moved from 50 feet away to 60 feet, 6 inches—the same distance it is today. The change was not only for the batter's protection, but for the pitcher's. Rusie himself was victimized by a line drive that struck him in the ear, causing him permanent hearing impairment.

He overmatched National League hitters for ten years, winning 243 games, including a four-year stretch when he won 30 or more each year. Ironically, considering how hard he threw to the plate, he hurt his arm in 1898 on a pickoff attempt and was never the same after that.

What made life interesting for National League batters was that Rusie, throwing as hard as he did, was often wild. He led the National League in strikeouts—and in walks—five times, and his lifetime total of 1,716 walks is fifth highest in baseball history, though he pitched only ten years. Rusie's career was marked by many contract disputes with Giants owner Andrew Freedman that resulted in Rusie sitting out one season and being suspended by Freedman in another. After the 1900 season, Freedman traded his troublesome pitcher to the Cincinnati Reds. It turned out to be a great deal for the Giants. Rusie had never recovered from his sore arm and pitched in only three games for the Reds before retiring. The Giants got the better of the deal. The player they got in return for Rusie was a young pitcher with a lot of potential: Christy Mathewson.

Year	Team	W-L	ERA	G	IP	H	BB	SO
1889	Ind (N)	13-10	5.32	33	225	246	128	113
1890	NY (N)	29-30	2.56	67	548.2	436	289	345
1891	NY	33-20	2.55	61	500.1	391	262	337
1892	NY	32-28	2.88	64	532	405	267	303
1893	NY	29-18	3.23	56	482	451	218	208
1894	NY	36-13	2.78	54	444	426	200	195
1895	NY	22-21	3.73	49	393.1	384	159	201
1897	NY	29-8	2.54	38	322.1	314	87	135
1898	NY	20-11	3.03	37	300	288	103	114
1901	Cin	0-1	8.59	3	22	43	3	6
10 years		**243-160**	**3.07**	**462**	**3769.2**	**3384**	**1716**	**1957**

Transactions: Dec. 15, 1900: Traded to Cincinnati for Christy Mathewson.

George Herman Ruth

Born February 6, 1895, in Baltimore, Maryland; died August 16, 1948, in New York City, New York. 6'2", 215 lbs., bats left, throws left. Years in minor leagues: 1. Major League debut: July 11, 1914. Years in Major Leagues: 22. Elected to Hall of Fame: 1936. Nickname: Babe—by some accounts, given to him when he was a youngster wanting to play ball with the bigger boys at St. Mary's Industrial School in Baltimore. Ruth himself gave two different accounts in biographies written two decades apart, but in both, he said the nickname was given to him in the minor leagues; also, The Bambino and the Sultan of Swat, given to him by sportswriters because of his power hitting.

Babe Ruth was the dominant player in baseball for two decades. He combined amazing physical ability, a brash personality and a penchant for always being in the spotlight, qualities that helped him become a household name. More important, he came along at baseball's lowest hour and lifted it out of the doldrums. Ruth was setting home run records as a member of the New York Yankees at a time when baseball was reeling from the Black Sox scandal in which eight members of the Chicago White Sox were banned for life in 1920 for conspiring with gamblers to fix the 1919 World Series.

Ruth, who began his career as a pitcher and quite possibly could have made it to the Hall of Fame as a hurler, hit a record 29 home runs for the Red Sox in 1919 and then was traded to the Yankees. It was in 1920, when the Black Sox scandal was threatening to steal all the baseball headlines, that Ruth came into his own, hitting more home runs than most other teams in the American League. He hit 54 homers in 1920, 59 in 1921, 35 in 1922 (when he played in only 110 games), 41 in 1923, 46 in 1924, 25 in 1925 (in 98 games), 47 in 1926, and 60 in 1927—a record number for a season until Roger Maris hit 61 in 1961. Ruth continued the home run onslaught with 54 in 1928, 46 in 1929, 49 in 1930, 46 in 1931, 41 in 1932, 34 in 1933 and 22 in 1934, his last year with the Yankees. He led the American League in home runs 12 times, in RBIs 6 times, in runs scored 8 times, in walks 11 times, in on-base percentage 10 times, and in slugging percentage 13 times. In 1924, he won the batting title with a .378 average, and he had a lifetime batting average of .342. He played in seven World Series with the Yankees, had a lifetime World Series average of .326 and twice hit three home runs in a World Series game. Two other statistics points to a little-recognized fact about Ruth. For a big man, he could run well: He had 123 stolen bases in his career, including 10 steals of home. Also, he hit 136 triples. By comparison, Willie Mays had 140 triples, playing the same number of seasons as Ruth.

He began his career as a pitcher for the Boston Red Sox. In his first three full seasons, he was 18–8, 23–12 and 24–13. Ruth was always a colorful character, even in his youth. As a Red Sox pitcher in 1917, he was involved in one of the most famous ejections of all time. On June 23, 1917, pitching against the Washington Senators, Ruth walked the first batter and became so incensed with home plate umpire Brick Owens' calls that Owens threw him out of the game. Ernie Shore relieved Ruth, picked the base runner off first, and retired the next 26 batters. Ruth appeared in two World Series as a Boston pitcher and was sensational—a fact obscured by his legendary feats with the Yankees. In the 1916 World Series, Ruth started and went 14 innings in a game the Red Sox eventually won for him, 2–1. In the 1918 World Series, Ruth won two games, giving him a lifetime World Series pitching record of 3–0 with an earned run average of 0.87. His $29\frac{2}{3}$ consecutive scoreless innings in World Series play was a record for more than 40 years, topped only by Whitey Ford. His lifetime totals as a pitcher show that he won twice as many as he lost. His 94–46 record includes five wins when he was called on to pitch while he was with the Yankees. He was sold to the Yankees in 1920 and was reunited with Ed Barrow, who became general manager of the Yankees and who had been Ruth's manager in Boston. Ruth's arrival also coincided with the end of the deadball era in baseball. The lively ball had arrived, and so had Ruth. At the end of his career he had 714 home runs, 2,211 RBIs, 2,174 runs scored (remarkably, the same number of runs as Henry Aaron), a slugging percentage of .690 (still the all-time record), and 2,056 walks.

Part of the Ruth mystique was his behavior off the field. He once collapsed at a railroad station, said to be suffering from "world's biggest belly-ache" caused by his enormous appetite for food and beverage. He also often thumbed his nose at authority and was suspended at times by both the Yankees and Commissioner Kenesaw Mountain Landis for his off-the-field escapades. Ruth was to baseball what Muhammad Ali was to boxing and Michael Jordan was to basketball later on. But no one did more for a sport at a time when the sport really needed it than George Herman Ruth—the Babe.

As a Pitcher

Year	Team	W-L	ERA	G	IP	H	BB	SO
1914	Bos (A)	2-1	3.91	4	23	21	7	3
1915	Bos	18-8	2.44	32	217.2	166	85	112
1916	Bos	23-12	1.75	44	323.2	230	118	170
1917	Bos	24-13	2.01	41	326.1	244	108	128
1918	Bos	13-7	2.22	20	166.1	125	49	40
1919	Bos	9-5	2.97	17	133.1	148	58	30
1920	NY (A)	1-0	4.50	1	4	3	2	0
1921	NY	2-0	9.00	2	9	14	9	2
1930	NY	1-0	3.00	1	9	11	2	3
1933	NY	1-0	5.00	1	9	12	3	0
10 years		**94-46**	**2.28**	**163**	**1221.1**	**974**	**441**	**488**

World Series

Year	Team	W-L	ERA	G	IP	H	BB	SO
1916	Bos (A)	1-0	0.64	1	14	6	3	4
1918	Bos	2-0	1.06	2	17	13	7	4
2 years		**3-0**	**0.87**	**3**	**31**	**19**	**10**	**8**

As a Hitter

Year	Team	G	AB	R	H	D	T	HR	RBI	AVE.
1914	Bos (A)	5	10	1	2	1	0	0	2	.200
1915	Bos	42	92	16	29	10	1	4	21	.315
1916	Bos	67	136	18	37	5	3	3	15	.272
1917	Bos	52	123	14	40	6	3	2	12	.325
1918	Bos	95	317	50	95	26	11	11	66	.300
1919	Bos	130	432	103	139	34	12	29	114	.322
1920	NY	142	458	158	172	36	9	54	137	.376
1921	NY	152	540	177	204	44	16	59	171	.378
1922	NY	110	406	94	128	24	8	35	96	.315
1923	NY	152	522	151	205	45	13	41	130	.393
1924	NY	153	529	143	200	39	7	46	121	.378
1925	NY	98	359	61	104	12	2	25	66	.290

Year	Team	G	AB	R	H	D	T	HR	RBI	AVE.
1926	NY	152	495	139	184	30	5	47	146	.372
1927	NY	151	540	158	192	29	8	60	164	.356
1928	NY	154	536	163	173	29	8	54	142	.323
1929	NY	135	499	121	172	26	6	46	154	.345
1930	NY	145	518	150	186	28	9	49	153	.359
1931	NY	145	534	149	199	31	3	46	163	.373
1932	NY	133	457	120	156	13	5	41	137	.341
1933	NY	137	459	97	138	21	3	34	103	.301
1934	NY	125	365	78	105	17	4	22	84	.288
1935	Bos (N)	28	72	13	13	0	0	6	12	.181
22 years		**2503**	**8399**	**2174**	**2873**	**506**	**136**	**714**	**2209**	**.342**

Transactions: January 3, 1920: Sold to New York for $125,000 and a $300,000 loan to Boston owner Harry Frazee.

WORLD SERIES

Year	Team	G	AB	R	H	D	T	HR	RBI	AVE.
1915	Bos (A)	1	1	0	0	0	0	0	0	.000
1916	Bos	1	5	0	0	0	0	0	1	.000
1918	Bos	3	5	0	1	0	1	0	2	.200
1921	NY (A)	6	16	3	5	0	0	1	4	.313
1922	NY	5	17	1	2	1	0	0	1	.118
1923	NY	6	19	8	7	1	1	3	3	.368
1926	NY	7	20	6	6	0	0	4	5	.300
1927	NY	4	15	4	6	0	0	2	7	.400
1928	NY	4	16	9	10	3	0	3	4	.625
1932	NY	4	15	6	5	0	0	2	6	.333
10 years		**41**	**129**	**37**	**42**	**5**	**2**	**12**	**33**	**.326**

Nolan Lynn Ryan

Born January 31, 1947, in Refugio, Texas. 6'2", 195 lbs., bats right, throws right. Years in minor leagues: 3; Major League debut: September 11, 1966; Years in Major Leagues: 27. Elected to Hall of Fame: 1999. Nickname: The Ryan Express—actually a description of his fastball that was applied to him as well.

Nolan Ryan was a fireballing righthander who set Major League records in almost every category of pitching. He threw 7 no-hitters and 12 one-hitters in his 27-year career in which opposing batters had a cumulative batting average of .204. He broke in with the New York Mets in 1966 and was a part of the "Miracle Mets" 1969 World Series championship team. He got into one game—his only appearance ever in the fall classic. He then spent eight years with the California Angels, nine years with the Houston Astros and five with the Texas Rangers.

He holds Major League records for most career strikeouts, 5,714; most career walks, 2,795; most complete games allowing one hit or less, 19; most 300 strike-out seasons, 6; most 200 strikeout seasons, 15; most 100 strikeout seasons, 24; most games with 15 or more strikeouts, 26; most games with 10 or more strike-outs, 215; most seasons in Major Leagues, 27; most strikeouts in a season, 383. Ryan tied the Major League record (since broken by Roger Clemens and Kerry Wood) when he struck out 19 Boston Red Sox batters in a nine-inning game on August 12, 1974. He set the single-season strikeout record of 383 in 1973, the first season that the American League had designated hitters instead of having weak-hitting pitchers in the lineup. As Ryan got older, he got better in some ways. Early in his career, he was wild. He led the league in walks eight times. Twice he walked more than 200 batters in a season and ten times walked more than 100, but he never did it past the age of 36. Ryan had three games past the age of 40 when he struck out 16 or more batters.

He led the league 11 times in strikeouts, 8 times in walks. He is second on the all-time list in games started with 773—only Cy Young, with 815, had more. Ryan ranks fifth in innings pitched with 5,387, twelfth in wins with 324, and aver-aged 9.55 strikeouts per every nine innings pitched over his 27-year career. The ultimate irony is that despite all of the records, Ryan never won a Cy Young Award. His best opportunity might have been 1974 when, pitching for the Angels, he won 22 games, led the league in innings pitched with 333, strikeouts with 367, had a 2.89 earned run average, 26 complete games; averaged 10 strikeouts per nine innings while allowing only six hits, and threw a no-hitter—all for a last-place team. The Cy Young Award that year went to Jim "Catfish" Hunter of Oakland's championship team.

Year	Team	W-L	ERA	G	IP	H	BB	SO
1966	NY (N)	0-1	15.00	2	3	5	3	6
1968	NY	6-9	3.09	21	134	93	75	133
1969	NY	6-3	3.54	25	89	60	53	92
1970	NY	7-11	3.41	27	132	86	97	125
1971	NY	10-14	3.97	30	152	125	116	137
1972	Cal	19-16	2.28	39	284	166	157	329
1973	Cal	21-16	2.87	41	326	238	162	383
1974	Cal	22-16	2.89	42	333	221	202	367
1975	Cal	14-12	3.45	28	198	152	204	341
1976	Cal	17-18	3.36	39	284	193	183	327
1977	Cal	19-16	2.77	37	299	198	204	341
1978	Cal	10-13	3.71	31	235	183	148	260
1979	Cal	16-14	3.59	34	223	169	114	223
1980	Hous	11-10	3.35	35	234	205	98	200
1981	Hous	11-5	1.69	21	149	99	68	140
1982	Hous	16-12	3.16	35	250.1	196	109	245
1983	Hous	14-9	2.98	29	196.1	134	101	183
1984	Hous	12-11	3.04	30	183.2	143	69	197
1985	Hous	10-12	3.80	35	232	205	95	209
1986	Hous	12-8	3.34	30	178	119	82	194
1987	Hous	8-16	2.76	34	211.2	154	87	270

Year	Team	W-L	ERA	G	IP	H	BB	SO
1988	Hous	12-11	3.52	33	220	186	87	228
1989	Texas	16-10	3.20	32	239.1	162	98	301
1990	Texas	13-9	3.44	30	204	137	74	232
1991	Texas	12-6	2.91	27	173	102	72	203
1992	Texas	5-9	3.72	27	157.1	138	69	157
1993	Texas	5-5	4.88	13	66.1	54	40	46
27 years		324-292	3.19	807	5387	3923	2795	5714

Transactions: Dec. 10, 1971: Traded with Don Rose, Leroy Stanton and Francisco Estrada to California Angels for Jim Fregosi. Nov. 19, 1979: Signed as free agent with Houston Astros. Dec. 7, 1988: Signed as free agent with Texas Rangers.

DIVISIONAL PLAYOFF

Year	Team	W-L	ERA	G	IP	H	BB	SO
1981	Hous	1-1	1.80	2	15	6	3	14

LEAGUE CHAMPIONSHIP SERIES

Year	Team	W-L	ERA	G	IP	H	BB	SO
1969	NY (N)	1-0	2.57	1	7	3	2	7
1979	Cal	0-0	1.29	1	7	4	3	8
1980	Hous	0-0	5.40	2	13.1	16	3	14
3 years		1-0	3.62	4	27.1	23	8	29

WORLD SERIES

Year	Team	W-L	ERA	G	IP	H	BB	SO
1969	NY (N)	0-0	0.00	1	2.1	1	2	3

Byrum Saam

Broadcaster. Elected to Hall of Fame: 1990.

By Saam has the distinction of broadcasting more losing games than anyone else—because he was the play-by-play man for the Philadelphia A's and Phillies from 1938 to 1975. During his tenure behind the mike, the Phils and A's finished last 19 times.

He had a habit—a lovable habit to his fans—of tripping over some of his words. Indeed, he signed on for his first broadcast by saying, "Hello, Byrum Saam, this is everyone speaking..."

Harold N. Saidt

Sportswriter. Elected to Hall of Fame: 1992. Nickname: Bus—origin unknown.

Bus Saidt was a sportswriter and columnist for the *Trenton (N.J.) Times* from 1967 until his death in 1989. His primary "beat" was the Philadelphia Phillies. He had a reputation for forthright reporting and columns in which he was not afraid to express strong opinions and criticisms.

Saidt's background was in acccounting. He worked for nearly 25 years as an accountant for the city of Trenton. But he had a love of sports, particularly baseball, that landed him a job as a radio sportscaster.

He was so well received as a sports commentator that in 1964, the *Trentonian* newspaper hired Saidt as a columnist. He was 45 at the time. He moved to the *Times* in 1967.

H.G. Salsinger

Sportswriter. Elected to Hall of Fame: 1968.

H.G. Salsinger was sportseditor of the *Detroit News* and covered the Tigers for nearly 50 years. His career allowed him to cover Tiger greats like Ty Cobb, Wahoo Sam Crawford, Harry Heilmann, Charlie Gehringer, Hank Greenberg, and Mickey Cochrane; the great pennant races of 1934, 1935 and 1945, all won by the Tigers; and the greats who played against the Tigers such as Babe Ruth, Lou Gehrig, the great Philadelphia A's teams and, of course, the Yankees. He died 10 years before his election and induction into the Hall of Fame.

Raymond William Schalk

Born August 12, 1892, in Harvel, Illinois; died May 19, 1970, in Chicago, Illinois. 5'7", 155 lbs., bats right, throws right. Years in minor leagues: 3; Major League debut: August 11, 1912; Years in Major Leagues: 18. Elected to Hall of Fame: 1955. Nickname: Cracker—origin unknown, even to Schalk.

Ray Schalk was a great defensive catcher for the Chicago White Sox who later managed the team. He was the first catcher to back up plays at first base and third base. He was so aggressive defensively that he once made a putout at second base, where he had run from his catcher's position to take a throw from the outfield.

He led American League catchers in fielding percentage eight times and caught 100 or more games in 12 seasons—11 of them in succession. In 1920, Schalk accomplished something behind the plate that has only happened one other time. He caught four 20-game winners: Red Faber, Ed Cicotte, Lefty Williams and Dickie

Kerr. Some catchers go through their entire careers without being behind the plate on a no-hitter. Schalk caught four no-hitters between 1914 and 1922, including Charlie Robertson's perfect game for the White Sox in 1922. The other no-hitters were by Jim Scott, Joe Benz and Cicotte. No catcher has ever caught more no-hitters. Schalk appreciated the catcher's role in such achievements, and after his retirement would send telegrams to catchers involved in them.

Schalk also had a strong throwing arm. He cut down so many base runners and base stealers that he holds the American League record for assists by a catcher. He was an adequate hitter, but, unquestionably, his defensive prowess, his handling of pitchers, his leadership and his integrity paved the way for Schalk's entrance to the Hall of Fame. He is believed to be the first White Sox player in the 1919 World Series to suspect that some of his teammates weren't playing as hard as they could. After eight players were suspended in the "Black Sox Scandal," proving Schalk's suspicions were correct, the catcher refused to talk about it for the next 50 years. He maintained, however, that the White Sox would have still won the World Series had Faber not been injured.

Year	Team	G	AB	R	H	D	T	HR	RBI	AVE.
1912	Chi (A)	23	63	7	18	2	0	0	8	.286
1913	Chi	129	401	38	98	15	5	1	38	.244
1914	Chi	135	392	30	106	13	2	0	36	.270
1915	Chi	135	413	46	110	14	4	1	54	.266
1916	Chi	129	410	36	95	12	9	0	41	.232
1917	Chi	140	424	48	96	12	5	2	51	.226
1918	Chi	108	333	35	73	6	3	0	22	.219
1919	Chi	131	394	57	111	9	3	0	34	.282
1920	Chi	151	485	64	131	25	5	1	61	.270
1921	Chi	128	416	32	105	24	4	0	47	.252
1922	Chi	142	442	57	124	22	3	4	60	.281
1923	Chi	123	382	42	87	12	2	1	44	.228
1924	Chi	57	153	15	30	4	2	1	11	.196
1925	Chi	125	343	44	94	18	1	0	52	.274
1926	Chi	82	226	26	60	9	1	0	32	.265
1927	Chi	16	26	2	6	2	0	0	2	.231
1928	Chi	2	1	0	1	0	0	0	1	1.000
1929	NY (N)	5	2	0	0	0	0	0	0	.000
18 years		**1761**	**5306**	**579**	**1345**	**199**	**49**	**11**	**594**	**.253**

WORLD SERIES

Year	Team	G	AB	R	H	D	T	HR	RBI	AVE.
1917	Chi (A)	6	19	1	5	0	0	0	0	.263
1919	Chi	8	23	1	7	0	0	0	2	.304
2 years		**14**	**42**	**2**	**12**	**0**	**0**	**0**	**2**	**.286**

Michael Jack Schmidt

Born September 27, 1949, in Dayton, Ohio. 6'2", 195 lbs., bats right, throws right. Years in minor leagues: 2; Major League debut: September 12, 1972; Years in Major Leagues: 18. Elected to Hall of Fame: 1995. Nickname: None.

Mike Schmidt edges out Eddie Mathews as the best power-hitting third baseman in National League history with his 509 homers as a third baseman and 548 overall, which is seventh on the all-time list. His offensive statistics are awesome. Schmidt led the National League in home runs eight times, a record. He won the National League's Most Valuable Player Award three times, tying him with Stan Musial and Roy Campanella for the National League record.

He hit 35 or more home runs in 11 seasons, ranking him second only to Babe Ruth in that category. Ruth did it 12 times. Schmidt hit 30 or more 13 times, placing him second to Henry Aaron who achieved it 15 times. He drove in more than 90 runs in 13 of his 18 Major League seasons and topped the 100 RBI mark nine times. Schmidt played his entire career with the Philadelphia Phillies and led them to division championships in 1976, 1977 and 1978, but they failed to get in the World Series each time. In 1980 and 1983, they made it all the way to the World Series. In between, in 1981, the strike-split season, the Phillies made it to divisional playoffs. Schmidt hit .381 with two home runs to become the MVP of the 1981 World Series.

Schmidt hit four consecutive home runs twice in his career. On April 17, 1976, he hit four in one game against the Cubs in Wrigley Field. Three years later, on July 6–7, 1979, it took him two games. He homered in his last at-bat on July 6 and in his first three at-bats on July 7. In addition to all of this, Schmidt was a great fielder who won 10 Gold Glove Awards. In 1974, his 404 assists at third base set a National League record. In 1977, he recorded 396 assists, second only to his mark three years earlier. Forty-two games into the 1989 season, Schmidt retired. He was still elected by the fans to be the starting third baseman in the All-Star game, an honor he declined to accept.

Year	Team	G	AB	R	H	D	T	HR	RBI	AVE.
1972	Phil	13	34	2	7	0	0	1	3	.206
1973	Phil	132	367	43	72	11	0	18	52	.196
1974	Phil	162	568	108	160	28	7	36	116	.282
1975	Phil	158	562	93	140	34	3	38	95	.249
1976	Phil	160	584	112	153	31	4	38	107	.262
1977	Phil	154	544	114	149	27	11	38	101	.274
1978	Phil	145	513	93	129	27	2	21	78	.251
1979	Phil	160	541	109	137	25	4	45	114	.253
1980	Phil	150	548	104	157	25	8	48	121	.286
1981	Phil	102	354	78	112	19	2	31	91	.316
1982	Phil	148	514	108	144	26	3	35	87	.280
1983	Phil	154	534	104	136	16	4	40	109	.255
1984	Phil	151	528	93	146	23	3	36	106	.277

Year	Team	G	AB	R	H	D	T	HR	RBI	AVE.
1985	Phil	158	549	89	152	31	5	33	93	.277
1986	Phil	160	552	97	160	29	1	37	119	.290
1987	Phil	147	522	88	153	28	0	35	113	.293
1988	Phil	108	390	52	97	21	2	12	62	.249
1989	Phil	42	148	19	30	7	0	6	28	.203
18 years		2404	8352	1506	2234	408	59	548	1595	.267

DIVISIONAL PLAYOFF

Year	Team	G	AB	R	H	D	T	HR	RBI	AVE.
1981	Phil	5	16	3	4	1	0	1	2	.250

LEAGUE CHAMPIONSHIP SERIES

Year	Team	G	AB	R	H	D	T	HR	RBI	AVE.
1976	Phil	3	13	1	4	2	0	0	2	.308
1977	Phil	4	16	2	1	0	0	0	1	.063
1978	Phil	4	15	1	3	2	0	0	1	.200
1980	Phil	5	24	1	5	1	0	0	1	.208
1983	Phil	4	15	5	7	2	0	1	2	.467
5 years		20	83	10	20	7	0	1	7	.241

WORLD SERIES

Year	Team	G	AB	R	H	D	T	HR	RBI	AVE.
1980	Phil	6	21	6	8	1	0	2	7	.381
1983	Phil	5	20	0	1	0	0	0	0	.050
2 years		11	41	6	9	1	0	2	7	.220

Albert Fred Schoendienst

Born February 2, 1923, in Germantown, Illinois. 6'1", 192 lbs., bats both, throws right. Years in minor leagues: 3; Major League debut: 1945; Years in Major Leagues: 19. Elected to Hall of Fame: 1989. Nickname: Red—for the color of his hair.

Switch-hitting Red Schoendienst was one of the best second basemen in baseball for almost two decades. He hit over .300 seven times, his tops being .342 in 1953 when Brooklyn's Carl Furillo edged him for the batting title with a .344 average. Schoendienst was not a spectacular fielder but was consistently better than anyone else in the National League. He led the league in fielding percentage seven times, which is still a National League record. The redhead was not a serious home run threat, yet his 14th inning shot in the 1950 All-Star Game provided the winning margin for the National League in its 4–3 victory at Comiskey Park. Schoendienst showed up at Sportsman Park in St. Louis in 1942 for a tryout with the Cardinals. It was the first time he had ever been in a Major League park. The Cardinals liked what they saw and signed him. He played parts of three seasons in the minor leagues and then came up in 1945 when the Cardinals, like many other teams, found their ranks depleted because of the war. Schoendienst showed he belonged, hitting .278 and leading the National League in stolen bases with 26.

He came to the Major Leagues as a shortstop, but the Cardinals already had Marty Marion. So first-year Cardinal manager Eddie Dyer took his first-year infielder and moved him to second base, a position he played in 1,834 Major League games. The Cardinals decided to go for a youth movement and traded Schoendienst to the Giants in 1956. The Giants peddled him to the Milwaukee Braves a year later, and he proved to be one of the factors that finally got the Braves over the hump. They won the pennant and beat the New York Yankees in the World Series in 1957, won the pennant again in 1958 and lost to the Yankees in the World Series.

Schoendienst felt weak at the end of the 1958 season and in the World Series. When the season was over, he found out why—he had contracted tuberculosis. He missed almost all of the 1959 season, playing in only five games for the Braves. After playing in 68 games in 1960, the Braves shipped him back to the Cardinals where he finished out his career. On November 19, 1964, Schoendienst succeeded Johnny Keane as Cardinal manager, a job he held longer than any other manager in Cardinal history—13 years. The Cardinals won National League pennants in 1967 and 1968 and the World Series in 1967. In all, he won 1,028 games as Cardinal manager. His tenure in baseball as player, manager and coach totals more than 50 consecutive years.

Year	Team	G	AB	R	H	D	T	HR	RBI	AVE.
1945	StL (N)	137	565	89	157	22	6	1	47	.278
1946	StL	142	606	94	170	28	5	0	34	.281
1947	StL	151	659	91	167	25	9	3	48	.253
1948	StL	119	408	64	111	21	4	4	36	.272
1949	StL	151	640	102	190	25	2	3	54	.297
1950	StL	153	642	81	177	43	9	7	63	.276
1951	StL	135	553	88	160	32	7	6	54	.289
1952	StL	152	620	91	188	40	7	7	67	.303
1953	StL	146	564	107	193	35	5	15	79	.342
1954	StL	148	610	98	192	38	8	5	79	.315
1955	StL	145	553	68	148	21	3	11	51	.268
1956	StL-NY	132	487	61	147	21	3	2	29	.302
1957	NY-Mil	150	648	91	200	31	8	15	65	.309
1958	Mil	106	427	47	112	23	1	1	24	.262
1959	Mil	5	3	0	0	0	0	0	0	.000
1960	Mil	68	226	21	58	9	1	1	19	.257
1961	StL	72	120	9	36	9	0	1	12	.300
1962	StL	98	143	21	43	4	0	2	12	.301
1963	StL	6	5	0	0	0	0	0	0	.000
19 years		**2216**	**8479**	**1223**	**2449**	**427**	**78**	**84**	**773**	**.289**

Transactions: June 14, 1956: Traded to New York Giants with Jackie Brandt, Bobby Stephenson, Dick Littlefield and Bill Sarni for Alvin Dark, Ray Katt, Don Liddle and Whitey Lockman. June 15, 1957: Traded to Milwaukee for Danny O'Connell, Ray Crone and Bobby Thomson.

WORLD SERIES

Year	Team	G	AB	R	H	D	T	HR	RBI	AVE.
1946	StL	7	30	3	7	1	0	0	1	.233
1957	Mil	5	18	0	5	1	0	0	2	.278
1958	Mil	7	30	5	9	3	1	0	0	.300
3 years		19	78	8	21	5	1	0	3	.269

Vin Scully

Broadcaster. Elected to Hall of Fame: 1992.

Vin Scully started his Major League Baseball broadcasting career at age 22 in Ebbetts Field in Brooklyn under the watchful eye of Red Barber. Scully is known for the vivid word pictures he paints as he describes the action on the field. He has done numerous network broadcasts and has won most of the major broadcasting awards, but he is best known as the voice of the Dodgers for more than 40 years. He was once voted the most memorable personality in Dodger franchise history.

George Thomas Seaver

Born November 17, 1944, in Fresno, California. 6'1", 210 lbs., bats right, throws right. Years in minor leagues: 1; Major League debut: April 13, 1967; Years in Major Leagues: 20. Elected to Hall of Fame: 1992. Nickname: Tom Terrific—given to him by New York sportswriters during the 1969 season when the "Miracle Mets" won the world championship.

Tom Seaver changed the New York Mets from one of baseball's worst teams to World Series champions in just three years. He played on Mets National League championship teams in 1969 and 1973 (the '69 team was the World Series winner) but had memorable moments playing for two other teams as well.

Seaver threw the only no-hitter of his career while pitching for Cincinnati and notched his 300th career win as a starter for the Chicago White Sox on August 4, 1985, at the age of 40. But he made his mark with the Mets. He was the National League Rookie of the Year in 1967 and strung together ten straight seasons of 200 or more strikeouts. He finished with 3,272 strikeouts in the National League, a league record for righthanded pitchers. His career strikeout total of 3,640 ranks him in fourth place all-time. He was 25–7 in the pennant-winning year of 1969 when he won the first of his three Cy Young awards. He won 311 games in his career, and in 16 of his 20 seasons his winning percentage was better than his team's.

On June 16, 1978, pitching for Cincinnati, he tossed a no-hitter against the St. Louis Cardinals, but Seaver said that wasn't his best game. The best he ever pitched came nine years earlier when Seaver had a perfect game going against the Cubs. Pinch hitter Jimmy Qualls broke it up with two outs in the ninth inning. On April 22, 1970, Seaver tied the then–Major League record when he struck out 19 San Diego Padres, finishing with 10 straight strikeouts—also a Major League record. He had the classic combination of a powerful arm with good control. He had an unusual stride in his delivery so that his right knee would touch the ground on almost every pitch. Seaver was elected to the Hall of Fame in 1992 with the highest percentage of ballots ever.

Year	Team	W-L	ERA	G	IP	H	BB	SO
1967	NY (N)	16-13	2.76	35	251	224	78	170
1968	NY	16-12	2.20	36	278	224	48	205
1969	NY	25-7	2.21	36	273.1	202	82	208
1970	NY	18-12	2.81	37	291	230	83	283
1971	NY	20-10	1.76	36	286	210	61	289
1972	NY	21-12	2.92	35	262	215	77	249
1973	NY	19-10	2.08	36	290	219	64	251
1974	NY	11-11	3.20	32	236	199	75	201
1975	NY	22-9	2.38	36	280	217	88	243
1976	NY	14-11	2.59	35	271	211	77	235
1977	NY-Cin	21-6	2.58	33	261.1	199	66	196
1978	Cin	16-14	2.87	36	260	218	89	226
1979	Cin	16-6	3.14	32	215	187	61	131
1980	Cin	10-8	3.64	26	168	140	59	101
1981	Cin	14-2	2.55	23	166	120	66	87
1982	Cin	5-13	5.50	21	111.1	136	44	62
1983	NY	9-14	3.55	34	231	201	86	135
1984	Chi	15-11	3.95	34	236.2	216	61	131
1985	Chi	16-11	3.16	35	239	223	69	134
1986	Chi-Bos	7-13	4.04	28	176	180	56	103
20 years		311-205	2.86	656	4782	3971	1390	3640

Transactions: June 15, 1977: Traded to Cincinnati for Pat Zachry, Doug Flynn, Steve Henderson and Dan Norman. Dec. 16, 1982: Traded to New York Mets for Charlie Puleo, Lloyd McClendon and Jason Felice. January 20, 1984: Claimed by Chicago in compensation draft.

LEAGUE CHAMPIONSHIP SERIES

Year	Team	W-L	ERA	G	IP	H	BB	SO
1969	NY (N)	1-0	6.43	1	7	8	3	2
1973	NY	1-1	1.62	2	16.2	13	5	17
1979	Cin	0-0	2.25	1	8	5	2	5
3 years		2-1	2.84	4	31.2	26	10	24

WORLD SERIES

Year	Team	W-L	ERA	G	IP	H	BB	SO
1969	NY (N)	1-1	3.00	2	15	12	3	9
1973	NY	0-1	2.40	2	15	13	3	18
2 years		1-2	2.70	4	30	25	6	27

Frank Gibson Selee

Born October 26, 1859, in Amherst, New Hampshire; died July 5, 1909, in Denver, Colorado. Years in Major Leagues: 16 (as manager). Elected to Hall of Fame: 1999.

Frank Selee is regarded as one of baseball's greatest managers. Much of his career was before the start of the 20th century—before the advent of the World Series. He was forced to retire because of illness in the 1905 season, but the Chicago Cubs team he developed won National League pennants in 1906, 1907, 1908 and 1910. Before managing the Cubs, Selee managed a Boston team that had a .607 winning percentage over a 12-year span. When he took over the Cubs in 1902, he moved Frank Chance from catcher to first base, acquired Joe Tinker from Portland and Johnny Evers from Troy, N.Y., thus establishing the fabled infield combination of Tinker-to-Evers-to-Chance. When he retired, Selee had a winning percentage of .598—which ranks fourth all time—and had five pennant winners in 16 years.

Year	Team	Record	Standing
1890	Bos (N)	76-57	Fifth
1891	Bos	87-51	First
1892*	Bos	52-22	First
1892*	Bos	50-26	Second
1893	Bos	86-43	First
1894	Bos	83-49	Third
1895	Bos	71-60	Fifth
1896	Bos	74-57	Fourth
1897	Bos	93-39	First
1898	Bos	102-47	First
1899	Bos	95-97	Second
1900	Bos	66-72	Fourth
1901	Bos	69-69	Fifth
1902	Chi (N)	68-69	Fifth
1903	Chi	82-56	Third
1904	Chi	93-60	Second
1905	Chi	37-28	Fourth
16 years		1284-862	

*1892 season was split into two seasons

Joseph Wheeler Sewell

Born October 9, 1898, in Titus, Alabama; died March 6, 1990, in Mobile, Alabama. 5'7", 155 lbs., bats left, throws right. Years in minor league: 1; Major League debut: September 10, 1920; Years in Major Leagues: 14. Elected to Hall of Fame: 1977. Nickname: None.

Joe Sewell was the toughest man to strike out in baseball history. In 14 seasons, he came to bat 7,132 times and fanned only 114 times, an average of one strikeout every 63 at-bats—and less than 10 strikeouts a year. He once went 115 consecutive games without going down on strikes. He had two years in which he only struck out three times, and three others when he struck out just four times.

His greatest day at the plate came in 1932 when Sewell, a lefthanded batter, went 5-for-5 against Lefty Grove, one of the greatest lefthanded pitchers of all time. Sewell played 11 years for the Cleveland Indians and three with the New York Yankees and finished with a lifetime batting average of .312. In addition to being tough to strike out, he was tough to get out of the lineup. Sewell played in 1,103 consecutive games, which would have been much longer had he not been benched for two games early in his career when manager Tris Speaker wanted to juggle his lineup.

Sewell entered the Major Leagues under the worst of circumstances. In 1920, he was playing shortstop for New Orleans in the Southern Association when Cleveland shortstop Ray Chapman was beaned by the Yankees' Carl Mays and died from the injury he received. To add more pressure, the Indians were in a hot pennant race at the time. Sewell came up and hit .329 in 22 games to help the Indians win the American League championship. He hit over .300 in 10 of his 14 seasons and led American League shortstops in fielding twice.

Year	Team	G	AB	R	H	D	T	HR	RBI	AVE.
1920	Cleve	22	70	14	23	4	1	0	12	.329
1921	Cleve	154	572	101	182	36	12	4	93	.318
1922	Cleve	153	558	80	167	28	7	2	83	.299
1923	Cleve	153	553	98	195	41	10	3	109	.353
1924	Cleve	153	594	99	188	45	5	4	104	.316
1925	Cleve	155	608	78	204	37	7	1	98	.336
1926	Cleve	154	578	91	187	41	5	4	85	.324
1927	Cleve	153	569	83	180	48	5	1	92	.316
1928	Cleve	155	588	79	190	40	2	4	70	.323
1929	Cleve	152	578	90	182	38	3	7	73	.315
1930	Cleve	109	353	44	102	17	6	0	48	.289
1931	NY (A)	130	482	103	146	22	1	6	64	.302
1932	NY	125	503	95	137	21	3	11	68	.272
1933	NY	135	524	87	143	18	1	2	54	.273
14 years		1903	7132	1141	2226	436	68	49	1053	.312

WORLD SERIES

Year	Team	G	AB	R	H	D	T	HR	RBI	AVE.
1920	Cleve	7	23	0	4	0	0	0	0	.174
1932	NY	4	15	4	5	1	0	0	3	.333
2 years		11	38	4	9	1	0	0	3	.237

Aloysius Harry Simmons

Born May 22, 1902, in Milwaukee, Wisconsin; died May 26, 1956, in Milwaukee, Wisconsin. 6', 210 lbs., bats right, throws right. Years in minor leagues: 3; Major League debut: April 15, 1924; Years in Major Leagues: 20. Elected to Hall of Fame: 1953. Nickname: Bucketfoot—a moniker that Simmons hated, bestowed upon him because of a batting stance in which he "stepped in the bucket," planting his back foot while his front foot would stride toward third base as he swung.

Al Simmons was the left fielder on one of baseball's early dynasties: Connie Mack's Philadelphia A's of 1929–31 that won three championships. Simmons contributed batting averages of .365, .381 and .390. In 1930, Washington owner Clark Griffith kept track of Simmons' hitting because he killed the Senators so often. Griffith said Simmons hit 14 home runs in the eighth or ninth innings that affected the outcome of ball games. Mack broke up the dynasty after the 1931 season to help him through the Depression. Simmons was one of the casualties, going to the White Sox in a cash deal. He bounced around with several clubs after that, and wound up in another World Series, playing for Cincinnati in 1939. Two of his most famous at-bats had far different outcomes. In 1929, the Cubs were beating the A's 8–0 in the seventh inning when Simmons broke the shutout with a home run. Later in the same inning, he singled and scored the A's 10th run of the inning—the most productive offensive inning in World Series history—to help seal an amazing comeback victory.

Five years later, he was one of five future Hall of Famers that Carl Hubbell struck out in succession in the All-Star game. The others were Babe Ruth, Lou Gehrig, Jimmie Foxx and Joe Cronin. Simmons had 11 consecutive seasons in which he hit over .300 and drove in over 100 runs. He finished with a lifetime batting average of .334 and had more hits, 2,927, than any other righthanded batter in the American League until Al Kaline surpassed him. He batted .329 in four World Series appearances and .462 in three All-Star games.

It was a stellar career for a man whose batting stance was so unorthodox. Simmons "stepped in the bucket" every time he swung the bat. Simmons was sensitive about criticism of his stance and didn't like his "Bucketfoot" nickname because he thought it was demeaning. He thought his results were what counted, and he did get results.

Year	Team	G	AB	R	H	D	T	HR	RBI	AVE.
1924	Phil (A)	152	594	69	183	31	9	8	102	.308
1925	Phil	153	658	122	253	43	12	24	129	.384
1926	Phil	147	581	90	199	53	10	19	109	.343
1927	Phil	106	406	86	159	36	11	15	108	.392
1928	Phil	119	464	78	163	33	9	15	107	.351
1929	Phil	143	581	114	212	41	9	34	157	.365
1930	Phil	138	554	152	211	41	16	36	165	.381
1931	Phil	128	513	105	200	37	13	22	128	.390
1932	Phil	154	670	144	216	28	9	35	151	.322
1933	Chi (A)	146	605	85	200	29	10	14	119	.331
1934	Chi	138	558	102	192	36	7	18	104	.344
1935	Chi	128	525	68	140	22	7	16	79	.267
1936	Det	143	568	96	186	38	6	13	112	.327
1937	Wash	103	419	60	117	21	10	8	84	.279
1938	Wash	125	470	79	142	23	6	21	95	.302
1939	Bos-Cin	102	351	39	96	17	5	7	44	.274
1940	Phil (A)	37	81	7	25	4	0	1	19	.309
1941	Phil	9	24	1	3	1	0	0	1	.125
1943	Bos (A)	40	133	9	27	5	0	1	12	.203
1944	Phil (A)	4	6	1	3	0	0	0	2	.500
20 years		2215	8761	1507	2927	539	149	307	1827	.334

Transactions: Sept. 28, 1932: Sold with Jimmy Dykes and Mule Haas to Chicago for $100,000. Dec. 10, 1935: Sold to Detroit for $75,000. April 4, 1937: Sold to Washington for $15,000. Dec. 29, 1938: Sold to Boston for $3,000. Aug. 31, 1939: Sold to Cincinnati (amount not known).

WORLD SERIES

Year	Team	G	AB	R	H	D	T	HR	RBI	AVE.
1929	Phil (A)	5	20	6	6	1	0	2	5	.300
1930	Phil	6	22	4	8	2	0	2	4	.364
1932	Phil	7	27	4	9	2	0	2	8	.333
1939	Cin	1	4	1	1	1	0	0	0	.250
4 years		19	73	15	24	6	0	6	17	.329

George Harold Sisler

Born March 24, 1893, in Manchester, Ohio; died March 26, 1973, in St. Louis, Missouri. 5'10", 170 lbs., bats left, throws left. Years in minor leagues: None; Major League debut: June 28, 1915; Years in Major Leagues: 15. Elected to Hall of Fame: 1939. Nickname: Gorgeous George—a name sportswriters called him because of his great ability in all phases of baseball.

George Sisler was the best ballplayer the St. Louis Browns ever had and, for a few years, was so good that even his contemporary, Ty Cobb, called him a near-perfect ballplayer. Sisler broke in with the Browns in 1915 and soon established himself as a great hitter. In his first four years, he averaged .338. Then, the dead ball era ended, and Sisler hit .407, .371 and .420 from 1920 to 1922, when he averaged 239 hits per year. His total of 257 hits in 1920 is still the Major League record. In 1922, he had a 41-game hitting streak—only Joe DiMaggio, Pete Rose and Wee Willie Keeler have done better. His 1920 season may be the best season any ballplayer ever had. Sisler batted .407, had 49 doubles, 18 triples, 19 home runs, 42 stolen bases, 122 RBIs and 137 runs scored. He played every inning of every game of the 154-game schedule.

Amazingly, Sisler came to the Major Leagues as a pitcher, not a hitter. Branch Rickey, later to become a great general manager, was Sisler's first field manager. In one of his first games, he outdueled Washington's Walter Johnson, 2–1. His prowess with the bat caused his transformation to a first baseman, and he excelled defensively at his new position.

Two defensive plays demonstrate his quick thinking and quick reflexes. In one game, he made a good stop of a hard hit ball and lobbed the ball toward first base, where he thought the pitcher would be covering. The pitcher wasn't, so Sisler scampered and caught his own toss to make the putout. In another game, Sisler was credited with an unassisted double play when he fielded a squeeze bunt, tagged the batter and then tagged the runner coming in from third base. In 1923 Sisler contracted a sinus infection that gave him double vision, forcing him to miss the whole season. He returned in 1924 and had a couple of good years but never returned to the form that made him one of baseball's greatest. He was the Browns' player-manager from 1924 to 1926. Sisler retired after the 1930 season.

Year	Team	G	AB	R	H	D	T	HR	RBI	AVE.
1915	StL (A)	81	274	28	78	10	2	3	29	.285
1916	StL	151	580	83	177	21	11	4	76	.305
1917	StL	135	539	60	190	30	9	2	52	.353
1918	StL	114	452	69	154	21	9	2	41	.341
1919	StL	132	511	96	180	31	15	10	83	.352
1920	StL	154	631	137	257	49	18	19	122	.407
1921	StL	138	582	125	216	38	18	11	104	.371
1922	StL	142	586	134	246	42	18	8	105	.420
1924	StL	151	636	94	194	27	10	9	74	.305
1925	StL	150	649	100	224	21	15	12	105	.345
1926	StL	150	613	78	178	21	12	7	71	.290
1927	StL	149	614	87	201	32	8	5	97	.327
1928	Wsh-Bos (N)	138	540	72	179	27	4	4	70	.331
1929	Bos	154	629	67	205	40	9	1	79	.326
1930	Bos	116	431	54	133	15	7	3	67	.309
15 years		**2055**	**8267**	**1284**	**2812**	**425**	**165**	**100**	**1175**	**.340**

Transactions: Dec. 14, 1927: Sold to Washington for $25,000. May 27, 1928: Sold to Boston for $7,500.

Enos Bradsher Slaughter

Born April 27, 1916, in Roxboro, North Carolina. 5'9", 190 lbs., bats left, throws right. Years in minor leagues: 3. Major League debut: April 19, 1938. Years in Major Leagues: 19. Elected to Hall of Fame: 1985. Nickname: Country—a name given to him by his minor league manager Burt Shotton at Columbus because of his background as a country boy.

Enos Slaughter was a career .300 hitter—.300 exactly, in fact—but he is best known for his hustle. Long before Pete Rose became "Charlie Hustle" in the Major Leagues, Slaughter was synonymous with hustle. His race home all the way from first base on a hit by Harry Walker in the seventh game of the 1946 World Series was the winning run for the Cardinals and solidified Slaughter's reputation for all-out play. He helped the Cardinals win two pennants in the 1940s. When he was traded to the Yankees in 1954, it broke his heart to leave his beloved Cardinals, but even as an aging ballplayer, he was still hustling and helped the Yankees to three championships.

Slaughter had ten seasons in which he hit over .300 and led the league in RBIs once and in triples twice. He broke in with the Cardinals in 1938 in the last days of the Gas House Gang and hit .276. The next year, he began his stronghold on .300 hitting with a mark of .320. His best year was in 1946 when he had his career high in home runs with 18 and in RBIs with 130, which was also the Major League high. Like many players in his era, Slaughter lost two years of playing time to military service.

Year	Team	G	AB	R	H	D	T	HR	RBI	AVE.
1938	StL (N)	112	395	59	109	20	10	8	58	.276
1939	StL	149	604	95	193	52	5	12	86	.320
1940	StL	140	516	96	158	25	13	17	73	.306
1941	StL	113	425	71	132	22	9	13	76	.311
1942	StL	152	591	100	188	31	17	13	98	.318
1946	StL	156	609	100	183	30	8	18	130	.300
1947	StL	147	551	100	162	31	13	10	86	.294
1948	StL	146	549	91	176	27	11	11	90	.321
1949	StL	151	568	92	191	34	13	13	96	.336
1950	StL	148	556	82	161	26	7	10	101	.290
1951	StL	123	409	48	115	17	8	4	64	.281
1952	StL	140	510	73	153	17	12	11	101	.300
1953	StL	143	492	64	143	34	9	6	89	.291
1954	NY (N)	69	125	19	31	4	2	1	19	.248
1955	NY-KC	118	276	50	87	12	4	5	35	.315
1956	KC-NY	115	306	52	86	18	5	2	27	.281
1957	NY	96	209	24	53	7	1	5	34	.254
1958	NY	77	138	21	42	4	1	4	19	.304
1959	NY-Mil	85	117	10	20	2	0	6	22	.171
19 years		2380	7946	1247	2383	413	148	169	1304	.300

Transactions: April 11, 1954: Traded to New York Yankees for Bill Virdon, Mel Wright and Emil Tellinger. May 11, 1955: Traded with Johnny Sain to Kansas City for Sonny Dixon and cash. Aug. 25, 1956: Sold to New York Yankees for waiver price. Sept. 12, 1959: Sold to Milwaukee Braves for waiver price.

WORLD SERIES

Year	Team	G	AB	R	H	D	T	HR	RBI	AVE.
1942	StL (N)	5	19	3	5	1	0	1	2	.263
1946	StL	7	25	5	8	1	1	1	2	.320
1956	NY (A)	6	20	6	7	0	0	1	4	.350
1957	NY	5	12	2	3	1	0	0	0	.250
1958	NY	4	3	1	0	0	0	0	0	.000
5 years		27	79	17	23	3	1	3	8	.291

Ken Smith

Sportswriter. Elected to Hall of Fame: 1983.

Ken Smith was a sportswriter who covered Lou Gehrig in both the minor and Major Leagues and was later a director of the National Baseball Hall of Fame. His career as a New York sportswriter covered the era of Ruth and Gehrig to Mantle and Maris. He wrote sports for New York newspapers from 1925 to 1962. Prior to that, he wrote for the *Hartford (Conn.) Courant*, reporting on the Hartford ball club when Gehrig and Leo Durocher were on the team.

Smith worked for the *New York Evening Mail* from 1925 to 1931, then moved to the *New York Mirror* in 1931 and remained there until the paper folded in 1963. He then took on responsibilities as director of the Hall of Fame for the next 13 years.

He was secretary of the Baseball Writers Association of America for 19 years, was director of the Hall of Fame for 13 years and was author of two books: one of the first on the Hall of Fame and one of the first biographies of Willie Mays. He died in 1991 at the age of 89.

Walter Wellesley Smith

Sportswriter. Elected to Hall of Fame: 1976. Nickname: Red.

Red Smith was a sportsreporter and columnist who was regarded as one of America's greatest sportswriters. His writing was full of detail, yet simple in style, elegantly phrased yet easy to understand. Smith spent 55 years in newspaper work, beginning as a $24-a-week reporter for the *Milwaukee Sentinel*, ending as a Pulitzer Prize–winning columnist for the *New York Times*. His last column was published five days before his death in 1982.

He worked for papers in Green Bay, St. Louis and Philadelphia before going to New York to work for the *Herald Tribune* and then the *New York Times.* His columns were syndicated all over the country, giving him national recognition. In 1976, he was awarded the Pulitzer Prize for Distinguished Commentary, the first sportswriter so honored.

Wendell Smith

Sportswriter. Elected to Hall of Fame: 1993.

Wendell Smith was a sportswriter for the *Pittsburgh Courier* and later a writer and columnist for the *Chicago American.* He was one of the nation's first prominent black sportswriters and played a unique behind-the-scenes role in helping Jackie Robinson adjust after breaking the color barrier in Major League Baseball.

He knew both Robinson and Brooklyn general manager Branch Rickey and roomed with Robinson in spring training and when the Dodgers were on the road in Robinson's rookie season. Smith also wrote extensively about the Negro leagues before he began covering Major League Baseball. In Chicago, Smith became a sports commentator on television in addition to his newspaper work.

Edwin Donald Snider

Born September 19, 1926, in Los Angeles, California. 6', 200 lbs., bats left, throws right. Years in minor leagues: 3; Major League debut: April 17, 1947; Years in Major Leagues: 18. Elected to Hall of Fame: 1980. Nickname: Duke— given to him by his father when he was a child.

Duke Snider was a great-hitting center fielder for the Brooklyn Dodgers at a time when New York had three Hall of Fame center fielders: Snider, Mickey Mantle and Willie Mays. Mantle and Mays posted higher individual numbers than Snider but the Duke of Flatbush provided enough power to help the Dodgers win their first World Series championship in Brooklyn in 1955 and in Los Angeles four years later. His 389 career home runs are the most by any Dodger. (He hit 18 more with the Mets and Giants to finish with a career total of 407.) His 11 home runs and 26 RBIs in World Series play are both National League records. He hit four home runs in both the 1952 and 1955 World Series.

Snider had five straight years in which he hit 40 or more home runs and had a career batting average of .295. Ralph Kiner is the only other National League player to have five straight 40-plus home run years. His greatest strength as a fielder was his arm. As a high school quarterback in Compton, California, he threw a 63-yard touchdown pass. He was capable of standing at home plate in Major League ballparks and throwing the ball over the outfield wall. The man in right field for Brooklyn was Carl Furillo, who also had a great arm.

Snider and Furillo developed a system so they would not collide going after flyballs. Snider would take a step forward and try to catch the ball high, while Furillo would step back and be prepared to catch the ball low if it got by Snider. Not many balls got by them. Snider retired after the 1964 season and bought avocado acreage in California. Before long, he was back in baseball, scouting and eventually broadcasting.

Year	Team	G	AB	R	H	D	T	HR	RBI	AVE.
1947	Brklyn	40	83	6	20	3	1	0	5	.241
1948	Brklyn	53	160	22	39	6	6	5	21	.244
1949	Brklyn	146	552	100	161	28	7	23	92	.292
1950	Brklyn	152	620	109	199	31	10	31	107	.321
1951	Brklyn	150	606	96	168	26	6	29	101	.277
1952	Brklyn	144	534	80	162	25	7	21	92	.303
1953	Brklyn	153	590	132	198	38	4	42	126	.336
1954	Brklyn	149	584	120	199	39	10	40	130	.341
1955	Brklyn	148	538	126	166	34	6	42	136	.309
1956	Brklyn	151	542	112	158	33	2	43	101	.292
1957	Brklyn	139	508	91	139	25	7	40	92	.274
1958	LA (N)	106	327	45	102	12	3	15	58	.312
1959	LA	126	370	59	114	11	2	23	88	.308
1960	LA	101	235	38	57	13	5	14	36	.243
1961	LA	85	233	35	69	8	3	16	56	.296
1962	LA	80	158	28	44	11	3	5	30	.278
1963	NY (N)	129	354	44	86	8	3	14	45	.243
1964	SF	91	167	16	35	7	0	4	17	.210
18 years		**2143**	**7161**	**1259**	**2116**	**358**	**85**	**407**	**1333**	**.295**

Transactions: April 1, 1963: Sold to New York Mets. April 14, 1964: Sold to San Francisco Giants.

WORLD SERIES

Year	Team	G	AB	R	H	D	T	HR	RBI	AVE.
1949	Brklyn	5	21	2	3	1	0	0	0	.143
1952	Brklyn	7	29	5	10	2	0	4	8	.345
1953	Brklyn	6	25	3	8	3	0	1	5	.320
1955	Brklyn	7	25	5	8	1	0	4	7	.320
1956	Brklyn	7	23	5	7	1	0	1	4	.304
1959	LA	4	10	1	2	0	0	1	2	.200
6 years		**36**	**133**	**21**	**38**	**8**	**0**	**11**	**26**	**.286**

Warren Spahn

Born April 23, 1921, in Buffalo, New York. 6', 183 lbs., bats left, throws left.
Years in minor leagues: 3; Major League debut: April 19, 1942; Years in Major Leagues: 21. Elected to Hall of Fame: 1973. Nickname: None.

Warren Spahn used a high leg kick to deceive batters for 21 years in becoming the winningest lefthanded pitcher in Major League history. His 363 wins include two no-hitters. He won 20 or games in 13 seasons, including six in a row. He led the National League in wins eight times and had the most complete games in the league in nine different years. He won the Cy Young Award in 1957 in helping the Braves to the World Series championship. Spahn still holds the record for most innings pitched in the National League with 5,246.

He made two appearances for the Braves in 1942 and then spent parts of three years in the military—or his lifetime statistics would have been even bigger. He surely would have topped Grover Cleveland Alexander and Christy Mathewson's 373 wins, which are third on the all-time list. In 1947, his first full season back, he won 21 games. The next year, he won only 15 but was half of the "Spahn and Sain and pray for rain" duo that helped the Boston Braves win the National League pennant—their first since the "Miracle Braves" of 1914.

He pitched his first no-hitter against the Phillies in 1960 at the age of 39 and his second against the Giants in 1961 at the age of 40. At age 42, he was 23-7 for Milwaukee in 1963. Spahn finished his career with stints with the Mets and the Giants. Spahn threw 63 shutouts in his career. His win total—363—matches the number of hits he got in his career. Another oddity: Spahn won his 100th game on August 15, 1951, against the Phillies, his 200th on September 13, 1956, also against the Phillies, and his 300th on August 11, 1961, against the Cubs. Fellow Hall of Famer Richie Ashburn witnessed all three milestones as a member of the losing team.

Year	Team	W-L	ERA	G	IP	H	BB	SO
1942	Bos (N)	0-0	5.74	4	15.2	25	11	7
1946	Bos	8-5	2.94	24	125.2	107	36	57
1947	Bos	21-10	2.33	40	289.2	245	84	123
1948	Bos	15-12	3.71	36	257	237	77	114
1949	Bos	21-14	3.07	38	302.1	283	86	151
1950	Bos	21-17	3.16	41	293	248	111	191
1951	Bos	22-14	2.98	39	310.2	278	109	164
1952	Bos	14-19	2.98	40	290	263	73	183
1953	Mil	23-7	2.10	35	265.2	211	70	148
1954	Mil	21-12	3.14	39	283.1	262	86	136
1955	Mil	17-14	3.26	39	245.2	249	65	110
1956	Mil	20-11	2.78	39	281.1	249	52	128
1957	Mil	21-11	2.69	39	271	241	78	111
1958	Mil	22-11	3.07	38	290	257	76	150
1959	Mil	21-15	2.96	40	292	282	70	143
1960	Mil	21-10	3.50	40	267.2	254	74	154
1961	Mil	21-13	3.02	38	262.2	236	64	115
1962	Mil	18-14	3.04	34	269.1	248	55	118
1963	Mil	23-7	2.60	33	259.2	241	49	102
1964	Mil	6-13	5.29	38	176	204	52	78
1965	NY-SF	7-16	4.01	36	197.2	210	56	90
21 years		363-245	3.09	750	5246	4830	1434	2583

Transactions: Nov. 23, 1964: Sold to New York Mets.

WORLD SERIES

Year	Team	W–L	ERA	G	IP	H	BB	SO
1948	Bos (N)	1–1	3.00	3	12	10	3	12
1957	Mil	1–1	4.20	2	15.1	18	2	2
1958	Mil	2–1	2.20	3	28.2	19	8	18
3 years		4–3	3.05	8	56	47	13	32

Albert G. Spalding

Born September 2, 1850, in Byron, Illinois; died September 9, 1915, in Point Loma, California. Baseball pioneer. Elected to Hall of Fame: 1939.

Albert Spalding won 47 games for the fledgling Chicago team in 1876 and won one more game in the next two years before turning his attention to the business side of baseball. He helped form the National League in 1876 while pitching for the Chicago White Stockings. He was concerned about gambling and other forms of corruption and worked diligently to try to keep the game clean.

In 1888, Spalding organized the first worldwide tour of baseball. He took two teams and visited 14 countries. By this time, he had founded a sporting goods company. When he returned from overseas, he found business was booming and he needed to devote his time to running his company.

He returned to the Major League scene briefly in 1901 to intercede in a dispute between the National League and a young league that was emerging. Through his efforts, an agreement was reached and the American League was created as a separate but equal partner in Major League Baseball.

Tristram E. Speaker

Born April 4, 1888, in Hubbard City, Texas; died December 8, 1958, in Lake Whitney, Texas. 5'11", 193 lbs., bats left, throws left. Years in minor leagues: 4; Major League debut: September 14, 1907; Years in Major Leagues: 22. Elected to Hall of Fame: 1937. Nickname: The Gray Eagle—because he was prematurely gray; also, Spoke—a takeoff on his last name.

Tris Speaker was a great hitter who had a lifetime batting average of .345. He hit over .380 four times: .386 in 1916, .388 in 1920, .380 in 1923 when he also drove in 130 runs, and .389 in 1925. Yet he won only only one batting title. Speaker played in the same era with Ty Cobb, who made a habit of winning batting titles. Speaker had 3,515 career hits and hit more doubles (793) than anyone in baseball history. His 223 triples are sixth highest, all-time. Speaker began his career with the Boston Red Sox in 1907. His first full season was in 1909 and he was the American League's Most Valuable Player just three years later when the Red Sox won the pennant. They won again in 1915. He was traded to Cleveland in 1916 for two players and $55,000 in cash. He loved Boston and threatened to quit baseball rather than report to Cleveland unless he was given $10,000 of the cash Boston was to get. His demand was met. Speaker became the Indians' player-manager in 1919.

The next year, he led the Indians to their first American League pennant with his .388 average. Defensively, he practically dared batters to hit the ball over his head as he played an extremely shallow center field. The result was that he caught a lot of balls that ordinarily would have dropped in for base hits. He also threw a lot of batters out. His 449 assists remain a record, and he got 35 of those in one year. He also made several unassisted double plays, including one in a World Series game. Because of his outstanding hitting and superb defensive skills, Speaker is generally considered to be one of baseball's greatest center fielders, if not the best.

Year	Team	G	AB	R	H	D	T	HR	RBI	AVE.
1907	Bos (A)	7	19	0	3	0	0	0	1	.158
1908	Bos	31	118	12	26	2	3	0	9	.220
1909	Bos	143	544	73	168	26	13	7	77	.309
1910	Bos	141	538	92	183	20	14	7	65	.340
1911	Bos	141	510	88	167	34	13	8	80	.327
1912	Bos	153	580	136	222	53	12	10	98	.383
1913	Bos	141	520	94	190	35	22	3	81	.365
1914	Bos	158	571	100	193	46	18	4	90	.338
1915	Bos	150	547	108	176	25	12	0	69	.322
1916	Cleve	151	546	102	211	41	8	2	83	.386
1917	Cleve	142	523	90	184	42	11	2	60	.352
1918	Cleve	127	471	73	150	33	11	0	61	.318
1919	Cleve	134	494	83	146	38	12	2	63	.296
1920	Cleve	150	552	137	214	50	11	8	107	.388
1921	Cleve	132	506	107	183	52	14	3	74	.362
1922	Cleve	131	426	85	161	48	8	11	71	.378
1923	Cleve	150	574	133	218	59	11	17	130	.380
1924	Cleve	135	486	94	167	36	9	9	65	.344
1925	Cleve	117	429	79	167	35	5	12	87	.389
1926	Cleve	150	96	96	164	52	8	7	86	.304
1927	Wash	141	523	71	171	43	6	2	73	.327
1928	Phil (A)	64	191	28	51	23	2	3	29	.267
22 years		**2789**	**10208**	**1881**	**3515**	**793**	**223**	**117**	**1559**	**.345**

Transactions: April 12, 1916: Traded to Cleveland for Sam Jones, Fred Thomas and $55,000.

WORLD SERIES

Year	Team	G	AB	R	H	D	T	HR	RBI	AVE.
1912	Bos (A)	8	30	4	9	1	2	0	2	.300
1915	Bos	5	17	2	5	0	1	0	0	.294
1920	Cleve	7	25	6	8	2	1	0	1	.320
3 years		**20**	**82**	**12**	**22**	**3**	**4**	**0**	**3**	**.306**

J.G. Taylor Spink

Sportswriter. Elected to Hall of Fame: 1962.

J.G. Taylor Spink was the longtime editor of *The Sporting News*, a publication founded by his uncle, that became the undisputed "Bible of Baseball" under his leadership and direction. At its peak, *The Sporting News* had a small core of full-time writers and more than 200 correspondents, including many of the nation's finest sportswriters. Spink took over as editor in 1914 and was a zealous guardian of the game, even helping to uncover clues that led to the banishment of eight Chicago White Sox players for fixing the 1919 World Series.

The Sporting News sponsored many awards for individual achievement in baseball and kept track of those achievements through its weekly publication of Major League box scores, news stories and columns from writers all over the country. The award honoring sportswriters as inductees into the Hall of Fame is named after Spink.

Wilver Dornel Stargell

Born March 6, 1941, in Earlsboro, Oklahoma. 6'2", 188 lbs., bats left, throws left. Years in minor leagues: 4; Major League debut: September 16, 1962; Years in Major Leagues: 21. Elected to Hall of Fame: 1988. Nickname: Pops—A name he gave himself in 1979, when, at the age of 38, he helped his younger teammates win a World Series championship.

Willie Stargell was not only well respected for his hitting, but for his team leadership and enthusiasm as well. In 1979, Stargell became "Pops" to a young ball club of overachievers who won the division championship on the last day of the season on a Stargell home run; won the National League championship series with Stargell leading the way, hitting .455; and won a come-from-behind effort in the World Series, with Stargell hitting what proved to be the game-winning homer in the seventh game.

He accomplished something no one else has in baseball history when, in 1979, he won three Most Valuable Player awards—for the league, for the playoffs and for the World Series. (Actually, he tied for league MVP with Keith Hernandez.) In the World Series, he had seven extra-base hits and 25 total bases, both records, and, at age 38, was the oldest player to be a Series MVP. Stargell led the National League in home runs in two different seasons, 1971 and 1973, when he hit 48 and 43, respectively. He hit three home runs in a game four different times in his career.

On July 22, 1964, he hit for the cycle against the St. Louis Cardinals. On June 4–5, 1966, he got nine straight hits in a two-game stretch. On August 1, 1970, Stargell tied a Major League record when he got five extra-base hits—three doubles and two home runs—in a game against the Braves.

Year	Team	G	AB	R	H	D	T	HR	RBI	AVE.
1962	Pitt	10	31	1	9	3	1	0	4	.290
1963	Pitt	108	304	34	74	11	6	11	47	.243
1964	Pitt	117	421	53	115	19	7	21	78	.273
1965	Pitt	144	533	68	145	25	8	27	107	.272
1966	Pitt	140	485	84	153	30	0	33	102	.315
1967	Pitt	134	462	54	125	18	6	20	73	.271
1968	Pitt	128	435	57	103	15	1	24	67	.237
1969	Pitt	145	522	89	160	31	6	29	92	.307
1970	Pitt	136	474	70	125	18	3	31	85	.264
1971	Pitt	141	511	104	151	26	0	48	125	.295
1972	Pitt	138	495	75	145	28	2	33	112	.293
1973	Pitt	148	522	106	156	43	4	44	119	.299
1974	Pitt	140	508	90	153	37	4	25	96	.301
1975	Pitt	124	461	71	136	32	2	22	90	.295
1976	Pitt	117	428	54	110	20	3	20	65	.257
1977	Pitt	63	186	29	51	12	0	13	35	.274
1978	Pitt	122	390	60	115	18	2	28	97	.295
1979	Pitt	126	424	60	119	19	0	32	82	.281
1980	Pitt	67	202	28	53	10	1	11	38	.262
1981	Pitt	38	60	2	17	4	0	0	9	.283
1982	Pitt	74	73	6	17	4	0	3	17	.233
21 years		**2360**	**7927**	**1195**	**2232**	**423**	**55**	**475**	**1540**	**.282**

LEAGUE CHAMPIONSHIP SERIES

Year	Team	G	AB	R	H	D	T	HR	RBI	AVE.
1970	Pitt	3	12	0	6	1	0	0	1	.500
1971	Pitt	4	14	1	0	0	0	0	0	.000
1972	Pitt	5	16	1	1	1	0	0	1	.063
1974	Pitt	4	15	3	6	0	0	2	4	.400
1975	Pitt	3	11	1	2	1	0	0	0	.182
1979	Pitt	3	11	2	5	2	0	2	6	.455
6 years		**22**	**79**	**8**	**20**	**5**	**0**	**4**	**12**	**.253**

WORLD SERIES

Year	Team	G	AB	R	H	D	T	HR	RBI	AVE.
1971	Pitt	7	24	3	5	1	0	0	1	.208
1979	Pitt	7	30	7	12	4	0	3	7	.400
2 years		**14**	**54**	**10**	**17**	**5**	**0**	**3**	**8**	**.315**

Charles Dillon Stengel

Born July 30, 1890, in Kansas City, Missouri; died September 29, 1975, in Glendale, California. 5'11", 175 lbs., bats left, throws left. Years in minor leagues: 3;

Major League debut: September 17, 1912; Years in Major Leagues: 39 (14 as player; 25 as manager). Elected to Hall of Fame: 1966. Nickname: Casey— taken from the letters of his hometown—KC; The Ole Professor—what sportwriters and broadcasters called him during his years as Yankee manager because of his philosophic (though often rambling) answers to questions.

Casey Stengel guided the New York Yankees to ten pennants and seven World Series championships in a 12-year span, obvious Hall of Fame credentials. Nobody has ever done better. But sandwiched around his stint with the Yankees were managerial duties with Brooklyn and Boston in the National League, where he could finish no higher than fifth, and with the New York Mets, who lost more than 100 games in their first years of existence with Stengel at the helm.

After his less than dazzling years managing Brooklyn and Boston, Stengel managed in the minors and won championships at Milwaukee and Oakland. It was then that the Yankees picked him to guide them to the top in the Major Leagues. He took an injury-riddled team and somehow, through platooning, lineup juggling, and getting the most out of his players, Stengel managed a pennant winner in his first year, and his second, third, fourth and fifth years with the Yankees. The Bronx Bombers won 103 games in 1954 but finished second to Cleveland, then won four more pennants, detoured to third place in 1959, and then won again in 1960.

After losing the 1960 World Series to the Pittsburgh Pirates on Bill Mazeroski's ninth inning home run, Stengel was relieved of his duties at the age of 70. A year later, the expansion New York Mets hired Casey to lead them. Stengel was a good ballplayer before his managing days and had a career .284 average over 14 years. In his first Major League game, he got four hits and a walk—in that order— in five at-bats as Brooklyn came from behind to beat Pittsburgh and snap the Pirates' 12-game winning streak. He played in World Series competition three years and had a .393 average. Ole Casey wouldn't have made it to the Hall of Fame on the strength of his playing career alone, but his zany ways as both player and manager, on and off the field, are an important part of the Stengel character.

As a player, he once caught a bird and put it under his hat while playing in the outfield for the Pirates in Brooklyn. The Dodgers had recently traded Stengel to Pittsburgh. So in his first at-bat back in Brooklyn, he came to the plate, doffed his cap to the crowd, and the bird flew out. In 1925, he was president, manager and outfielder for Worcester in the Eastern League. At the end of a dismal season, Stengel the manager released Stengel the outfielder and Stengel the president released Stengel the manager. Then he quit as president.

His career in baseball spanned enough time that he played against Babe Ruth (in the 1923 World Series) and managed Mickey Mantle 30 years later.

As a Player

Year	Team	G	AB	R	H	D	T	HR	RBI	AVE.
1912	Brklyn	17	57	9	18	1	0	1	13	.316
1913	Brklyn	124	438	60	119	16	8	7	43	.272

Year	Team	G	AB	R	H	D	T	HR	RBI	AVE.
1914	Brklyn	126	412	55	30	13	10	4	60	.316
1915	Brklyn	132	459	52	109	20	12	3	50	.237
1916	Brklyn	127	462	66	129	27	8	8	53	.279
1917	Brklyn	150	549	69	141	23	12	6	79	.257
1918	Pitt	39	122	18	30	4	1	1	12	.246
1919	Pitt	89	321	38	94	10	10	4	43	.293
1920	Phil	129	445	53	130	25	6	9	50	.292
1921	Phil-NY (N)	42	81	11	23	4	1	0	6	.284
1922	NY	84	250	48	92	8	10	7	48	.368
1923	NY	75	218	39	74	11	5	5	43	.339
1924	Bos (N)	131	461	57	129	20	6	5	39	.280
1925	Bos	12	13	0	1	0	0	0	2	.077
14 years		**1277**	**4288**	**575**	**1219**	**182**	**89**	**60**	**535**	**.284**

Transactions: Jan. 9, 1918: Traded with George Cutshaw to Pittsburgh for Chuck Ward, Burleigh Grimes and Al Mamaux. August 1919: Traded to Philadelphia for Possum Whitted. July 1, 1921: Traded with Johnny Rawlings and Red Causey to New York for Goldie Rapp, Lee King and Lance Richbourg. Nov. 12, 1923: Traded with Dave Bancroft and Bill Cunningham to Boston for Billy Southworth and Joe Oeschger.

WORLD SERIES

Year	Team	G	AB	R	H	D	T	HR	RBI	AVE.
1916	Brklyn	4	11	2	4	0	0	0	0	.364
1922	NY (N)	2	5	0	2	0	0	0	0	.400
1923	NY	6	12	3	5	0	0	2	4	.417
3 years		**12**	**28**	**5**	**11**	**0**	**0**	**2**	**4**	**.393**

AS A MANAGER

Year	Team	W-L	Standing
1934	Brklyn	71-81	Sixth
1935	Brklyn	70-83	Fifth
1936	Brklyn	67-87	Seventh
1938	Bos (N)	77-75	Fifth
1939	Bos	63-88	Seventh
1940	Bos	65-87	Seventh
1941	Bos	62-92	Seventh
1942	Bos	59-89	Seventh
1943	Bos	68-85	Fifth
1949	NY (A)	97-57	First
1950	NY	98-56	First
1951	NY	98-56	First
1952	NY	95-59	First
1953	NY	99-52	First
1954	NY	103-51	Second
1955	NY	96-58	First

Year	Team	W-L	Standing
1956	NY	97-57	First
1957	NY	98-56	First
1958	NY	92-62	First
1959	NY	79-75	Third
1960	NY	97-57	First
1962	NY (N)	40-120	Tenth
1963	NY	51-111	Tenth
1964	NY	53-109	Tenth
1965	NY	31-64	Tenth
25 years		**1926-1867**	

Robert Stevens

Sportswriter. Elected to Hall of Fame: 1999.

Bob Stevens covered the San Francisco Giants for the *San Francisco Chronicle* for 31 years. He also covered the Oakland A's during their three World Championship years, 1972–74. Prior to his Major League work, Stevens' "beat" was the San Francisco Seals for 17 years. Early in his career, he used the pen name of "Lefton Base" as a baseball writer for the *Chronicle*.

J. Roy Stockton

Sportswriter. Elected to Hall of Fame: 1972.

J. Roy Stockton was sports editor of the *St. Louis Post-Dispatch* back in the days when the Cardinals and the Browns were baseball's "western" teams. Because of that, his reports had a wide following as he covered the great Cardinal pennant teams of the 1940s, the Brown's one and only championship team of 1944, and one of baseball's earliest franchise moves when the Browns left for Baltimore. Stockton was succeeded as *Post-Dispatch* sportseditor by Bob Broeg who is also in the Hall of Fame.

Donald Howard Sutton

Born April 2, 1945, in Clio, Alabama. 6'1", 185 lbs., bats right, throws right. Years in minor leagues: 2; Major League debut: April 14, 1966; Years in Major Leagues: 23. Elected to Hall of Fame: 1998. Nickname: Black and Decker— like the saw by the same name, because of his reputation for "cutting" or scuffing the ball to give him an edge in gripping and throwing sharply breaking pitches.

Don Sutton won 324 games by finesse and cunning, battling hitters rather than blowing the ball by them. He is the only pitcher in baseball history to have more than 300 wins while having only one 20-win season: 1976, when he was 21–10 with the Dodgers. He pitched about half his career with the Dodgers, but also spent time with Houston, Milwaukee, Oakland and California. He joined the Brewers late in 1982 and helped them win their only pennant by going 4–1 down the stretch and providing veteran leadership on a young team.

His strikeout statistics are as impressive—and as unusual—as his win totals. He is one of the all-time leaders in career strikeouts with 3,574, but never once in his 23 years in the Majors did he lead the league in strikeouts. By way of comparison, Walter Johnson had 3,506 strikeouts and led the league 12 times.

Sutton had 11 seasons when he won 15 or more, including 2 in which he won 19 and another when he won 18. He also tossed five one-hitters in his career. He appeared in three World Series with the Los Angeles Dodgers as well as the one with the Milwaukee Brewers.

Year	Team	W-L	ERA	G	IP	H	BB	SO
1966	LA (N)	12-12	2.99	37	225.2	192	52	209
1967	LA	11-15	3.95	37	232.2	223	57	169
1968	LA	11-15	2.60	35	207.2	179	59	162
1969	LA	17-18	3.47	41	293	269	91	217
1970	LA	15-13	4.08	38	260	251	78	201
1971	LA	17-12	2.55	38	265	231	55	194
1972	LA	19-9	2.08	33	272.2	186	63	207
1973	LA	18-10	2.42	33	256.1	196	56	200
1974	LA	19-9	3.23	40	276	241	80	179
1975	LA	16-13	2.87	35	254	202	62	175
1976	LA	21-10	3.06	35	267.2	231	82	161
1977	LA	14-8	3.19	33	240	207	69	150
1978	LA	15-11	3.55	34	238	228	54	154
1979	LA	12-15	3.82	33	226	201	61	146
1980	LA	13-5	2.21	32	212	163	47	128
1981	Hous	11-9	2.60	23	159	132	29	104
1982	Hous-Mil	17-9	3.06	34	249.2	224	64	175
1983	Mil	8-13	4.08	31	220.1	209	54	134
1984	Mil	14-12	3.77	33	212.2	224	51	143
1985	Oak-Cal	15-10	3.86	34	226	221	59	107
1986	Cal	15-11	3.74	34	207	192	49	116
1987	Cal	11-11	4.69	35	192	199	41	99
1988	LA	3-6	3.93	16	87	91	30	44
23 years		**324-256**	**3.26**	**774**	**5282**	**4692**	**1343**	**3574**

Transactions: Dec. 4, 1980: Signed with Houston as free agent. Aug. 30, 1982: Traded to Milwaukee for Kevin Bass, Frank DiPino, Mike Madden and cash. Dec. 7, 1984: Traded to Oakland for Ray Burris and Eric Barry.

LEAGUE CHAMPIONSHIP SERIES

Year	Team	W-L	ERA	G	IP	H	BB	SO
1974	LA (N)	2-0	0.53	2	17	7	2	13
1977	LA	1-0	1.00	1	9	9	0	4

Year	Team	W–L	ERA	G	IP	H	BB	SO
1978	LA	0–1	6.35	1	5.2	7	2	0
1982	Mil	1–0	3.52	1	7.2	8	2	9
4 years		**4–1**	**2.06**	**5**	**39.1**	**31**	**6**	**26**

WORLD SERIES

Year	Team	W–L	ERA	G	IP	H	BB	SO
1974	LA (N)	1–0	2.77	2	13	9	3	12
1977	LA	1–0	3.94	2	16	17	1	6
1978	LA	0–2	7.50	2	12	17	4	8
1982	Mil	0–1	7.84	2	10.1	12	1	5
4 years		**2–3**	**5.26**	**8**	**51.1**	**55**	**9**	**31**

William Harold Terry

Born October 30, 1898, in Atlanta, Georgia; died January 9, 1989, in Jacksonville, Florida. 6'2", 200 lbs., bats left, throws left. Years in minor leagues: 2; Major League debut: September 24, 1923; Years in Major Leagues: 14. Elected to Hall of Fame: 1954. Nickname: Memphis Bill—because his home was in Memphis.

Bill Terry did not get into the Hall of Fame for his personality. He was strictly business, brash, and argumentative—but he could hit. Memphis Bill hit over .320 nine years in a row, and his lifetime batting average of .341 is the highest of any National League lefthanded batter.

The New York Giants first baseman is the last National League player to hit over .400. Terry hit .401 in 1930 and won the league's Most Valuable Player Award. He got over 200 hits in six seasons. In 1931, he, Jim Bottomley and Chick Hafey battled for the batting title that Hafey won by less than a percentage point over the other two.

Terry was a good fielding first baseman who didn't get the credit he deserved for his glove, because his batting was what made headlines. As good as he was, he played in the shadow of two first basemen making bigger headlines in the American League: Lou Gehrig and Jimmie Foxx. When his playing career was over, he succeeded John McGraw as manager of the Giants and won three pennants.

Year	Team	G	AB	R	H	D	T	HR	RBI	AVE.
1923	NY (N)	3	7	1	1	0	0	0	0	.143
1924	NY	77	163	26	39	7	2	5	24	.239
1925	NY	133	489	75	156	31	6	11	70	.319
1926	NY	98	225	26	65	12	5	5	43	.289
1927	NY	150	580	101	189	32	13	20	121	.326
1928	NY	149	568	100	185	36	11	17	101	.326

Year	Team	G	AB	R	H	D	T	HR	RBI	AVE.
1929	NY	150	607	103	226	39	5	14	117	.372
1930	NY	154	633	139	254	39	15	23	129	.401
1931	NY	153	611	121	213	43	20	9	112	.349
1932	NY	154	643	124	225	42	11	28	117	.350
1933	NY	123	475	68	153	20	5	6	58	.322
1934	NY	153	602	109	213	30	6	8	83	.354
1935	NY	145	596	91	203	32	8	6	64	.341
1936	NY	79	229	36	71	10	5	2	39	.310
14 years		1721	6428	1120	2193	373	112	154	1078	.341

WORLD SERIES

Year	Team	G	AB	R	H	D	T	HR	RBI	AVE.
1924	NY (N)	5	14	3	6	0	1	1	1	.429
1933	NY	5	22	3	6	1	0	1	1	.273
1936	NY	6	25	1	6	0	0	0	5	.240
3 years		16	61	7	18	1	1	2	7	.295

Chuck Thompson

Broadcaster. Elected to Hall of Fame: 1993.

Chuck Thompson's introduction to baseball came from one of his grandmother's rooming house tenants: Connie Mack. He has broadcast for the Phillies, A's and Senators, but fans up and down the East Coast have known him as the melodic voice of the Orioles.

Samuel Luter Thompson

Born March 5, 1860, in Danville, Indiana; died November 7, 1922, in Detroit, Michigan. 6'2", 207 lbs., bats left, throws left. Years in minor leagues: 2; Major League debut: 1885; Years in Major Leagues: 12. Elected to Hall of Fame: 1974. Nickname: Big Sam—because of his size.

Big Sam Thompson was a 19th century slugger who became the best run producer in baseball history. Playing for Detroit and Philadelphia over a 12-year period, he averaged .923 runs batted in per game. In 1887, 1894 and 1895 Thompson averaged better than one RBI a game. His career total of 128 home runs was second only to Roger Connor among players who performed in the 19th century. In 1889, he became the first Major League player to hit 20 home runs. Two years earlier, he was the first player to get 200 hits and 300 total bases in a season. He hit .407 in 1894 and followed that with .392. Twice he drove in more than 160 runs.

Year	Team	G	AB	R	H	D	T	HR	RBI	AVE.
1885	Det (N)	63	254	58	77	11	9	7	44	.303
1886	Det	122	503	101	156	18	13	8	89	.310
1887	Det	127	545	118	203	29	23	11	166	.372
1888	Det	56	238	51	67	10	8	6	40	.282
1889	Phil (N)	128	533	103	158	36	4	20	111	.296
1890	Phil	132	549	116	172	41	9	4	102	.313
1891	Phil	133	554	108	163	23	10	7	90	.294
1892	Phil	153	609	109	186	28	11	9	104	.305
1893	Phil	131	600	130	222	37	13	11	126	.370
1894	Phil	99	437	108	178	29	27	13	141	.407
1895	Phil	119	538	131	211	45	21	18	165	.392
1896	Phil	119	517	103	154	28	7	12	100	.298
1897	Phil	3	13	2	3	0	1	0	3	.231
1898	Phil	14	63	14	22	5	3	1	15	.349
1906	Det (A)	8	31	4	7	0	1	0	3	.226
15 years		1407	5984	1256	1979	340	160	127	1299	.331

Joseph Bert Tinker

Born July 27, 1880, in Muscotah, Kansas; died July 27, 1948, in Orlando, Florida. 5'9", 175 lbs., bats right, throws right. Years in minor leagues: 3; Major League debut: April 17, 1902; Years in Major Leagues: 15. Elected to Hall of Fame: 1946. Nickname: None

Joe Tinker is perhaps best known today as the shortstop in the Franklin P. Adams poem immortalizing "Tinker to Evers to Chance." He played 15 years in the Major Leagues, mostly for the Chicago Cubs, where he was a good hitter and an outstanding fielder. He had a career batting average of .264. He led the National League in fielding average five times, in assists twice and in putouts twice. He also had 336 career steals. Tinker was a main cog in the Cub machine that won four pennants in five years between 1906 and 1910. He also was the player-manager for Cincinnati, the Chicago Federals and then back with the Cubs.

Tinker always hit Christy Mathewson well, and that was important because the Cubs were always battling the Giants for the pennant and consequently were up against Mathewson in many important games. He hit .400 against Mathewson in 1908 and had a big triple against him on October 8 that helped the Cubs beat the Giants, 4–2 for the National League pennant. That game was necessary because on September 23, the Giants thought they had beaten the Cubs, 2–1, on a run-scoring hit in the bottom of the ninth inning. But the Giants' Fred Merkle, who had been the runner on first, turned and headed for the clubhouse when the apparent winning run scored—before he touched second base. The Cubs noticed, called for the ball, and touched the base for a force out. The game ended in a 1–1 tie which eventually led to the October 8 playoff. There would have been no playoff, and the Giants would have won the September 23 game 1–0, except that early on, Tinker had homered—off Mathewson.

Tinker spent one year as player-manager at Cincinnati then hopped to the Federal League for two years, then managed the Cubs for a year. In retirement, he suffered from diabetes and had to have one leg amputated. He lived in Orlando, Florida, where the ballpark, Tinker Field, was named in his honor. He died on his 68th birthday in 1948.

Year	Team	G	AB	R	H	D	T	HR	RBI	AVE.
1902	Chi (N)	131	494	55	129	19	5	2	54	.261
1903	Chi	124	460	67	134	21	7	2	70	.291
1904	Chi	141	488	55	108	12	13	3	41	.221
1905	Chi	149	547	70	135	18	8	2	66	.247
1906	Chi	148	523	75	122	18	4	1	64	.233
1907	Chi	117	402	36	89	11	3	1	36	.221
1908	Chi	157	548	67	146	22	14	6	68	.266
1909	Chi	143	516	56	132	26	11	4	57	.256
1910	Chi	134	473	58	136	25	9	3	69	.288
1911	Chi	144	536	61	149	24	12	4	69	.278
1912	Chi	142	550	80	155	24	7	0	75	.282
1913	Cin	110	382	47	121	20	13	1	57	.317
1914	Chi (F)	126	438	50	112	21	7	2	46	.256
1915	Chi (F)	31	67	7	18	2	1	0	9	.269
1916	Chi (N)	7	10	0	1	0	0	0	1	.100
15 years		1804	6434	774	1687	263	114	31	782	.264

Transactions: Dec. 15, 1912: Traded with Grover Lowdermilk and Harry Chapman to Cincinnati for Bert Humphries, Red Corriden, Pete Knisely, Art Phelan and Mike Mitchell. December 1913: Traded to Brooklyn for Dick Egan and $6,500. Tinker demanded $2,000 of the purchase price. When he didn't get it, he jumped to the Federal League and the deal was voided.

WORLD SERIES

Year	Team	G	AB	R	H	D	T	HR	RBI	AVE.
1906	Chi (N)	6	18	4	3	0	0	0	1	.167
1907	Chi	5	13	4	2	0	0	0	1	.154
1908	Chi	5	19	2	5	0	0	1	5	.263
1910	Chi	5	18	2	6	2	0	0	0	.333
4 years		21	68	12	16	2	0	1	7	.235

Harold Joseph Traynor

Born November 11, 1899, in Framingham, Massachusetts; died March 16, 1972, in Pittsburgh, Pennsylvania. 6', 175 lbs., bats right, throws right. Years in minor leagues: 2; Major League debut: September 15, 1920; Years in Major Leagues: 17 years. Elected to Hall of Fame: 1948. Nickname: Pie—several accounts of how he got the name; most involve his appetite for pastries as a child; another version alludes to his father's profession, a printer. When lead type was spilled, the printer's expression is that it was "pied" and some believe Traynor's father called his son "Pie" in a loving manner, referring to him being mixed up.

Pie Traynor was a mainstay on the great Pittsburgh Pirate teams of the 1920s. He hit over .300 ten times in his career, finishing with a lifetime batting average of .320. He drove in more than 100 runs seven times, including five years in a row. He scored more than 100 runs twice, and topped the 90 mark six times. Traynor was a superb fielder. He led the National League in putouts seven times and assists three times, but only once did he lead the league in overall fielding percentage.

Despite all of these statistics, what made Traynor stand out were assets that don't show up in a record book. John McGraw, the great manager, said Traynor was the greatest team player he had ever seen. Ty Cobb selected Traynor as the third baseman on his "all time" team because of his consistency. On Pirate teams that featured the Waner brothers—Lloyd and Paul—and Kiki Cuyler, Traynor provided that invisible ingredient of leadership that helped hold it all together.

He was an aggressive yet graceful third baseman. No one in his day was better at charging bunts and slow-rolling ground balls and throwing runners out or moving swiftly to his left or right to snare hotly hit ground balls or line drives. The secret, he said, was that he used a felt lining instead of leather inside his glove because if the ball glanced off the glove, it wouldn't go as far. Traynor managed the Pirates from 1934 to 1939 and was in the dugout when Gabby Hartnett hit the famous home run into the darkness of Wrigley Field against Pittsburgh that catapulted the Cubs into first place and an eventual pennant.

Year	Team	G	AB	R	H	D	T	HR	RBI	AVE.
1920	Pitt	17	52	6	11	3	1	0	2	.212
1921	Pitt	7	19	0	5	0	0	0	2	.263
1922	Pitt	142	571	89	161	17	12	4	81	.282
1923	Pitt	153	616	108	208	19	19	12	101	.338
1924	Pitt	142	545	86	160	26	13	5	82	.294
1925	Pitt	150	591	114	189	39	14	6	106	.320
1926	Pitt	152	574	83	182	25	17	3	92	.317
1927	Pitt	149	573	93	196	32	9	5	106	.342
1928	Pitt	144	569	91	192	38	12	3	124	.337
1929	Pitt	130	540	94	192	27	12	4	108	.356
1930	Pitt	130	497	90	182	22	11	9	119	.366
1931	Pitt	155	615	81	183	37	15	2	103	.298
1932	Pitt	135	513	84	169	27	10	2	68	.329
1933	Pitt	154	624	85	190	27	6	1	82	.304
1934	Pitt	119	444	62	137	22	10	1	61	.309
1935	Pitt	57	204	24	57	10	3	1	36	.279
1937	Pitt	5	12	3	2	0	0	0	0	.167
17 years		1941	7559	1183	2416	371	164	58	1273	.320

WORLD SERIES

Year	Team	G	AB	R	H	D	T	HR	RBI	AVE.
1925	Pitt	7	26	2	9	0	2	1	4	.346
1927	Pitt	4	15	1	3	1	0	0	0	.200
2 years		11	41	3	12	1	2	1	4	.293

Clarence Arthur Vance

Born March 4, 1891, in Adair County, Iowa; died February 16, 1961, in Homosassa Springs, Florida. 6'1", 200 lbs., bats right, throws right. Years in minor leagues: 10; Major League debut: April 16, 1915; Years in Major Leagues: 14. Elected to Hall of Fame: 1955. Nickname: Dazzy—An expression he learned from a cowboy when he was youngster and he used in describing his change-up, saying, "ain't it a dazzy?"

Dazzy Vance pitched five complete games in seven days in the minor leagues, hurting his arm and postponing his trip to the Major Leagues. He languished in the minors for ten years. He didn't make it to the Major Leagues until he was 31 years old and still managed to win 197 games in 14 years. In his first full year with the Brooklyn Dodgers in 1922, he led the National League in strikeouts and won the strikeout title the next six years as well—a National League record.

Vance was blessed with an 83-inch reach. His long arm and high leg kick made him a formidable opponent for National League hitters his entire career. Cincinnati's Rube Bressler described how tough Vance was to hit against when he said, "You couldn't hit him on a Monday." He told of how Monday was wash day in Brooklyn and women would hang their white clothes on a line behind the outfield wall. When Vance pitched, with that big windup, high leg kick, and the white background of the clothes on the line, he was impossible to hit, said Bressler. He had the league's lowest earned run average three years and led the league in wins twice. His greatest year was 1924 when he was 28–6, including a 15-game winning streak. Vance was voted the league's Most Valuable Player even though Rogers Hornsby of the St. Louis Cardinals hit .424. In 1925, Vance threw the only no-hitter of his career, beating the Philadelphia Phillies 10–1.

Vance was the cause of Babe Herman's famed hit in which three men wound up on third base. The bases were loaded with Hank DeBerry on third, Vance on second and Chick Fewster on first. Herman belted a sure double into the outfield and took off running. DeBerry scored. Vance rounded third and headed for the plate when he suddenly turned and decided to go back to third. Fewster had gone from first to third and was standing on the bag. While all this was going on, Herman rounded second and headed for third. He slid into third from one direction while Vance slid back into third from another direction, while Fewster remained standing on third. All three were tagged out. Since, technically, the base belonged to Vance, the other two men were ruled out for one of the most unusual double plays in baseball history. In 1929, the Dodgers paid him $25,000, making him the highest paid pitcher in history. In 1933, he played for the Cardinals, giving him the chance to play in his only World Series. When asked what was his best pitch, Dazzy answered, "the unexpected one."

Year	Team	W-L	ERA	G	IP	H	BB	SO
1915	Pitt-NY (A)	0-4	4.11	9	30.2	26	21	18
1918	NY	0-0	15.43	2	2.1	9	2	0
1922	Brklyn	18-12	3.70	36	245.2	259	94	134
1923	Brklyn	18-15	3.50	37	280.1	263	100	197
1924	Brklyn	28-6	2.16	35	308.2	238	77	262
1925	Brklyn	22-9	3.53	31	265.1	247	66	221
1926	Brklyn	9-10	3.89	24	169	172	58	140
1927	Brklyn	16-15	2.70	34	273.1	242	69	184
1928	Brklyn	22-10	2.09	38	280.1	226	72	200
1929	Brklyn	14-13	3.89	31	231.1	244	47	126
1930	Brklyn	17-15	2.61	35	258.2	241	55	173
1931	Brklyn	11-13	3.38	30	218.2	221	53	150
1932	Brklyn	12-11	4.20	27	175.2	171	57	103
1933	StL (N)	6-2	3.55	28	99	105	28	67
1934	StL-Cin	1-3	4.56	25	77	90	25	42
1935	Brklyn	3-2	4.41	20	51	55	16	28
16 years		**197-140**	**3.24**	**442**	**2967**	**2809**	**840**	**2045**

March 1915: Sold to New York Yankees. February 1933: Traded with Gordon Slade to St. Louis for Jake Flowers and Owen Carroll. June 25, 1934: Picked up by Cincinatti for waiver price.

WORLD SERIES

Year	Team	W-L	ERA	G	IP	H	BB	SO
1933	StL (N)	0-0	0.00	1	1.1	2	1	3

Joseph Floyd Vaughan

Born March 9, 1912, in Clifty, Arkansas; died August 30, 1952, in Eagleville, California. 5'11", 185 lbs., bats left, throws right. Years in minor leagues: 1; Major League debut: April 17, 1932; Years in Major Leagues: 14. Elected to Hall of Fame: 1985. Nickname: Arky—short for Arkansas, his home state.

The Pittsburgh Pirates can lay claim to two of the greatest shortstops of all time: Honus Wagner and Arky Vaughan. Vaughan's lifetime batting average of .318 is second only to Wagner's .329 for shortstops. Vaughan played for the Pirates the first ten years of his career and hit over .300 in each of those years. His best season was 1935 when he hit .385. Nobody hit higher in the National League for nearly 60 years. Tony Gwynn hit .394 in 1994, a seasoned shortened by a strike. Vaughan was the first man to hit two home runs in an All-Star game. He hit a pair of two-run homers in the 1941 game, an achievement lost in the record books because of Ted Williams's three-run, game-winning homer in the ninth inning. Arky was a guardian of the strike zone, fanning only 276 times in over 6,000 at-bats. He also led the National League in walks for three straight years: 1934, 1935 and 1936. He was not much of a power hitter but was fast on the base paths. He led the league in triples three times and in stolen bases once. He was also an excellent, consistent fielder, leading National League shortstops in putouts and assists three times each. He never drove in 100 runs, but had more than 90 RBIs in four of his 14 seasons. Vaughan was a man of integrity and proved it when he quit in a dispute with Dodger manager Leo Durocher, who Vaughan felt had lied about a situation in which a teammate was suspended. Arky went back to the family farm in California. He wound up staying there for four years, helping out on the farm while his brother was in the service in World War II.

He came back to the Dodgers in 1947, when Durocher was suspended for a year. It gave him the opportunity to play in his one and only World Series. In 1952, while fishing with a friend, their boat capsized and both men drowned. It is believed Vaughan may have suffered a heart attack while trying to rescue his friend. He was 40 years old.

Year	Team	G	AB	R	H	D	T	HR	RBI	AVE.
1932	Pitt	129	497	71	158	15	10	4	61	.318
1933	Pitt	152	573	85	180	29	19	9	97	.314
1934	Pitt	149	558	115	186	41	11	12	94	.333
1935	Pitt	137	499	108	192	34	10	19	99	.385
1936	Pitt	156	568	122	190	30	11	9	78	.335
1937	Pitt	126	469	71	151	17	17	5	72	.322
1938	Pitt	148	541	88	174	35	5	7	68	.322
1939	Pitt	152	595	94	182	30	11	6	72	.306
1940	Pitt	156	594	113	178	40	15	7	95	.300
1941	Pitt	106	374	69	118	20	7	6	38	.316
1942	Brklyn	128	495	82	137	18	4	2	49	.277
1943	Brklyn	149	610	112	186	39	6	5	66	.305
1947	Brklyn	64	126	24	41	5	2	2	25	.325
1948	Brklyn	65	123	19	30	3	0	3	22	.244
14 years		1817	6622	1173	2103	356	128	96	926	.318

Transactions: Dec. 12, 1941: Traded to Brooklyn for Pete Coscarat, Luke Hamlin, Babe Phelps and Jimmy Wasdell.

WORLD SERIES

Year	Team	G	AB	R	H	D	T	HR	RBI	AVE.
1947	Brklyn	3	2	0	1	1	0	0	0	.500

Bill Veeck

Born February 9, 1914, in Chicago, Illinois; died January 2, 1986, in Chicago, Illinois. Years in Major Leagues: 15 (as owner of three teams). Elected to Hall of Fame: 1991.

Bill Veeck was an innovative owner of three Major League teams. He pulled off some of the most outlandish stunts—for the entertainment of his audience—in baseball history. Veeck believed that if you got people into the ballpark once, they would return. So he dreamed up bizarre promotions to attract fans.

Some of his most famous shenanigans:

• A night for St. Louis Browns fans in 1951 in which they got a chance to manage the team—with flash cards. A Browns official held up a sign toward the crowd, asking about a particular game situation. For instance, the sign might say: "Bunt?" Fans would respond by holding up cards that said either "Yes" or "No." The Browns won the game.

• Five days later, 3-foot, 6-inch Eddie Gaedel pinch-hit for Frank Saucier in a game against the Detroit Tigers and walked on four pitches.

• In 1979, a promotion bombed—literally. At "Disco Demolition Night" at Comiskey Park, fans were invited on the field between games of a twi-night doubleheader to put their disco records into a huge bonfire. Damage to the field was so extensive that the second game had to be cancelled, and the White Sox forfeited.

Veeck introduced exploding scoreboards and players' names on the backs of their uniforms. He installed showers in the stands so sunbathers could cool off and created many giveaway days such as Bat Day. He was a showman, to be sure, but he was also a good baseball man. Veeck's 1948 Cleveland Indian team won the American League pennant and the World Series with the help of Larry Doby, who Veeck signed in 1947 as the first black player in the American League, and Satchel Paige, a rookie sensation in 1948 at the age of 42. A few years later, he bought the St. Louis Browns and used promotions to get the fans' minds off of what was taking place on the field—a lot of Browns losses. In 1959, he bought the Chicago White Sox and they won the American League pennant. They played in a World Series for the only time since 1919 and lost to the Los Angeles Dodgers in six games.

Veeck learned his trade from his father, Bill Veeck, Sr., who was general manager of the Chicago Cubs. One of the jobs that young Bill Veeck handled was planting the ivy on the walls of Wrigley Field, making it, as it remains today, one of baseball's most cherished landmarks.

George Edward Waddell

Born October 13, 1876, in Bradford, Pennsylvania; died April 1, 1914, in San Antonio, Texas; 6'1", 195 lbs., bats left, throws left. Years in minor leagues: 2.

Major League debut: September 8, 1897; Years in Major Leagues: 13. Elected to Hall of Fame: 1946. Nickname: Rube—what city people called farm boys who came into the big city; a nickname Waddell tolerated from friends but he disliked strangers calling him that.

Rube Waddell was a great pitcher for a few years and a good one the rest of the time. He had good control on the field but was often out of control off the field, and few managers could deal with his eccentric nature for very long.

The manager who got the most out of him was Connie Mack of the Philadelphia A's. Waddell won at least 20 games in each of his first four seasons under Mack and helped Philadelphia win two pennants. In 1905, Waddell finished the season with an earned run average of 1.45, one of three seasons in which his earned run average was under 2.00 His lifetime ERA of 2.16 is the sixth best in baseball history. Mack said Waddell had the best combination of speed and curveball that he had ever seen.

"Eddie," as he liked his friends to call him, would sometimes get so absorbed in whatever he was doing—whether it was fishing, playing marbles or drinking—that he would lose all track of time. He loved to chase fire engines and once climbed over an outfield fence during a game to chase one. After the 1907 season, Mack tired of the "odd ball" in Waddell and dealt him to the St. Louis Browns. The first time he faced his old teammates, he struck out 16—an American League record at the time. He died of tuberculosis in 1914 at the age of 37.

Year	Team	W-L	ERA	G	IP	H	BB	SO
1897	Louis	0-1	3.21	2	14	17	6	5
1899	Louis	7-2	3.08	10	79	69	14	44
1900	Pitt	8-13	2.37	29	208.2	176	55	130
1901	Pitt-Chi (N)	13-17	3.01	31	251.1	249	75	172
1902	Phil (A)	24-7	2.05	33	276.1	224	64	210
1903	Phil	21-16	2.44	39	324	274	85	302
1904	Phil	25-19	1.62	46	383	307	91	349
1905	Phil	26-11	1.45	46	328.2	231	90	287
1906	Phil	15-17	2.21	43	272.2	221	92	196
1907	Phil	19-13	2.15	44	284.2	234	73	232
1908	StL (A)	19-14	1.89	43	285.2	223	90	232
1909	StL	11-14	2.37	31	220.1	204	57	141
1910	StL	3-1	3.55	10	33	31	11	16
13 years		**191-145**	**2.16**	**407**	**2961.1**	**2460**	**803**	**2316**

Transaction: January 1900: Traded to Pittsburgh with Patsy Flaherty, Deacon Phillippe, Walt Woods, Honus Wagner, Icebox Chamberlain, Chief Zimmer, Tacks Latimer, Claude Ritchey, Fred Clarke, Tommy Leach, Mike Kelly, Conny Doyle and Tom Massitt for Jack Chesbro, Paddy Fox, John O'Brien, Art Madison and $25,000. (Sale of the chief assets of the Louisville team after Louisville was dropped by the National League.) May 1901: Sold to Chicago Cubs. Feb. 7, 1908: Sold to St. Louis Browns.

John Peter Wagner

Born February 24, 1874, in Carnegie, Pennsylvania; died December 6, 1955, in Carnegie, Pennsylvania. 5'11", 200 lbs., bats right, throws right. Years in minor leagues: 6; Major League debut: July 19, 1897; Years in Major Leagues: 21. Elected to Hall of Fame: 1936. Nickname: Honus—German for John; also, The Flying Dutchman—because of his ancestry (German/Dutch) and his great speed.

Honus Wagner was the National League's first superstar and is still regarded as one of the best all-around players of all time. In the first Hall of Fame balloting, in 1936, Wagner finished behind Ty Cobb—and ahead of Babe Ruth. There was no Rookie of the Year award when Wagner played, but had there been, he would have won it with his .344 batting average in his first year with the Pittsburgh Pirates. He hit over .300 for 17 consecutive seasons and won eight batting titles in a 12-year period, all the while dazzling fans and opponents alike with sensational plays at his shortstop position. His 3,430 hits rank him sixth on the all-time list.

Wagner led the National League in stolen bases six times and finished with 722 career steals. Though records are sketchy, Wagner is credited with stealing second, third and home in the same game three times in his career. He stole seven bases in the 1909 World Series, a record that stood until Lou Brock broke it in 1967. The Dutchman was awkward in appearance and looked even more awkward with a bat in his hand. He was bow-legged, and his batting stance, according to one writer, looked like a man sitting on a bar stool. He held the bat with his hands apart and flailed at pitches, hitting the ball to all fields. Wagner was a kind, gentle man off the field who would not allow his picture to be used in cigarette advertising because he thought it was not the right image to project to children. He was involved in one the biggest "trades" in baseball history in 1900 when the Louisville owner moved his franchise to Pittsburgh, which involved the exchange of 17 players, including Wagner. He would never be traded again.

Wagner was a coach with the Pirates from 1933 to 1951, a time in which he is remembered for telling outlandish stories about his playing days. As a shortstop, he had the reputation of scooping up everything in sight when a ball came near him, and is said to have sometimes thrown ball, dirt and pebbles toward first base. Wagner told young ballplayers that a dog ran on the field one day, just as he was fielding a ground ball, and he scooped up the dog and threw it to first.

Year	Team	G	AB	R	H	D	T	HR	RBI	AVE.
1897	Louis (N)	61	241	38	83	17	4	2	39	.344
1898	Louis	151	591	80	180	31	4	10	105	.305
1899	Louis	144	549	102	197	47	13	7	113	.359
1900	Pitt	135	528	107	201	45	22	4	100	.381
1901	Pitt	141	556	100	196	39	10	6	126	.353
1902	Pitt	137	538	105	177	33	16	3	91	.329

Year	Team	G	AB	R	H	D	T	HR	RBI	AVE.
1903	Pitt	129	512	97	182	30	19	5	101	.355
1904	Pitt	132	490	97	171	44	14	4	75	.349
1905	Pitt	147	548	114	199	32	14	6	101	.363
1906	Pitt	142	516	103	175	38	9	2	71	.339
1907	Pitt	142	515	98	180	38	14	6	82	.350
1908	Pitt	151	568	100	201	39	19	10	109	.354
1909	Pitt	137	495	92	168	39	10	5	100	.339
1910	Pitt	150	556	90	178	34	8	4	81	.320
1911	Pitt	130	473	87	158	23	16	9	89	.334
1912	Pitt	145	558	91	181	35	20	7	102	.324
1913	Pitt	114	413	51	124	18	4	3	56	.300
1914	Pitt	150	552	60	139	15	9	1	50	.252
1915	Pitt	151	566	68	155	32	17	6	78	.274
1916	Pitt	123	432	45	124	15	9	1	39	.287
1917	Pitt	74	230	15	61	7	1	0	24	.265
21 years		**2786**	**10427**	**1740**	**3430**	**651**	**252**	**101**	**1732**	**.329**

Transaction: January 1900: Traded to Pittsburgh with Patsy Flaherty, Deacon Phillippe, Walt Woods, Rube Waddell, Icebox Chamberlain, Chief Zimmer, Tacks Latimer, Claude Ritchey, Fred Clarke, Tommy Leach, Mike Kelly, Conny Doyle and Tom Massitt for Jack Chesbro, Paddy Fox, John O'Brien, Art Madison and $25,000. (Sale of the chief assets of the Louisville team after Louisville was dropped by the National League.)

WORLD SERIES

Year	Team	G	AB	R	H	D	T	HR	RBI	AVE.
1903	Pitt	8	27	2	6	1	0	0	3	.222
1909	Pitt	7	24	4	8	2	1	0	6	.333
2 years		**15**	**51**	**6**	**14**	**3**	**1**	**0**	**9**	**.275**

Roderick John Wallace

Born November 4, 1874, in Pittsburgh, Pennsylvania; died November 3, 1960, in Torrance, California. 5'8", 175 lbs., bats right, throws right. Years in minor leagues: None; Major League debut: September 15, 1894; Years in Major Leagues: 25. Elected to Hall of Fame: 1953. Nickname: Bobby—origin unknown; also, Mr. Shortstop—because of his ability to field his position.

Bobby Wallace was the first American League shortstop elected to the Hall of Fame. He began his career as a pitcher and won 24 games one year. Sixty years later, he ended his career as a scout. In the decades in between, he was a player, manager and umpire. Playing for the St. Louis Browns, he led the American League in assists three times and once had 27 assists in a game—a record that seems secure. In 1902, he may have become the first Major League player with a long-term contract when the Browns signed him to a six-year deal for $32,500—and a signing bonus of $6,500. That made him easily the highest paid player in baseball.

He started his career as a pitcher with the Cleveland Spiders and, after a brief appearance in 1894 (a loss), he was 12–13 in 1895 and 10–7 in 1896 before making the transition to the infield. As a shortstop, he discovered that too many runners were beating out hits by a fraction of a second. He developed a style of picking up ground balls and throwing to first base in one fluid motion, instead of picking up the ball, coming to standing position, and then throwing. It is the way every infielder plays today.

He managed the Browns for a little over a year, with only an eighth place finish to show for it, and umpired with veteran American League umpire Billy Evans for about a year, but decided he'd rather play than ump. Wallace played in the Majors for 25 years and never really had a spectacular year at the plate. But people who saw him play remember him for his fielding. He did not play in an era of nationwide television and radio, so the word couldn't spread as quickly about Wallace as it does today about such great fielding stars as Brooks Robinson and Ozzie Smith. But 35 years after he retired, enough people remembered his abilities to elect him to the Hall of Fame in 1953.

Year	Team	G	AB	R	H	D	T	HR	RBI	AVE.
1894	Cleve (N)	4	13	0	2	1	0	0	1	.154
1895	Cleve	30	98	16	21	2	3	0	10	.214
1896	Cleve	45	149	19	35	6	3	1	17	.235
1897	Cleve	130	516	99	173	33	21	4	112	.335
1898	Cleve	154	593	81	160	25	13	3	99	.270
1899	Cleve	151	577	91	170	28	14	12	108	.295
1900	StL (N)	126	485	70	130	25	9	4	70	.268
1901	StL	134	550	69	178	34	15	2	91	.324
1902	StL (A)	133	494	71	141	32	9	1	63	.285
1903	StL	135	511	63	136	21	7	1	54	.266
1904	StL	139	541	57	149	29	4	2	69	.275
1905	StL	156	587	67	159	25	9	1	59	.271
1906	StL	139	476	64	123	21	7	2	67	.258
1907	StL	147	538	56	138	20	7	0	70	.257
1908	StL	137	487	59	123	24	4	1	60	.253
1909	StL	116	403	36	96	12	2	0	35	.238
1910	StL	138	508	47	131	19	7	0	37	.258
1911	StL	125	410	35	95	12	2	0	31	.232
1912	StL	99	323	39	78	14	5	0	31	.241
1913	StL	55	147	11	31	5	0	0	21	.211
1914	StL	26	73	3	16	2	1	0	5	.219
1915	StL	9	13	1	3	0	1	0	4	.231
1916	StL	14	18	0	5	0	0	0	1	.278
1917	StL	8	10	0	1	0	0	0	2	.100
1918	StL	32	98	3	15	1	0	0	4	.153
25 years		2382	8618	1057	2309	391	143	34	1121	.268

Edward Augustine Walsh

Born May 14, 1881, in Plains, Pennsylvania; died May 26, 1959, in Pompano Beach, Florida. 6'1", 193 lbs., bats right, throws right. Years in minor leagues: 4; Major League debut: May 7, 1904; Years in Major Leagues: 14. Elected to Hall of Fame: 1946. Nickname: Big Ed—more for his pitching statistics than for his size.

Ed Walsh was the master of the spitball when it was a legal pitch and won an average of 25 games a year for six years for the Chicago White Sox. He was known for his durability—and the best example of which is his performance during the 1908 season when the White Sox battled unsuccessfully for a pennant. Walsh pitched 41⅓ innings—the equivalent of almost five complete games—in an eight-day stretch. On September 29, 1908, he beat Boston in both ends of a doubleheader, allowing just one run. The next day, he pitched another complete game, this one against Cleveland. Although Walsh gave up only one run and struck out 15, Addie Joss of the Indians threw a perfect game to beat him.

Walsh worked 464 innings in that 1908 season, a modern Major League record, and won 40 games, including 12 shutouts. He started 49 games and relieved in 17. Although "saves" weren't officially counted back then, historians have determined Walsh would have had six saves in addition to those 40 wins. He pitched during an era when the White Sox were known as the "Hitless Wonders," and sometimes even great pitching couldn't bail them out. In 1910, Walsh had a stunning earned run average of 1.27—but lost 20 games. His teammates had a combined batting average of .211 and hit only seven home runs. The "Hitless Wonders" won the pennant in 1906. Walsh won 17 games, 10 by shutout. In the third game of the World Series, he struck out 12 Cubs, a Series record that lasted many years. On average, he gave up a home run once every 124 innings during his career. He threw a no-hitter in 1912. His lifetime ERA of 1.82 is one of those records that may never be broken. He ended his Major League career not as a pitcher but as an umpire. Walsh was an American League umpire in 1922 but gave it up after one season.

Year	Team	W-L	ERA	G	IP	H	BB	SO
1904	Chi (A)	6-3	2.60	18	110.2	90	32	57
1905	Chi	8-3	2.17	22	136.2	121	29	71
1906	Chi	17-13	1.88	41	278.1	215	58	171
1907	Chi	24-18	1.60	56	422.1	341	87	206
1908	Chi	40-15	1.42	49	464	343	56	269
1909	Chi	15-11	1.41	28	230.1	166	50	127
1910	Chi	18-20	1.27	36	369.2	242	61	258
1911	Chi	27-18	2.22	37	368.2	327	72	255
1912	Chi	27-17	2.15	41	393	332	94	254
1913	Chi	8-3	2.58	14	97.2	91	39	34
1914	Chi	2-3	2.82	5	44.2	33	20	15
1915	Chi	3-0	1.33	3	27	19	7	12

Year	Team	W-L	ERA	G	IP	H	BB	SO
1916	Chi	0-1	2.70	2	3.1	4	3	3
1917	Bos (N)	0-1	3.50	4	18	22	9	4
14 years		**195-126**	**1.82**	**430**	**2964.1**	**2346**	**617**	**1736**

WORLD SERIES

Year	Team	W-L	ERA	G	IP	H	BB	SO
1906	Chi (A)	2-0	1.80	2	15	7	6	17

Lloyd James Waner

Born March 16, 1906, in Harrah, Oklahoma; died July 22, 1982, in Oklahoma City, Oklahoma. 6'1", 175 lbs., bats left, throws right. Years in minor leagues: 3; Major League debut: April 12, 1927; Years in Major Leagues: 18. Elected to Hall of Fame: 1967. Nickname: Little Poison—not because he was "poison" to opposition pitching, the common thought about the derivation of his nickname; it is actually a version of how a New York fan, with a decidedly East Coast accent, pronounced the word "person" in referring to him. A New York sportswriter picked up on the term. It is not known why Lloyd was "Little Poison" and his brother, Paul, was "Big Poison," with Lloyd actually being the bigger of the two men, physically.

Lloyd Waner was a fleet-footed center fielder and a great lead-off hitter who liked to slap the ball to all fields. Waner and his brother, Paul, were two-thirds of the Pittsburgh Pirate outfield for 14 years. Lloyd broke in with the Pirates in their pennant winning year of 1927. His first Major League hit was a routine grounder to short that he beat out—a signal of the type of player he was going to be. By season's end, he had a .355 batting average with 223 hits—still a Major League record for rookies—and 198 of those hits were singles, which is also a Major League record.

Nobody ever got off to a faster start in a Major League career. Waner followed his rookie season by getting 221 hits in 1928 and 234 in 1929—a three-year total of 678. He only played part of the 1930 season, sidelined with an appendectomy, but came back in 1931 to get 214 hits. He hit over .300 in 10 of his first 12 seasons and finished with a lifetime batting average of .316. Waner only struck out 173 times in his career, an average of once every 45 at-bats.

Though Pittsburgh ran into a buzz saw in the 1927 World Series—the Yankees murdered them in a four-game sweep—Waner hit .400 from his lead-off position. He was an outstanding defensive center fielder, largely because of his speed and the jump he got on balls. He led National League outfielders in putouts four times. An irony of his great career is that he never played in an All-Star game.

Year	Team	G	AB	R	H	D	T	HR	RBI	AVE.
1927	Pitt	150	629	133	223	17	6	2	37	.355
1928	Pitt	152	659	121	221	22	14	5	61	.335
1929	Pitt	151	662	134	234	28	20	5	74	.353
1930	Pitt	68	260	32	94	8	3	1	36	.362
1931	Pitt	154	681	90	214	25	13	4	57	.314
1932	Pitt	134	565	90	188	27	11	2	38	.333
1933	Pitt	121	500	59	138	14	5	0	26	.276
1934	Pitt	140	611	95	173	27	6	1	48	.283
1935	Pitt	122	537	83	166	22	14	0	46	.309
1936	Pitt	106	414	67	133	13	8	1	31	.321
1937	Pitt	129	537	80	177	23	4	1	45	.330
1938	Pitt	147	619	79	194	25	7	5	57	.313
1939	Pitt	112	379	49	108	15	3	0	24	.285
1940	Pitt	72	166	30	43	3	0	0	3	.259
1941	Pitt-Bos-Cin	77	219	26	64	5	1	0	11	.292
1942	Phi (N)	101	287	23	75	7	3	0	10	.261
1944	Brklyn-Pitt	34	28	5	9	0	0	0	3	.321
1945	Pitt	23	19	5	5	0	0	0	1	.263
18 years		**1993**	**7772**	**1201**	**2459**	**281**	**118**	**27**	**598**	**.316**

Transactions: May 7, 1941: Traded to Boston Braves for Nick Strincevich. June 12, 1941: Traded to Cincinnati Reds for Johnny Hutchings. March 9, 1943: Traded to Brooklyn with Al Glossop for Babe Dahlgren.

WORLD SERIES

Year	Team	G	AB	R	H	D	T	HR	RBI	AVE.
1927	Pitt	4	15	5	6	1	1	0	0	.400

Paul Glee Waner

Born April 16, 1903, in Harrah, Oklahoma; died August 29, 1965, in Sara-sota, Florida. 5'8½", 153 lbs., bats left, throws left. Years in minor leagues: 3; Major League debut: April 13, 1926; Years in Major Leagues: 20. Elected to Hall of Fame: 1952. Nickname: Big Poison—not because he was "poison" to opposition pitching but a reference to how a New York fan—with an East Coast accent—pronounced the word "person" in talking about him.

Paul Waner was the more spectacular of the Waner brothers, both on and off the field. He won three batting titles—in 1927, 1934 and 1936. In 1927, he won the National League's Most Valuable Player Award when he hit .380 and his Pittsburgh Pirates won the pennant. Waner hit over .300 14 times, including 12 straight seasons. He got more than 200 hits in eight of those seasons. He finished with 3,152 hits and a lifetime batting average of .333.

Big Poison had more power than his little brother but was not concerned with home runs. He liked to stand far back in the batter's box with his feet almost together. As the pitch came in, Waner would raise his right foot and try to knock the ball down either foul line. The results are impressive: 603 career doubles and 190 triples. He was known to be a heavy drinker who often showed up at the ball-park drunk or hungover. Ironically, his middle name was Glee.

A favorite story that Waner never denied: Teammate Fred Lindstrom arrived at his home one morning for a golf date. His wife told Lindstrom that Paul had gone to the store for a loaf of bread. Lindstrom waited a while and then asked Mrs. Waner when Paul had left. "Last night," she said. He got his 3,000th hit as a member of the Boston Braves in 1942. Waner had beaten out an infield hit that could have been called an error. Standing on first, he motioned to the official scorer not to rule it a hit. Later, he got a clean single off his old teammate, Rip Sewell of the Pirates, and, fittingly, celebrated with a party that night.

Year	Team	G	AB	R	H	D	T	HR	RBI	AVE.
1926	Pitt	144	536	101	180	35	22	8	79	.336
1927	Pitt	155	623	113	237	40	17	9	131	.380
1928	Pitt	152	602	142	223	50	19	6	86	.370
1929	Pitt	151	596	131	200	43	15	15	100	.336
1930	Pitt	145	589	117	217	32	18	8	77	.368
1931	Pitt	150	559	88	180	35	10	6	70	.322
1932	Pitt	154	630	107	215	62	10	8	82	.341
1933	Pitt	154	618	101	191	38	16	7	70	.309
1934	Pitt	146	599	122	217	32	16	14	90	.362
1935	Pitt	139	549	98	176	29	12	11	78	.321
1936	Pitt	148	585	107	218	53	9	5	94	.373
1937	Pitt	154	619	94	219	30	9	2	74	.354
1938	Pitt	148	625	77	175	31	6	6	69	.280
1939	Pitt	125	461	62	151	30	6	3	45	.328
1940	Pitt	89	238	32	69	16	1	1	32	.290
1941	Brk-Bos	106	329	45	88	10	2	2	46	.279
1942	Bos	114	333	43	86	17	1	1	39	.258
1943	Brklyn	82	225	29	70	16	0	1	26	.311
1944	Brk-NY	92	143	17	40	4	1	0	17	.280
1945	NY (A)	1	0	0	0	0	0	0	0	.000
20 years		**2549**	**9459**	**1626**	**3152**	**603**	**190**	**113**	**1309**	**.333**

WORLD SERIES

Year	Team	G	AB	R	H	D	T	HR	RBI	AVE.
1927	Pitt	4	15	3	5	1	0	0	3	.333

John Montgomery Ward

Born March 3, 1860, in Bellefante, Pennsylvania; died March 4, 1925, in Augusta, Georgia. 5'9", 165 lbs., bats left, throws right. Years in minor leagues: 1; Major League debut: July 15, 1878; Years in Major Leagues: 17. Elected to Hall of Fame: 1964. Nickname: Monte—a shortening of his middle name.

John "Monte" Ward not only could do it all—he did it all in professional baseball. He was an outstanding pitcher until he hurt his right arm, his pitching arm, in a baserunning mishap. So, while his right arm was mending, he taught himself to throw lefthanded and played center field for a year. The next season, with his right arm healed but not strong enough to pitch, he switched to short-stop and stayed there for the rest of his career.

Ward was a manager for six years and compiled a .562 winning percentage. He also was a union organizer, forming the first players' association, but it could not withstand the owners' pressure and was short-lived. In 1911, he was part of an ownership group that purchased the Boston club in the National League, but he was bought out a year later. Nonetheless, his career as pitcher, outfielder, short-stop, manager, union organizer and and club owner is one of the most remarkable sagas in baseball history.

Johnny Ward was a brash teenager with a quick temper when he joined the Providence team in 1888 and had the lowest earned run average in the league at 1.51. The next year, at the age of 19, he won 47 for Providence's pennant winning ball club. The year after that, he threw a perfect game. He had the baserunning accident in 1884 and turned his concentration to hitting. In the next 12 years, he hit over .300 three times and finished with 2,123 hits. As a pitcher, Ward is the answer to a classic baseball trivia question: Who invented the intentional walk?

AS A HITTER

Year	Team	G	AB	R	H	D	T	HR	RBI	AVE.
1878	Prov (N)	37	138	14	27	5	4	1	15	.196
1879	Prov	83	364	71	104	10	4	2	41	.286
1880	Prov	86	356	53	81	12	2	0	27	.228
1881	Prov	85	357	56	87	18	6	0	53	.244
1882	Prov	83	355	58	87	10	4	0		.245
1883	NY (N)	88	380	76	97	18	7	7		.255
1884	NY	113	482	98	122	11	8	2		.253
1885	NY	111	446	72	101	8	9	0		.226
1886	NY	122	491	82	134	17	5	2	81	.273
1887	NY	129	545	114	184	16	5	1	53	.338
1888	NY	122	510	70	128	14	5	2	49	.251
1889	NY	114	479	87	143	13	4	1	67	.299
1890	Brklyn	128	561	134	207	15	12	4	60	.369
1891	Brklyn	105	441	85	122	13	5	0	39	.277
1892	Brklyn	148	614	109	163	13	3	2	47	.265
1893	NY (N)	135	588	129	193	27	9	2	77	.328
1894	NY	136	540	100	143	12	5	0	77	.265
17 years		1825	7647	1408	2123	232	97	26	686	.278

AS A PITCHER

Year	Team	W-L	ERA	G	IP	H	BB	SO
1878	Prov	22-13	1.51	37	334	308	34	116

Year	Team	W-L	ERA	G	IP	H	BB	SO
1879	Prov	47-17	2.15	70	587	571	36	239
1880	Prov	40-23	1.74	70	595	501	45	230
1881	Prov	18-18	2.13	39	330	326	53	119
1882	Prov	19-13	2.59	33	278	261	36	72
1883	NY (N)	12-14	2.70	33	277	278	31	121
1884	NY	1-3	3.40	9	60.2	72	18	23
7 years		161-101	2.10	291	2461.2	2317	253	920

As Manager

Year	Team	W-L	Standing
1884	NY (N)	6-8	Fourth
1890	Brklyn	76-56	Second
1891	Brklyn	61-76	Sixth
1892	Brklyn	95-59	Third
1893	NY (N)	68-64	Fifth
1894	NY	88-44	Second
6 years		394-307	

Earl Weaver

Born August 14, 1936, in St. Louis, Missouri. Years in minor leagues: 13; Years in Major Leagues: 17 (as a manager). Nickname: None.

Earl Weaver managed the Baltimore Orioles for 17 years. In 12 of those years, his team won more than 90 games. Five times, they won 100 games or more, a Major League record he shares with Joe McCarthy. Under Weaver, the Orioles won six division titles, four league championships and one World Series championship. His overall managerial record was 1,480 wins and 1,060 losses for a winning percentage of .583.

Weaver was a minor league ballplayer for 13 years but never climbed any higher than the Double A level. Like Sparky Anderson, Whitey Herzog, Walter Alston and others, Weaver was a much better manager than he was a player. He managed in the minor leagues for several years and was the winning manager at Elmira in the longest scoreless game in professional baseball history in 1965. His Elmira team was tied with Springfield, 0–0, after 25 innings. Amazingly, both teams scored in the 26th and Elmira pushed over the winning run in the 27th.

Weaver became manager of the Orioles in 1968, replacing Hank Bauer. Three future Hall of Famers—Brooks Robinson, Frank Robinson and Jim Palmer—helped Weaver lead the Orioles to consecutive division titles in 1969, 1970 and 1971, winning 318 games—an average of 106 wins a year. The 1970 team won 108 games and defeated Cincinnati in the World Series. His Orioles were back in the World Series in 1979 but lost in seven games to a Pittsburgh Pirate team led by Willie Stargell.

Weaver, who often said his managerial strategy was to wait for a three-run homer, had some classic run-ins with umpires. Once, in the heat of a pennant race in Toronto, Weaver refused to have his players take the field until a tarp down the right field line was moved. Home plate umpire Marty Springstead saw no need to move the tarp and told Weaver to put a team on the field. After five minutes and no movement from the Oriole dugout, Springstead forfeited the game to the Blue Jays. One of Weaver's tricks was to pull his cap down tightly on his head. Then, in arguments with umpires, Weaver would get close enough to scrape their faces with the bill of his cap. Weaver was suspended six times and ejected from games almost 100 times. He is 1 of only 14 managers in the Hall of Fame.

Year	Team	W-L	Standing
1968	Balt	48-34	Second
1969	Balt	109-53	First
1970	Balt	108-54	First
1971	Balt	101-57	First
1972	Balt	80-74	Third
1973	Balt	97-65	First
1974	Balt	91-71	First
1975	Balt	90-69	Second
1976	Balt	88-74	Second
1977	Balt	97-64	Second
1978	Balt	90-71	Fourth
1979	Balt	102-57	First
1980	Balt	100-62	Second
1981	Balt	59-46	(strike shortened)
1982	Balt	94-68	Second
1985	Balt	53-52	Fourth
1986	Balt	73-89	Seventh
17 years		**1480-1060**	

League Championship Series

Year	Team	W-L
1969	Balt	3-0
1970	Balt	3-0
1971	Balt	3-0
1973	Balt	2-3
1974	Balt	1-3
1979	Balt	3-1
6 years	**15-7**	

World Series

1969	Balt	1-4
1970	Balt	4-1
1971	Balt	3-4
1979	Balt	3-4
4 years		**11-13**

George Weiss

Born June 23, 1895, in New Haven, Connecticut; died August 13, 1972, in
Greenwich, Connecticut. Years in Major Leagues: 28 years (as farm director
and general manager). Elected to Hall of Fame: 1971.

George Weiss was general manager of the New York Yankees from 1948 to
1960 during which his teams won ten pennants and seven World Series. As general
manager he was able to reap what he had sown in his earlier days. As farm
director of the Yankees, beginning in 1932, he developed one of the greatest farm
systems ever. During his tenure as farm director, the Yankees won nine pennants
and eight world championships. Weiss was a winner and he had the track record
to prove it.

As farm director, he teamed with general manager Ed Barrow to be a formidable
combination. They had one celebrated disagreement: when Weiss wanted to
bring up a kid named Joe DiMaggio and Barrow resisted. Weiss lobbied the Yankee
ownership and won. When he became general manager, he hired a fellow
named Casey Stengel as his manager, and they remained together until the end of
the 1960 season when both were fired in a Yankee youth movement. As Yankee
general manager, Weiss made many trades with the Kansas City A's and acquired
players who later starred for the Yankees—and gave the A's the dubious nickname
of being a Yankee farm team.

For all his baseball brilliance, Weiss is also known for being slow to bring a
black player to the Major Leagues. Elston Howard was the Yankees' first black in
1956. Weiss was also known for being a penny-pincher who was not overjoyed
when Yankee players had such great years that big pay raises were expected.

Michael Francis Welch

Born July 4, 1859, in Brooklyn, New York; died July 30, 1931, in Nashua,
New Hampshire. 5'10", 185 lbs., bats right, throws right. Years in minor
leagues: 2; Major League debut: May 1, 1980; Years in Major Leagues: 13 years.
Elected to Hall of Fame: 1973. Nickname: Smiling Mickey—given to him by
a cartoonist of his day because of his sunny disposition and because he had a
habit of grinning anytime he was in a tight spot on the mound.

Mickey Welch was one of the great pitchers of the 19th century, using an early
version of the screwball to keep hitters off balance. He was one of the first pitchers
to win 300 games—only Pud Galvin and Tim Keefe, a teammate, beat him to
the 300 mark.

His durability was incredible. In 1882, he started 44 games and completed
them all. In 1883, he pitched more than 400 innings. In 1884, he started 65 games
and completed 62 of them. His most remarkable season was 1885 when he won
44 games, including a stretch in which he won 17 in a row. Between 1884 and

1886, Welch averaged over 500 innings a year and once had a streak of 104 complete games in a row.

When the Giants won their first pennant in 1888, Welch and Keefe accounted for 61 of the team's 84 victories. Welch was part of a baseball first in 1889 when he was called on as a pinch hitter. That had never been done before. Welch struck out, but his role as a pinch hitter is one that has become part of baseball strategy for more than 100 years.

Year	Team	W-L	ERA	G	IP	H	BB	SO
1880	Troy	34-30	2.54	65	574	575	80	123
1881	Troy	20-18	2.67	40	368	371	78	104
1882	Troy	14-16	3.46	33	281	334	62	53
1883	NY (N)	27-21	2.73	54	426	431	66	144
1884	NY	39-21	2.50	65	557.1	528	146	345
1885	NY	44-11	1.66	56	492	372	131	258
1886	NY	33-22	2.99	59	500	514	163	272
1887	NY	23-15	3.36	40	346	339	91	115
1888	NY	26-19	1.93	47	425.1	328	108	167
1889	NY	27-12	3.02	45	375	340	149	125
1890	NY	18-13	2.99	37	292.1	268	122	97
1891	NY	6-9	4.28	22	160	176	97	46
1892	NY	0-0	14.40	1	5	11	4	1
13 years		**311-207**	**2.71**	**564**	**4802**	**4587**	**1297**	**1850**

Willie James Wells Sr.

Born 1905; died 1989. 5'9", 160 lbs., bats right, throws right. Years in minor leagues (Negro Leagues): 30; Years in Major Leagues: None. Elected to Hall of Fame: 1997. Nickname: The Devil—origin unknown.

Willie Wells was a good hitter for three decades in the Negro leagues, but earned his reputation for being the best shortstop in the Negro leagues in the 1930s and 1940s. He hit .404 for the St. Louis Stars in 1930. He had a career batting average of .392 against Major League competition in exhibition games.

In 1947, when Jackie Robinson broke the color line by playing for the Brooklyn Dodgers, Wells, who would have been a sure bet for the Major Leagues ten years earlier, had to continue to toil in the Negro leagues because he was 42 years old. The next year, at age 43, Wells hit .328 for Indianapolis. His playing career was over two years later. Wells is regarded as being somewhat of a pioneer in two areas. Playing for the Newark Eagles in 1936, he was beaned with a pitch and was knocked unconscious. Returning to the lineup several days later, Wells sported a construction helmet—believed to be the first batting helmet worn in professional baseball.

His other innovation was in the infield, to help make up for his average throwing arm. Instead of staying at the stationary position between short and third, Wells studied the hitters and moved in one direction or another to help him get a jump on the ball, a common practice in baseball today.

Zachariah Davis Wheat

Born May 23, 1888, in Hamilton, Missouri; died March 11, 1972, in Sedalia, Missouri. 5'10", 170 lbs., bats left, throws left. Years in minor leagues: 2; Major League debut: April 14, 1915; Years in Major Leagues: 18. Elected to Hall of Fame: 1959. Nickname: Buck, short for buckwheat, used occasionally in newspapers; but most often, Zack—a shortening of his first name.

Zack Wheat was one of the most popular players ever to play for the Brooklyn Dodgers. He played left field for 19 years, all but one year with the Dodgers, and hit over .300 in 14 of those years. Wheat was a contemporary of Babe Ruth's and once rated higher than Ruth in a New York newspaper poll asking fans to choose their favorite ballplayer. Wheat was a line drive hitter who had a special knack for hitting a curveball. He also seemed to get better with age. In 1924, at age 38, he hit .375. The following year, the 39-year-old hit .359 and batted in 103 runs.

He finished with a lifetime batting average of .317 with one batting title to his credit—one that took a special ruling from the commissioner. He hit .335 in 1918. Billy Southworth of the Pittsburgh Pirates hit .341, but played in only 64 games. Edd Rousch of Cincinnati hit .333, two points lower than Wheat, but he played in 113 games—eight more than Wheat. National League president John Heydler considered all the factors and granted the title to Wheat. Two other highlights of Wheat's career were his 29-game hitting streak in 1916 and his participation in the 26-inning, 1–1 tie between Brooklyn and Boston in 1920.

Year	Team	G	AB	R	H	D	T	HR	RBI	AVE.
1909	Brklyn	26	102	15	31	7	3	0	4	.304
1910	Brklyn	156	606	78	172	36	15	2	55	.284
1911	Brklyn	140	534	55	153	26	13	5	76	.287
1912	Brklyn	123	453	70	138	28	7	8	65	.305
1913	Brklyn	138	535	64	161	28	10	7	58	.301
1914	Brklyn	145	533	66	170	26	9	9	89	.319
1915	Brklyn	146	528	64	136	15	12	5	66	.258
1916	Brklyn	149	568	76	177	32	13	9	73	.312
1917	Brklyn	109	362	38	113	15	11	1	41	.312
1918	Brklyn	105	409	39	137	15	3	0	51	.335
1919	Brklyn	137	536	70	159	23	11	5	62	.297
1920	Brklyn	148	583	89	191	26	13	9	73	.328
1921	Brklyn	148	568	91	182	31	10	14	85	.320
1922	Brklyn	152	600	92	201	29	12	16	112	.335
1923	Brklyn	98	349	63	131	13	5	8	65	.375
1924	Brklyn	141	566	92	212	41	8	14	97	.375
1925	Brklyn	150	616	125	221	42	14	14	103	.359
1926	Brklyn	111	411	68	119	31	2	5	35	.290
1927	Phil (A)	88	247	34	80	12	1	1	38	.324
19 years		2410	9106	1289	2884	476	172	132	1248	.317

WORLD SERIES

Year	Team	G	AB	R	H	D	T	HR	RBI	AVE.
1916	Brklyn	5	19	2	4	0	1	0	1	.211
1920	Brklyn	7	27	2	9	2	0	0	2	.333
2 years		12	46	4	13	2	1	0	3	.283

James Hoyt Wilhelm

Born July 26, 1923, in Huntersville, North Carolina. 6', 190 lbs., bats right, throws right. Years in minor leagues: 6; Major League debut: April 18, 1952; Years in Major Leagues: 21. Elected to Hall of Fame: 1985. Nickname: None— He was known by his middle name.

Hoyt Wilhelm was the first knuckleball pitcher to be elected to the Hall of Fame, as well as the first relief pitcher. His career statistics would be even greater except for two things: He did not make it to the Major Leagues until he was almost 29 years old; and the role of a relief pitcher was much different in his era than it is today. When Wilhelm pitched, a short reliever was summoned in the late innings of a close game, regardless of the score. It was his job to either preserve the win or hold the other team to keep the game within reach. Today's short relievers usually only enter the game in "save" situations. Wilhelm's career total of 227 saves, considering the late start he got and the number of times he pitched in nonsave situations, is especially noteworthy. His easy style gave him durability that allowed him to last 21 years, pitching in the Major Leagues until a week before his 49th birthday. His knuckleball was often as deceiving to catchers as it was to hitters. Five of Wilhelm's catchers hold records for most passed balls in an inning. Paul Richards, his manager at Baltimore, even designed an enlarged catcher's mitt that was used exclusively when Wilhelm was pitching.

Wilhelm served in World War II and was wounded in the Battle of the Bulge. He returned with a Purple Heart and began his professional career at Mooresville in Class D ball in 1946 and posted a 21–8 record. For some reason, he remained in D ball where he was 20–7 the next year. After that, he started to move up the ladder but did not make it to the Major Leagues until 1952. As a rookie with the New York Giants, Wilhelm was 15–3 and led the National League in appearances with 71. He made his Major League debut on April 18, but five days later made his first big impression: He pitched 5⅓ innings of relief in a 9–5 win over the Boston Braves. He also batted for the first time and hit a home run—and never hit another one in his 21-year career. Wilhelm and Earl Averill are the only two Hall of Famers to have homered in the their first Major League at-bats. Wilhelm's lifetime batting average was .088.

Wilhelm was well-traveled, pitching for the Giants, Cardinals, Indians, Orioles, White Sox, Braves and Dodgers. On September 20, 1958, pitching for

Baltimore and making a rare start, Wilhelm threw a no-hitter against the New York Yankees. He threw 99 pitches, 87 of them knuckleballs in the 1–0 victory. In 1964, a year in which he turned 41 in the middle of the season, he made 71 relief appearances for the Chicago White Sox and had an earned run average of 1.99, the fifth time in his career when his ERA was under 2.00. In that same season, Wilhelm had 12 wins and 27 saves. Another distinction for Wilhelm: He is the only Hall of Famer selected in an expansion draft. The Kansas City Royals picked him in 1968 but traded him to the Angels two months later, so he never threw a single pitch for Kansas City. When his career ended, he held the following records: most game appearances, 1,070; most relief wins, 124; most relief appearances, 1,018; most games finished, 651; and most innings as relief pitcher, 1,870. Although he saved 227 games, he never led the league in saves.

Year	Team	W-L	ERA	G	IP	H	BB	SO
1952	NY (N)	15-3	2.43	71	159.1	127	57	108
1953	NY	7-8	3.04	68	145	127	77	71
1954	NY	12-4	2.10	57	111.1	77	52	64
1956	NY	4-1	3.93	59	103	104	40	71
1957	StL-Cleve	2-4	4.14	42	58.2	54	22	29
1958	Cleve-Balt	3-10	2.34	39	131	95	45	92
1959	Balt	15-11	2.19	32	226	178	77	139
1960	Balt	11-8	3.31	41	147	125	39	107
1961	Balt	9-7	2.30	51	109.2	89	41	87
1962	Balt	7-10	1.94	52	93	64	34	90
1963	Chi (A)	5-8	2.64	55	136.1	106	30	111
1964	Chi	12-9	1.99	73	131.1	94	30	95
1965	Chi	7-7	1.81	66	144	88	32	106
1966	Chi	5-2	1.66	46	81.1	50	17	61
1967	Chi	8-3	1.31	49	89	58	34	76
1968	Chi	4-4	1.73	72	93.2	69	24	72
1969	Cal-Atl	7-7	2.20	52	77.2	50	22	67
1970	Atl-Chi (N)	6-5	3.40	53	82	73	42	68
1971	Atl-LA (N)	0-1	2.70	12	20	12	5	16
1972	LA	0-1	4.62	16	25.1	20	15	9
21 years		**143-122**	**2.52**	**1070**	**2254**	**1757**	**778**	**1610**

Transactions: Feb. 26, 1957: Traded to St. Louis Cardinals for infielder Whitey Lockman. Sept. 21, 1957: Sold to Cleveland Indians. Aug. 23, 1958: Picked up by Baltimore Orioles for waiver price. Jan. 14, 1963: Traded with infielder Pete Ward, infielder Ron Hansen and outfielder Dave Nicholson to Chicago White Sox for infielder Luis Aparicio and outfielder Al Smith. Dec. 12, 1968: Traded by Kansas City Athletics to California Angels for infielder Ed Kirkpatrick and catcher Dennis Paepke. Sept. 8, 1969: Sold to Atlanta Braves. Sept. 21, 1970: Sold to Chicago Cubs. Nov. 30, 1970: Traded to Atlanta Braves for infielder Hal Breeden.

WORLD SERIES

Year	Team	W-L	ERA	G	IP	H	BB	SO
1954	NY (N)	0-0	0.00	2	2.1	1	0	3

Billy Leo Williams

Born June 15, 1938, in Whistler, Alabama. 6'1", 170 lbs., bats left, throws right. Years in minor leagues: 4; Major League debut: August 6, 1959; Years in Major Leagues: 18. Elected to Hall of Fame: 1987. Nickname: None.

Billy Williams is remembered by those who saw him play for his "sweet swing." He always seemed graceful, never off balance, and he got a lot of results. Williams was never spectacular but was consistently good and had some great games and great seasons. He batted third in a Chicago Cub lineup that featured Williams, Ron Santo and Ernie Banks as one of the most powerful middle lineups of his era. Williams batted over .300 five times and won the National League batting championship in 1972 with a .333 average. His best offensive year was 1970 when he led the league in hits with 205, runs with 137, hit 42 home runs, had 129 RBIs and hit .322.

Williams did not play high school baseball because his school did not have a team, but he played plenty of summer ball. He turned down a football scholarship at Grambling with its noted coach Eddie Robinson because he wanted to play baseball instead. He played four years of minor league ball and at one time barnstormed on a black team where two of his teammates were Henry Aaron and Satchel Paige. His first full season in the Majors was 1961, and he made an immediate impression. He hit 25 home runs, including two grand slams, and drove in 86 runs while hitting .278. He was selected as the National League's Rookie of the Year.

Williams had some spectacular individual performances while playing 16 years for Cub teams that never won a pennant. He had three games in which he got four extra-base hits, including one in which all of his hits were doubles. He had one three-homer game in his career. He also had a game in which his four hits were the only Cub hits of the game. Williams played in 1,117 consecutive games for the Cubs, a National League record since broken by Steve Garvey. He finished his career with the Oakland A's but still did not manage to get into a World Series.

Year	Team	G	AB	R	H	D	T	HR	RBI	AVE.
1959	Chi (N)	18	33	0	5	0	1	0	2	.152
1960	Chi	12	47	4	13	0	2	2	7	.277
1961	Chi	146	529	75	147	20	7	25	86	.278
1962	Chi	159	618	94	184	22	8	22	91	.298
1963	Chi	161	612	87	175	36	9	25	95	.286
1964	Chi	162	645	100	201	39	2	33	98	.312
1965	Chi	164	645	115	203	39	6	34	108	.315
1966	Chi	162	648	100	179	23	5	29	91	.276
1967	Chi	162	634	92	176	21	12	28	84	.278
1968	Chi	163	642	91	185	30	8	30	98	.288
1969	Chi	163	642	103	188	33	10	21	95	.293
1970	Chi	161	636	137	205	34	4	42	129	.322
1971	Chi	157	594	86	179	27	5	28	93	.301

Year	Team	G	AB	R	H	D	T	HR	RBI	AVE.
1972	Chi	150	574	95	191	34	6	37	122	.333
1973	Chi	156	576	72	166	22	2	20	86	.288
1974	Chi	117	404	55	113	22	0	16	68	.280
1975	Oak	155	520	68	127	20	1	23	81	.244
1976	Oak	120	351	36	74	12	0	11	41	.211
18 years		**2488**	**9350**	**1410**	**2711**	**434**	**88**	**426**	**1475**	**.290**

Transaction: Oct. 23, 1974: Traded to Oakland A's in exchange for pitchers Darold Knowles and Bobby Locker and infielder Manny Trillo.

LEAGUE CHAMPIONSHIP SERIES

Year	Team	G	AB	R	H	D	T	HR	RBI	AVE.
1975	Oak (A)	3	8	0	0	0	0	0	0	.000

Joseph Williams

Born April 6, 1886, in Seguin, Texas; died March 12, 1946, in New York, New York. 6'4", 200 lbs., bats right, throws right. Years in minor leagues: 27 (Negro Leagues); Years in Major Leagues: None; Elected to Hall of Fame: 1999. Nickname—Smokey Joe, because of the speed of his fastball.

Smokey Joe Williams is regarded as one of baseball's greatest pitchers, but he never got a shot at the Major Leagues because he was black and he pitched before the color line was broken in the big leagues. Williams won more than 100 games in five seasons with the San Antonio Black Bronchos from 1905 to 1909. Then he played for several clubs in the Negro leagues for the next 20 years. His most memorable game occurred on August 2, 1930, when Williams, pitching for the Homestead Grays, struck out 27 batters while throwing a complete game as the Grays beat the Monarchs, 1–0, in 12 innings. Williams was 45 years old. The 1931 Grays team rivals some of the great Major League teams as being one of the best ever assembled. It featured Williams, Josh Gibson and Oscar Charleston, all Hall of Famers.

Theodore Samuel Williams

Born August 30, 1918, in San Diego, California. 6'4", 198 lbs., bats left, throws right. Years in minor leagues: 3; Major League debut: April 20, 1939; Years in Major Leagues: 19. Elected to Hall of Fame: 1966. Nicknames: The Splendid Splinter—because he was tall and thin; also, The Thumper, because of his hitting ability; also—Teddy Ballgame, a nickname he gave himself.

It is hard to know where to begin in listing Ted Williams' accomplishments. But a good starting point would be 1941 when Williams hit .406, the last time any

Major League player hit over .400. In the All-Star game that year, Williams hit a three-run homer in the bottom of the ninth inning to give the American League a 7–5 victory. On the last day of the 1941 season, Williams had a .39955 batting average which, rounded off, would give him a .400 average. He was given the option of sitting out a doubleheader with the Philadelphia A's, but Williams chose to play both games, got six hits in eight at-bats and finished with the .406 average. His on-base percentage that year was .551, a Major League record that still stands.

He did not win the Most Valuable Player Award in 1941—that honor went to Joe DiMaggio, who hit safely in 56 straight games. Williams had many near misses in his career. He won the Triple Crown in 1942 but again was passed over for the MVP award, which went to Joe Gordon. In 1949, he would have won his third Triple Crown but lost the batting title to George Kell by two-tenths of a percentage point. So much for the near misses. The accomplishments are phenomenal. Williams won two Triple Crowns, two MVP awards, six batting titles and four home run titles. He played in 18 All-Star games and hit another famous All-Star homer—off Rip Sewell's famed "Blooper pitch," a slow ball thrown with a high arc—in 1946. He led the league in runs scored six times and in RBIs four times. He led the league in slugging percentage nine times and in walks eight times. He finished with a lifetime batting average of .344 with 521 home runs.

He doubled off of Red Ruffing of the New York Yankees in his first Major League game and homered off Jack Fisher of the Baltimore Orioles in his last Major League at-bat. His lifetime statistics would be much higher if Williams hadn't missed nearly five seasons due to military service. In 1957, at the age of 39, Williams hit .388, the highest batting average of any player since 1941—when Williams hit .406. After his playing days were over, Williams managed the Washington Senators and followed them to Texas. His managerial career earned him Manager of the Year honors once, but after four years Williams was out of baseball, leaving with him the legacy of being one of the greatest hitters of all time.

Year	Team	G	AB	R	H	D	T	HR	RBI	AVE.
1939	Bos (A)	149	565	131	185	44	11	31	145	.327
1940	Bos	144	561	134	193	43	14	23	113	.344
1941	Bos	143	456	135	185	33	3	37	120	.406
1942	Bos	150	522	141	186	34	5	36	137	.356
1946	Bos	150	514	142	176	37	8	38	123	.342
1947	Bos	156	528	125	181	40	9	32	114	.343
1948	Bos	137	509	124	188	44	3	25	127	.369
1949	Bos	155	556	150	194	39	3	43	159	.343
1950	Bos	89	334	82	106	24	1	28	97	.317
1951	Bos	148	531	109	169	28	4	30	126	.318
1952	Bos	6	10	2	4	0	1	1	3	.400
1953	Bos	37	91	17	37	6	0	13	34	.407
1954	Bos	117	386	93	133	23	1	29	89	.345
1955	Bos	98	320	77	114	21	3	28	83	.356
1956	Bos	136	400	71	138	28	2	24	82	.345

Year	Team	G	AB	R	H	D	T	HR	RBI	AVE.
1957	Bos	132	420	96	163	28	1	38	87	.388
1958	Bos	129	411	81	135	23	2	26	85	.328
1959	Bos	103	272	32	69	15	0	10	43	.254
1960	Bos	113	310	56	98	15	0	29	72	.316
19 years		2292	7706	1798	2654	525	71	521	1839	.344

WORLD SERIES

Year	Team	G	AB	R	H	D	T	HR	RBI	AVE.
1946	Bos	7	25	2	5	0	0	0	1	.200

Victor Gazaway Willis

Born April 12, 1876, in Wilmington, Delaware; died August 3, 1947, in Elkton, Maryland. 6'2", 185 lbs., bats right, throws right. Years in minor leagues: 3; Major League debut: April 20, 1898; Years in Major Leagues: 13. Elected to Hall of Fame: 1995. Nickname: None.

When baseball fans talk about durable pitchers, names like Alexander, Johnson and Mathewson usually come up. Vic Willis was a contemporary of all of them, and he set the standard for all of them in terms of durability. Willis pitched 13 years in the Major Leagues, started 471 games and completed 388 of them. In 1902, pitching for the Boston Braves, Willis made 46 starts and completed 45, which is still a National League record. That same year he led the league in innings pitched with 410, hits allowed with 372 and strikeouts with 225.

He won more than 20 games and pitched more than 300 innings in eight of his 13 seasons, including four 20-win seasons in a row. Using a big curveball as his best weapon, Willis tossed 50 shutouts in his career. By comparison, Sandy Koufax, who pitched for 12 seasons, had 40 career shutouts. Anyone who pitches as much as Willis did is bound to have some bad games and bad seasons. He had seasons in which he lost 25 and 29 games.

The highlight of his career came on August 7, 1899, when he threw a no-hitter against Washington. For many years, he was considered one of the finest pitchers not in the Hall of Fame. In 1995, he was finally enshrined, 85 years after his playing days were over and 48 years after his death.

Year	Team	W-L	ERA	G	IP	H	BB	SO
1898	Bos (N)	24-13	2.84	41	311	264	148	160
1899	Bos	27-10	2.50	41	341.2	277	117	120
1900	Bos	10-17	4.19	32	236	258	106	53
1901	Bos	20-17	2.36	38	305.1	262	78	133
1902	Bos	27-19	2.20	51	410	372	101	225
1903	Bos	12-18	2.98	33	278	256	88	125
1904	Bos	18-25	2.85	43	350	357	109	196

Year	Team	W-L	ERA	G	IP	H	BB	SO
1905	Bos	11-29	3.21	41	342	340	107	149
1906	Pitt	22-13	1.73	41	322	295	76	124
1907	Pitt	22-11	2.34	39	292.2	234	69	107
1908	Pitt	23-11	2.07	41	304.2	239	69	97
1909	Pitt	22-11	2.24	39	289.2	243	83	95
1910	StL (N)	9-12	3.35	33	212	224	61	67
13 years		247-206	2.63	513	3996	3621	1212	1651

Transactions: Dec. 15, 1905: Traded to Pittsburgh for Dave Brain, Del Howard and Vive Lindaman. January 1910: Sold to St. Louis Cardinals.

WORLD SERIES

Year	Team	W-L	ERA	G	IP	H	BB	SO
1909	Pitt	0-1	4.76	2	11.1	10	8	3

Lewis Robert Wilson

Born April 26, 1900, in Ellwood City, Pennsylvania; died November 23, 1948, in Baltimore, Maryland. 5'6", 190 lbs., bats right, throws right. Years in minor leagues: 3; Major League debut: September 29, 1923; Years in Major Leagues: 12. Elected to Hall of Fame: 1979. Nickname: Hack—short for Hackenschmidt, a burly professional wrestler of the early 20th century, because of Wilson's unusual size.

Hack Wilson was one of the most colorful ballplayers of his day—but his day didn't last long. He played only 12 years in the Major Leagues, but won four home run titles as well as most of the fights that he got in on and off the field. He was a notorious drinker who was not a "happy drunk." He earned good money in the big leagues but died penniless at the age of 48, and donations had to be taken to pay for his funeral.

But his glory days were sensational. In 1930, as a member of the Chicago Cubs, Wilson had one of the greatest offensive seasons in baseball history. He hit 56 home runs, drove in 190 runs—still the Major League record—and hit .356. Wilson had a unique presence on a ball field because of the way he was built. Barely five feet, six inches tall, he weighed close to 200 pounds and had a size 18 neck—but he wore size 6 shoes. He played for the New York Giants, Chicago Cubs and Brooklyn Dodgers—and fell from grace even faster than he had risen. In 1931, the year after his 56-homer, 190-RBI year, Wilson hit just 13 home runs and drove in 61 runs. Three years later, he was out of baseball.

In 1929, he led the Cubs to the National League pennant. In the fourth game of the World Series, the Cubs were beating the Philadelphia A's 8-0 in the seventh inning when Mule Haas hit a fly ball to center. Wilson circled around, trying to find it, but lost it in the sun. It dropped for a three-run homer. The A's scored 10 runs in the inning and wound up winning the game, 10–8. Wilson was known as a man who could throw a knockout punch—literally—and he thought about becoming a professional boxer in the off-season. That idea was nixed by Commissioner Kenesaw Mountain Landis. Perhaps Hall of Fame sportswriter Warren Brown best summed up Wilson's career—and life—when he said, "Wilson was a highball hitter on and off the field."

Year	Team	G	AB	R	H	D	T	HR	RBI	AVE.
1923	NY (N)	3	10	0	2	0	0	0	0	.200
1924	NY (N)	107	383	62	113	19	12	10	57	.295
1925	NY (N)	62	180	28	43	7	4	6	30	.239
1926	Chi (N)	142	529	97	170	36	8	21	109	.321
1927	Chi (N)	146	551	119	175	30	12	30	129	.318
1928	Chi (N)	145	520	89	163	32	9	31	120	.313
1929	Chi (N)	150	574	135	198	30	5	39	159	.345
1930	Chi (N)	155	585	146	208	35	6	56	190	.356
1931	Chi (N)	112	395	66	103	22	4	13	61	.261
1932	Brklyn	135	481	77	143	37	5	23	123	.297
1933	Brklyn	117	360	41	96	13	2	9	54	.267
1934	Brk-Phil	74	192	24	47	5	0	6	30	.245
12 years		**1348**	**4760**	**884**	**1461**	**266**	**67**	**244**	**1062**	**.307**

Transactions: December 1931: Traded with Bud Teachout to St. Louis for Burleigh Grimes. Jan. 23, 1932: Traded to Brooklyn for minor league pitcher Bob Parkham and $45,000

WORLD SERIES

Year	Team	G	AB	R	H	D	T	HR	RBI	AVE.
1924	NY (N)	7	30	1	7	1	0	0	3	.233
1929	Chi (N)	5	17	2	8	0	1	0	0	.471
2 years		**12**	**47**	**3**	**15**	**1**	**1**	**0**	**3**	**.319**

Robert Wolff

Broadcaster. Elected to Hall of Fame: 1995.

Bob Wolff was both the television and radio voice of the Senators from 1947 until 1960, an era in which Washington earned its reputation of being "first in war, first in peace and last in the American League."

He went with the team to Minnesota where he broadcast for one year and then went to NBC to be part of its baseball broadcasting team. He also broadcast many sports from Madison Square Garden.

One of the highlights of Wolff's long career was broadcasting the last three innings of Don Larsen's perfect game in the 1956 World Series.

George Wright

Born January 28, 1847, in New York, New York; died August 31, 1937, in Boston, Massachusetts. Years in Major Leagues: None; was a pioneer ballplayer and manager prior to formation of Major Leagues. Elected to Hall of Fame: 1937

George Wright was a shortstop on the first professional baseball team, his brother Harry's Cincinnati Red Stockings in 1869. He was an outstanding hitter and was an innovative defensive shortstop. He once hit 49 home runs in 56 games for the Red Stockings, who put together a 130-game winning streak in 1869 and 1870. At shortstop, he was the first to play back, rather than in the base path, and also fielded the ball with his legs close together to prevent the ball from going through his legs.

He was player-manager of the Boston Red Stockings, a team that won four straight championships, and later managed the Providence Grays. While visiting England, his parents' native land, he was introduced to tennis and developed a love for the game. He set up tours in the United States involving young tennis players so that Americans could develop the same love for the game that he had. One of the touring young players was Harvard student Dwight Davis, for whom the Davis Cup would be named years later. Wright's son, Beals, was to become a member of the U.S. Davis Cup team.

George and Harry Wright are honored in the Hall of Fame for their early and lasting contributions to baseball, but not everyone shared their early enthusiasm for the sport. *The Cincinnati Enquirer*, in covering George Wright's team's first game in 1869, reported that both teams played poorly—and the story did not tell a final score. Apparently, the reporter got bored and left.

Harry Wright

Born January 10, 1835, in Sheffield, England; died October 3, 1895, in Atlantic City, New Jersey. Years in Major Leagues: None; was active player, manager and promoter of baseball long before Major Leagues were formed. Elected to Hall of Fame: 1953. Nickname: The Father of Professional Baseball—more of an identifier than a nickname, for all of his work in in promoting the sport in its earliest days.

Harry Wright came by his love of sports naturally; his father was a professional cricket player in England. Wright was playing cricket on a New York field one day when he noticed a group of men playing a different game on a nearby field. It was his introduction to baseball. Wright later joined the team he had been watching, the New York Knickerbockers, but enjoyed his greatest success as the organizer and field manager of the Cincinnati Red Stockings, the greatest team prior to the 20th century. The Red Stockings won 56 games in 1869 and continued the streak in 1870 with 74 more wins before losing to Brooklyn in extra innings, stopping the amazing streak at 130. He also managed the Boston team from 1871 to 1875 and later managed both the Providence and Philadelphia teams. Wright outfitted his team in the first baseball uniform of sorts: knickers, a style that has lasted for more than a century, with modifications. Players still wear uniform pants that resemble knickers (with stirrups). Wright also patented the first scorecard and was the first to take a team on a foreign tour.

When the National League was founded in 1876, Wright was its first secretary. In his later years, when his days on the field were over, the National League named him as its first supervisor of umpires.

Early Wynn Jr.

Born January 6, 1920, in Hartford, Alabama. 6', 235 lbs., bats left, throws right. Years in minor leagues: 3; Major League debut: September 13, 1939; Years in Major Leagues: 23. Elected to Hall of Fame: 1972. Nickname: Gus—because teammate Ellis Clary on Sanford in the Florida State League in 1937, who first started calling him "Gus" said he did it because Wynn just looked like a Gus.

Early Wynn, a burly righthanded pitcher, has the distinction of playing on the only two teams between 1948 and 1965 that beat out the New York Yankees for the American League pennant. Wynn won 23 games for the 1954 Cleveland Indians and 22 for the 1959 Chicago White Sox. He was the Cy Young Award winner in 1959 at the age of 39.

Wynn won exactly 300 games, pitching for the Washington Senators, Cleveland, Chicago and back with Cleveland again, but he didn't start out like a Hall of Famer. After his first eight seasons, all with Washington, Wynn had a lifetime record of 72 wins and 87 losses. He was then traded to Cleveland, and his career took off. He won 20 or more games five times and led the American League in innings pitched three times.

Wynn was a colorful player who was also a good hitter, and was prone to oddities in his career. In 1939, when the Senators gave him a look, he was just a big, mediocre pitcher whose biggest asset was his determination. But he is best remembered in that year for bunting into a triple play. Wynn is also the only man in Major League history to hit a pinch-hit grand-slam home run—and to give one up.

At the end of the 1961 season, Wynn needed just eight wins to become a 300-game winner. He worked out hard to stay in shape and, at the age of 42, won seven games for the White Sox in 1962. He was released at the end of the season and had to wait until the middle of the 1963 season to get one last chance at 300. His old team, the Indians, signed him, and on June 21 he pitched the first five innings of a game the Indians won 7–4—and Wynn became the 14th man to win 300 games.

Year	Team	W-L	ERA	G	IP	H	BB	SO
1939	Wash	0-2	5.75	3	20.1	26	10	1
1941	Wash	3-1	1.58	5	40	35	10	15
1942	Wash	10-16	5.12	30	190	246	73	58
1943	Wash	18-12	2.91	37	256.2	232	83	89
1944	Wash	8-17	3.38	33	207.2	221	67	65
1946	Wash	8-5	3.11	17	107	112	33	36
1947	Wash	17-15	3.64	33	247	251	90	73
1948	Wash	8-19	5.82	33	198	236	94	49
1949	Cleve	11-7	4.15	26	164.2	186	57	62
1950	Cleve	18-8	3.20	32	213.2	166	101	143
1951	Cleve	20-13	3.02	37	274.1	227	107	133
1952	Cleve	23-12	2.90	42	285.2	239	132	153
1953	Cleve	17-12	3.93	36	251.2	234	107	138
1954	Cleve	23-11	2.73	40	270.2	225	83	155
1955	Cleve	17-11	2.82	32	230	207	80	122
1956	Cleve	20-9	2.72	38	277.2	233	91	158
1957	Cleve	14-17	4.31	40	263	270	104	184
1958	Chi (A)	14-16	4.13	40	239.2	214	104	179
1959	Chi	22-10	3.17	37	255.2	202	119	179
1960	Chi	13-12	3.49	36	237.1	220	112	158
1961	Chi	8-2	3.51	17	110.1	88	47	64
1962	Chi	7-15	4.46	27	167.2	171	56	91
1963	Cleve	1-2	2.28	20	55.1	50	15	29
23 years		**300-244**	**3.54**	**691**	**4564**	**4291**	**1775**	**2334**

Transactions: Dec. 14, 1948: Traded with infielder Mickey Vernon to Cleveland for for Joe Haynes, Larry Milbourne, Pete Filson and cash. Dec. 4, 1957: Traded with outfielder Al Smith to Chicago White Sox for outfielder Minnie Minoso and infielder Fred Hatfield.

WORLD SERIES

Year	Team	W-L	ERA	G	IP	H	BB	SO
1954	Cleve	0-1	3.86	1	7	4	2	5
1959	Chi (A)	1-1	5.54	3	13	19	4	10
2 years		**1-2**	**4.95**	**4**	**20**	**23**	**6**	**15**

Carl Michael Yastrzemski

Born August 22, 1939, in Southampton, New York. 5'11", 185 lbs., bats left, throws right. Years in minor leagues: 2; Major League debut: April 11, 1961; Years in Major Leagues: 23. Elected to Hall of Fame: 1989. Nickname: Yaz— a shortening of his last name.

Carl Yastrzemski had more than big shoes to fill when he came up with the Boston Red Sox in 1961; the shoes were huge. Yastrzemski took over in left field for the retiring Ted Williams—and stayed there for 23 years. When he retired after the 1983 season, Yaz was the only American League player to have more than 400 home runs and more than 3,000 hits. He also had played in more games than any other American League player, 3,308, won three batting titles and won the Triple Crown in 1967 when he hit .326, hit 44 home runs and drove in 121 runs.

He helped the Red Sox into the World Series in 1967 and again in 1975, but they lost both in seven games. Yastrzemski, who holds most of the Red Sox offensive records not held by Williams, was spectacular in postseason play, hitting .405 in the 1975 League Championship Series and .400 and .310 in his two World Series appearances. He played in 17 All-Star games. Yaz won batting titles in 1963, 1967 (the Triple Crown year) and in 1968—"the year of the pitcher" in Major League Baseball—when an average of .301 was good enough to win the batting championship.

His great clutch hitting was further demonstrated in the last week of the 1967 season when the Red Sox were fighting for the pennant and the pressure was on. Yastrzemski, by then unquestionably the team leader, responded by getting 10 hits in his last 13 at-bats. Ted Williams said that for one month—September of 1967—Yastrzemski was the greatest player who ever lived. The Red Sox went into the final weekend in a four-way race for the pennant and won it on the final day with a doubleheader sweep of the Twins in which Yastrzemski got seven hits in eight at-bats. Yaz was also a great defensive player and was adept at playing balls off the "Green Monster," Boston's tall left-field wall. He won Gold Glove awards seven times and was also a seven-time leader in assists. Yastrzemski holds a Major League record for getting at least 100 hits in his first 20 seasons in the Majors and shares a record for remaining with the same team for 23 consecutive seasons.

Year	Team	G	AB	R	H	D	T	HR	RBI	AVE.
1961	Bos	148	583	71	155	31	6	11	80	.266
1962	Bos	160	646	99	191	43	6	19	94	.296
1963	Bos	151	570	91	183	40	3	14	68	.321
1964	Bos	151	567	77	164	29	9	15	67	.289
1965	Bos	133	494	78	154	45	3	20	72	.312
1966	Bos	160	594	81	165	39	2	16	80	.278
1967	Bos	161	579	112	189	31	4	44	121	.326
1968	Bos	157	539	90	162	32	2	23	74	.301
1969	Bos	162	603	96	154	28	2	40	111	.255
1970	Bos	161	566	125	186	29	0	40	102	.329
1971	Bos	148	508	75	129	21	2	15	70	.254
1972	Bos	125	455	70	120	18	2	12	68	.264
1973	Bos	152	540	82	160	25	4	19	95	.296
1974	Bos	148	515	93	155	25	2	15	79	.301
1975	Bos	149	543	91	146	30	1	14	60	.269
1976	Bos	155	546	71	146	23	2	21	102	.267
1977	Bos	150	558	99	165	27	3	28	102	.296
1978	Bos	144	523	70	145	21	2	17	81	.277
1979	Bos	147	518	69	140	28	1	21	87	.270
1980	Bos	105	364	49	100	21	1	15	50	.275

Year	Team	G	AB	R	H	D	T	HR	RBI	AVE.
1981	Bos	91	338	36	83	14	1	7	53	.246
1982	Bos	131	459	53	126	22	1	16	72	.275
1983	Bos	119	380	38	101	24	0	10	56	.266
23 years		3308	11988	1816	3419	646	59	452	1844	.285

LEAGUE CHAMPIONSHIP SERIES

Year	Team	G	AB	R	H	D	T	HR	RBI	AVE.
1975	Bos	3	11	4	5	1	0	1	2	.455

WORLD SERIES

Year	Team	G	AB	R	H	D	T	HR	RBI	AVE.
1967	Bos	7	25	4	10	2	0	3	5	.400
1975	Bos	7	29	7	9	0	0	0	4	.310
2 years		14	54	11	19	2	0	3	9	.352

Tom Yawkey

Born February 20, 1903, in Detroit, Michigan; died July 9, 1976, in Boston, Massachusetts. Years in Major Leagues: 43 (as owner of the Boston Red Sox). Elected to Hall of Fame: 1980.

Tom Yawkey was one of baseball's most popular owners. As a young man he inherited a fortune and in 1930 invested much of it by purchasing the Boston Red Sox. He developed a reputation early on for spending millions of dollars in acquiring quality players and in refurbishing Fenway Park, the home of the Red Sox. Today, long after Yawkey's death, his ballpark is still regarded as one of the old treasures because of its friendly fan atmosphere and unique characteristics such as the "Green Monster," the famed left-field wall.

Yawkey had an amazing quality for developing friendships with ballplayers. As a youngster growing up in Detroit, his hero was Ty Cobb, and the two men became friends. Yawkey bought the Red Sox at Cobb's suggestion. Not long after he took over the club, Yawkey hired Hall of Fame second baseman Eddie Collins as his general manager. Yawkey had money; Collins had expertise in picking players.

Together, they put together some classic deals, acquiring such notables as Lefty Grove, Jimmie Foxx and Joe Cronin and signing a youngster named Ted Williams. For all the wheeling and dealing, the Red Sox were only able to produce three pennants for Yawkey, in 1946, 1967 and 1975—and lost each World Series in seven games.

Denton True Young

Born March 29, 1867, in Gilmore, Ohio; died November 4, 1955, in Peoli, Ohio. 6'2", 220 lbs., bats right, throws right. Years in Major Leagues: 22.

Elected to Hall of Fame: 1937. Nickname: Cy—because, supposedly when Young was a youthful pitcher, he fired pitches against a wooden fence, leaving it looking like a cyclone hit it.

Cy Young is clearly an example where the record speaks for itself. He averaged 23 wins a year for 22 years and his lifetime total of 511 wins is the most ever—far ahead of any other pitcher. In fact, only one other pitcher, Walter Johnson, has won more than 400.

Young won 30 or more games five times and 20 or more games 16 times, including 14 seasons in a row. He pitched three no-hitters in his career, including a perfect game against the Philadelphia Athletics in 1904 which was part of a string of 24 consecutive hitless innings. He pitched over 300 innings in 16 seasons, and in five of those he had over 400 innings pitched. He pitched a record total of 7,356 innings and had 751 complete games. At the end of his career he had 76 shutouts and a career earned run average of 2.63. He led the league in most strikeouts and fewest walks 11 times and averaged only 1.5 walks per game for his entire career. Another record that Young has a firm grip on: most lifetime losses: 313, the result of a durable pitcher who lasted a long time. Young appeared in only one World Series in his career, in 1903 with Boston. He started three games and completed them all and also appeared in one game in relief. He won two and lost one but he had a spectacular earned run average of 1.59. In the last game of his brilliant career, he pitched well enough to get career win 512 but lost a 12-inning heartbreaker to a rookie just beginning to make his mark: Grover Cleveland Alexander. Long after he retired, his greatness on the mound was institutionalized when the Major Leagues began awarding the Cy Young Award to the best pitcher in each league.

Year	Team	W-L	ERA	G	IP	H	BB	SO
1890	Cleve (N)	9-7	3.47	17	147.2	145	30	36
1891	Cleve	27-20	2.85	55	423.2	431	140	147
1892	Cleve	36-11	1.93	53	453	363	118	167
1893	Cleve	32-16	3.36	53	422.2	442	103	102
1894	Cleve	25-22	3.94	52	408.2	488	106	101
1895	Cleve	35-10	3.24	47	369.2	363	75	121
1896	Cleve	29-16	3.24	51	414.1	477	62	137
1897	Cleve	21-18	3.79	46	335	391	49	87
1898	Cleve	25-14	2.53	46	377.2	387	41	107
1899	StL (N)	26-15	2.58	44	369.1	368	44	111
1900	StL	20-18	3.00	41	321.1	337	36	119
1901	Bos (A)	33-10	1.62	43	371.1	324	37	158
1902	Bos	32-11	2.15	45	384.2	350	53	160
1903	Bos	28-9	2.08	40	341.2	294	37	176
1904	Bos	26-16	1.97	43	380	327	29	203
1905	Bos	18-19	1.82	38	320.2	248	30	208
1906	Bos	13-21	3.19	39	287.2	288	25	140
1907	Bos	22-15	1.99	43	343.1	286	51	147
1908	Bos	21-11	1.26	36	299	230	37	150
1909	Cleve (A)	19-15	2.26	35	295	267	59	109

Year	Team	W–L	ERA	G	IP	H	BB	SO
1910	Cleve	7–10	2.53	21	163.1	149	27	58
1911	Cl-Bos (N)	7–9	3.78	18	126.1	137	28	55
22 years		**511–313**	**2.63**	**815**	**7356**	**7092**	**1217**	**2799**

Transactions: Feb. 18, 1909: Traded from Boston to Cleveland for Charlie Chech, Jack Ryan and $12,500. July 1911: Picked up by Boston on waivers.

WORLD SERIES

Year	Team	W–L	ERA	G	IP	H	BB	SO
1903	Bos (A)	2–1	1.59	4	34	31	4	17

Dick Young

Sportswriter. Elected to Hall of Fame: 1978.

Dick Young was a longtime New York sportswriter who gained fame and sometimes notoriety as a columnist for the *New York Post*. He was highly opinionated and therefore widely read in the sports haven of New York City. Former Commissioner Ford Frick, in his autobiography, maintains that it was Young and not Frick who suggested an asterisk be placed next to Roger Maris's name in the record book if he were to break Babe Ruth's single season home run record in 1961—which he did. The remark was a sarcastic reply to Frick's ruling that Maris should get a separate entry since he would have played in more games than Ruth.

Young, who was intensely loyal to the city of New York, once wrote a column about how Comiskey Park in Chicago was in such a rough neighborhood that it was dangerous just getting to the ballpark. Not long after that, Young was mugged in Chicago outside the "friendly confines" of Wrigley Field.

Ross Middlebrook Youngs

Born April 10, 1897, in Sweet Home, Texas; died October 22, 1927, in San Antonio, Texas. 5'8", 162 lbs., bats left, throws right. Years in minor leagues: 5; Major League debut: September 25, 1917; Years in Major Leagues: 10. Elected to Hall of Fame: 1972. Nickname: Pep—short for peppy, a reference to his enthusiasm.

Ross Youngs was an outstanding outfielder for the New York Giants for ten years. His manager, John McGraw, who was not known for lavish compliments, called Youngs the greatest outfielder he ever saw. Youngs bounced around in the minor leagues for five years before coming up with the Giants at the end of the 1917 season. He batted only 26 times and hit .346. The next season he hit .302 with 474 at-bats to immediately become a big-league star.

Between 1921 and 1924, the Giants won four straight pennants, and Youngs, in addition to being an outstanding defensive outfielder, hit .327, .331, .336 and .356, respectively. In the 1922 World Series, Youngs hit .375. His counterpart on the Yankees, Babe Ruth, hit .118. Youngs hit over .300 for seven consecutive seasons and led all National League outfielders in assists in three seasons. He seemed destined for superstardom when suddenly he seemed to lose his touch.

In 1925, Youngs' batting average dropped to .264. Before the start of the 1926 season, a physical examination revealed that he had Bright's disease, a serious kidney ailment. He continued to play but the Giants hired a male nurse to stay with him on the road. He toughed it out and hit .306 but was never to play again and died a year later at the age of 30. During that 1926 season, knowing his career was probably going to end prematurely, Youngs spent a lot of time training the man who would succeed him—Mel Ott—who was to hit 511 home runs in his career and earn a spot for himself in the Hall of Fame.

Year	Team	G	AB	R	H	D	T	HR	RBI	AVE.
1917	NY (N)	7	26	5	9	2	3	0	1	.346
1918	NY	121	474	70	143	16	8	1	25	.302
1919	NY	130	489	73	152	31	7	2	43	.311
1920	NY	153	581	92	204	27	14	6	78	.351
1921	NY	141	504	90	165	24	16	3	102	.327
1922	NY	149	559	105	185	34	10	7	86	.331
1923	NY	152	596	121	200	33	12	3	87	.336
1924	NY	133	526	112	187	33	12	10	74	.356
1925	NY	130	500	82	132	24	6	6	53	.264
1926	NY	95	372	62	114	12	5	4	43	.306
10 years		**1211**	**4627**	**812**	**1491**	**236**	**93**	**42**	**592**	**.322**

WORLD SERIES

Year	Team	G	AB	R	H	D	T	HR	RBI	AVE.
1921	NY (N)	8	25	3	7	1	1	0	3	.280
1922	NY	5	16	2	6	0	0	0	2	.375
1923	NY	6	23	2	8	0	0	1	3	.348
1924	NY	7	27	3	5	1	0	0	1	.185
4 years		**26**	**91**	**10**	**26**	**2**	**1**	**1**	**9**	**.286**

Robin R. Yount

Born September 16, 1955, in Danville, Illinois. 6', 175 lbs., bats right, throws right. Years in minor leagues: None; Major League debut: April 5, 1974; Years in Major Leagues: 20. Elected to Hall of Fame: 1999. Nickname: None.

Robin Yount spent his entire 20-year career with the Milwaukee Brewers as a shortstop and center fielder. He is one three players in Major League history to

win Most Valuable Player awards at two positions. (The others are Hank Greenberg and Stan Musial.) He played more than 1,000 games at each of the two positions. Yount was a sure-handed fielder with a good arm when he took the field for
the Brewers in 1974 at the age 18. But he was a late bloomer as a batter and didn't
hit over .300 until his ninth year. He then hit over .300 in six of the next eight
seasons. He was a spray hitter who had more than 20 doubles in 16 out of his 20
years.

He holds Milwaukee club records for games played, at-bats, runs, hits, singles, doubles, triples, home runs, RBIs and stolen bases. He is 15th on the all-time
list with his 3,142 hits, and he was the third youngest player to get 3,000 hits—
only Ty Cobb and Henry Aaron did it sooner. Yount is also one of three players
to have 3,000 hits, 250 home runs and 100 triples, the others being George Brett
and Willie Mays.

His best year—and his first MVP season—was 1982, when he hit .331 and
led the American League in hits with 210 and in doubles with 46. He had his career
highs of 29 home runs and 114 runs batted in, in leading the Brewers to their only
World Series appearance. They lost to the Cardinals in seven games, but Yount
was outstanding. He had 12 hits and hit .414, including a pair of four-hit games,
which is a World Series record.

Year	Team	G	AB	R	H	D	T	HR	RBI	AVE.
1974	Mil	107	344	48	86	14	5	3	28	.250
1975	Mil	147	558	67	149	28	2	8	52	.267
1976	Mil	161	638	59	161	19	3	2	54	.252
1977	Mil	154	605	66	174	34	4	4	49	.288
1978	Mil	127	502	66	147	23	9	9	71	.293
1979	Mil	149	577	72	154	26	5	8	51	.267
1980	Mil	143	611	121	179	49	10	23	87	.293
1981	Mil	96	377	50	103	15	5	10	49	.273
1982	Mil	156	635	129	210	46	12	29	114	.331
1983	Mil	149	578	102	178	42	10	17	80	.308
1984	Mil	160	624	105	186	27	7	16	80	.308
1985	Mil	122	466	76	129	26	3	15	68	.277
1986	Mil	140	522	82	163	31	7	9	46	.312
1987	Mil	158	635	99	198	25	9	21	103	.312
1988	Mil	162	621	92	190	38	11	13	91	.306
1989	Mil	160	614	101	195	38	9	21	103	.318
1990	Mil	158	587	98	145	17	5	17	77	.247
1991	Mil	130	503	66	131	20	4	10	77	.260
1992	Mil	150	557	71	147	40	3	8	77	.264
1993	Mil	127	454	62	117	25	3	8	51	.258
20 years		**2856**	**11008**	**1632**	**3142**	**583**	**126**	**251**	**1406**	**.285**

Divisional Playoff Series

Year	Team	G	AB	R	H	D	T	HR	RBI	AVE.
1981	Mil	5	19	4	6	0	1	0	1	.316

LEAGUE CHAMPIONSHIP SERIES

Year	Team	G	AB	R	H	D	T	HR	RBI	AVE.
1982	Mil	5	16	1	4	0	0	0	0	.250

WORLD SERIES

Year	Team	G	AB	R	H	D	T	HR	RBI	AVE.
1982	Mil	7	29	6	12	3	0	1	6	.414

Bibliography

Books

Alexander, Charles C. *John McGraw*. New York: Viking Press, 1988.

_____. *Ty Cobb*. New York: Oxford University Press, 1984.

Anderson, Dave. *Pennant Races: Baseball at Its Best*. New York: Doubleday, 1994.

Asinov, Eliot. *Eight Men Out: The Black Sox and the 1919 World Series*. New York: Holt, Rinehart and Winston, 1963.

Aylesworth, Thomas, and Benton Minks. *The Encyclopedia of Baseball Managers*. New York: Crescent Books, 1990.

Berkow, Ira. *Red: A Biography of Red Smith*. New York: Times Books, 1986.

Brown, Gene. *The Complete Book of Baseball*. New York: New York Times Co., 1980.

Carmichael, John P. *My Greatest Day in Baseball*. New York: Grossett & Dunlap, 1965.

Clark, Dick, and Larry Lester. *The Negro Leagues Book*. Cleveland: The Society for American Baseball Research, 1994.

Creamer, Robert W. *Stengel: His Life and Times*. New York: Dell, 1984.

Curran, William. *Mitts: A Celebration of the Art of Fielding*. New York: William Morrow, 1985.

DeGregorio, George. *Joe DiMaggio: An Informal Biography*. New York: Stein and Day, 1983.

Dickson, Paul. *Baseball's Greatest Quotations*. New York: HarperCollins, 1991.

Einstein, Charles. *The Baseball Reader: Favorites from the Fireside Books of Baseball*. New York: Lippincott & Crowell, 1980

Feller, Bob, with Bill Gilbert. *Now Pitching: Bob Feller*. New York: Carol, 1990.

Ford, Whitey, Mantle Mickey and Joe Durso. *Whitey and Mickey*. New York: Viking, 1977.

Frick, Ford C. *Games, Asterisks and People*. New York: Crown, 1973.

Frisch, Frank, and Roy J. Stockton. *Frank Frisch: The Fordham Flash*. Garden City, N.Y.: Doubleday & Co., 1962.

Gallagher, Mark. *Day by Day in New York Yankees History*. New York: Leisure Press, 1983.

Helyar, John. *Lords of the Realm: The Real History of Baseball*. New York: Villard, 1994.

Holway, John. *Blackball Stars: Negro League Pioneers*. Westport, Conn.: Meckler, 1988

_____. *Voices from the Great Black Baseball Leagues*. New York: Dodd, Mead, 1975.

Honig, Donald. *Baseball America*. New York: Macmillan, 1985.

Ivor-Campbell, Frederick, Robert L. Tiemann, and Mark Rucker. *Baseball's First Stars*. Cleveland: The Society for American Baseball Research, 1996.

James, Bill. *The Politics of Glory: How Baseball's Hall of Fame Really Works*. New York: Macmillan, 1994.

Kahn, Roger. *The Boys of Summer.* New York: Harper & Row, 1972.

Kiner, Ralph, and Joe Gergen. *Kiner's Korner: At Bat and on the Air: My 40 Years in Baseball.* New York: Arbor House, 1987.

Leptich, John, and Dave Baranowski. *This Date in St. Louis Cardinals History.* New York: Stein & Day, 1983.

Lewis, Franklin. *The Cleveland Indians.* New York: G.P. Putnam's Sons, 1949.

Lyons, Jeffrey, and Douglas B. Lyons. *Out of Leftfield.* New York: Random House, 1998.

Marazzi, Rich, and Len Fiorito. *Aaron to Zuverink.* New York: Stein and Day, 1982.

Martin, Billy, and Peter Golenbock. *Number One: Billy Martin.* New York: Delacorte, 1980.

Meany, Tom. *Baseball's Greatest Teams.* New York: A.S. Barnes, 1949.

Miller, James Edward. *The Baseball Business: Pursuing Pennants and Profits in Baltimore.* Chapel Hill: University of North Carolina Press, 1990.

Musial, Stan, and Bob Broeg. *Stan Musial: The Man's Own Story.* New York: Doubleday, 1964.

Okrent, Daniel and Lewine Harris. *The Ultimate Baseball Book.* Boston: Houghton Mifflin, 1988.

Peary, Danny. *Baseball's Finest: The Greats, the Flakes, the Weird and the Wonderful.* North Dighton, Mass.: JG Press, 1990.

Peterson, Robert. *Only the Ball Was White.* New York: McGraw-Hill, 1970.

Pope, Edwin. *Baseball's Greatest Managers.* New York: Doubleday, 1960.

Quigley, Martin. *The Crooked Pitch: The Curveball in American Baseball History.* Chapel Hill, N.C.: Algonquin Books, 1984.

Rathgeber, Bob. *Cincinnati Reds Scrapbook.* Virginia Beach, Va.: JCP Corp., 1982.

Reichler, Joseph. *The Baseball Encyclopedia.* New York: Macmillan, 1996.

Reidenbaugh, Lowell. *Baseball's Hall of Fame, Cooperstown: Where the Legends Live Forever.* New York: Random House, 1997.

Ritter, Lawrence S. *The Glory of Their Times.* New York: Random House, 1985.

Robinson, Brooks, and Jack Tobin. *Third Base Is My Home.* Waco, Texas: Word Books, 1974.

Robinson, Frank, and Barry Stainback. *Extra Innings.* New York: McGraw Hill, 1988.

Ruscoe, Michael. *Baseball: A Treasury of Art and Literature.* China: Hugh Lauter Levin Associates, 1993.

Sahadi, Lou. *The Pirates: We Are Family.* New York: Times Books, 1980.

Schoor, Gene. *Seaver.* Chicago: Contemporary Books, 1986.

_____. *The Pee Wee Reese Story.* New York: Julian Messner, 1956.

Skipper, James K. *Baseball Nicknames: A Dictionary of Origins and Meanings.* Jefferson, N.C.: McFarland, 1992.

Skipper, John C. *Inside Pitch: A Closer Look at Classic Baseball Moments.* Jefferson, N.C.: McFarland, 1996.

_____. *Umpires: Classic Baseball Stories from the Men Who Made the Calls.* Jefferson, N.C.: McFarland, 1997.

Smalling. R.J. *Baseball America's Baseball Address List,* Durham, N.C.: Baseball America, 1996.

Society for American Baseball Research. *The Home Run Encyclopedia.* New York: Macmillan, 1996.

_____. *Baseball Research Journal.* Cooperstown, N.Y.: SABR, 1981.

Thorn, John, and Pete Palmer. *Total Baseball.* New York: Warner Books, 1989.

_____. *The Ol' Ball Game: A Collection of Baseball Characters & Moments Worth Remembering.* New York: Barnes & Noble, 1993.

Tygiel, Jules. *Baseball's Great Experiment: Jackie Robinson and His Legacy.* New York: Random House, 1983.

Magazines

Kazuba, David. "Inventor of the Box Score." *Editor & Publisher*, June 14, 1997.

Markusen, Bruce. "Expansion Drafts Seldom Yield Impact Players." *Baseball Digest*, April 1998.

Nack, William. "Lost in History." *Sports Illustrated*, Aug. 19, 1996.

National Baseball Hall of Fame and Museum Yearbook. Cooperstown, N.Y.: 1997.

Tannenbaum, Teddy. "Diamond Fever: Cuba's Passion for Baseball Rivals America's Love of Its National Pastime." *Home Cigar Aficionado*, 1993.

Newspapers

Dolson, Frank. "Inquirer's Allen Lewis Will Enter Hall of Fame." *Philadelphia Inquirer*. May 16, 1982.

Drebinger, John. "Dodgers Capture First World Series; Podres Wins, 2-0." *New York Times*, Oct. 5, 1955.

Dryden, Charles. "Hitless Wonders Rally and Turn Apparent Yankee Victory into Defeat." *Chicago Tribune*, July 13, 1906.

Etkin, Jack. "McGuff Rides Words of Emotion, Respect into Cooperstown." *Kansas City Star*, July 29, 1985.

Fullerton, Hugh. "Is Big League Baseball Being Run for Gamblers with Ballplayers in the Deal?" *New York World*, Dec. 15, 1920.

Finch, Frank. "Bob Hunter Chucked Law Career to Earn Success as Scrivener." *The Sporting News*, Feb. 28, 1962.

Gauger, Jim. "Hall's Guilfoile: Tremendous Respect for Times' Bus Saidt." *Trenton Times*, Aug. 2, 1993.

Lieb, Fred. "Spink Award to Mercer, Early Giants Writer." *The Sporting News*, Dec. 6, 1969.

"This Year, Cooperstown Has Even More Charm for Collett." *Dayton Daily News*, Aug. 3, 1992.

Index